A Handbook of the Museum of Art

RHODE ISLAND SCHOOL OF DESIGN

A Handbook
of the
Museum of Art

RHODE ISLAND SCHOOL OF DESIGN

PROVIDENCE, RHODE ISLAND 1985

This catalogue has been made possible
by grants from the Prospect Hill Foun-
dation, the National Endowment for the
Arts, a Federal agency, the Museum
Associates, and the friends and family of
Helen M. Danforth.

Edited by Carla Mathes Woodward
and Franklin W. Robinson

COVER:
Edouard Manet, *Le Repos,* oil on canvas,
page 252

FRONTISPIECE:
The facade of the Museum on Benefit
Street, taken from the north, with
Pendleton House in the foreground and
the tower of Memorial Hall in the background. This photograph was taken in
the 1920's; the tower was removed in
1950, due to damage from the hurricane
in 1938.

This Handbook is dedicated to the memory of

Helen Metcalf Danforth (1887–1984),

in gratitude for her leadership of the Museum for four decades.

Authors

MARIE J. AQUILINO

TANYA B. BARTER

JOHN CARPENTER

JUDITH HOOS FOX

FLORENCE M. FRIEDMAN

MARTA GARSD

JOHN T. GOTJEN

MAUREEN HARPER

R. ROSS HOLLOWAY

DEBORAH J. JOHNSON

THOMAS W. LENTZ

JANICE LIBBY

THOMAS MICHIE

WILLIAM E. MIERSE

CHRISTOPHER P. MONKHOUSE

JANE OHLY

HOLLY RICHARDSON

FRANKLIN W. ROBINSON

DANIEL ROSENFELD

CAROL C. SANDERSON

WENDY SHAH

ELLEN SPENCER

LAURA VOOKLES

SUSAN D. WALTHER

ROLF WINKES

ROBERT WORKMAN

Table of Contents

Foreword

This Museum has a special character. The Rhode Island School of Design was founded in 1877 to teach the fine arts and the industrial and applied arts, and to exhibit works of art for the education of students and the general public. From the first, then, this Museum has been an integral part of an art school, and this fact, the interests and enthusiasms of the students and faculty, has shaped its collecting policies. The reader of this Handbook will note the remarkable collections of furniture and textiles, costumes and ceramics, not to speak of unusually deep holdings in such areas as wallpaper and architectural drawings. To a great degree, this focus on the collection has been shaped by the Museum's role as part of a large and vital School of Design.

At the same time, this is the major art museum in the state of Rhode Island. As such, it serves and draws strength from the community, and that community in itself is special. Providence is (in American terms) an old city, and many parts of it retain a grace and beauty one might not expect in a modern state capital. The Museum itself is on perhaps the most beautiful street in the city. Although the space the Museum occupies is constricted on all sides, the very fact that it is an integral part of the community, at the very center of a city rich in architectural tradition, adds to its vitality and relevance. In 1913, the first year for which we have such records, classes from every primary and secondary school in the city of Providence were given tours of the Museum, and this tradition of service has continued.

The School and the city have been two major factors in forming the special character of the Museum; the third is our donors. This institution has been fortunate in having attracted supporters throughout its history who were unusually farsighted, generous, and dedicated to the cause of art and museums. Chief among these, of course, are the various members of the Metcalf family; the group that founded the School of Design in 1877 was led by Mrs. Jesse Metcalf, and this quiet but energetic family has built each of the three buildings that make up the museum complex, purchased outright or given endowments for the purchase of most of the works of art, and provided leadership to various trustee committees for over a century. The history of the Museum written by Carla Mathes Woodward for this volume documents this involvement in greater detail, but two women of extraordinary energy and discrimination from this family must be mentioned here, Mrs. Eliza G. Radeke and Mrs. Helen M. Danforth, to the latter of whom this volume is dedicated.

The leadership of the Metcalf family attracted many other collectors, and the reader will note the appearance in these pages of superb works given by Isaac C. Bates, Lucy Truman Aldrich, and Charles L. Pendleton, among so many others, while there are other collections of extraordinary interest in memory of Albert Pilavin and Nancy Sayles Day. Our graphics collections have been enriched by the Fazzano family and by a donor of more than 500 British watercolors who wishes to remain anonymous. The list is endless, but its lesson is clear: this is an institution whose main function has been to acquire works of art of the highest quality.

A happy consequence of such generous and perceptive donors has been a sequence of directors and curators who were scholars, connoisseurs, and teachers. Again, Mrs. Woodward's essay documents their contribution, but their paradigm is surely L. Earle Rowe, director of the Museum for 25 years, a man of modesty and patience whose acquisitions ranged from the great Japanese Buddha to the Babylonian lion to Monet and Picasso.

Together, the School of Design, the city of Providence, and the Metcalf family and other great donors have created a museum with a special character: a one-story facade is succeeded by a series of small galleries on three floors, with works of art drawn from a collection of over 60,000 objects. At certain times, there are children everywhere, working with crayons and paper, and college students writing essays or making careful copies of the old masters. The atmosphere is one of deep and genuine involvement with the work of art itself, a confrontation with quality. This institution fulfils the primary purpose of museums and art itself, as a place where one can learn and grow and be refreshed.

There are many people who must be thanked for making this Handbook a reality. The funding for this volume has come from the Prospect Hill Foundation, the National Endowment for the Arts, a Federal agency, the Museum Associates, and the friends and family of Helen M. Danforth. Carla Mathes Woodward worked on this project for well over a year, preparing the history of the Museum, a fascinating document in itself, and working with the authors of the entries. These authors also deserve special praise; curators, interns, graduate students, and friends of the Museum have contributed essays that are remarkably scholarly and remarkably concise. Janet Phillips undertook the vital task of reading and editing the manuscript and guiding the volume as a whole through the various stages of the printing process. Houghton P. Metcalf, Jr., and Estise Mauran have kindly read the history of the Museum and commented on it; much of that history has been based on research done by Jane Reeder. Murray S. Danforth, Jr., has kindly provided the photograph of his mother, and has taken special interest in this project. Gilbert Associates has designed the handsome volume the reader holds in his hands; Ira Garber, Amanda Merullo, and Robert O. Thornton took most of the photographs for it. We thank the Gorham Company, Providence, for permission to use their color photograph of the Gorham writing table. We are also grateful to Joyce M. Botelho, Mrs. Edmund Capozzi, Mrs. Ernest Nathan, and Wm. McKenzie Woodward for their kind help. Many present and former members of the staff of the Museum and the School have collaborated on this book, most particularly Kathleen Bayard and Jean Waterman, and also: Julie Alton, Carol Anderson, Elizabeth T. Casey, Edward Dwyer, Robert P. Emlen, Jean S. Fain, Eleanor Fayerweather, Susan B. Glasheen, Susan Handy, Laura C. Luckey, June Massey, Hannah Myers, Joan Patota, Thomas C. Pautler, Louann Skorupa, Laura Stevens, Diane Stratton, and L. Jean Zimmerman.

We are grateful to all these dedicated people for making this Handbook possible.

F.W.R.

Frank Benson, *Portrait of Mrs. Jesse Metcalf*, oil on canvas. Gift of Mrs. William C. Baker, Mrs. Manton B. Metcalf, Mrs. Stephen O. Metcalf and Mrs. Gustav Radeke. 06.060

ACQUISITION, PRESERVATION, AND EDUCATION:
A History of the Museum

CARLA MATHES WOODWARD

A Three-Fold Challenge

On March 22, 1877, "An Act to Incorporate the Rhode Island School of Design" was enacted by the Rhode Island General Assembly. The corporation, including C. A. L. Richards, William B. Weeden, Francis W. Goddard, Charles D. Owen, Helen A. Metcalf, Sarah E. Doyle, Mary H. Drake, Clifton A. Hall, Claudius B. Farnsworth, and their associates and successors, was formed "for the purpose of aiding in the cultivation of the arts of design. . . ." In objectives set forth in the By-Laws of the Rhode Island School of Design, a balanced and challenging three-fold plan aimed for:

1. The instruction of artisans in drawing, painting, modeling and designing so that they may successfully apply the principles of art to the requirements of trade and manufacture.

2. The systematic training of students in the practice of art in order that they may understand its principles, give instruction to others and become artists.

3. The general advancement of public art education by the collection and exhibition of works of art and by lectures and by other means of instruction in the fine arts.

The Roots of RISD

At the Rhode Island exhibition of the Philadelphia Exposition of 1876, the Women's Centennial Commission, led by Mrs. Jesse Metcalf, was left with $1,675 after meeting the exhibit's expenses; with this amount they determined to found the School of Design. A small sum, for a bold move; yet the need for such an institution in Rhode Island had been felt for some years. Elsie S. Bronson recorded the School's background for the 50th Anniversary Celebration,[1] showing what the community's leaders in the mid-19th century did on behalf of art in Rhode Island. In 1854, the Rhode Island General Assembly chartered the Rhode Island Art Association, of which William W. Hoppin was president, to establish "a permanent Art Museum and Gallery of the Arts of Design . . . and to use all other appropriate means for cultivating and promoting the Ornamental and Useful Arts" – interestingly, rejecting any notion of a discrepancy between usefulness and beauty. (This was a pioneering plan, as only three major municipal art

---

1. Elsie S. Bronson, *The Rhode Island School of Design: A Half-Century Record (1878– 1928)*, Providence, 1928, n.p. Typewritten copies in the Library of the Rhode Island School of Design.

museums existed in the United States by 1850: the Philadelphia Academy of Fine Arts, the Boston Atheneum, and the Wadsworth Atheneum in Hartford.) Plans for the Rhode Island Art Association included an annual exhibit, a possible periodical on art, and a school program with good instruction and materials. All this would require an endowment which, unfortunately, was never raised.[2]

The group did, in fact, enjoy a major accomplishment: the purchase of Asher B. Durand's oil painting of 1855, *Chocorua Peak*. (This was placed on loan to RISD after the institution was established, and came into the Museum's permanent collection almost 100 years after it was purchased.) The Durand acquisition was the first step toward a permanent Rhode Island public art collection, and shows a commitment to the collecting of contemporary American art, a continuing practice at the Museum.

Two exhibitions also took place under the aegis of the Rhode Island Art Association: one, in September 1854, was mounted in Westminster Hall, later the site of the Hospital Trust Building. According to Providence newspaper accounts in 1897 reviewing the early history and background of the Rhode Island School of Design:

"The [1854] exhibition was miscellaneous, consisting of oil-paintings, statuary, prints and copies, loaned by wealthy residents of Newport and Providence. The catalogue was interesting, and among the numbers were a horse and cart by Géricault, owned by Robert H. Ives, and two portraits of horses, painted by Rosa Bonheur, owned by P. Allen, Jr.; also a painting by DeBrakeleer of the Dutch School. The eminent family of Ives took a decided interest in the exhibition, and loaned most valuable works of art. . . . It was a promising beginning."

Subsequently, "There was a second exhibition in 1855, held in the little gallery at the foot of Waterman Street, adjoining the present School of Design. At that time the Rhode Island Art Association was endeavoring to establish in Providence a School of Design for persons of both sexes; the object, the same as the present School of Design."

Precedent for the industrial arts school could be found abroad. England, having felt the challenge of superior art industrial skills in Germany and France, responded by establishing the technical schools of South Kensington and an accompanying museum – the Victoria and Albert – at the time of the First International Exposition of 1851. (The English also exhibited at the Philadelphia Exposition of 1876 – where Mrs. Metcalf and her friends gathered their funds for RISD – to the great interest and attention of Americans.) In Rhode Island, and other states as well, the art and design education movement might have rapidly accelerated in mid-century, but the Civil War interrupted Rhode Island's plans.

The post-war climate proved ever more fertile for training designers. In 1870 Massachusetts had provided legislation for art education; 1872 saw the establishment of the Lowell School of Practical Design, which concentrated especially on training textile designers. Rhode Island was looking toward new industrial prosperity at this time, with the manufacturing of silverware, jewelry, tools, and textiles. With educational facilities for training similar to those in Massachusetts, local industry would reap great benefits.

2. Dr. Blumer, historian for RISD's 50th Anniversary, assessed the Rhode Island Art Association as "a pompous beginning and an early failure" (Providence *Evening Bulletin*, October 6, 1928).

The president of Brown University – the obvious institution to promote these educational measures – recognized the situation in his annual report for 1873:

> "Adequate as the College may have been to the wants of the past, it manifestly is not equal to the needs of today. . . . that in a community like ours which in some sense is a center of manufactures for a population of millions, if not for our whole country, liberal provision should be made for instruction in the applications of science to the mechanic arts is too evident to need discussion. . . . Unless I am misinformed, a large number of the intelligent citizens of our State are now desirous that a Scientific School of high order – a school which, in addition to its more immediate aims shall not fail to provide also for sub-schools of Design, of Drawing, of Civil Engineering, of Architecture, of the Fine Arts, – may speedily be established in Rhode Island and if possible may be established in conjunction with, and in a sense, as a part of Brown University."[3]

Since Brown could not fund the areas of fine and applied arts at the time, leadership for Rhode Island's art and technical training was wide open. Three years later, the Philadelphia Exposition produced not only a nest egg, but a leader – Helen Adelia Rowe Metcalf – and her friends of the Women's Centennial Commission from Rhode Island. Moving rapidly and decisively, they met on March 5, 1877 to choose 12 trustees to fund and organize the school. On March 22, Rhode Island School of Design was incorporated for "the cultivation of the arts of design."

Growing Pains – The Search for Space
Plans for teachers, curriculum, catalogue, and – most important – space for classrooms and equipment took more than a year before the School opened on October 7, 1878, in Room 34 of the Hoppin Homestead Building at 283 Westminster Street. The actual planning was conducted by Claudius B.

3. From RISD President John R. Frazier's *History of Rhode Island School of Design*, an address to the Rhode Island Historical Society, November 13, 1960.

Steel engraving of the Hoppin Homestead Building, Westminster Street, 1881. Courtesy of the Rhode Island Historical Society

William L. Loring, *Portrait of Mrs. Gustav Radeke*, oil on canvas. Gift of the Estate of Mrs. Gustav Radeke. 31.600

Farnsworth, a lawyer and treasurer of a textile manufacturing company, Clifton A. Hall, an architect, and Mrs. Metcalf, whose husband manufactured woolen textiles.

Mrs. Metcalf's dreams and determination for the future of Rhode Island School of Design cannot be underestimated. As President Frazier remarked in 1960, "The School was her idea. She had been active on the committee at Philadelphia and it was her motion that prompted the committee to vote its remaining funds to found a school. The school was not only sponsored by the trustees, it was managed by them to a degree that is unheard of today. Management was in the hands of the Executive Committee and Mrs. Metcalf was its chairman. Though a mother of five children, she is said to have appeared every day on the school premises to act as its Director. She chose the teachers. She managed the finances. No detail or item for purchase was too insignificant for her personal attention. She was known on occasion to sweep and dust the classrooms."

Mrs. Metcalf's commitment was extraordinary, yet others of her family also joined actively in the early work of funding and forming the institution, a role still played by their descendants today. Jesse Metcalf paid the annual operating deficits. Their son, Stephen O. Metcalf, became Treasurer in 1884 after the resignation of Henry R. Chace. Of great importance, especially in the building of the Museum, is the part played by their daughter, Eliza Radeke, who succeeded her mother in managing the School as well as endowing the Museum collections. Dr. Gustav Radeke, Eliza's husband, brought back from Germany tin and wood models of objects, ornamental and architectural casts from antique sculpture, and industrial materials, a collection he had assembled with the advice of Dr. O. Jessen, a distinguished scholar and director of Prussian industrial schools, and which he donated in 1885. These were added to collections for the industrial museum of the School, which had opened in 1880, holding its first exhibition of technical drawings in that year.

Exhibition activity had been part of the School of Design's program from its first year at the Hoppin Homestead under the headmaster, Mr. Charles Barry. The first catalogue of the School, published in 1878, included a proviso for a museum in reiterating the original goals of the institution. As early as 1879, an annual student exhibition was held each spring – the only exhibitions of record for several years. The early years of activity concentrated on increasing enrollment in day, evening, and Saturday classes (the latter for children), and the seeking of state appropriations, which were mainly for student scholarships. (In 1884, $1,000 from the Rhode Island General Assembly was acclaimed as "the first public effort to provide a basis for the higher forms of mechanical and industrial education.") In March of 1884, an alumni exhibition was held; graduates and present members of the School were invited to send one or two works of art in plaster, charcoal, crayon, watercolor, or oil. The year 1885 was a landmark for exhibitions; the First Annual Exhibition of American Artists opened in the same year that Dr. Radeke's study collection was presented by him, Mrs. Metcalf, and Mr. Edward I. Nickerson.

The year 1887, a decade after its incorporation, produced positive events for the growth of the School and its Museum – and the start of growing pains. According to Elsie Bronson, a lecture "Does Art Pay," given before the Providence Commercial Club, had induced an encouraging feeling toward a museum of the fine and industrial arts, and at the 1887 annual meeting of the School, a committee was appointed from the directors to promote interest in the community. Free public lectures were given by the directors and friends on such topics as "Couplings for Shafting," "Lithography," "Mechanical Engineers," "Architecture," and "Industrial Schools." The collection was enlarged in 1887–88 with gifts of textiles and casts in bas-relief. All of this made obvious the inadequacy of the space in the Hoppin Homestead, and beginning with the Tenth Anniversary catalogue of June 1888, and for the next five years, membership in the association of Rhode Island School of Design was sought for endowment, special lectures, and "adequate space for the industrial museum, museum of fine arts, and library which were in the making; and the one great thing on which all others must depend, a permanent building to house the school."

Waterman Building

A Permanent Site

The circular for RISD of 1891–92 allowed, "The Committee on Building has as yet been unable to obtain a satisfactory site, but it is confidently expected that before many months we shall see the fulfillment of our hopes in the growing walls of a suitable home. So much has been achieved with the small resources at our disposal that we are encouraged to hope for further recognition and support when a substantial building shall mark our establishment as a permanent factor in the progress and prosperity of our State."

The way would be cleared legally in 1892 when the General Assembly enlarged the powers of the Corporation to hold possessions up to $500,000, plus works of art, and exempted school property from taxation. It took Jesse Metcalf's gift of a building to make the property a reality in brick and mortar. The dedication of the "Waterman Building" at 11 Waterman Street was held on October 24, 1893. At the ceremony, William C. Baker (Mrs. Metcalf's son-in-law), a member of the Museum committee, said he hoped that the building would house not only the School "but also a rare and beautiful collection of works of art."

The collection had, in fact, been started. In addition to the Durand, 71 etchings by Salvator Rosa and the gift of a Campanian amphora had been among the earliest acquisitions. Also in 1890, engravings from the collection of Royal C. Taft had been exhibited.[4] No longer were exhibition offerings limited to student, or contemporary American, works.

The entire first floor of the Waterman Building showcased the Museum, with classes and lectures occupying the rest. Mrs. Bronson's chapter "On Firm Ground" relates:

> "The galleries on the first floor of the School building had been opened with an exhibition of paintings, casts of ancient sculpture, bronzes, pottery, modern silverware, embroideries and other objects of artistic interest, many loans supplementing the possessions of the school. When the loans were removed, a permanent exhibition was arranged and opened free to the public every afternoon beginning January 15, 1894. The room at the right of the entrance contained a new collection of classical and renaissance casts given chiefly by Mrs. Radeke. In April the large room opposite was hung with the 233 framed and catalogued "autotypes," illustrating the history and masterpieces of the art of painting, which for thirty years was to give the room its familiar name. This large addition to the educational equipment of the school was made possible by subscriptions of $250 each from Mr. Isaac C. Bates, Mr. Louis H. Comstock, Mr. Joseph Davol and Mr. Walter A. Peck."

Bates, who would figure prominently in the formation of the Museum's collection through purchases and the bequest of his collection, gave at this time 270 wood-engravings and the etchings of Anthonie Waterloo, and joined Jesse Metcalf in gifts of several oil and watercolor paintings.

Mrs. Metcalf died on March 1, 1895. In the next year, Jesse Metcalf presented funds for a fitting memorial: three new exhibition galleries, which were completed and opened on March 11, 1897.[5] Many gifts followed the unveiling of the spacious new museum area, which adjoined the main building; the former exhibit spaces became offices, the library, and a place to exhibit student work continuously.

4. Mr. Taft became President of the RISD Corporation in 1888. He was governor of Rhode Island, 1888–89. 169 prints from his collection were given to the Museum by Mrs. Taft in 1945.
5. These galleries are now used as the special exhibition area on C-Floor.

The Autotype Room, looking into the Waterman Building Museum galleries

The opening exhibit featured loans of 100 paintings, engravings from Charles Bradley and Isaac Bates, 77 pen and ink drawings from Charles G. Bush of the New York *Herald*, and Japanese pottery and bronzes from Mrs. William C. Baker and Mr. Bates, who later gave his to the Museum.

The thrust of the Museum clearly had changed from industrial arts to fine arts. With the death of Dr. Radeke in 1892, the School had lost possibly its staunchest supporter of the purely industrial museum. It was to fall to Mrs. Radeke, among the Metcalfs, to mold the art museum into definite shape – with the help of her brothers.

Endowment, Prosperity, and Charles L. Pendleton

Jesse Metcalf's death in 1899 followed not long after his wife's. A significant boost to the potential of the Museum came from his children in 1900 as a memorial: an endowment fund of $50,000, to be called the Jesse Metcalf Memorial Fund, for the purchase of works of art. The Museum was now both a physical and a financial entity.

Rumblings were heard from other areas of the School. Mrs. Bronson explains, ". . . large subscriptions and expenditures were made for the museum, and the museum had been endowed, while the school was handicapped by lack of necessary equipment – perhaps also by lack of effective organization." The days of management in Helen Metcalf's manner clearly could not continue; a director was needed as well as a volunteer committee.

Frank Benson, *Portrait of Isaac C. Bates*, oil on canvas. Bequest of Isaac C. Bates. 13.910

Waterman galleries (now C-9) with schoolchildren, showing Copley portraits and John Alexander's *Blue Bowl*, ca. 1910

Waterman galleries, early 20th century,
now C-9. Portraits of Mr. and Mrs. Jesse
Metcalf on the end wall

Accordingly, in 1901, Eleazer Bartlett Homer was appointed director of Rhode Island School of Design.

Ironically, one of Homer's earliest successes directly benefited the Museum. The main event of his first fall term was an exhibit of contemporary American paintings in the Museum, including 18 artists, and the selection of Winslow Homer's *On a Lee Shore* as the first purchase from the income of the Jesse Metcalf Fund. A fine purchase, as well, from the artist's point of view; writing to his dealer on October 19, 1900, Winslow Homer stated, "I have a *very excellent* painting 'On a Lee Shore,' 39 x 39 . . . I will send it to you if you desire to see it. *Good* things are scarce. Frame not ordered yet, but I can send it by the time McKinley is elected."[6] The opening of this auspicious exhibit was a welcoming reception for Mr. and Mrs. Eleazer B. Homer.

Further financial stability was provided in 1901 by the offer of an endowment fund of $50,000 from Eliza Radeke, Jesse H. Metcalf, Stephen O. Metcalf, and Manton B. Metcalf, on condition that the same amount be raised from outside sources by June 1, 1902 – terms that were met. The family also gave several lots of land behind the School building. Additional physical space for the School and Museum came in 1902 with the donation by Mrs. Radeke and her brothers of the Old Congregational Church on Benefit Street, designed ca. 1850 by Thomas A. Tefft. Appropriately, Tefft himself had been a director of the Rhode Island Art Association and was well aware of the deficiencies in art education in the state in the middle years of the 19th century. The church was renovated and dedicated on November 24, 1903. Space was available for a mechanical department, sculpture, and the rapidly developing department of textile design. In the large hall where dedication exercises took place, a space "for lectures, concerts, plays, pageants, student exhibitions, and other artistic and educational uses" came to be used for many years as the site of Museum lectures.

The generosity of the Metcalf family would inspire an exciting, innovative gift from Charles Pendleton of Providence. By agreement with Rhode Island School of Design, Stephen O. Metcalf, and Eliza G. Radeke on May 25, 1904, Pendleton donated his entire collection of 18th century English and American furniture, paintings, china, pottery, and rugs provided: ". . . said collection shall remain forever in the State of Rhode Island, and be kept separate and intact in a suitable building and under proper care, for the benefit of the public, as a perpetual memorial of himself and of his family, and be forever held and known as 'THE CHARLES L. PENDLETON COLLECTION.'"

Since no such "suitable building" existed, the Metcalfs set about quickly to create one. They provided property on Benefit Street, and S. O. Metcalf donated the building costs. Failure to complete the building would have meant a loss of the collection to the Boston Museum of Fine Arts. Fortunately, this was not to be. Pendleton died soon after the agreement had been signed, and the collection came to be housed in a handsome "Georgian" building designed by a local architectural firm agreed to by all parties, Stone, Carpenter and Willson. The firm had produced many fine Providence edifices, including Royal C. Taft's house (1895), based on the Joseph Brown House (1774) of 50 South Main Street, as well as the Union Station (1896–98), the Old Stone Bank (1896–98), and the Providence Public Library (1900) on Empire Street. Edmund R. Willson's design of 1904 – "to be so far as practi-

---

6. Winslow Homer had exhibited his work previously at RISD, in the summer of 1898, along with Edmund C. Tarbell and Frank W. Benson, who is heavily represented in the collections of the Museum.

cable, of fire-proof construction" – has the distinction of being the first American wing added to a museum in this country. It was completed in 1906, the year Willson died.

The Pendleton building, known as Colonial House, was similar in dimensions and arrangement to Pendleton's actual residence at 72 Waterman Street. Its holdings revealed a strong collecting preference on Charles Pendleton's part for English and Philadelphia Chippendale-style furniture. The building opened in October 1906, with a bound catalogue of the collection for subscribers prepared by Luke Vincent Lockwood. Daily hours for the Pendleton Collection were 2–4 p.m., while the rest of the Museum was open 10–5 weekdays and Saturdays, 2–5 on Sundays. An admission fee of 25¢ was charged on Monday, Wednesday, and Friday; "all members of the corporation received free tickets admitting four persons, however, and students and artists who applied were granted free admission on any day."[7]

In 1905, the year prior to the opening of Colonial House, the objects in the Museum were catalogued. A characteristic diversity was already evident; included were examples of pottery (especially a large collection of peasant pottery given and lent by Mrs. Radeke), metalwork, particularly Japanese ornaments and bronzes, lacquer and textiles, the autotypes and casts, and paintings, especially purchases from the Jesse Metcalf Fund. These were works by Winslow Homer, George Hitchcock, William Merritt Chase, R. Swain Gifford, J. Alden Weir, Childe Hassam, Mary Cassatt, and John W. Alexander. Typically, Mrs. Radeke recognized the problems of space with this rapidly growing collection, as well as the logistical problems of separation between Colonial House and the 1897 galleries. Accordingly, as the School reported in 1905–06, "A new gallery has also been built to connect the Pendleton collection with the present galleries of the School of Design and will be fitted up to contain the increasing collections of porcelains and metalwork. This building is the gift of Mrs. Gustav Radeke." This elegant space was designed by Charles Platt.

The year of the opening of the Pendleton Collection and the new corridor galleries, Museum attendance reached a new high: 60,941.

7. Bronson, p. 58.

The Museum and Memorial Hall, formerly the Old Congregational Church, given to RISD in 1902 (photograph taken ca. 1935)

Connector gallery designed by Charles
Platt, with metalwork and pottery,
prior to the installation of the Lucy
Truman Aldrich Collection of European
Porcelain Figures of the 18th Century

New Growth, Greater Goals

Eleazer B. Homer's directorship of Rhode Island School of Design ended in
1907. His greatest contribution to the Museum was undoubtedly his negotia-
tions for Charles Pendleton's collection; although his major preoccupation
was with enlargement of the library, he recognized the Museum's importance for the School. As Elsie Bronson reports, "With the Museum Mr. Homer
had little to do, but he conceived it as a potential laboratory for student
research, and urged that a larger number of industrial and artistic objects of
historic value be acquired to that end. An excellent beginning was being
made in textiles, of which there were also frequent loan exhibitions. . . ."
Metalwork and jewelry collecting, with the advice of Engelhart C. Ostby,
also commanded attention.

Mrs. Radeke became acting director on September 11, 1907. The School
report of that year commented, "The Rhode Island School of Design now
has 62,010 square feet of floor space devoted to the work of its school and
Museum. Even with the recent expansion of areas the rooms remain
crowded." When Huger Elliott became RISD's director in 1908, he agreed
with Mrs. Radeke's assessment of space problems – particularly for the
textile department. The Metcalf brothers subsequently purchased the Breck
Building on North Main Street for textiles; it was renamed West Hall.

The collections of the Museum continued to grow nearly as rapidly as
space could be made, and in unexpected areas. In 1910, the interior of Colonial
House gained a new look from the bequest by Hope Brown Russell of the

collection of her mother, Anne Allen Ives. This remarkable gathering of paintings, china, glass, and silver was housed in one room unto itself.[8] Colonial House would eventually include other gifts and purchases in the decorative arts field as permanent exhibits, in addition to Charles Pendleton's own bequest.

A concerted effort to raise funds for expansion resulted in the formation of an Endowment Committee in 1909–10, chaired by Theodore Francis Green. A brochure for endowment solicitation emphasized the needs of the industrial department and the Museum as well. The Museum was actively serving as a resource for students – Elliott even had it opened periodically for the evening students. He also started public educational services, giving the first of the Sunday docent talks in December 1911. Elliott opened the library to the public and published a bulletin of the School's activities and acquisitions. The community was drawn to this growing enterprise of Rhode Island School of Design, and responded to its potential contribution to society. The year 1912 would provide fruitful new directions and signal the beginning of a vital new regime.

A Perfect Partnership

Huger Elliott resigned in May 1912 to become education director at the Museum of Fine Arts, Boston. In summer of 1912, L. Earle Rowe came from that museum to be the director of Rhode Island School of Design. Not a creative artist, he was instead "an historian of the arts with the enthusiasms of a collector." He would find a perfect match in the person of Eliza Radeke. As President Frazier pointed out, "Eliza Radeke, who fell heir to her mother's role of manager, had a larger view of that role. Not only were her sights set higher but she also had a respect for expert opinion and a willingness to be guided by professional direction . . . . " In all, four men would serve as School Director under her management – a seemingly awkward task. Yet Frazier felt, "Why it worked at all was probably due to Mrs. Radeke's personality. She was the personification of devotion and dedication. These qualities inspire like devotion. She was quiet, retiring and kind, but she had a strong will and could be arbitrary without causing resentment. She sailed a taut ship but everyone respected the skipper. And with those of us who knew her well respect was mixed with admiration and affection." Rowe's knowledge of the great museums of the world, his five years' experience as docent and curator in Boston, his archaeological work in Greece and Egypt – and his insistence on works for the collection being of "museum quality" – made him well-suited to the interests of RISD, its Museum, and Mrs. Radeke.

Rowe came to a busy place as far as the Museum was concerned. Attendance the previous year was 81,321. Elliott had started the popular Sunday docent talks that year, which Rowe continued. As the School report pointed out in 1911–12, the Museum's contribution to the community was significant:

> "In addition to the permanent collection in the Museum, two hundred and fifty-seven special loan exhibitions have been shown in the galleries since the School occupied the new building on Waterman Street. These exhibitions have given the people of Providence an opportunity to see

8. Eleazer Homer would have been pleased that the bequest also benefited the library; engravings and 312 books were added from Mrs. Ives's holdings.

representative collections of paintings and sculpture by many American artists. Eight large loan exhibitions of paintings by great French and Dutch artists have been held and architectural work has also been shown."

Growth and pressing space needs continued. The death of Isaac C. Bates, President of the Corporation from 1907 until his death on January 1, 1913, yielded the Museum a large bequest of American paintings, watercolors and drawings, prints, 193 pieces of jewelry, table glass, and 214 pieces of Japanese and Chinese porcelain, as well as decorative arts, metalwork, East Indian and Javanese textiles – and $55,000. Mrs. Radeke became President of the Corporation. Elsie Bronson puts the relationship neatly: "It was a time when firm principles and steady judgment were needed for the guidance of a school grown large in numbers and complicated in activities; and Mr. Rowe's work for the museum was the more possible because he could depend upon Mrs. Radeke's experience and cooperation in the affairs of the school."

At this point, however, the textile department took precedence. It was the only department in the school that essentially ran itself. Receiving a state grant in 1913 for expansion, it would function, in effect, as Rhode Island's textile school. A fine new textile building, rising four stories high, was built in 1913–15 on land donated by the three Metcalf brothers; $10,400 was donated by 23 individuals and businesses for equipment.

Further potential for expansion came with the bequest in 1916 of $3,000,000 from Lyra Brown Nickerson, daughter of Edward I. Nickerson, in equal shares to Rhode Island School of Design and the Providence Public Library. This would be known as the Museum Appropriation Fund (later to be added to anonymously). With permission from the Rhode Island General Assembly to accept unlimited holdings, RISD was now in a position to reconsider the issue of museum space. A wood building next to Colonial House was torn down, and a committee of five was appointed to consider an addition to the museum building.

World War I: Delay, Opportunity, Delay
With the advent of the War, there would be no new building. However, opportunities for museum collecting soared with the flooding of the art market by collections in European hands, and Earle Rowe wasted no time. The annual Museum Appropriation was raised from $25,000 to $40,000 from the Nickerson bequest. Rowe acquired paintings by Aert de Gelder, El Greco, Whistler, Sargent, and Chinese and Byzantine paintings as well as a collection of Persian art, all principally from the Museum Appropriation. In January of 1919, after the Armistice, S. O. Metcalf again raised the issue of building plans. Two pressing problems existed: the Museum, and a much-needed extension to the textile building for the jewelry and silversmithing departments. Since the jewelry industry in the state was at peak production following World War I, it seemed prudent and logical to favor the textile addition. West Hall was torn down for space. And the Museum plans continued to languish.

The Museum: A Metcalf Monument
A major blow to the Metcalf family was felt with the death of Manton B. Metcalf in 1923. In 1924, his bequest of $50,000, and his collection, greatly enriched the Museum's holdings. An exhibit of his gifts, December 12, 1923 – January 9, 1924, included the Flemish *Adoration of the Magi*, the Collantes *Hagar and Ishmael*, the Basaiti *Portrait of a Man*, and the Cologne *Deposition*.

November 26, 1924: excavation of the hill for the museum building, looking toward Benefit Street from North Main Street

As if galvanized by this event, his brothers Stephen O. and Jesse H. decided the time had come for a proper museum building. In May of 1924, they presented $400,000 for the building, to be named for their sister, Eliza Greene Radeke, whose personal attention had very largely shaped the Museum's collection to that point.

The Boston architect William T. Aldrich[9] was engaged for this challenging task. His site problems included a steeply sloping hill and achieving compatibility with the existing facade of Colonial (Pendleton) House on Benefit Street, where the front entrance of the Museum would be located. His solution proved to be a brilliant synthesis: the creation of new space with a continuing sense of intimacy.

Ground was broken on November 10, 1924. On April 24, 1926, the Eliza G. Radeke Museum was dedicated. Its innovative plan achieved substantial recognition. *The Art News* remarked at the time,

"A distinctive new note in museum planning has been struck in the Providence edifice, the major part of the building being given over to rooms, or 'galleries' . . . restricted in size, where a few exhibits can be seen and enjoyed at close range without incurring that scourge – museum fatigue."

The *Providence Journal* acclaimed the "appointments and attractiveness of installation" as among the best of the country's museums. Its very complexity of site permitted six floors with some 30 or more galleries that brought out a range of objects never before seen for lack of space. From a gracious entrance hall, the visitor could walk directly into Colonial House, or to the left into a

9. Brother of Lucy Truman Aldrich, whose collections and role in planning the galleries will be subsequently examined.

Visitors in the Main Gallery, late 1920's

ring of 12 rooms arranged around a large, two-level exhibition gallery hung with paintings. The tapestry hall led to the classical gallery, followed by early American paintings and furniture; the Spanish room and John Nicholas Brown's collection; further Spanish paintings; modern French paintings; Dutch and Flemish, and Barbizon School; and another painting and sculpture space, followed by three galleries of watercolors and drawings, with windows overlooking the open exterior court. Access to the original Museum galleries was through a deep stairwell that provided still more space to hang large paintings. The upper story above Benefit Street also displayed many treasures. Around the upper level of the main gallery (not accessible from the gallery itself) were the Renaissance room, Gothic, Chinese, Japanese, and Persian galleries, and three galleries for prints and drawings.

Three floors below provided necessary museum services. The lowest level, on North Main Street, contained general storage. Above, a pottery exhibit and painting storage were housed. Next, just below the main exhibition floor, administrative offices, and textile and American furniture exhibits, were to be found. The old galleries, built in 1897, could also be reached directly from this level, and contined to be used to exhibit major works of art.

Visitors in the Asian collections (later the Ethnographic Gallery), late 1920's

A thoroughly modern building for its time, the Museum was fireproof, the skylight over the main gallery had a unique "light mixing" chamber, and the air flowing through the galleries was "washed of atmospheric impurities as it heated or cooled the space."

Great care was taken by the staff to acquaint the public with the richness of space, including a series of *Providence Journal* articles in 1927, written by curator Miriam A. Banks, on different galleries. Art in Providence had definitely achieved its full flowering of setting.

A Further Tribute: The Radeke Memorial Garden

Following Mrs. Radeke's death in 1931, a further addition to the exterior Museum space was contributed in her honor. The open courtyard, devoid of planting, was transformed in 1934 into the Radeke Memorial Garden. As remarkable as Mrs. Radeke herself, the garden's planting scheme made a barren space into a rich arrangement of terraces and seating areas surrounding a central pool; plants and trees ranged from the Oriental maidenhair tree (ginkgo) to yew, holly and boxwood, with spring color provided by white azaleas and rhododendrons.[10] The statue of Pan from Mrs. Radeke's own garden at 92 Prospect Street was placed in a niche in the building wall. An article by curator Miriam Banks appearing in the July 1934 *Bulletin* described the rich variety of the plants and their meaning and appropriateness to such a place. In closing, she remarked: "A great English statesman once so loved his garden that he ordered his heart when he died to be buried there in a silver box under a sundial. Instead of burying her heart, the family of Eliza Greene Radeke have chosen to enshrine her memory in living beauty in the heart of the Institution she so deeply loved."

10. Although the central pool has since been filled in, the garden was restored to its original scheme of green and white 50 years later by the Perennial Planters Garden Club.

Photograph of Mrs. Radeke in her own garden, with statue of Pan and pool, at 92 Prospect Street

The Radeke Garden, with center pool and statue of Pan, in the 1930's

Other Spaces: A Postscript

For a time, the Museum enjoyed the possession of a building not connected
to the main plant on Benefit Street. In 1936, the Edward Carrington House
at 66 Williams Street was given to the Museum by a Carrington descendant,
Margarethe L. Dwight. Built in 1810 and purchased in 1812 by Carrington – a
merchant and American consul in China from 1802 to 1811 – the house
functioned as a museum of the China Trade in New England and was
particularly active in its programs during the mid-1940's under Marguerite
Appleton of the Education Department. However, winter closings (for lack
of fuel) predicted the house's doomed future as a permanent part of the
RISD plant. Ultimately the house itself was sold for a private residence, in
1961. Carrington objects, nonetheless, are still part of the Museum's collection.

Having achieved a building of its own by 1926, the Museum of Art, as it
came to be known, was in a position to move into RISD's second half-century
with full confidence in its own visible identity. It is well to remember that
the Museum – any museum – does not consist solely of architecture, but of
individuals. To look over the first 50 years of foundation building, and to
move into the history of the following era to the present, requires an understanding of the people who made the policies, formed the collections, and
gave of their time, their wealth, and their knowledge.

Directors and Donors: Dynamic Partnerships

"The history of a Museum is the history of its collecting, and the perceptive
   visitor may learn a great deal about the history of collecting within the
   state simply by examining the source and accession number of each object.
   The fact that the Museum is especially rich in classical material, in eighteenth century furniture, in Oriental textiles and Japanese prints, and in
   nineteenth century French pictures is due to the continuing, passionate,
   and dedicated enthusiasm of two or three people for more than half a
   century." — *Treasures in the Museum of Art, Rhode Island School of Design,*
   1956

Though the roots of the Museum were established in the 19th century, the
real growth of RISD and its Museum came at the start of the 20th with the
first appointment of a professional head for the institution: Eleazer Bartlett
Homer, who served from 1901 to 1907. In inaugurating endowment campaigns, he benefited both School and Museum. Under him were held exhibits
of American painters (from one of which the renowned Winslow Homer
painting was purchased), of Rhode Island painters, and in April 1903, the
best teacher and pupil work of the Rhode Island School of Design's first 25
years. Certainly, the Pendleton Collection, and the 1905 Museum catalogue,
could be considered his most important achievements in building and consolidating the Museum. By bringing to public attention the work of the
textile department, the new jewelry design department, and the achievements of RISD graduates (such as pottery from New Orleans by William and
Ellsworth Woodward, shown in 1903), he established the School as a serious
and vital community presence. Aside from the Pendleton Collection and
purchases of American art through the Jesse Metcalf Fund, however, his
goals for Museum acquisitions focused on materials directly related to
departmental programs.

Following Homer and the year 1907–08, when Mrs. Radeke served as
acting director, Isaac Comstock Bates became President of the Corporation.

Having served as a trustee since 1885, and vice-president from 1891 to 1907, Bates had been involved in the School, with particular interest in the Museum, from its early days. He shared with Mrs. Radeke a love of American art; as a member of the Providence Art Club, he knew and encouraged many local artists and formed an important tie between them and the Museum. He collected for himself, and frequently with the Museum in mind; the William Merritt Chase *Lady in Pink* given in 1894 is an example. He joined others in acquiring significant works for the collection, such as the Copley portraits of Governor and Mrs. Gill. As described in his memorial exhibit catalogue, 1913: "His taste was not only sensitive and sure, it was catholic and comprehensive." In these important early years, Bates was a staunch supporter of Mrs. Radeke.

The arrival of Huger Elliott in 1908 as director began further efforts toward a raising of standards for the School and students, as well as the important steps of the establishment of the Endowment Committee and the bequest of Hope Brown Russell to the Museum and library, mentioned earlier. Elliott proposed new courses in decorative design, illustration, and the history of costume – and he wanted the Museum to serve as an active educational force. Some of his best students, who went on to teach at the School, included Arthur W. Heintzelman, William H. Drury, and John R. Frazier (later President of the School).

Another of Elliott's achievements was a wider recognition of the importance of the School to the public. With the start of the Sunday docent programs, he established a continuing tradition. In December 1911, he gave the first; the artist Sydney R. Burleigh gave the second; and the third was presented by L. Earle Rowe.

Earle Rowe: Toward "A Museum of Distinction"
When Huger Elliott left Rhode Island School of Design in May 1912 for Boston, he and Rowe exchanged cities. Coming from Boston to Providence, Rowe found a good basis for building a strong museum collection, and he had definite ideas of his own. The Museum had good American paintings, a good start in classical art, and excellent textiles (which Rowe augmented in his first year.) As Elsie Bronson commented, Rowe had a firm acquisition policy: "Two lists were to be kept in mind, one of the things to be acquired in due course, when good examples were offered and terms were favorable, the other of things rare, supreme of their kind, to be taken at the first oppor-

L. Earle Rowe

tunity." In his first year, Rowe collected Chinese mortuary figures and Peruvian pottery and textiles – adding to a collection that would eventually be comprehensive in Peruvian weaving history.

By 1913, Rowe was designated secretary of the Museum Committee, to prepare quarterly and annual reports. The first issue of the official *Bulletin of the Rhode Island School of Design*, with L. E. Rowe as General Editor, appeared in January 1913, devoted principally to information about the Museum:

"With the issue of this bulletin, the Rhode Island School of Design joins the institutions dealing with the teaching of art through schools or museums which have such official organs. The practical value of a bulletin as a means of reaching and interesting the supporters and friends of the museum or school has already been abundantly proved . . . . interest on the part of the general public should be fostered as far as possible. The feeling should be universal that the museum or art gallery is not a treasure-house for a privileged few but a center of art-interests for all."

The January *Bulletin* had already been prepared when Corporation President Isaac C. Bates died on January 1. The April 1913 issue was a memorial to Bates: "It is difficult to attempt to give any adequate account of the extent and the worth of what he did for the School, and of his benefactions to it" – which comprised his various offices performed as Trustee, Vice-President, and President, as well as his collection given without restrictions and a bequest of $55,000. A representative collection of George Inness, Alexander Wyant, and Edward M. Bannister added depth to his extensive American landscape holdings, characterized by small paintings exhibited in his home. Larger canvases included several by Frank W. Benson, as well as Chase and Charles W. Hawthorne. Winslow Homer watercolors of the same period as his oil *Fishin'* showed Bates's taste for Homer's studies of children. Japanese and Chinese works in many media rounded out the diversity of the collection, along with prints and other objects in the decorative arts.

To fill the void left by Bates's death, Mrs. Gustav Radeke was elected President of Rhode Island School of Design. Although the loss of Bates was severe, the presence of Mrs. Radeke as true head, as well as interested supporter, was critically important for Earle Rowe. With her experience in the School and Museum, as well as her cooperation, Rowe's shaping of the collection was considerably facilitated.

Very soon, Mrs. Radeke offered the collection two works in the area most interesting to herself and Earle Rowe. In 1915, she presented a handsome Attic Greek amphora (490–480 B. C.) and an Attic funerary lion of the 4th century B. C. in Pentelic marble. The vase is particularly important to the collection, since its style is distinctive and the hand can be recognized in other works. The RISD piece has given the name to this "Providence Painter," whose elegant figures make the vase's decoration singularly appealing.

Mrs. Radeke continued to give heavily to the Museum in the area of Classical art. Of the vases described in Fascicule I of the *Corpus Vasorum Antiquorum, United States of America*, one-third are Radeke gifts. Her partnership with Rowe in building the Classical collection was certainly not exclusive; she was advised during the 1920's by Edward Perry Warren of Lewis, England. In 1925, 25 vases were acquired through Warren, who sometimes "tossed in" a few gifts of his own.

The 1920's saw many additions to the Classical collection, of the high standard of quality sought by both Earle Rowe and Eliza Radeke: the

Pamphylian Sarcophagus, the Republican head, the head of Augustus, a large collection of ancient jewelry, and the bronze figure of a shepherd. In the year of the opening of the Radeke building, 1926, the beautiful bronze *Aphrodite* was acquired with the help of E. P. Warren. Given Mrs. Radeke's enthusiasm for the Classical collection, it seems highly suitable that, upon her death in 1931, the Attic grave stele with a figure of a mourning woman was acquired in her memory.

Rowe was highly fortunate in the financial support he received beyond that of Mrs. Radeke. The previously mentioned Lyra Brown Nickerson bequest – the largest ever received by the institution – yielded the annual Museum Appropriation Fund, which was added to by others, with Mrs. Radeke as a guiding force. It was this fund that purchased the *Aphrodite* in 1926. The increasing complexity of acquisitions made clear the need for additional professional help for Rowe, and in 1921, Miriam A. Banks was appointed to the staff, and an assistant superintendent of buildings assigned to care for the Museum.

1926: A Banner Year
The successful completion of the Eliza Greene Radeke Building, opening in 1926, was not the only landmark for that year. The Museum announced a bequest of $50,000 from Benjamin Jackson, to be known as the Mary Bixby Jackson Fund, for the purchase of works of art. Many important works of art have been purchased through the years with the Jackson Fund, including two directly in the realm of the Radeke-Rowe shared interest – the bronze Umbrian warrior and the bronze situla. The situla could be said to be one of Earle Rowe's most important acquisitions. It has been widely published and, with one other example, is the most elaborate and intact example known of a north Italian group of situlae. Its presence adds distinction to the antiquities collection of the sort enjoyed by the Providence Painter Vase.

Further windfalls came from other quarters. In 1927, a gift was announced that strikes a strange note today in the history of the Museum's collections and buildings. Marsden J. Perry announced that his home and its furnishings would eventually come to Rhode Island School of Design as "The John Brown House – Marsden J. Perry Trust," along with an endowment fund of $200,000. This offer was received with great rejoicing and fanfare, as RISD envisioned acquiring a link to historic Providence and the prosperity of the four Brown brothers. However, during the Depression, Perry lost his fortune, the furniture was auctioned, and RISD questioned the value of the house without its decorative arts collection. The house was purchased by John Nicholas Brown, who later gave it to the Rhode Island Historical Society; it is the Society's historic museum today.

A Deep, Comprehensive Collection
The successful partnership of President Radeke and Director Rowe was by no means limited to the collecting of Classical art. Mrs. Radeke had a particular interest in 18th century American furniture and participated in the purchase of the Mary Hadley chest, while giving a fine continuous-arm Windsor chair, along with the rest of her furniture collection, as part of her bequest. Sharing an interest in American painting and drawing with her presidential predecessor, Isaac Bates, Mrs. Radeke gave the Museum various works over the years including the American Impressionist John Twachtman's *Spring*, John LaFarge's *The Great Pali* (both of which derived directly

from the artists or their estates), paintings by Emil Carlsen and Willard Metcalf, a charming portrait of his daughter *Eleanor* by Frank W. Benson, and Maxfield Parrish's *Cowboys, Hot Springs, Arizona*.

Mrs. Radeke's strongest mark on the collection was undeniably in the area of 19th century French paintings and drawings. Drawings were her personal passion, and she and Dr. Radeke had collected in many areas; his old masters came to the collection first. It is Mrs. Radeke's French drawings, however, that are truly extraordinary. Her gifts to the Museum during the decade of the 1920's, when she and Earle Rowe essentially laid the groundwork for the tone of the Museum in many of the collection areas, included Edouard Manet's drawing, *Mlle. V. in the Costume of an Espada,* the pride of both Radekes.

The Radeke tradition of collecting French drawings was to be carried on by her niece, Mrs. Murray S. Danforth, with the same high standards of quality. In 1942, Mrs. Danforth gave the Museum a large group of objects, including ten French drawings. Among these, remarkable for their technical diversity and significance in the total *oeuvre* of each artist, are Seurat's conté crayon drawing, *Café Concert,* Cézanne's *Card Player,* and two pastels by Degas, *Dancer with Bouquet* and *Before the Race,* part of an important group of Degas pastels that was collected mainly by members of the Metcalf clan. The quality of the French drawing collection is very largely based on the taste and good collecting sense of Mrs. Radeke and Mrs. Danforth.

Mrs. Radeke was also in the vanguard in gifts of 19th century French painting. Monet seems to have been a particular favorite, and as early as 1920, Mrs. Radeke presented the Museum with *Pont d'Argenteuil,* an unusual view of the river and shoreline seen under a T-shaped section of the bridge.[11] Earle Rowe commented, "Mrs. Radeke did not collect works of art to grace her home, and defer the time of the public's having a chance to see them infrequently on loan to the Museum, or to have them in the permanent collection; rather did she give the larger part of her works of art to be of immediate and permanent use." These early gifts were anonymous, acknowledged and identified only at the time of her death in 1931.

Sharing this interest and appreciation of French painting of the previous century with Mrs. Radeke, Rowe purchased a number of French paintings during the 1920's, including Degas's *La Savoisienne,* the only Degas oil in the collection.

With this strong nucleus of French art established at the Museum during the 1920's, it is not surprising that the following decade was characterized by a growing awareness of French art in Rhode Island and at the Museum. In 1930, the exhibition *Modern French Art* presented works by Picasso, Cézanne, Van Gogh, Gauguin, Dufy, Seurat, Matisse, and others. Great interest was generated, and a lecture given on March 19 by Paul J. Sachs, Associate Director of the Fogg Art Museum at Harvard, was attended by over 800 people – certainly a record for the time. The following year, the Museum presented an exhibition of work by Matisse in a variety of media. Assistance in mounting the exhibit and providing loans came from the artist's son, Pierre Matisse, as well as from a number of collectors. One of these,

11. During the 1920's, several Monets were acquired by gift and purchase through the Museum Appropriation: *Rouen Cathedral, Cliff at Etretat, The Waterlilies,* as well as the 1934 purchase, *Gare St. Lazare.* However, through sale and exchange, this group is totally different from the group of four Monet paintings in the collection today, one of which, *Le Bassin d'Argenteuil,* was the gift of Helen Danforth in 1942.

John Nicholas Brown, wrote in the *Bulletin:* "More public interest in the Museum's activities was aroused by the retrospective exhibition of the works of Henri Matisse than by any single enterprise of recent months. For this reason . . . this venture in the realm of modern art can be called an outstanding success." Perhaps not quite as popular, though certainly pioneering, was the 1933 exhibition of work by André Dunoyer de Segonzac, his first in the United States.

The Other Facets of Rowe
The role of Mrs. Radeke in establishing areas of collecting depth for the Museum is undeniable. Appropriately, following her death, her niece Mrs. Murray S. Danforth succeeded her as President of the Board of Trustees on June 11, 1931. With her similar interests and support, Earle Rowe would continue on an active course for several fruitful years.

Mrs. Murray S. Danforth

Rowe's goal, apart from his areas of interest shared with Eliza Radeke, was to gather a truly encyclopedic collection of art historical objects – always of "museum quality." He believed that "the three great phases of activity which characterize the museums of today are acquisition, preservation and education," and he satisfied the first of these by acquiring 15,000 objects during the 1920's and 30's. Always an archaeologist at heart and by training, his ventures in collecting comprised not only Greek and Roman works, but Etruscan, Egyptian, and New World (especially Peruvian) art, which he sought from his earliest days at RISD.

Another particular interest of Earle Rowe was Asian art. Within three months after arriving at the School, he had collected Chinese mortuary figures and a Chinese hanging scroll painting. Chinese stone steles, a Sung ivory statue, and early ritual bronzes were later incorporated into the collection. In this area, Rowe involved another member of the Metcalf family – Mrs. Radeke's brother, Manton B. Metcalf – in his enthusiasm for Chinese works. The Museum was able to enjoy the fruits of this mutual interest in the generous bequest of Manton B. Metcalf in 1924, received while Earle Rowe was still director of the School.

Persian art was a pioneering field of collecting at the time. Among Rowe's magnificent acquisitions was a large collection of Persian miniatures, in 1917, and later the splendid "turbeh" (tomb cover) of Abdul-Ghassem of 1375. This was to play an unusually important role as part of the *International Exhibition of Persian Art* held at Burlington House, London, in 1931, which was to increase collection building in England and America from recent excavations in the Mesopotamian Valley, Samarra, Rakka, and other areas rich in ceramics. All this, of course, was dear to Rowe's heart. Fortunately, Manton Metcalf's bequest included Rakka pottery; Persian textiles and tiles also formed part of the collection of the artist Florence Koehler, received through Mr. and Mrs. Henry D. Sharpe in 1926. Mrs. Sharpe would continue to be one of the Museum's most discriminating donors.

The 1920's also saw the beginnings of the medieval collection for the Museum. This would take its present installation form after the days of Rowe, but he, with Mrs. Radeke's help, acquired some of the most important pieces. The *St. Peter* from the lost Abbey Church of Cluny and the acquisition in 1922 of a beautiful French Gothic diptych in ivory set a standard for the medieval collection that is unsurpassed.

The Metcalf family had helped Rowe to shape the Renaissance holdings. In 1912, Mrs. Jesse H. Metcalf presented the 15th century Italian terracotta relief depicting the Entombment of Christ. In 1916, when collecting had focused primarily on American painting, Manton Metcalf donated Marco Basaiti's *Portrait of a Venetian Gentleman* and Andrea Previtali's *The Risen Christ;* Jesse Metcalf gave the Florentine panel of the early 15th century, *St. Anthony Abbot.* With this base, the Renaissance collection was given further dimension in the 1920's with the Museum Appropriation purchases of Lippo Memmi's *Mary Magdalen* and the 15th century French sculpture of *Saint Roch.* Clearly, the 1920's was a period of building great diversity in the Museum, as well as depth in certain fields.

In other periods, welcome gifts carried out Rowe's collecting mandate. In 17th century art, the acquisition of Francisco Collantes's *Hagar and Ishmael,* a Spanish landscape of brooding power, revealed the breadth of Manton Metcalf's bequest as well as the collecting taste of the time. The 1920's were, in fact, a time of revival of interest in Baroque art in American collecting.

Rowe actually started the Egyptian collection before arriving at RISD, for while he was in Egypt working under Dr. George A. Reisner of the Harvard University – Museum of Fine Arts Egyptian Expedition, he suggested that objects be sent to the Rhode Island School of Design. From 1911 to 1915, 15 examples of pottery were received from the Egyptian Exploration Fund. In May of 1923, Rowe delivered a public lecture at RISD that has ironic overtones in light of the sweeping interest in his subject in our own day. Speaking on "With the Excavators in Egypt" – or "Tut-Ankh-Amen and others" – according to the Providence *Evening Bulletin,* Rowe:

" . . . minimized the importance of the recent discoveries in the Valley of the Kings, criticised the press for its headlines of the Luxor finds, classified the objects unearthed in the tomb of Tut-Ankhamen as characteristic but by no means the finest examples of the art of the 18th dynasty, and labelled the publicity campaign growing out of the discoveries as an attempt fostered by the Egyptian Government to again attract to Egypt the tourist trade, which had been practically stopped by a number of recent political murders."

Given Earle Rowe's impressive achievements in carrying out the aims of the founders of the School so successfully and vividly, the 50th Anniversary of RISD in 1928 should have been an occasion of great rejoicing. However, Rowe had given too much of himself to the various enterprises of School and Museum, and fell ill in 1928. After a necessary year's leave of absence, he returned in one capacity: as Director of the Museum. Therefore, Earle Rowe can be considered the first "real" Museum Director. Royal Bailey Farnum was appointed Director of Education of the School.

With his time and energies in one place, Rowe could perform at his best for the Museum. The year 1930, just before Mrs. Radeke's death, was particularly active, with an attendance of 101,255 visitors. Twenty special exhibits were mounted, and the exhibition *Modern French Art* alone attracted 13,000 viewers.

New Ventures and Variety

Rowe had spent the winter of his leave in Italy, where his attention was drawn to Etruscan antiquities. As an extension of his Classical art collecting, this specific focus allowed him to enrich the collection with some of its major monuments. The bronze situla – almost a unique survivor of its type – was purchased in 1932 through the Mary B. Jackson Fund. He acquired many exquisite examples of ancient jewelry. Bucchero ware pottery and other bronze articles, such as the urn with handles in the shape of human hands, rounded out this area. The quality of acquisitions remained high in 1932 in several areas, the Tiepolo ceiling fresco from the Palazzo Labia in Venice being an outstanding example.

Programs had a special boost at this time. Sunday gallery talks continued, featuring familiar personalities such as Professor C. A. Robinson, Jr., Mrs. George E. Downing, and Miss Elizabeth T. Casey. In 1932, a special experimental program was launched, the Community Art Project. Operated by the School of Design and Brown University and funded by a Carnegie Grant, this was intended to coordinate the arts in Rhode Island. At first, this took the form of the "Institute of Art," which brought to Providence well-known figures such as Frank Lloyd Wright. In 1935, the Project's "Art Caravan" put on tour two exhibits, one of models of 17th century Rhode Island homes, the other of 20th century landscape painting. Twelve thousand people throughout Rhode Island saw these, and the idea of small shows touring the state became extremely popular. Neighboring Massachusetts and Connecticut towns also participated, and a show of the Project's history, in photographs, was sent to Canada. After three years, the Art Caravan was replaced by the Picture Lending Library, sending to homes and schools examples of good art. By 1940, the Project's Wednesday evening series of lectures and concerts began, held at the Museum itself, allowing participants to enjoy programs and the current exhibitions. The project was discontinued at the time of World War II with gas and travel restrictions; its chief functions were taken over completely by the Museum of Art. Its beginnings in the Rowe era indicated the increasing awareness of the need, and the potential, for art to reach the entire state.

Rowe's directorship gathered momentum, and 1933–35 marked its height in activities, acquisitions, and special achievements. In the Annual Report of 1933–34, curator Miriam Banks wrote of the completion of the beautiful Radeke Garden, truly a living memorial. RISD participated in a significant archaeological venture in the acquisition of the Babylonian lion tile mosaic (which would figure prominently in later Museum exhibit schemes) from the Ishtar gate of Nebuchadnezzar. Other examples went to major museums in New York, Boston, Philadelphia, Detroit, and Chicago, and it was stipulated that, if sold, the mosaic should go to another museum. Other outstanding purchases included Salomon van Ruysdael's *Ferryboat*, a major example of Dutch 17th century landscape, Cézanne's *Jas de Bouffan*, and Maxfield Parrish's *Shepherds*. Mrs. Danforth provided Toulouse-Lautrec drawings of singular variety and quality, giving depth to this area, as well as silver by Samuel Vernon. In a totally different area Rowe found one of the stars of the collection: the bronze *Shiva Nataraja*, a South Indian depiction of the god Shiva as Lord of the Dance. And purchases were made from Museum Appropriation funds to give further depth to earlier 19th century French art, such as the acquisition of Delacroix's *Arabs Traveling*, an oil based on sketches made during the artist's trip in 1832 to North Africa.

Collecting Strength

The years 1934–35 were important not only for individual acquisitions. A sudden clustering of large collections came into the Museum through gift and purchase, and set off a chain reaction of gallery improvements.

In 1934, the opportunity arose to purchase through the Mary B. Jackson Fund a group of over 500 pieces of French wallpaper collected by M. and Mme. Charles Huard of Paris. This important and rare assemblage of scenic, floral, figural, and *trompe l'oeil* papers dates from 1740 to 1840; the Museum has one of the few such collections in this country. Also in 1934, a gift of 623 Japanese color woodblock prints of birds and flowers was received from Mrs. John D. Rockefeller, Jr. (Abby Aldrich Rockefeller). It was her intention to have the prints shown in groups and rotated. Appropriately, the following year three galleries were redecorated to provide a harmonious setting for the prints; the Chinese galleries also received attention.

As if sparked by her sister's gift of the woodblock prints, Miss Lucy Truman Aldrich gave her outstanding collection of Japanese priest robes and costumes for No drama in 1935. She also presented her collection of 18th century European porcelain figures, a fine and varied group, which would be formally catalogued in 1965 by the curator for the Aldrich collections, Elizabeth T. Casey. Mrs. Rockefeller had a hand in the installation of the porcelains, for she, Lucy Aldrich, and Helen Danforth gave an 18th century English pine-paneled room as the setting, transforming the corridor gallery between the original three museum galleries and Pendleton House.

With such important new acquisition assets coming in rapidly, Earle Rowe attempted new experiments in exhibitions. To reach out to the various populations of the state, Rowe mounted an exhibit in 1935 of Portuguese handicrafts as the first of a series showing "folk art" of "Rhode Island citizens of foreign birth." The following year, a similar show for the Swedish Rhode Island population took place. The year 1935 also saw the Thirty-Second Annual Exhibit of Contemporary American Painting, and an important show of Cubist and abstract art from the Museum of Modern Art, shown partially at Brown because of size, opened just after Rowe's death in 1937. The *Tercentenary Exhibit*, emphasizing Rhode Island's contribution to art, was mounted in February and March of 1936.

The last years of Rowe's career – and life – at the Museum truly bear out his credo of 1914: "The three great phases of activity which characterize the museums of today are acquisition, preservation, and education." Individual acquisitions, preservation through collection maintenance as well as safe-guarding intact collections, and educational efforts for the public were evident:

1935 – A large number of school tours was made possible with bus service privately subsidized by "several interested friends."

1936 – Rowe accepted the gift of Carrington House, preserving intact the possessions of three generations of the Carrington family.

1937 – Hubert Robert's painting, *An Architectural Scene – An Old Palace*, was purchased through the Museum Appropriation Fund. This had a distinguished exhibition history and was the only Robert from the United States to be exhibited in Paris for the 200th anniversary of the birth of the artist; it was a great addition to the growing 18th century collection.

1937 – The large Harold Brown collection of French Empire decorative arts – furniture, porcelains, and Chinard's bust of Mme. Récamier – was the last collection Rowe acquired and preserved.

In 1936, the last major purchase of Rowe's career proved especially appropriate. The great Japanese Buddha Dainichi, considered by many to be the symbol of the Museum, the largest wooden Japanese Buddha in a Western museum, was purchased through the Museum Appropriation. Earle Rowe lived long enough to see it installed in its special gallery on the upper floor of the Museum.

On February 17, 1937, Earle Rowe was dead. As part of a series of published tributes, the dealer Robert W. Macbeth said,

"His death is a real blow not only to me, but I feel, to the cause of art in America. He was one man who stood with his feet on the ground, and there are so few of those that we can't spare one."

The Buddha in its gallery setting, ca. 1940

A Dedicated Curator

As Earle Rowe's living memorial, "the building itself and the contents of the Museum show his wide and sympathetic interest, his scholarship, his excellent taste, and his splendid planning. No man could have a better monument." The question of who should and could succeed him, at least temporarily, had an obvious answer: his curator, Miriam A. Banks. She became acting director in March 1937, continuing until December of that year.

Miss Banks had been a strong figure in the background for many years. As she reported in her memorial tribute to Rowe in the *Bulletin*, the collection had increased by approximately 15,000 items in a little over two decades, and she had been personally present for much of that activity. In her own term as acting director, the high point for acquisitions was the purchase of the most important painting from Picasso's Blue Period, *La Vie*, which was later sold and found its way to the Cleveland Museum of Art. From her role as public spokesman, historian, and general commentator, her writings provide much of the flavor of her era in the Museum. Her background was broad; she wrote extensively on the Rockefeller Japanese prints as well as on floral symbolism in the Radeke Garden, on Classical art, and on the history of Earle Rowe's career.

Under Miriam Banks, the Lucy T. Aldrich Collection of Japanese No Drama Costumes and Priest Robes opened in four galleries, two halls on the upper floor, and the main gallery. Installed under Miss Aldrich's personal direction, it was the fruition of a great deal of planning. A lecture was given for the opening by Kojiro Tomita, Curator of Asiatic Art of the Museum of Fine Arts, Boston. The east end gallery on the upper floor had been redecorated with Japanese shoji at the windows, a black lacquer floor, gray walls, and parchment lamps; the collection could thus be shown in rotation in a congenial atmosphere.

The Aldrich porcelain collection opened at the same time, with 150 English and Continental objects specially displayed in the new 18th century English paneled room. Miss Aldrich's extraordinarily eclectic taste included a Benin bronze from Nigeria and American naive painting as well as porcelains and Asiatic costumes. Her contributions to the Museum have added great depth and dimension to the whole collection.

Miriam Banks kept the Museum visible, active, and afloat for a busy year. A new year – and a new director – would shortly bring many changes.

Alexander Dorner: Consolidation and Education

The next Museum director would have as clear a philosophy and style as L. Earle Rowe. Alexander Dorner, recently arrived from Germany where he had been Director of the Landes Museum of Hannover, was offered the Providence directorship in January 1938 with the recommendation of Alfred Barr of the Museum of Modern Art and the sponsorship of John Nicholas Brown. The Museum Committee that endorsed him enthusiastically included such Museum supporters and board members as Mrs. Danforth, Mrs. Rockefeller, Miss Aldrich, Mr. Brown, the artist William Brigham, and the Providence lawyer William Edwards.

Dorner found the attitude of American museums compatible with his own; they were educational, with an emphasis on service to the public. Many years before, Earle Rowe had written: " . . . the art Museum of the future . . . will emphasize the educational function in ways and to a degree not at present realized." Alexander Dorner made education his prime responsibility.

In Germany, Dorner had been attracted to the comprehensive approach to art espoused by the Bauhaus. A suitable space, integrated with the works it contained, could permit better understanding by the spectator of the objects themselves. At RISD, Dorner set out to create "atmosphere galleries," evoking the feeling and look of a particular period by integrating the exhibit arrangements, lighting, colors, labels and recordings, and supplementary material. The visitor would ideally feel immersed in the ambience of the period.

Although Dorner was unable, in his relatively short tenure as director, to carry out all his plans, he did construct atmosphere galleries for Egyptian, Mesopotamian, Classical, and Medieval art. In each gallery, window transparencies were created by Gordon Peers of the School to suggest restorations of buildings which, lit from behind, gave the illusion of space. Modern cases were eliminated and, as far as possible, a feeling for the original situation of a work was sought; for example, the Babylonian lion mosaic was placed on a wall that reproduced, in tones of gray, portions of the original frieze as found by the German archaeologists at the turn of the century. Labels were inconspicuous. Floors were black. The Classical gallery had blue walls "like the Aegean sky"; the Medieval gallery had two large stained glass windows lit from the rear to simulate "the light of heaven." Each of the galleries had an earphone and speaker for music, literature, and gallery talks.

Dorner's penchant for evoking the "original" feeling for a work sometimes led to extremes. In the case of an Egyptian tomb sculpture, Dorner had the arms and chest reconstructed and eyeballs inserted, done to show how the work would have looked, but in such a way that the restorations were easy to differentiate from the original material.

Gothic window being installed as a doorway in the Medieval Gallery, 1940

In acquisitions, Dorner made clear his plans from the beginning. The April 1938 *Bulletin* – sporting a vivid new format with large, compelling photographs – stated that "the buying program should gradually fill in the gaps in the collections." This, rather than broad acquisition of collections or specialization in any one area, was especially true in those periods covered by the new "atmosphere galleries." Perhaps Dorner's best known acquisition is the mummy and coffin of the Egyptian priest Nesmin; he also enriched the Egyptian collection with Coptic mummy portraits and a bronze figure of the seated Horus. The Classical gallery achieved increased architectural verisimilitude with the addition of numerous wall paintings from Boscotrecase and the well-known parakeet mosaic, as well as mosaics from Antioch acquired by exchange from the Worcester Art Museum. Dorner acquired a Coptic doorway, a Romanesque doorway, and a Gothic window and had them installed, piece by piece, as the permanent entrances to the Medieval gallery. The two stained glass windows were also newly acquired.

Contemporary art always fascinated Dorner. He acquired the splendid Ozenfant *Jug* and Franz Marc's watercolors, *Antelope* and *Two Horses*; he had previously bought the Marc works in Germany prior to their subsequent sale by the Nazis. Certainly, it was an unusual distinction for objects to be acquired twice by the same man as director of two different museums.

Alexander Dorner's exhibitions followed closely in the spirit of his acquisitions. Believing Dutch painting to be an important area of need, he not only purchased in the field but mounted a show, *Dutch Paintings*, as his first major special exhibit. With characteristic thoroughness, Dorner included some important Dutch paintings as loans, such as Jacob van Ruisdael's *Jewish Cemetery*, and published a full catalogue for the show, written by Wolfgang Stechow.

The publication of thorough exhibition catalogues was part of Dorner's educational philosophy. In 1939, he founded the Rhode Island Museum

Press; the first publication was *Dutch Painting*, and the second – and last – was Henry-Russell Hitchcock's *History of Rhode Island Architecture*, for the exhibition of the same name. The latter exhibition presented a display of models and oversize photographs, the first show to survey thoroughly the architecture of one state.[12] In producing the Museum's familiar *Bulletin*, Dorner changed not only the look but also the content. Guest specialists wrote extensively on the collections; for example, Professor C.A. Robinson, Jr., covered the history of styles of "Greek and Roman Vases" using the Museum's collection. In selecting this method of publishing the collection, Dorner in effect put guides to the objects into the hands of all the members, with solid art historical content.

Dorner's exhibition schedule could produce surprises. To show the importance of popular contemporary art, Dorner staged a show that created a sensation, *American Cartoonists of Today*. According to his biographer Samuel Cauman, "The popular romantic notion of the art museum as a temple where only the most exalted outpourings of the human spirit may dwell has never been exposed so vividly as by the general shock of surprise that the Museum of the Rhode Island School of Design would gather and display a cartoon show!"

Formal Educational Endeavors
In addition to his didactic gallery schemes, completed through the Medieval period, Dorner also consolidated the Museum's educational efforts by appointing Carolyn MacDonald to head the new Museum Education Department (she later wrote her Ph.D. dissertation on her work at RISD). Educational activity was constantly increasing, with school tours, concerts, and Dorner's own series of art history lectures to 800 public school teachers wanting to use the Museum; an administrator clearly was necessary. Carolyn MacDonald also introduced Dorner to a number of education theories and philosophies, including those of John Dewey and William James.

Docent training became an active part of Museum educational life. Docents were to increase and encourage the participation of the public, particularly school groups. According to Dr. Carolyn Sherman of the University of Rhode Island, "The Museum of Art under Alexander Dorner became a functioning resource in the community life." Dorner felt strongly about art education for children and acted upon his beliefs. In a Providence radio talk, November 2, 1938, he said:

"One usually does not like what one does not understand. (To make this understanding possible through the senses and the intellect is the aim of the rearrangement of our art museum.) The children are our future. Therefore, to start with the children in this new kind of art education seems to me of first importance. . . . I wish to thank the superintendent of our schools, Mr. Hanley, for his understanding and active help in this task."

Dorner the Philosopher
In assessing the contribution of Alexander Dorner, it is necessary to think of him as a philosopher as well as an administrator. His goal in arranging the Museum was, simply put, to express notions of the dynamic growth of man and civilization, and the "progress" of art through the ages. He came

12. This was to be followed up in 1982 by the Museum's exhibit, *Buildings on Paper: Rhode Island Architectural Drawings 1825 – 1945*.

increasingly to view art as an integral part of the history of man, not an isolated phenomenon.

Dorner, as much as Earle Rowe – and other directors to follow – had a very specific theory of museums. How successful he was in a brief span of time has been debated; but his ideas were clear from the start, as his 1938 report to the Museum Committee declares:

> "Being in the first place an educational institution . . . the entire museum collection needs to be rearranged in historical succession. . . . No separation should be made between . . . fine . . . and . . . applied arts. They have never been separated in history. . . . *The rearrangement of the collection* will give the basis for a plan of . . . future . . . acquisitions. Important lacks must be filled out, including . . . examples of interior architecture, furniture, and . . . applied arts. There should be . . . a scholarly annual *publication*, a more popular quarterly . . . and educational papers for children . . . suitable for use in public and private schools . . . if possible, *educational films* on international and Rhode Island art history. . . . In each gallery should be shown a richly illustrated . . . booklet to . . . show the cultural background of each period and so explain the works of art displayed. In this way . . . the succession of the galleries would make clear that the development of art and culture is in active relation to our own age.
>
> "All educational work should result in an understanding of our age."

Time proved to be too short. On September 5, 1941, came the announcement that Alexander Dorner would leave RISD. He subsequently taught art history at Brown, and later continued his career at Bennington College.

Another Interregnum

Once again, Miriam Banks stepped in for a year as acting director until June 1942. It was a quiet year for exhibits. Among the offerings was the Fifth Rhode Island National Salon of Photography. For the public, the Chamber Music series proved to be popular.

Museum Efforts in War and Peace

In July 1942, Gordon B. Washburn arrived from the Albright Art Gallery in Buffalo to serve as Director. His personal mission was to make the Museum of Art "a vital part of the community." This would take rather innovative forms as the Museum found itself serving the public not only in peace, but in war.

To improve communication, Washburn radically changed the style and content of the *Bulletin*, creating a monthly *Museum Notes* in a newsletter format. *Museum Notes* provided information on new acquisitions, special exhibitions (especially their public appeal and educational value), staff activities, public programs such as the Chamber Music series (to which considerable space was devoted), and the Museum's war efforts, which took the form of thematic and benefit exhibits and an unusual but treasured institution: the Gallery Canteen.

The Gallery Canteen provided a note of stability in an otherwise disruptive era. Taking over three galleries in the heart of the Museum, it opened in early December of 1942 with a game room complete with piano and jukebox, a lounge with a card area and milk bar, and a writing room. Mrs. Ralph Eaton was director and from all reports created a true "home away from

The Gallery Canteen

home" for servicemen. The Canteen was supported from contributions, partly those solicited from the Corporation.

At the same time, the private sector was not neglected. The Education Department featured a Junior Room with activities for children. Carrington House opened and provided a new focus for tours. In 1943, a members' room, available for rent by outside groups, was opened in the dining room in Pendleton House.

Members of the Fruit Hill Garden Club at tea in Pendleton House, 1944

A Talented Staff

Washburn made great strides in expanding the staff of the Museum, hiring several highly competent individuals who would change the course of their departments.

The first appointment, Dr. Heinrich Schwarz, brought new organization to the collections. Dr. Schwarz, the former curator of the Austrian State Gallery in Vienna, had come to the Albright Art Gallery in 1940 when Washburn was director there. After two years he was called to Providence with the task of researching and documenting the collection. His fields of specialization and interests were broad: Baroque, 19th century and modern art, and the history of photography. Schwarz's contributions to Museum publications were of a consistently high scholarly level. He was responsible for building the Print Department and for cataloguing the works in that collection.

Since Washburn's interests focused on community involvement, it is not surprising that he worked constantly to strengthen educational programs. In 1943 he appointed Mrs. Harford Powel education director. Her assistant was Eleanor Sayre, who was to play an important role in acquiring objects for traveling exhibits sent to schools and libraries by the Education Department. Miss Sayre, who later became the distinguished Curator of Prints and Drawings at the Museum of Fine Arts, Boston, had a remarkable eye; many of the pieces she collected, particularly North American Indian material, have proved to be rare and valuable, and are on exhibit permanently in the Museum today.

A new Director of Education arrived in 1945: Roberta Fansler Alford. Having been at the Metropolitan Museum's Education Department for 18 years, she would serve at RISD not only in her original capacity, but also as acting director from 1949 to 1952. Mrs. Alford's husband, John, became head of History of Art for the School and she also assisted in the School's art history courses, thus creating a link in the educational efforts of both School and Museum.

An area of the Museum which required particular attention was decorative arts. Accordingly, Washburn selected a new curator, Dr. Rudolf P. Berliner, who came to serve in 1946. In the 1920's and 30's he had been Curator of Decorative Arts at the Bavarian State Museums in Munich and then worked at the Cooper Union (now Cooper-Hewitt) Museum in New York. Dr. Berliner's field was ornament, and he devoted several exhibits to this theme.

Other new staff in the early years of Washburn's tenure included Marguerite Appleton, appointed as Museum lecturer, and Narcissa Williamson in Education (who later became Keeper of Musical Instruments at the Museum of Fine Arts, Boston).

A Surge of Activity

From the start, Washburn declared his interest in "having the Museum play an active part in the community war effort." One of his earliest shows in 1943 was of a group of Russian icons, an exhibit intended to "do its bit" in the drive for Russian war relief. Other shows were also intended to remind the public of the presence of overseas allies. February 1944 was a time for *Blitzed Architecture of London*, which showed London buildings before and after bombing. The exhibit in the fall of 1944, *Old and New England*, was a war bond sale during its first week. The student exhibit in May of 1943 focused on the School's war program, with signal flags from the textile department, camouflage, posters, and war machinery designs. October 1943 featured *Wings over America*, an exhibition of photographs of the training of Army fliers. In 1944 a show of drawings by servicemen was presented, including the work of William Grosvenor Congdon, the young Providence artist who created a portrait of S. O. Metcalf for the foyer of the new College Building.

Many exhibits during the war years had a very limited geographic focus – on Rhode Island, or New England – and Americana was much in evidence. In May of 1943, Washburn continued the tradition of an exhibit of Rhode Island artists; feeling communication had been a problem, he had met with all the artists to work out plans. This became an annual event. The next September, *American Rooms in Miniature*, created by Mrs. James Ward Thorne, was shown along with *Speak Their Language*, a cartoon show investigating the differences between American and British temperament. A special event was a showing of American costumes, modeled by students, from the collections of the Museum, Carrington House, and the RISD Costume Department. The next month, a show of silver made by Paul Revere and other Americans continued the native emphasis. Just after the war, in 1946, an exhibition called *The Negro Artist Comes of Age* showed the Museum's painting by Horace Pippin, *Quaker Family*, for the first time and included prints by Wilmer Jennings, who became a jewelry designer in Rhode Island.

Under Rudolf Berliner, major exhibits in decorative arts took place. The *Ornamentation* series began. The *Textile Panorama* of February – March 1947, based on a similar show held at the Brooklyn Museum the year before, presented a wide range of materials including Coptic, Peruvian, and

European. The next year, Daniel Tower organized a show of *Furniture of Today*. This gathering of American furniture – all in mass production – featured well-known designers such as Charles Eames and Alvar Aalto. The main gallery was specially installed, imitating a trellised garden. The opening included a lecture by Edgar C. Kaufman, Jr., director of the Department of Industrial Design at the Museum of Modern Art, on "Modern Interiors of the Last 50 Years."

Of even more immediate interest to the Providence audience was the November 1948 exhibit on the physical future of the city, *Providence Looks Ahead*. Sponsored by the Chamber of Commerce, the City Plan Commission, the Redevelopment Agency, the Museum, and 40 other civic organizations, the show looked at areas of civic improvement in recreation, traffic, parking, and housing. Photographs and models of Corliss Park and Valley View Housing, as well as a model built by RISD students of the proposed Mashapaug Community, gave tangible evidence of civic dreams.

By the late 1940's, several staff members who would serve with distinction for many years had arrived. Elmina Malloy succeeded Herwin Schaefer as Registrar; Sofia Vervena became Assistant to the Director of Education; and Eleanor Fayerweather joined the staff of the School in 1947 as instructor in clothing and fashion, to become curator of the costume center after its move to the Museum in 1956.

Gordon Washburn leapt into acquisitions early, in 1943. Out of a show of 19th century French painting, he enriched the Museum's holdings in the early part of that century by purchasing Corot's youthful work, *Honfleur, le vieux bassin*. Two important later French paintings came shortly thereafter, Cézanne's *Au Bord d'une Rivière* and Monet's *La Seine à Giverny*. By sale and exchange, Washburn gathered Géricault's *Cart Loaded with Kegs* and Renoir's *Young Shepherd*, and ventured into more diverse fields with the acquisition of the Spanish Romanesque *Crucified Christ*.

As if in summation of his career at the Museum, Washburn exhibited 73 paintings in February 1949, representing the major movements in art since 1800. As an effort in interpretation, which Washburn published in a handbook for the show, it was consistent with his overriding museum philosophy: involve and reach the community, and make the Museum – and art – vital and immediate.

An Active Acting Director

After Gordon Washburn's departure, Roberta Alford became acting director for three years, from 1949 to 1952. She had established herself as an active museum educator and had been involved with several exhibitions, particularly the 1947 show of *Painting in the Ancient World*, which had focused on the new Classical gallery installation incorporating Pompeiian murals (bought in 1938) and three 4th century A.D. floor mosaics acquired by exchange with the Worcester Art Museum in 1939.

Mrs. Alford had a coherent, comprehensive scheme for the Museum which she proposed in *Museum Notes* of January 1950 as "A Philosophy and a Plan." The galleries should follow an historical sequence so the "Museum can function as a kind of historical compass." Acquisitions would "serve a specific educational need in filling out the panorama of cultural history" (a return to Dorner's point of view). The biggest gaps she perceived to be in contemporary art and the art of 1500–1800.

According to Mrs. Alford, works must, of course, be of highest quality. This was true of recent purchases, including the German (formerly called

Italian) brass candlestick in the shape of a man, and the pen and bistre wash Rembrandt drawing, *Landscape with Farm Buildings and High Embankment*, acquired through the Jesse Metcalf and Mary B. Jackson Funds and published with extensive documentation by Heinrich Schwarz.

Loan exhibits would be reduced in number to allow more showing of the permanent collection, especially in neglected areas of strength; she cited American paintings and sculpture, and the Steinert collection of early keyboard and string instruments.

Mrs. Alford planned to continue Dorner's scheme of "cultural period rooms" beyond the medieval, and to move the French paintings to the top floor "where their popularity will overcome the psychological barrier of a flight of stairs." Art from 1500 to 1800 would replace French art on the main floor.

A new architectural feature was planned for that winter: the enclosed bridge over the Radeke Garden between Pendleton House and the European galleries. The north room in Pendleton would be reserved for changing exhibits of Rhode Island furniture.

Mrs. Alford was especially concerned that the Decorative Arts collection should maintain a high level of acquisitions, with particular attention to the objects' potential usefulness for students of design. Appropriately, in 1949 the Jacob Ziskind Collection of textile drawings and samples, formerly the property of the Arnold Print Works in North Adams, Massachusetts, was accepted by the Museum.

The 1951 exhibit, *The Albert M. Steinert Collection of Keyed and Stringed Instruments,* which included two important harpsichords by the Ruckers family, fulfilled a dream of Mrs. Alford. In 1950, she had written on the history of the very popular chamber music series, which for space reasons had been moved to the RISD Auditorium in 1946. Mrs. Alford hoped to have some concerts back in the galleries, using instruments from the Steinert collection. The April 1951 concert did, in fact, employ the Hans Ruckers harpsichord on exhibit.

Several major purchases were added to the collection during Roberta Alford's term as acting director. Heinrich Schwarz acquired the exquisite oil by Sébastien Bourdon, *Landscape with a Mill,* a remarkable classicizing 17th century work that helped to fill the 300-year gap in history remarked upon by Mrs. Alford. She and her husband visited Henry Moore in England and acquired two drawings as well as his bronze sculpture, *Interior-Exterior.*

A New Look

Before relinquishing her position, Roberta Alford succeeded in reinstalling the galleries as she had proposed. The Pendleton Collection of English and American furniture received special attention. Three new galleries were established: High Renaissance and Baroque, 18th century, and early 19th century Napoleonic art. The French paintings of the later 19th century had been moved upstairs. The nucleus of these collections was acknowledged by Mrs. Alford to be the Hope Brown Russell bequest of 1909, the Isaac Bates bequest, the Brownell gift of 1929, and the Susan Martin Allien bequest of 1935. Once again, it was clear that preserving large collections was the stuff of which the Museum was made.

By the end of Mrs. Alford's directorship, new faces on the staff included Graeme Keith as Assistant Decorative Arts Curator, Betty Burroughs Wood-house, Instructor, and John McCarville, Preparator, known familiarly as "Mr. Mac."

The Lucy Truman Aldrich Japanese and
Chinese robes in renovated gallery
(photograph taken in May 1968)

John Maxon: An Eclectic Eye

John Maxon assumed the Director's post in July 1952. He continued reorganizing the Museum galleries in the spirit of Mrs. Alford, and succeeded ultimately in opening all the major galleries. In 1953, the time was right for a new look for the Oriental galleries on the top floor, which had been named in memory of Abby Aldrich Rockefeller. Her sister, Lucy Truman Aldrich, engaged William G. Perry of Perry, Shaw and Hepburn to renovate and redesign the room containing Japanese No Drama costumes and priest robes. Miss Aldrich also persuaded her nephews, Nelson A. and David Rockefeller, to commission the architect Philip C. Johnson (then Director of the Department of Architecture at the Museum of Modern Art) to reinstall Mrs. Rockefeller's print collection in a specially designed gallery, as well as to redesign the third gallery, which at that time held a 17th century Brussels tapestry given by Winthrop W. Aldrich, three Kashmir rugs lent by Miss Aldrich, and, in two specially made steel and glass cases, a group of 17th century Chinese porcelains lent by John D. Rockefeller, Jr.

Miss Aldrich's support of the collections and their exhibit spaces was generous and varied. At her death in 1955, when John Maxon was Director, her gifts had included two items in welcome areas in addition to the Asiatic: the Elizabethan *Portrait of a Lady of the Hampden Family*, and the 17th century Benin bronze ancestor portrait head, a highly valued part of the African art holdings and a work of unmatched quality. According to Maxon, Miss Aldrich "was distinguished by the firmest of Yankee character, a real warmth, and an extraordinary sparkle" – and consummate taste.

Maxon's plans for the look of the rest of the Museum were well thought out and definite. In *Museum Notes* of Spring 1954, he expressed the notion that the usual chronological ordering was not the only possible presentation, "but it is didactically logical and convenient." He planned no radical changes, but rather a perfecting of the scheme. As an example of this refining, he created a new coat area to free the handsome lobby for a gallery of Greek sculpture to honor Eliza Radeke. This space, as well as the Roman and Greek vase galleries, was repainted, and new backgrounds were created for the Medieval, Renaissance, Baroque, and Rococo galleries. An "Empire Salon" was designed for the Harold Brown decorative arts collection.

The Waterman galleries were hung with American 19th and 20th century paintings, many of which had not been seen by the public for years. The stairwell gallery leading to this area contained the Sargent *Portrait of Manuel Garcia*, Eastman Johnson's large oil sketch for *Sugaring Off*, Washington Allston's *Head*, the Sully portrait, Winslow Homer's *On a Lee Shore*, the Opper *Fire Engine*, and the Providence Theatre drop curtain of 1808, lent by the Rhode Island Historical Society.

Maxon believed in "islanding" an object, so that the viewer was undistracted by other – even related – material. Unlike Dorner, he wanted to avoid didactic treatment. The Museum should be informal in feeling with "an un-museumlike atmosphere" so that the viewer leaves "exhilarated, not exhausted."

The mandate for acquisitions was clear to Maxon. In pointing out great areas of Rhode Island collecting that had come to the Museum – Aldrich and Rockefeller for Asiatic, Radeke for Classical, Danforth for 19th century – he asserted: "I have long felt that the presence of an important collection in a museum is the best reason for augmenting that collection, and I firmly believe that a small museum should concentrate on developing its strengths and only incidentally attempt the impossible task of telling in detail the whole

The Neo-classical gallery during the Maxon era

story of art." He felt that Earle Rowe had done a superb job, but that now further diversification was not the most crucial task of collection building.

There were gaps, however, that Maxon wished to address. Contemporary art needed increased exhibition exposure *and* acquisitions. Maxon would expand the 19th century collections to embrace new areas, particularly work by Tissot and other Victorian painters. William Frith's *Salon d'or at Bad Homburg* is one of a group of English acquisitions, in an area not previously popular at the Museum, which Maxon said should be appreciated on literary as well as formal grounds. In general, Maxon was interested in building up the English painting collection, and purchased oils by Edward Matthew Ward and William Etty, gratefully accepted Mrs. Danforth's gift of the Joshua Reynolds caricature, and lamented the lack of major works by artists such as Turner or Constable.

By far the greatest area of acquisition under Maxon was in Italian painting, particularly Baroque; he was assisted by Anthony M. Clark, who became Secretary of the Museum in 1955. Additionally, Clark participated in exhibitions and took over the editing of *Museum Notes* in November 1955. This publication had returned in 1953 to the size and format of the Rowe era, in booklet form, published three times a year. Clark had plenty to report about the active collecting pursuits of John Maxon.

Maxon was nothing if not eclectic in his acquisitions: the Archaic Greek *Kouros*; Carpeaux's painting, *Bathers*, purchased in memory of Earle Rowe; Prud'hon's oil sketch for *Divine Vengeance and Justice Pursuing Crime*, the gift of Mrs. Danforth in memory of Mrs. Radeke, on the occasion of the 75th anniversary of the School; works from the Venetian school, such as Francesco Bassano's *Birth of the Virgin*,[13] Francesco Guardi's *Scuola di San Marco*, and Tintoretto's oil sketch, *The Combat between Tancred and Clorinda*; the magnificent *Christ at the Column* by Mathias Stomer, a Dutch follower of Caravaggio; Poussin's *Venus and Adonis*; and Francesco Vanni's altarpiece of *The Vision of St. Francis* from the church of Nôtre-Dame-des-Anges in Lyon. A particular coup turned out to be the terracotta bust of a *Venetian Nobleman*, purchased in 1954 as a work by Alessandro Vittoria, a pupil of the Florentine/Venetian master sculptor, Jacopo Sansovino. Nearly 30 years later, John Pope-Hennessy reattributed the work to Sansovino himself.

The Museum's holdings of decorative arts were enriched by a number of major acquisitions. Through Jack Linsky, who had given the Museum many objects over the years, a Louis XV console table arrived. The Providence Art Club lent its superb secretary desk by Guillaume Beneman, a major asset to the Empire Gallery. When in 1980 the Art Club was forced to sell the desk, a signed work with handsome decorative mounts reflecting the influence of Napoleon's Egyptian Campaign of 1800–01, the Museum was able to purchase it through the Helen M. Danforth Fund and thus assure its permanent position as the focal point for the French Empire collection.

Some of the Museum's most significant acquisitions during Maxon's directorship came from the oldest, as well as the most recent, periods of art. The anonymous gift of a Greek marble koré, as well as the purchase of a very rare Greek marble head from the 5th century B.C., continued the fine tradition of Classical collecting of the Radeke era. Perhaps the single most

13. See the article by W. R. Rearick on Leandro Bassano and the Dal Ponte family, note 1, *Museum Notes*, 1982. This painting has been variously attributed to both Jacopo and Francesco Bassano.

important work acquired in the Maxon period is Edouard Manet's masterpiece, *Le Repos*, bequeathed in 1959 by Edith Stuyvesant Vanderbilt Gerry. It is a painting which had sparked extreme reactions, ranging from harsh criticism at the 1873 Salon to this tribute from the dealer Durand-Ruel: "C'est une des oeuvres les plus remarquables de Manet. Sa valeur est immense." Théodore Duret had bought it from Durand-Ruel, sold it, and Durand-Ruel bought it back. At that point, Berthe Morisot herself wanted it, "but through an error of her bidder, she lost it." Of such errors is museum history made.

Maxon also offered contemporary art shows, planned an annual exhibition by young Rhode Island artists, and featured a 1959 show of "a collection in the making," *Paintings since 1945*, owned by Richard Brown Baker, whose collection has appeared several times at the Museum.

Giving

Maxon was quick to recognize the importance of his donors. With such an active acquisition program, he sought increased support and a broader base of such support from the membership in a *Museum Notes* article on "Giving," in March 1958. Maxon mentioned several important objects that the Museum could not have acquired by itself, or that filled gaps not in the current buying program. A special gift in the 19th century area was the Degas pastel of *Jockeys*, virtually a pendant to one previously presented by Mrs. Murray Danforth; it was given by G. Pierce Metcalf, who also donated Monet's *Honfleur*, by bequest. Maxon also pointed out another source, or rather cause, of giving: the enticing exhibition (such as *The Age of Canova*, which resulted in the gift of six Italian drawings from Janos Sholz).

Staff Changes

By 1956, the middle of Maxon's term, the staff had shifted and expanded. Bernice Davidson was the Chief Curator, Graeme Keith and Betty Burroughs Woodhouse were now their respective department heads, Anita Glass was Keeper of Photographs, Thomas F. Ryan had become Superintendent, and Marguerite Appleton had retired. A new department was created in that year. The Costume Center moved from the School to the Museum, and with it came Eleanor Fayerweather. She had come to the School in 1947 as instructor in clothing and fashion. Having worked previously at the Brooklyn Museum with a fine costume collection for teaching, Miss Fayerweather saw the need for such a collection at RISD.

Textiles were already under Dr. Berliner's care in the Museum, but costumes were scattered around, if they existed at all; many things had been given to the School's drama department, and Eleanor Fayerweather had to rescue them. Two years after Miss Fayerweather's arrival, she was approached by Edna Lawrence (who created the School's Nature Lab); Miss Lawrence had gathered and saved a number of costume items, especially North African works, which she placed in Miss Fayerweather's care.

John Maxon appreciated the costume collection and its value and, in fact, had been part of the "rescue" mission himself, having found some Poiret evening wraps in the Woods-Gerry mansion which are now valued items in the Museum's costume holdings. He instigated the move of costumes to the Museum, and thus an important study resource for apparel design students, as well as gems for public viewing, established itself and grew. The collection was added to by local donors as well as others; eventually large representative

Eleanor Fayerweather

holdings included designs by Fortuny, Bonnie Cashin, Vera Maxwell, and Charles James.

In June of 1959, John Maxon left RISD for the Art Institute of Chicago. Appropriately, the Museum Committee gave the Degas drawing, *Two Seated Women*, in his honor, adding strength to strength.

David Giles Carter: Education and Building on Strengths
The Museum's new director, David Carter, arrived in 1959 from the John Herron Art Museum in Indianapolis. After a year he was prepared to issue his policy for the Museum, "The Museum Surveyed." He neatly summarized John Maxon's accomplishments and style:

" . . . astute and significant acquisitions, a reorganization of the Museum's galleries, a series of important exhibitions, a recasting of *Museum Notes* [devoting it to scholarly articles], new publications [through Anthony Clark], and a stimulation of new interest in the Museum."

Beyond this, Carter urged increased university and secondary school use of the Museum and a change in its image of exclusiveness, feeling that increased attention to young people would help. "This year, through the generosity of the Junior League of Providence, Inc., our small staff is supplemented by the part-time services of Mrs. Frederick Thomas as Public School Coordinator and Supervisor of Volunteers." This resulted in greater services through the training and use of volunteers and was the true start of the Education Department docent program as it exists today.

Pearl Nathan lecturing to a school group in front of the mummy

Carter planned to maintain the chronological order of the galleries, with a few changes, but felt that the objects should be handled as little as possible for their safety. The collection should "reveal the countenance of our western culture" and become a "Mecca" for scholars in areas of strength.

"Considering our funds and the supply of material, the public may expect to see a building up of existing strengths such as the Classical field and a marked interest in Medieval, Renaissance, Northern Baroque and to a lesser extent, Far Eastern Art. The administration must have the conviction to buy quality advantageously in areas not currently popular."

New Look, New Faces, and the Museum Forum

The installation of the Museum would remain essentially the same, but Carter planned some changes reflecting his own interests. There would be a new setting for the Miller bequest of American furniture and silver, four cases created for the George H. Warren collection of swords, and other arms and armor, and a complete reorganization of the Northern Renaissance and Italian Quattrocento collection.

New staff appointments were announced. Elaine P. Loeffler was Chief Curator, and Hugh J. Gourley III became Curator of Decorative Arts and editor of *Museum Notes*. Carter also credited Eleanor Fayerweather with the successful growth of the costume collection and announced that, in addition to her faculty duties, she had officially been named Curator of the Costume Center of the Museum. During Carter's term, the first full-fledged showing of the costume collection was held in the South Gallery of the Museum.

The Education Department had developed a new scheme: the Museum Forum. Its intention was teaching by using a relatively permanent exhibit of historically arranged material and changing school projects. Dr. Charles L. Kuhn of the Busch-Reisinger Museum at Harvard had helped the Museum to obtain 35 groups of casts; maps and photomurals would be installed; and study pieces would include some works too damaged for the main exhibit areas – "noble wrecks if you like" was Carter's assessment.

Mrs. Thomas was put in charge, the hope being that with increased educational activity, legislation securing state support for educational programs would allow her to be put on regular staff. Other possibilities for increased programming included using the Museum's teacher training program to set up several affiliated art centers coordinated by the Museum, and more circulating exhibits – almost a revival of aspects of the Community Arts Program under Rowe.

The Forum opened on November 1, 1961, with an exhibit on Egypt and the Ancient Near East displayed in the South Gallery. Designed by Mac-Donald Associates of Providence, the space consisted of movable partitions for flexible use. Gordon Peers again provided replication material, this time a painted reconstruction of the Ishtar Gate; the lion mosaic had been installed in the Egyptian Gallery on the upper floor. The Forum could be used with guides or as a self-teaching area.

Plans for future expansion included the addition of Greek, Roman, and Byzantine material and, in the gallery across the hall, Medieval, Renaissance, and 18th and 19th century art. Twentieth century art would appear in the foyer on the level below, to complete the cultural progression.

Education was not the only area pressed for funds. Carter recognized the need for greater endowment, and the projects he proposed are a very familiar list for staff even today: maintenance, an auditorium with a capacity for 350 people, the Forum, air-conditioning, conservation, larger exhibits, more guards and other staff, publications, and acquisitions.

Major Acquisitions in New Areas

As he had promised, Carter looked to new areas of collecting immediately. Northern art was enriched shortly after his arrival with the purchase of the Tilman Riemenschneider lindenwood *Pietá* from the Museum Works of Art Fund. Further accessions concentrated heavily on Northern painting: Joachim Wtewael's *The Marriage of Peleus and Thetis*, Hendrick Goltzius's *Christ on the Cold Stone*, and Pieter Lastman's *St. Matthew and the Angel*.

One of the most distinguished acquisitions under David Carter was the 15th century Utrecht panel, *The Crucifixion with the Two Thieves*, whose author came to be known as the Providence Master. With justifiable pride, Carter wrote, "It is not often that a museum or art historian can announce in one breath both a significant addition to its collection and an extension of our knowledge of a little known school of painting. The Museum may claim that distinction for its new acquisition . . . the first fifteenth century Utrecht panel to enter the permanent collection of an American museum," purchased with the aid of an anonymous gift.

David Carter started a Museum tradition in 1962 with the first exhibition of "Art For Your Collection." To encourage collectors in the community, this consisted of works of art in all media, gathered by members of the staff and offered in an exhibit/sale lasting about one week. The public flocked to see this appealing assortment of pieces which could be added to their personal collections. With one interruption, these popular shows have occurred annually ever since, and the 20th anniversary of this event was celebrated in the fall of 1983 with a special retrospective of past purchases.

After several busy years in the early 1960's, David Carter left the Museum in June of 1964 for another directorship in Montreal. As a tribute to his role, particularly in increasing the collection of Northern European works, the Board Chairman, Mrs. Danforth, presented a German 11th century bronze lion in David Carter's honor. Hugh Gourley became acting director for the following year.

Daniel Robbins: Contemporary Collections
With the arrival of Daniel Robbins on the Museum scene in May 1965, the Museum entered the contemporary world in full force. Robbins started important new collections of modern art and presented Providence with a galaxy of contemporary exhibitions and events that brought new vitality to Museum offerings.

It was traditional for the Museum to build solid, coherent collections: witness the Bates bequest, the Pendleton Collection, the Huard wallpapers, the Harold Brown collection, the Radeke and Danforth 19th century French paintings and drawings, to name just a few. Robbins was able to open a new collection in a little more than a year after his arrival: the Nancy Sayles Day Collection of Latin American Art, whose opening exhibit and catalogue appeared in the fall of 1966. Latin American art was of great interest to Robbins, and as he stated in the catalogue, "The Museum of Art, Rhode Island School of Design, has been presented with a unique opportunity to form a collection in this new and adventurous area. We owe this opportunity to the children of Nancy Sayles Day, who suggested and made possible the beginning of this contemporary Latin American Collection. They believed that this is the type of exciting, creative project that she would have enjoyed and have taken pleasure in sharing with Providence – her birthplace. . . . The Nancy Sayles Day Collection gives the Museum of Art a chance to take a chance . . . to participate vigorously in what is happening now. . . ." The collection came eventually to include many media and artists, and continues to receive additions.

Another special opportunity presented itself when Selma Pilavin (now Mrs. Murry Robinson) established in 1967 the Albert Pilavin Memorial Collection of Twentieth Century American Art in memory of her husband, "whose progressive ideas . . . would be sympathetic to these first acquisitions." Collecting contemporary art had been a tradition at the Museum from the start; the purchase of Winslow Homer's *On a Lee Shore* was just the beginning, and Isaac Bates contributed substantially to the contemporary American holdings. Yet there had been a lull in the collecting of American art following World War II, and the Pilavin Collection gave new impetus and direction, reviving what was in many ways a basic Museum practice. Running the gamut of styles, including major compositions by Cy Twombly and Ellsworth Kelly, Wayne Thiebaud's popular teaser *Wimbledon Cup*, and, more recently, the forceful lead sculptures by Robert Wilson, *The Stalin Chairs*, the collection has become an essential part of the fabric of taste and thought of the Rhode Island museum public. Selma Pilavin Robinson's dedication to this ideal has inspired the Museum – and other collectors – ever since.

In the area of graphics, the 20th century has received further emphasis from the Robbins era through the present, particularly with gifts from Mr. and Mrs. Bayard Ewing and their endowment of the Twentieth Century Graphics Fund. The Ewings, along with other donors, also purchased a large painting by Mark Rothko in honor of Daniel Robbins in September 1971. The graphics collection has been enriched by their generosity with works by Lichtenstein, Rosenquist, Rauschenberg, and Frank Stella.

Exhibits during Robbins's tenure also focused heavily on the contemporary area. In 1964, *Paintings and Constructions of the 1960's from the Richard Brown Baker Collection* presented the second selection from this great collection. The 1966 retrospective of Walter Murch, the showing of the Roy Neuberger Collection and *The Jazz Age* in 1968, followed by *Contemporary Black Artists* in 1969 and *Joaquín Torres-García* (who is richly represented in the Nancy Sayles Day Collection) in 1970, are good examples. Perhaps the best remembered show, also of 1970, was *Raid the Icebox*, when none other than Andy Warhol pulled works from the Museum's storage for exhibition, from Romanesque stone columns to French shoes to American hatboxes.

Other Directions

While contemporary art received much attention, the staff was busy in other areas of exhibits and acquisitions. In 1965, Hugh Gourley mounted a major show, *The New England Silversmith,* covering three centuries of craftsmanship, for which, perhaps, the exhibition in 1983 of Gorham silver was the logical successor. In 1968, Eleanor Fayerweather's department presented *Russian Stage and Costume Designs.*

Growth in areas other than contemporary art posed increased problems and obligations. Visiting Curator of Paintings and Graphics Henri Zerner stressed the Museum's need for an extensive print collection, changing exhibits, and a good, separate print study room. He praised Heinrich Schwarz's "shrewd purchase policy" and the Museum's generous donors for the formation of a remarkable collection, including good 19th century works, 18th century Venetian etchings, Neo-classical prints, important sheets by Rembrandt, Dürer, and Goya, "as well as less familiar treasures such as two admirable softground etchings by Gainsborough so rare that very few print collections include them."

The year 1966 was a landmark for Robbins. A fund drive for $70,000 resulted in 372 donations toward the purchase of Rodin's bronze, *Study for the Monument to Balzac.* Perhaps the most controversial of several studies created by Rodin for this commission, it is a highly important, powerful

Daniel Robbins and Thomas Ryan with Rodin's statue of Balzac dramatically
unveiled in the Radeke Garden

sculpture and was a significant addition to the 19th century bronzes in the
Museum.

Later acquisitions of particular interest included the purchase of Raymond
Duchamp-Villon's *Seated Woman*, a Cubist bronze with gold leaf patina, and
its preparatory drawing in charcoal. A gift in 1968 held special significance
for Rhode Island: an oil by Martin Johnson Heade, *Brazilian Jungle,* 1864,
was probably purchased directly from Heade by Henry Lippitt (later
Governor of Rhode Island) to furnish his handsome house at 199 Hope Street.
In 1938, the painting passed to his grandson, C. Richard Steedman, in whose
house at 271 Angell Street it remained until being given by the Steedmans to
the Museum.

Publications Policy

Robbins turned *Museum Notes* to new usefulness by taking the existing
publication and adapting it into a full catalogue for special shows and
collections. By 1967, periodic exhibits of *Recent Accessions* were begun, with
Museum Notes as an accompanying catalogue, under the direction of Dr.
Stephen E. Ostrow, who became Chief Curator in 1967.

The Brown University faculty became increasingly involved in the activities
of the Museum; in 1966, Presidents Albert Bush-Brown of RISD and Barnaby
Keeney of Brown arranged a joint curatorial appointment whereby art history
professors at Brown spent one semester in an exclusively curatorial capacity
at the Museum of Art. Stephen Scher surveyed the Medieval collection, and
Henri Zerner returned to Prints and Drawings. Carl Goldstein followed
Scher in Northern Baroque art. These exchanges were to involve new acqui-
sition possibilities in addition to publications and major exhibits, such as
The Renaissance of the Twelfth Century produced by Scher in 1969, and the
Tissot catalogue prepared by Zerner.

The Pace Quickens

In 1967-68, the Pilavin Collection had begun, with the rare painting by Patrick Henry Bruce, *Still-Life-Forms*, 1920-21, and Andy Warhol's *Race Riot*. The Tissot retrospective was held. Pendleton House was completely refurbished, a project of the Museum Associates under the direction of John Kirk, Consultant Curator for Pendleton House. Elizabeth Casey rearranged all of the Oriental collection. With the publications program moving along under

Elizabeth Temple Casey with friends at her retirement party in the Radeke Garden, June 23, 1978

Ostrow's direction, guest author Brunilde Ridgway completed the Classical Stone Sculpture catalogue. The walls seemed to burst, with over 96,500 visitors the next year.

The Robbins term ended in June 1971, upon his departure to direct the Fogg Art Museum at Harvard.

Stephen Ostrow: Research and Reassessment

When he became Director of the Museum in July 1971, Dr. Stephen E. Ostrow took hold of the publication program of the collection, revived under Daniel Robbins, and began a long-range coordinated group of publications: the *Selection* series. The purpose was straightforward in theory and complex in execution: to research and catalogue, then publish and exhibit, the whole collection. In effect, Ostrow was continuing the path established by Heinrich Schwarz almost 30 years earlier.

New staff came to assist in the endeavor. Since Ostrow's appointment as Director left no Chief Curator, he selected J. Patrice Marandel for that position. R. Ross Holloway of Brown became Consultant Curator of Antiquities to supervise the editing and production of the catalogues of the Classical collection. Diana L. Johnson had already arrived, in 1969, as Assistant Curator of Prints and Drawings, where she was working to organize and transfer the graphics storage to a new area for storage, study, and exhibition. A Print Room was opened to students and the general public, though at the loss of some of the Costume Center's space.

The task was great for the publication program, since over 28,000 objects had been accessioned by the time Stephen Ostrow became Director. However, all over the country this type of reevaluation and consolidation prevailed in museums. The first endeavor, *Selection I: American Watercolors and Drawings from the Museum's Collection,* appeared as the December 1971 issue of *Museum Notes.* It was followed in April 1972 by *Selection II: British Watercolors and Drawings from the Museum's Collections.* This exhibit and catalogue was occasioned by the anonymous gift over several years of more than 500 British watercolors and drawings of the 18th and 19th centuries. Overnight, the Museum had become a center for British studies. Malcolm Cormack came from the Fitzwilliam Museum in Cambridge, England, for six months as Consultant Curator, as well as Visiting Professor at Brown; from his research and the work done in his seminar, the British drawings were published, and this extraordinary treasure trove became accessible to the widest public.

The completion of *Selection VII: American Paintings from the Museum's Collection, ca. 1800-1930* was a time of celebration, for it coincided with the Centennial of Rhode Island School of Design. Over 100 paintings from a collection of more than 400 were mounted for exhibit, while others received conservation care and documentation. The history of the institution was evident in many respects, such as the large holdings from the Isaac Bates bequest. Following the exhibit, in 1978, Mrs. Houghton P. Metcalf, Sr., gave the marvelous painting, *A Boating Party,* by John Singer Sargent, in memory of her husband; they had acquired it 30 years earlier. This gift marked a return to the acquisition of 19th century paintings with a work of great quality and importance. Also exhibited at that time was another 19th century American painting acquired in Ostrow's term, William Morris Hunt's *La Bouquetière* (The Violet Girl) of 1856, the gift of Mrs. S. Foster Damon of Providence in 1972.

The program instituted by Robbins continued whereby the Museum and Brown University co-sponsored the annual scholarly exhibition and catalogue required for Brown candidates for a master's degree in art history. Shows of considerable variety ensued: *Early Lithography, The Portrait Bust, Jacques Callot, Caricature, To Look on Nature, Drawings and Prints of the First Maniera,* and *Europe in Torment.* Following the latter show, the exhibition was held at Brown because of construction at the Museum.

The thrust in collecting continued to look "significantly and experimentally" at contemporary art, aided with several matching grants from the National Endowment for the Arts, yet acquisitions and exhibitions of earlier periods did occur. One of the most spectacular shows of this time was held in 1973: *Ceremonial Costumes,* prepared by Eleanor Fayerweather, including coronation robes from the Russian and Napoleonic courts.

Educational Efforts
Stephen Ostrow had appointed Cora Lee Gibbs Curator of Education in 1971; she had previously served as Assistant Curator. Finances for educational programs were as tight as for exhibits, and grants were secured from the Rhode Island State Council on the Arts/Arts in Education Project for more slide units for the Museum Resources Program. Educational projects included a special program for gifted children in East Providence, which continues; a tour called "Getting to Know Your Museum," as well as after-school "Seeing and Doing" and "Sketching in the Galleries" for members' children, Saturday tours, some Sunday parent and child activities, and a high school seminar on modern art, were among the offerings. Activities took place virtually every day the Museum was open.

New Air
Programs continued despite the upheaval caused by the realization of a long-cherished dream: the installation of an atmospheric control system,

which began in August 1974. Many galleries closed, except the special exhibit galleries, which continued to show a nucleus of the permanent collection, the Porcelain Gallery, Pendleton House, and the Ancient galleries. In October 1975, the main exhibit areas were reinstalled, and all was completed in the spring of 1976. The project was undertaken with great care, for *every* object in the collection was moved at least twice during 20 months of construction. Programs carried on, often taking place outside the Museum.

During this period of a "closed" Museum, nonetheless, more than three fourths of the usual attendance was maintained. Because school tours had to be curtailed, docents increased in-school lectures.

Ostrow summed up 1974–1975 as a year of "hiatus and watershed." The atmospheric control project – the largest capital improvement to the Museum since the main building was completed in 1926 – was a commitment to the preservation of the collections. As "watershed," that year saw the creation of the Museum Council, a body unique in the Museum's history, whose purpose was to oversee the activities and long-range planning of the Museum.

In the same year, when acquisitions included the gift of 60 more British watercolors and George Rickey's kinetic sculpture from Selma Pilavin, austerity forced some reduction of staff and the search for more operational funds. In 1976, Christopher P. Monkhouse was chosen as Curator of Decorative Arts; he has since demonstrated a sensitivity to Rhode Island, both in its heritage and its collectors. Just at this time, the Department of Decorative Arts received a major bequest of European ceramics from Abby Rockefeller Mauzé, niece of Lucy Truman Aldrich, in fields complementary to the ceramics given by Miss Aldrich.

The winter of 1978 was unprecedented. Bizarre weather – a huge blizzard – caught Rhode Island unawares. Just before, an exhibit of paintings by Cleve Gray had opened, and a show planned by Christopher Monkhouse, *Napoleon in Rhode Island* (of Napoleonic material largely collected in this area), almost stalled, but managed to open on schedule. Stephen Ostrow left that summer to go into academic life at the University of Southern California. His able Chief Curator, Diana Johnson, succeeded him – with a special plan to unveil.

A Fantastic Year: 1978–79

Diana Johnson had been at work since 1972 on an exhibit which achieved realization as *Fantastic Illustration and Design in Britain, 1850–1930*. George Landow of Brown University, an expert in Victorian literature and art, collaborated on the show, which was a relatively unpublished area. "Fantasy," as it was popularly called, captivated the public, and a number of special programs, such as related readings performed by Trinity Square Repertory Company of Providence, kept attendance high.

Mrs. Johnson had recently served as full Curator for the Graphics Department, collecting not only contemporary graphics but photography as well. She had also assumed responsibility for the installation of the atmospheric control system and the refurbishing of galleries as Ostrow's Chief Curator.

Although her term as Acting Director was brief, Mrs. Johnson was able to leave a record of strong acquisitions and improvements behind her. Her year was also made easier by the presence of many volunteers, including members of the original founding family – the Metcalfs.

Into the 1980's

With a new Director, Franklin W. Robinson, the Museum set its course into a lively new decade.

The commitment to building contemporary art collections had been well established with the Nancy Sayles Day and Pilavin collections as well as the NEA-supported graphics acquisitions. A new series of exhibits, the "Installation" shows, started in the winter of 1980 with a piece designed by Richard Fleischner filling C-9 gallery. Prints from the 1970's by Jasper Johns had been displayed that fall, and video installations accompanied the Fleischner work. A new curatorial position in Painting and Sculpture, with an emphasis on contemporary art, was filled with the appointment of Judith Hoos Fox.

Pendleton House was completely repainted, following a scheme close to the original colors planned by Edmund Willson, and a new area for exhibiting the Huard wallpaper collection was created out of the stairwell designed by Charles Platt. The Department of Decorative Arts also ventured into the contemporary, planning the innovative show *Clay* with RISD ceramics professor Jacquelyn Rice; a fluid mussel server by ceramist Betty Woodman was one of several Museum purchases from that exhibit.

For public interest, Museum Month, held each May, presented special exhibitions, events, and lectures – all free, all month. It was not the only occasion for new, special programs. Activities to facilitate museum going for the handicapped public were undertaken by the Education Department, including a Braille gallery guide and an annual *Concert of Song and Sign* in December, in which students from the Rhode Island School for the Deaf and Cranston East High School participated. A new facility opened for the Providence public with the start of the Three for All Gallery at the Arcade, co-sponsored with the Rhode Island Historical Society and the Providence

The Museum Ball, 1980, in the Main Gallery

RISD Professor Howard Newman with students in the Baroque Gallery, 1984

Preservation Society; special lectures and shows were designed to acquaint visitors with arts "on the hill."

Acquisitions were many, and major purchases filled historical gaps. Adding to Earle Rowe's acquisitions in Peruvian art, a large Nasca burial cloth was bought with the Helen M. Danforth Fund in 1979; and the representation of the Bassano family in the collection was rounded out by the acquisition in 1981 of Leandro Bassano's major canvas, *The Adoration of the Shepherds,* through the bequest of Lyra Brown Nickerson, by exchange. Other areas, such as photography, Indian and Japanese painting, and costumes and textiles, became the focus of major emphasis in acquisitions.

Exhibitions: The Stamp of Rhode Island
As mentioned earlier, two exhibitions, both undertaken by Christopher Monkhouse, carried out themes of decades earlier: *Buildings on Paper: Rhode Island Architectural Drawings 1825–1945,* and *Gorham: Masterpieces in Metal* celebrated the extraordinary heritage of Rhode Island art and design.

The main gallery was devoted to these handsome shows. It also featured other long-term exhibits of important areas of the permanent collection: several Pilavin collection shows; a selection of Classical vases and sculptures; Islamic art; and French painting. Curators from all departments contributed to the planning, and the richness and variety of the Museum's collection was never more apparent.

Important exhibitions also came out of the Print Room, under the leadership of a new curator, Deborah J. Johnson. *A Century of Black Photographers, 1840–1960* and a selection of old master drawings from the permanent collection were organized as travelling shows, with scholarly catalogues that became major contributions to their fields.

Publications tied all past threads together. *Museum Notes* was resumed as an annual publication of departmental reports on activities and acquisitions. Numerous catalogues accompanied shows; the *Roman Paintings and Mosaics* catalogue was completed by Rolf Winkes of Brown in 1982. Orientation materials were produced, including gallery guides (available at the reception desk, and installed as maps on different gallery levels); a short guidebook on the collection, *Masterpieces,* was prepared. By the 1980's, there was no apparent philosophical division between the remarkably esthetic exhibition and the well-grounded educational publication, label, or exhibit handout.

Adult programs received a major boost with new lecture courses in art history offered by Ronnie Zakon Siegel, who became Curator of Education in 1980. The Museum added nine new staff positions, from the installation crew to curators of Asian art and antiquities, galleries were repainted and floors refinished (finally removing traces of black paint), and storage areas were renovated. In addition, the commitment to collectors continued not only with "Art For Your Collection," but with the creation of a Collectors' Club.

By the mid-1980's, the Museum had met the three-fold challenge of the Rhode Island School of Design's original incorporators, as a permanent gallery and an educational tool, by simply striving for a clear-cut goal: the bringing together of art and people, and keeping them there. As Earle Rowe put it even more simply, many years ago, the Museum's mission is acquisition, preservation, and education.

PUBLICATIONS/BIBLIOGRAPHY

Sources for "Acquisition, Preservation, and Education: A History of the Museum" are principally the publications, reports and catalogues of the Rhode Island School of Design and the Museum of Art, as well as articles and histories commissioned by the institution.

Bulletin of the Rhode Island School of Design

Bronson, Elsie S. *The Rhode Island School of Design: A Half-Century Record (1878–1928)*. A typescript, available at the Rhode Island School of Design library, prepared for the 50th Anniversary Celebration.

Cauman, Samuel. *The Living Museum. Experiences of an Art Historian and Museum Director – Alexander Dorner*. New York: New York University Press, 1958.

Frazier, John R. *The History of the Rhode Island School of Design* (text of an address to the Rhode Island Historical Society, November 13, 1960).

Reeder, Jane. *A History of the Museum of Art*, RISD (unpublished).

Rhode Island School of Design scrapbooks of newspaper clippings, especially from the *Providence Journal*.

Color Plates

Babylonian, *Lion Relief*, ca. 605–562 B.C., glazed polychrome brick. (entry 2)

Egyptian, *Coffin of Nesmin*,
ca. 250 B.C., wood, stucco,
polychrome. (entry 4)

Greek, *Amphora with Twisted Handles*,
ca. 490–480 B.C., ceramic. (entry 10)

Hellenistic, *Aphrodite*, last quarter of 2nd
century B.C., bronze. (entry 25)

Roman, *Portrait of a Man*, ca. A.D. 150–160,
tempera (?) on wood. (entry 36)

Japanese, *Buddha Dainichi Nyorai*, ca.
1150, cryptomeria wood. (entry 42)

Japanese, *No Robe*, late 17th century, silk with embroidered and stenciled decoration. (entry 44)

Toshusai Sharaku, *Matsumoto Koshiro IV in the Role of Fishmonger Gorobei*, 1794, polychrome woodblock print, with mica background. (entry 46)

Indian, *Wine Cup of the Emperor Jahangir*, 1612–13, fine-grained green hardstone. (entry 66)

Indian, *Tent Hanging (qanat)*, ca. 1700, stenciled, painted and dyed cotton. (entry 70)

Attributed to Lippo Memmi, *Mary Magdalen*, first half of 14th century, tempera and gold leaf on panel. (entry 84)

Jacopo Sansovino, *Venetian Nobleman*, ca. 1560, terracotta. (entry 86)

Leandro Bassano, *Adoration of the Shepherds*, ca. 1592–94, oil on canvas. (entry 87)

Giovanni Battista Tiepolo, *The Angel of Fame*, ca. 1750, fresco, mounted on canvas. (entry 91)

Joachim Wtewael, *The Marriage of Peleus and Thetis*, 1610, oil on panel. (entry 99)

Salomon van Ruysdael, *The Ferryboat*, 1645, oil on canvas. (entry 100)

Sébastien Bourdon, *Landscape with a Mill,* after 1658, oil on canvas. (entry 104)

Eugène Delacroix, *Arabes en Voyage,* 1855, oil on canvas. (entry 109)

Edouard Manet, *Le Repos,* ca. 1870, oil on canvas. (entry 110)

Claude Monet, *Le Bassin d'Argenteuil*, 1874, oil on canvas. (entry 113)

Auguste Rodin, *Balzac*, 1893, bronze.
(entry 117)

Paul Cézanne, *Au Bord d'une Rivière*, 1904–05, oil on canvas. (entry 118)

Raymond Duchamp-Villon, *Seated Woman*, 1914–15, bronze with applied gold-washed patina. (entry 121)

John Singleton Copley, *Rebecca Boylston Gill*, ca. 1773, oil on canvas. (entry 124)

Winslow Homer, *On a Lee Shore*, 1900, oil on canvas. (entry 135)

Jackson Pollock, *Magic Lantern*, 1947, oil, oil-based enamels, aluminum paint, and tacks. (entry 143)

Wayne Thiebaud, *Wimbledon Trophy*, 1968, oil on canvas. (entry 146)

Fernando Botero, *La Familia Pinzón*, 1965, oil on canvas. (entry 150)

Giovanni Benedetto Castiglione, *Christ on the Cross Adored by Angels*, ca. 1650's, brush and paint. (entry 153)

Joseph Mallord William Turner, *Rainbow: Osterspey and Feltzen on the Rhine,* ca. 1819–25, blue and brown washes heightened with white. (entry 166)

David Cox, *The Hayfield,* 1833, watercolor. (entry 168)

Edgar Degas, *Dancer with a Bouquet*, ca. 1877–80, pastel and black chalk over monotype, and gouache. (entry 184)

Edgar Degas, *Six Friends*, ca. 1885, pastel and black chalk.
(entry 188)

Winslow Homer, *Waiting for the Start*, 1889, watercolor over pencil. (entry 201)

Mary Cassatt, *Antoinette's Caress*, ca. 1906, pastel. (entry 203)

Albanian, *Surcoat*, late 19th century,
velvet with metallic embroidery and
brocade ribbon; silk lining. (entry 214)

Flemish, *Grand Verdure with Animals*, ca. 1530, tapestry weave; linen warp, wool and silk weft. (entry 217)

English, *Casket*, mid-17th century, silk satin with silk embroidery, with pearls, mica, metal purl, and metallic thread. (entry 218)

French, *Ballgown,* ca. 1775, brocaded and embroidered silk faille. (entry 221)

French, *Man's Suit,* ca. 1775, printed silk velvet. (entry 221)

Jean-Baptiste Isabey, *Court Train,* 1804, velvet embroidered with silver purl, lined with satin. (entry 224)

Nabby Martin, *Sampler,* 1786, linen plain weave,
silk and metallic embroidery. (entry 229)

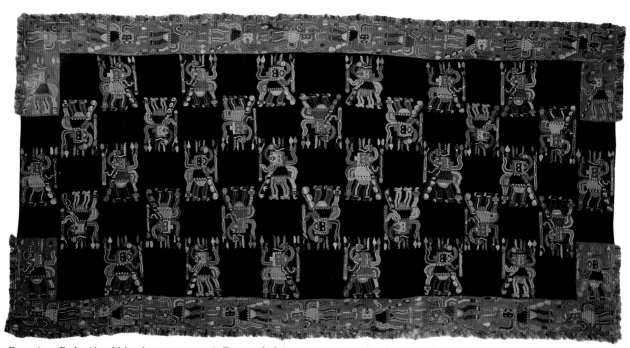

Peruvian, *Embroidered Mantle,* 1st century A.D., wool plain weave, cotton borders; wool embroidery. (entry 239)

Italian, Venice, *Bowl*, late 15th–early 16th century, glass. (entry 244)

Johann Joachim Kändler, *Dancing Lady*,
ca. 1740, porcelain. (entry 247)

Hugnet Frères, *Fireplace Surround*, ca. 1900, walnut, ceramic and copper.
(entry 254)

American, Philadelphia, *Pier Table*, 1760–80,
mahogany, pine, marble. (entry 267)

Townsend and Goddard School, *Desk and Bookcase*, ca. 1760–90, mahogany, pine, tulip poplar, chestnut, and cedar. (entry 270)

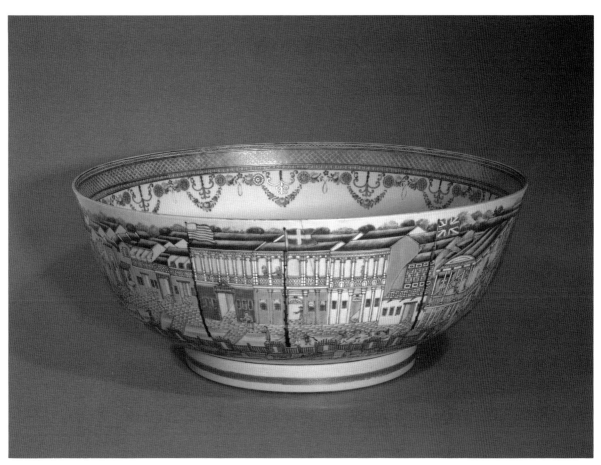

Chinese Export, *Punch Bowl*, ca. 1785–1800, porcelain. (entry 273)

William C. Codman, *Lady's Writing Table and Chair*, 1903, ebony, mahogany, boxwood, redwood, ivory, mother-of-pearl, tooled leather, and silver. (entry 284)

The Collection

All dimensions are in inches; height is followed by width, and, where appropriate, by depth. The entries are arranged by department within the Museum. Within each department, they are arranged by country, and chronologically by date of execution within each country. Abbreviations of catalogues of the permanent collection, referred to under "Publications" in the entries, are listed in full on page 332.

1

SYRO-HITTITE, ca. 14th century B.C.

Seated Goddess, Astarte (?)
Cast copper. 5½ x 1¼

Helen M. Danforth Fund. 82.039

Publication: *Museum Notes*, RISD, 1982, p. 7.

Based on a close parallel in the Louvre, this statuette may represent Astarte, goddess of fertility in ancient Canaan and later Phoenicia. Her head, held high and tilted slightly backward with its tall cylindrical headdress, imparts an air of elegance and power to the piece. The slender, rounded forms of her neck, head and headdress contrast markedly with the flattened and attenuated treatment of her body, broad at the shoulders, tapering at the waist, and following the contour of a chair or throne. That she originally sat in a chair is suggested by the presence of projecting tangs extending from her seat and feet.

The features of the goddess are simply yet forcefully rendered. The large eyes, once inlaid, are framed by arched brows which flow into the lines of the nose. And her ears, though disproportionately large, are felicitously balanced by the elongated neck and headdress. The figure's only sign of movement is her gesture. With arms held at almost right angles to her body, she raises her right hand in a typical Near Eastern gesture of benediction, which even for the modern viewer carries a sense of immediacy and divine pronouncement. Her left hand, held in a tight fist and pierced, may once have gripped a scepter.

The modeling of the figure's body and its strict frontality bespeak strong Egyptian influence, well represented in Syrian art from the beginning of the 2nd millennium until after the 8th century B.C. The RISD piece may derive from the 14th century B.C. during Egypt's 18th Dynasty, when the goddess Astarte was introduced into Egypt and served as protectress of the King's horses and chariotry. She was frequently identified with Isis, who was also depicted as a seated goddess.

While Syro-Hittite figures are sometimes decorated with gold or silver leaf, the RISD statuette shows no grooves for such attachments. Its function, however, probably parallels that of comparable figurines, serving as a dedicatory offering in a temple.

2

BABYLONIAN, ca. 605–562 B.C.

Lion Relief
Glazed polychrome brick. 41 x 90

Museum Appropriation. 34.652

Growing up along the Tigris and Euphrates rivers, ancient Mesopotamian civilization began centuries before the 5th millennium B.C., and ended with a final native dynasty in the neo-Babylonian period (ca. 612 – 539 B.C.). Under a series of neo-Babylonian kings the chief city of the south, Babylon, became one of the wonders of the ancient world. The kings reconstructed the city with temples, palaces (one with a museum of antiquities), the famous hanging gardens, and a ziggurat (stepped temple platform) known from the Old Testament as the Tower of Babel.

One of Babylon's most splendid structures was a four-tower gatehouse dedicated to the goddess of love and war, Ishtar. The gate, which provided access to the inner city, was fronted by a broad street used for religious processions; the street was lined on either side by walls, the lower portions of which were decorated with over 100 lion reliefs, the RISD lion among them. As visitors approached the gateway, the lions appeared to stride forward to meet them.

The lion relief is made of molded bricks which were baked and glazed with yellow, blue and cream color. Other examples can be found in the Museum of Fine Arts, Boston, the Metropolitan Museum of Art, Yale University Art Gallery, the Detroit Institute of Arts, and the Oriental Institute Museum, University of Chicago.

Color plate, page 61

3

EGYPTIAN, Early Dynasty 12, ca. 1900 B.C.
Probably from Meir in Middle Egypt

Funerary Statuette
Wood. H. 11½

Museum Appropriation. 11.033

Publication: *Bulletin*, RISD, July 1939, p. 14.

Small wooden statuettes, often placed within or beside the coffins of wealthy Egyptian noblemen and officials of the Middle Kingdom, served as a residence for the spirit of the deceased should his corpse suffer damage or annihilation. Based on close parallels with examples in other museums, the RISD statuette probably depicts an early Twelfth Dynasty steward named Seneb who lived in Meir, a site in Middle Egypt. Seneb wears a white kilt, indicating his "white-collar" status. The kilt's long, triangular starched apron represents a variation on the plain wrap-around kilt which was also worn in shorter and pleated versions.

Carved from a soft wood (there are no hard woods indigenous to Egypt), the figurine is composed of separately joined pieces. The arms are joined, probably by tenons, to the head and torso which have been carved in a single piece. The front portions of the feet are separately attached to the foot-and-leg sections. As with all striding Egyptian statuary the left foot is stretched forward, and the figure stands in a strictly frontal pose. Unlike stone statues, however, wooden examples do not make use of a back pillar.

The face and torso of the RISD statuette are executed with care and sensitivity. The shape of the ovoid, shaven head, and its delicately modeled facial features and clavicles betray the hand of a skilled artist. Unlike the individualized treatment of the face, however, the long arms and somewhat clumsy legs and feet are handled more summarily.

4

EGYPTIAN, Ptolemaic Period, ca. 250 B.C.

Coffin and Mummy of Nesmin
Wood, stucco, polychrome (coffin).
70½ x 17
Linen, cartonnage (mummy; not
illustrated).

Museum Appropriation and Mary B.
Jackson Fund. 38.206.2

Provenance: Lady Meux, Theobald's
Park; William Randolph Hearst

Publication: Winkes/RISD, 1974, p. 8.

Some of the earliest Egyptian coffins
were simple reed constructions, one surviving example being a crude reed tray
on which the body was laid in a contracted position. Wooden chests were
also used as coffins. Occasionally paneled on the outside, they resembled the
exterior of First Dynasty mud-brick
tombs. The shape of the traditional
Egyptian coffin, however, was rectangular or anthropoid (i.e., mummiform) like
the Museum's coffin of the Ptolemaic
priest Nesmin. The purpose of the coffin
(or series of coffins, each one nested
within the other) was to protect and
house the body for eternity. Without an
intact corpse, life after death was
considered impossible. To prevent the
corpse from decomposing, mummification was developed. This process
consisted of removing the internal
organs, drying out the body, stuffing it
to its original shape, and then tightly
bandaging the entire corpse.

During the Ptolemaic Period when
Nesmin lived, the quality of mummification had declined, and greater
attention was devoted to the coffin.
Nesmin's coffin, which comes from
Akhmim in Middle Egypt, is decorated
with registers of hieroglyphic text
interspersed with images of protective
deities. Nut, goddess of heaven with a
sun disk atop her head, kneels below
Nesmin's broad floral collar and extends
in each winged hand an ostrich feather,
symbol of order and truth (Maat).
Beneath Nut, Nesmin is shown in a
funerary bier, his bird-soul (Ba) hovering
above. Below are pictured his four
canopic jars which (in theory) held his
embalmed organs. Sixteen registers of
hieroglyphic text reaching almost to the
foot of the case detail his titles and
genealogy. On either side six gods stand
ready to protect Nesmin from the perils
of the Afterlife. An additional form of
protection is provided by the scarab

beetle, symbol of resurrection, which
surmounts the coffin mask. The beard,
separately attached to the deceased's
chin, signifies that Nesmin is united in
death with Osiris, benevolent god of the
underworld.

While most Ptolemaic coffins are made
of cartonnage (plastered and molded
layers of linen), Nesmin's is composed
of wood. A careful system of dovetailing
can be seen under the foot of the base. In
order for the traditional religious
symbols and text to be applied, the
coffin was first plastered and then
painted.

Color plate, page 62

5

EGYPTIAN, Ptolemaic, ca. 150–100 B.C.
Said to come from Tanis in Egypt

Male Portrait Head
Mottled (gray) granite. 9⁵/₁₆ x 6½

Gift of Mrs. Murray S. Danforth. 58.001

Publication: Ridgway/RISD, 1972, no. 7.

While a tradition of realism developed in Egyptian portraiture as early as the beginning of the Old Kingdom (ca. 2700 B.C.), the rendering of idealized, youthful faces was far more common. When Egypt fell under Greek domination in the Ptolemaic Period (ca. 305–30 B.C.), however, the Hellenistic interest in depicting age, emotion, and inner personality in portraiture encouraged the ancient Egyptian tradition of verism to become a dominant trend. The result was the production of a number of exceptional, lifelike Ptolemaic portraits, one of which is the RISD head.

Depicting an elderly and unknown man, this granite head probably once formed part of a nearly lifesize statue. A surviving portion of the back pillar, an ancient Egyptian convention, hugs the rear of the neck. The pillar would once have been inscribed with the man's names and titles. The quiet and restrained quality of this work is achieved in part through the rendering of the frontal, oval face with thin, horizontal lips and calm, narrow eyes. An attempt at portraying an individual, as opposed to a type, is illustrated by the asymmetrical furrows running from the outer edges of the nose to the mouth and from the corners of the mouth downward. The subdued nature of second century B.C. portraits would give way in the following century to more emotionally realistic examples which can be suitably compared with Roman Republican portraits of the same period.

6

GREEK, Attic, Late Geometric,
ca. 750 B.C.

Skyphos (Drinking Cup)
Painted ceramic. 3¾ x 5½

Anonymous gift in memory of
C. A. Robinson, Jr. 83.025

Publication: *Museum Notes,* RISD, 1983,
p. 9.

With the collapse of Mycenaean civilization ca. 1200 B.C., Greek culture fell into
a period of obscurity known as the Dark
Ages: trade virtually ceased, poverty
was widespread, and the arts of architecture, sculpture, painting, and writing
disappeared amidst waves of migratory
peoples and barbarian invaders. Pottery
making, however, continued, and in a
rebirth of Greek art in the 10th century
B.C. a new form of pottery decoration

was invented. Today called the Geometric Style, it appears to have been the
brilliant innovation of Athenian (Attic)
potters whose city, according to tradition, went untouched by the barbarian
invaders.

The Geometric Style consists of a
variety of abstract, linear motifs, some of
which may derive from contemporary
textiles. Classed by shape of pot and
form of decoration, the Geometric Style
is divided by present-day scholars into
Proto-, Early, Middle, and Late Geometric phases (ca. 1050–700 B.C.). While
the earliest stages utilize few painted
elements, subsequent periods add
increasing numbers of motifs until a
tapestrylike profusion of small-scale
ornamentation covering the entire
surface of the vessel results in the latest
phase.

While lacking some of the last-named
features, the RISD vase, a two-handled
drinking cup called a *skyphos,* represents
an early stage of the late Geometric. The
pot can be dated through parallel
examples based especially on its deep

vertical lip, reflex ribbon handles, and
skyphoid body, which would subsequently evolve into the high-rimmed
bowl form.

The main surface decoration of the pot
includes a chain of dotted lozenges on
the lip, and below, in the handle frieze,
is a central metope panel with a mean-
der design flanked by columns of zig-
zags and dots. The lower portion of the
vessel, covered with a dark, rich glaze,
lends a well-balanced effect to the total
Geometric decoration.

7

GREEK, Corinthian, ca. 600 B.C.

Column Crater Fragment
Ceramic. 4½ x (estimated) 10

Walter J. Kimball Fund. 62.059

Publication: Ashmead and Phillips/RISD, 1976, no. 16.

Painted ceramics provide the only complete record of developments in painting as they took place on the Greek mainland from the 8th through the 5th centuries B.C. The monumental paintings have disappeared for the most part, and the painted ceramics supply some glimpse of what these more ambitious models must have been like. Yet the painted pots can be artistically important in their own right. They were household objects used for dining and for the important evening drinking parties, the *symposia*, popular with men. In the case of the city of Corinth, the painted pottery was an important export item. Perhaps the distinctive painting styles and the often unique shapes made it easier for the city's merchants to sell the contents of the vases. Whatever the reason, Corinthian pottery is found at ancient sites all over the Mediterranean.

This fragment comes from the shoulder of a vessel used for mixing wine with water at the *symposium*. The preserved fragment shows a cavalcade of warriors moving to the left towards a sphinx. The similar treatment of the warriors and the horses establishes a rhythmic regularity which is interrupted by the slight differences in the rendering of specific features. The sphinx is a mythical beast that was invented in the Near East and was borrowed by the Greeks.

There is a narrative contained on this fragment but too little remains of the scene to reconstruct the story. The introduction of narrative content into Greek pictorial art was a major breakthrough and would continue to dominate Greek painting for the next 600 years.

8

GREEK, Archaic, 6th century B.C.
Said to be from Messenia

Man in a Cloak
Bronze. 4½ x 1⅜

Gift of Mrs. Gustav Radeke. 20.056

Provenance: Pozzi; A. Sambon;
E. P. Warren

Publication: Mitten/RISD, 1975, no. 12.

This is a small bronze solid cast figure of
a shepherd dressed in a long cloak, a
conical hat called a pilos, and boots. His
dress is not unlike that which is still
worn in some mountainous regions of
Greece and Turkey. The drapery wraps
tightly around the body defining the
contours of the chest, the folded arms,
the back, and the buttocks. The legs are
defined where they appear beneath the
cloak and are shown as large calves with
what may be conventional markings for
musculature.

The undecorated expanses of the robe
and the pilos offset the detailed treatment
of the face and boots. The mustache,
beard, and hair are rendered with carefully incised lines. The boots are clearly
represented as laced with three tie
crosses over the tongue. The figure's
posture is static, but is made more
informal by the placement of the feet
in two different positions which suggest
that the figure is in the process of
balancing himself rather than being
firmly balanced.

It has long been maintained that there
was a school of bronze sculptors in
Arcadia during the archaic and classical
periods. There are several small bronzes
in American and foreign collections
which are attributed to the Arcadian
area. They share in common their small
size and were probably votive offerings,
and at least one of them carries a dedication to the god Pan. Our small peasant
figure may have been likewise intended
as an offering to this Arcadian god of the
flocks.

9

GREEK, ca. 540 B.C.
Said to be from the sanctuary of Apollo
on Mt. Ptoon, Boeotia

Inscribed Kouros
Bronze. 3⅞ x 1¹⁄₁₆

Mary B. Jackson and Jesse Metcalf
Funds. 54.001

Publication: Mitten/RISD, 1975, no. 11.

From about 620 to 480 B.C., Archaic
Greek sculptors made a series of innovations in the treatment of the human male
figure which changed the course of
figurative sculpture in the round. Beginning in the 7th through 6th centuries
B.C., sculptural advances moved from
stiff, blocklike figures with patterned
anatomical detail toward a progressively
convincing rendering of the naked male
youth in a relaxed contrapposto stance
by the beginning of the 5th century B.C.
The stone figures exemplifying this
development are known as *kouroi*:
statues of nude, beardless youths rendered on the whole like Egyptian statues
in a rigid, frontal pose, with the left foot
forward but parallel to the right. Though
the pose and carving technique appear
to be Egyptian-inspired, important
Egyptian elements were eliminated: the
back pillar and connective stone
webbing between it and the figure were
omitted by the Greeks, whose concept of
a statue differed from that of the
Egyptians. They, unlike other ancient
peoples up to that time, wanted to
endow their statuary with the potential
for movement in space.

The RISD *kouros*, a mid-6th century
B.C. bronze miniature rendition of its
type, presents the curious "Archaic
smile" and stiff proportions of this
period, while leaning forward as if about
to stride forth from its plinth. The arms
are rigidly bent at the elbows, and the
fists are clenched and perforated to hold
rodlike instruments, perhaps sections of
bronze handles to a container on which
the *kouros* and a companion piece were
symmetrically attached.

The meaning and function of the
kouroi are by no means fully understood.
Intended, it appears, to represent either
Apollo, the divine guardian of the dead,
or a deceased mortal perhaps likened to
Apollo, they have been found in both
temple sanctuaries as votive offerings to
Apollo and in cemeteries as funerary
monuments to the dead. The meaning of
the RISD *kouros* is perhaps elucidated by
its dedicatory inscription. Running
down the right leg and up the left, it
reads: "Amphias made this dedication
from the tithe to the farshooter,"
indicating that the statuette (as well as
the container on which it stood) represents a percentage of the dedicator
Amphias's harvest or battle gains
offered up in thanks to Apollo, the
farshooter.

10

GREEK, Attic, ca. 490–480 B.C.

Amphora with Twisted Handles
Ceramic. 20 x 10 (at rim)

Gift of Mrs. Gustav Radeke. 15.005

Provenance: Basseggio and Jekyll
collections

Publication: Luce/RISD, 1933, pl. 18.

Pottery manufacturing was a mainstay
of the economic life of the Greek mainland from the time of the first neolithic
settlers. The elastic nature of the clay in
and around Athens makes it particularly
suitable to the production of vases with
unusual and elegant shapes. The matrix
of the clay when it is suspended in water
forms a fine paint-like slip that can be
used to decorate the surface of the pot.
During the second half of the 6th
century B.C., changes in the manner of
firing the kiln led to the creation of a
new and distinctive style known as red
figure ware. The figures in a scene are
presented in red while the details of
their garments and the background are
rendered in black. The style retained its
popularity into the middle of the 4th
century B.C.

Our vase is a fine example of the fully
developed red figure style. The shape is
that of an amphora designed to hold
wine, but the decoration has nothing to
do with the pot's use. On one side
stands the god Apollo, who can be
recognized from his lyre or *cithara,* his
long hair, and the laurel wreath. On the
other side is half of a female figure; her
head was lost when the vessel was
broken. Though she carries no attributes,
she is probably intended to represent the
goddess Artemis, Apollo's sister.

The names of several potters and
painters of red figure ware have come
down to us, for many signed their
works. Unfortunately, this is not the
case with the amphora. However, the
style of painting is distinctive enough
that works in other collections are now
recognized as having been done by the
same hand, and the RISD amphora has
become the "name piece" of an artist
called the Providence painter. His work
can be identified by the elongated,
attenuated, and elegant forms of the
figures, which are usually placed alone
on a ground line against an undefined
black background.

Color plate, page 62

11

GREEK, Attic, ca. 540 B.C.

Amphora
Signed by Nikosthenes
Ceramic. H. 11¾

Museum Appropriation. 23.303

Provenance: Castellani, Paravey, and Darthès collections

Publication: Luce/RISD, 1933, pl. 9, 2a–c.

This intact and extremely well-preserved amphora was found in 1865 in Italy, at the ancient Etruscan site of Caere, known today as Cerveteri. Beneath one handle of the vase an inscription reads "Nikosthenes epoisen" (Nikosthenes made [this].) The well-known signature of this famous late 6th century B.C. potter and workshop owner appears on over 100 vases found from sites as diverse as the Crimea, Egypt, Sicily, and Etruria.

An astute businessman as well as a skilled potter, Nikosthenes produced vase shapes to suit specific foreign tastes. His atelier especially catered to the Italian Etrurian market which favored pottery in the form of metallic ware. The RISD vase, one of the best examples of the distinctive Nikosthenic amphora, features the broad flat handles and angular body typical of this export ware. The black-figure decoration, by an unknown hand, depicts several horsemen and standing male figures on the shoulder of the pot. Ivy leaves and palmette and lotus motifs, traditional forms of pottery decoration, embellish the rest of the vase.

12

GREEK, Archaic, early 5th century B.C.

Oinochoe in the Form of a Woman's Head
Ceramic. 9½ x 5

Gift of Mrs. Gustav Radeke. 22.213

Provenance: Hope collection

Publication: Luce/RISD, 1933, no. 26.

Plastic (i.e., sculpted) vases have been found in both archaic and classical Greek contexts in the Mediterranean. Their production seems to have begun in the eastern Greek world in the 7th century B.C., and by the late 6th century B.C. they were being manufactured in Athens. Though the earliest versions were cups decorated with a face in relief, the later archaic and classical versions are, like the RISD example, representations of the neck and head of the figure, which form the body of the vessel, and a separate top portion attached to the crown of the skull. This sculptural rendition in terracotta allowed the potter and vase painter to experiment with the effects of modeled decoration, as on the face and the front of the hair, in contrast to painted passages; for example, on the sides of the head where the hair is treated as lozenges and chevrons. Although they in no way duplicate archaic and early classical sculpture, the plastic vases with their painted surfaces do give some hint of what the polychromed statuary of the same period looked like.

The first coined money was made by the Greeks or by their neighbors in Asia Minor, the Lydians, in the 7th century B.C. Within a century the use of coinage had spread throughout the Greek world (which at this time included much of southern Italy and almost all of Sicily), and for many cities the artistic quality of their coinage became a matter of civic pride. Closely allied to the art of the gem engraver, the work of the master engravers of Greek coinage was often conceived with a height of relief and a feeling for design in the round or oval field of the coin that has rarely been equaled in modern times.

In the Greene Collection of almost 400 Greek coins the Museum possesses a widely representative selection, and more than a few outstanding specimens, of the finest Greek coins, both of the city states and of Hellenistic monarchies which came into being following the death of Alexander the Great (323 B.C.).

13

EGYPTIAN, ca. 311–305 B.C.

Tetradrachm
Silver. D. 1¹⁄₁₆
Obv: Head of Alexander III, right
Rev: Athena Alkis, right

Museum Appropriation. 40.015.58

Provenance: Henry A. Greene Collection

14

SYRACUSAN, ca. 415–405 B.C.
From Sicily

Dekadrachm
Silver. D. 1⁷⁄₁₆
Obv: Galloping quadriga, left; Nike, right, crowning charioteer
Rev: Head of Arethusa, left

Museum Appropriation. 40.015.25

Provenance: Henry A. Greene Collection, R. Hobart Smith Collection

Publication: *Museum Notes*, RISD, May 1951, vol. 8, no. 4.

15

SYRIAN, 149–148 B.C.

Tetradrachm
Silver. D. 1¼
Obv: Head of Alexander I, right
Rev: Zeus Nikephoros, enthroned, left

Museum Appropriation. 40.015.318

Provenance: Henry A. Greene Collection

16

ELEAN, ca. 421–365 B.C.

Stater
Silver. D. ⅞
Obv: Head of Eagle, left
Rev: Thunderbolt

Museum Appropriation. 40.015.5

Provenance: Henry A. Greene Collection

Publication: C. T. Seltman, *The Temple Coins of Olympia*, Cambridge, England, 1921, p. 7.

17

CORINTHIAN, 4th century B.C.

Stater
Silver. D. ⅞
Obv: Pegasos flying to left
Rev: Head of Athena, left, with Nike

Museum Appropriation. 40.015.326

Provenance: Henry A. Greene Collection

18

ATHENIAN, 5th or 4th century B.C.

Tetradrachm
Silver. D. ⅞
Obv: Head of Athena, right
Rev: Owl, right

Museum Appropriation. 40.015.268

Provenance: Henry A. Greene Collection

19

GREEK, ca. 420 B.C.

Head of a Goddess
Marble. 10⅛ x 7⁵⁄₁₆ x 8¾

Museum Appropriation. 55.027

Provenance: Professor Vladimir G. Simkhovitch, New York

Publication: Ridgway/RISD, 1972, no. 8.

In this superb head the Museum of Art possesses a treasure unique among American collections: this is an original from a statuary group which once decorated one of the temples of Greece in the 5th century B.C. The subject was a youthful goddess. In the original pose of the figure, the head was turned slightly left. We should imagine her lips, eyes, and hair painted in lifelike, though perhaps to modern eyes over-vivid, colors. The hairband across her forehead was also painted and emphasized at each end by ornaments in bronze fixed in dowel holes drilled for the purpose. The sculpture thus mimicked a hairband around which the hair was rolled, while the embroidered material was exposed over the forehead.

The head is executed with the majestic simplicity characteristic of the best art of the later 5th century. The chisel rather than the drill is the tool the sculptor has employed in his work, resulting in the shallow grooving of the hair and the simplicity of the conception of the facial features. The skin was then polished, giving the surface finish, of which traces remain despite the weathering the head has suffered on its left side.

Close examination of the head shows that the features are not symmetrical. The right eye is set more deeply than the left; the left eye is smaller, and it is given a curious tilt. The impression of awkwardness thus created disappears if the head is viewed from below and to the viewer's left. A sharp angle from below is the natural sight line for a sculpture displayed in the opening of the pitched roof of a Greek temple, high above its colonnade. It is just this "optical correction" which identifies our head as coming from a pedimental group. A hole for a metal dowel in the crown of the head probably received a pin which secured the complete figure to the ceiling of the pedimental opening.

The dignified style and the technique of execution combine to identify this as a 5th century original, and the head bears strong resemblances to the sculpture of Athens and Attica, the center of Greek art of the day, in the late 5th century. But there is no known Attic temple of the period surely decorated with pedimental sculpture to which the Providence head may be attributed. The dimensions of the head do not fit any of the surviving or hypothetical groups. It seems therefore that we must look outside Attica, to the Greek islands or to northern Greece, both areas where Attic influence was strong, for the home of the goddess.

The Providence goddess is also potentially helpful in answering a question which has long plagued the study of Greek temple sculpture: how was the labor of these vast sculptural programs carried out? If we remember that Michelangelo spent three years to produce seven sculptures for the Medici Chapel in Florence, the man-hours of skilled sculptors necessary to complete the Parthenon sculpture (40 pedimental figures and at least two chariot groups, the central figure 10 feet in height, 92 sculptured metopes, and a frieze 524 feet in length) seem almost incalculable. Two small drill holes just below the temples and a third on the head midway between the hair band and the crown of the head are possibly the traces of the blocking out of the head by means of a mechanical device called a pointing machine which permits transfer of "points" from a model (even in another material such as clay or plaster) to a stone block. After the points defining the sculpture are drilled into the block, the cortex of stone can be quickly chipped away, leaving the rough form of the desired sculpture which then need only receive its final treatment. Because of the traces of drilling to significant points defining the overall shape of the head, the Providence goddess becomes a document of the technique, as well as the noble conception, of Greek architectural sculpture in its finest hour.

20

GREEK, Attic (Spata?), ca. 390 – 380 B.C.
Funerary Lion
Pentelic marble. 18⅜ x 38⅜ x 10⅝

Gift of Mrs. Gustav Radeke. 15.003

Publication: Ridgway/RISD, 1972, no. 10.

Though real lions were absent from the Greek mainland before recorded history, their image, perhaps reintroduced from the east, appears in Greek art as early as the Mycenaean period when a sculpted pair of facing lions were set atop the gateway to the citadel at Mycenae. The lion as a symbol of violence and destruction was kept alive in the myth of Heracles and the Nemean lion. It was as a ferocious beast that the lion re-emerged in archaic Greek sculpture, in representations on pedimental groups of some temples and as funerary guardians.

The RISD lion is a fine example of the funerary lion type which continued to be produced into the mid-4th century B.C.; a similar example can be found at the Museum of Fine Arts, Boston. Lions were represented in a conventionalized rather than naturalistic manner since no actual lions served as models. Our lion betrays this schematizing in the head, which is too small for the body and is slightly squarish, and in the treatment of the mane, which is rendered more as a patterned surface than as real fur.

Funerary lions were created most often in pairs to sit on either side of large mortuary monuments popular in Athens during the 5th and 4th centuries B.C. Though the RISD lion is sculpted in the round, one side is more finished than the other, and the finished side must have been the one the artist intended to display. The conventionalized treatment of the lion does not detract from the stress on the animal's strength and suppleness. The lion served both as a guardian of the grave and as a symbol of the nobility and valor of the deceased.

21

SOUTH ITALIAN, Tarentine, ca. 350 –
340 B.C.

Bull's Head Rhyton
Ceramic. 7 x 3½ (at rim)

Museum Appropriation. 26.166

Publication: Ashmead and Phillips/RISD,
1976, no. 60.

Taranto, an ancient city in southern
Italy, specialized in the 4th century
before Christ in a distinctive form of
ceramic ware known as the rhyton, a
type of drinking vessel modeled on popular Greek red-figure examples which
had been imported from Athens during
the previous century. With the defeat of
Athens in the Peloponnesian War (404
B.C.), however, the export of Attic
pottery was severely curtailed, and the
rhyton shape was subsequently abandoned by Attic potters. The Tarentine
populace continued to prize their rhyton
imports, however, treasuring them
perhaps as family heirlooms or as sacred
temple objects. By the middle of the 4th
century, local demand prompted Taranto
to manufacture its own variant of the
Athenian model. Unlike the Greek
examples, however, the more fragile
Tarentine rhyta are almost always non-
functional, rarely show signs of wear,
and their purpose, it seems, was
funerary. The subjects of their decoration
were often associated with themes of the
afterlife.

The RISD Tarentine rhyton, naturalistically modeled in the form of a bull's
head, is decorated along the separately
made bowl with a nude satyr. The figure
moves to the right, holding a tympanum
(tambourine) in his left hand and a
thyrsos (an ivy- or vine-covered staff
terminating in a pinecone) in his right.
Both the shape and decoration of the
vessel reflect funerary themes associated
with Dionysus. Dionysus was the South
Italian's favorite god of the underworld
and also the god of wine. The mold-made
bull's head may allude to this god, who
was worshiped in southern Italy as a
bull; the satyr, who carries Dionysiac
attributes and is a follower of the underworld god, is perhaps to be understood
as part of a larger scene of Dionysiac
satyrs and initiates reveling in the
mysteries of their lord.

22

HELLENISTIC (Knidos?), ca. 300 B. C.

Statue of a Youth (The "Bebenburg Youth")
Marble (Parian?). 19 x 7¹¹⁄₁₆

Museum Appropriation and Special
Gifts. 23.342

Provenance: Freiherr Theodor
von Karg-Bebenburg, Munich

Publication: Ridgway/RISD, 1972, no. 19.

A hallmark of Hellenistic sculpture (300–
30 B. C.) is the soft outline, especially of
the features, often described by the term
"sfumato," or misty. This development
was already underway in the 4th century, for Lysippos's portrait of Alexander
the Great was famous for the "melting"
quality of the expression. In the Bebenburg Youth we see a small sculpture
which belongs to the tradition stemming
from the work of Lysippos. Its prototypes
are the athletes of the great Sikyonian
master, some of which we know through
contemporary copies of one Lysippan
group dedicated at Delphi (the so-called
Daochos Group). Lysippos worked by
preference in bronze and within the last
few years a bronze statue of an athletic
victor has been acquired by the J. Paul
Getty Museum in Malibu, California,
and, with some reason, has been attributed to Lysippos himself. Needless to
say, the Getty bronze is also a close
cousin of the Bebenburg Youth.

What is the subject of the statue? A
nude male figure is a god or a divinely
favored mortal, most often an athletic
victor. The Bebenburg Youth is not easily
identified with any divinity and almost
surely represents a victorious mortal.
Such symbolism, however, could be
extended from the actual athletic victor
or fallen soldier to generalized funeral
symbolism, suggesting that precious
goal of all mankind, victory over death.
The Bebenburg Youth, therefore, may be
thought of as a victor's dedication to a
god or a funeral statue from a tomb.

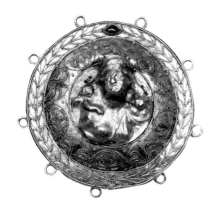

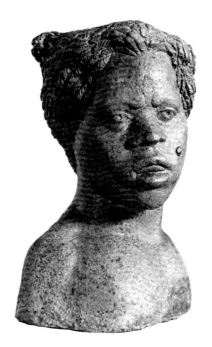

23

HELLENISTIC , mid to late
3rd century B.C.

Medallion-Disc: Bust of Aphrodite
Gold. 2½ x 9/10 (relief)

Museum Appropriation. 29.256

Publication: M.J. Acquilino in *Gold
Jewelry*, ed. by Tony Hackens and Rolf
Winkes, Louvain-la-Neuve, 1983,
pp. 72-74.

This unfinished medallion-disc with
relief bust, said to be from Pagasai
(Thessaly), is a common type of jewelry
found in the 4th through 2nd centuries
B.C. Numerous medallions have been
unearthed from tombs in northern
Greece, Tarentum, South Russia, and
Egypt.

The centerpiece of the disc in the form
of Aphrodite and Eros is typical of the
iconography of such medallions. The
goddess, her head turned slightly to her
right, has a small Eros perched on her
shoulder, who reaches across her chest
in a playful attempt to loosen the knot
that secures her drapery. This relief
emblem, which reveals only preliminary
embossing, was constructed from a
separate sheet of gold. The gold was
hammered over a wooden mold and
attached to the disc with three pieces of
hollow wire, which were inserted
through the medallion and twisted
together at the back. Palmette designs
outlined in filigree and inlaid with dark

blue enamel surround the central
emblem; the flat outer rim is decorated
with a tightly drawn floral motif.
Whereas the interest in the highly
modeled figure is a Greek contribution,
the ornamental motifs were derived
from Egyptian prototypes, transmitted
through Persian artisans and transformed by Greek craftsmen.

The function of the medallion is not
clear. It may have served as the cover for
a small metal container for cosmetics or
other personal possessions; or possibly it
was a breast ornament, worn over a
girdle and held in place by leather cross-
straps.

24

HELLENISTIC (Samandhond, Egypt?), late
3rd century through end of 2nd century
B.C.

Balsamarium
Bronze. 8⅛ x 3¹⁵⁄₁₆

Gift of Mrs. Gustav Radeke. 11.035

Publication: Mitten/RISD, 1975, no. 19.

This bronze *balsamarium* (perfume vase),
consisting of lid and container, portrays
the bust of a Nubian youth. Judging
from the boy's shoulders, which appear
forcefully pulled behind him, he is
probably to be understood as a Negro
captive. Such a small-scale rendering of
the bound Negro probably represents an
abbreviated (and now lost) version of a
full-length sculpture of the same theme.

While many Hellenistic renderings
present the black as a grotesque caricature, this realistically modeled bronze
treats the figure with sensitivity and
restraint. The youth turns his head
angrily, staring up contemptuously at
his captor, his lips parted and brow
furrowed. The boy's corkscrew curls,
part of which serve as the lid of the
container, display an ancient Nubian
hairstyle still fashionable today.

The individualized treatment of the
facial features, powerful expression of
emotion, and empathetic treatment of
the subject indicate a Hellenistic date
and possibly an Alexandrian workshop.

25

HELLENISTIC , last quarter
of 2nd century B.C.

Aphrodite
Bronze. 18½ x (max.) 9⁷⁄₁₆

Museum Appropriation and Special
Gift. 26.117

Provenance: Prince Belosselski-
Belosorski, Leningrad; Dr. von Frey,
Vienna

Publication: Mitten/RISD, 1975, pp. 66-
76.

While the taut, athletic beauty of the
naked male figure was a favorite subject
in the Classical art of 5th century B.C.
Greece, the depiction of female nudity
was generally relegated to images of
courtesans or women of inferior status.
This attitude abruptly shifted, however,
with the 4th century B.C. masterwork of
Praxiteles, the first Greek sculptor to
portray the goddess of love, Aphrodite,
in unclothed elegance. The RISD Aphrodite, a late Hellenistic variant of a
Praxitelean model, captures the nude
goddess at the moment of adjusting a
necklace. Her left forearm, incorrectly
restored, may have grasped one end of
the necklace or may possibly have been
extended to hold a mirror. Much of the
aesthetic force of this statuette derives
from the natural, balanced pose of the
figure, her right hip thrust outward, her
torso describing a graceful S-curve. The
delicate features, once enlivened by
copper inlays for the lips and possibly
silver for the pupils, together with the
subtle tilt of the head and her downward
glance, impart to the work a contemplative, almost sacred, air befitting a
goddess.

Color plate, page 63

26

SARDINIAN, 6th century B.C.

Warrior
Bronze. 5⅛ x 1⅜

Gift of Mrs. Murray S. Danforth. 55.030.

Publication: Mitten/RISD, 1975, no. 2.

This diminutive bronze figure, probably a votive offering for a local sanctuary, depicts a helmeted warrior in a short jacket of armor (much like the padding worn by a baseball umpire) and trunklike shorts. Probably representing an archer, the figure's once outstretched left hand perhaps held a bow, while his right hand drew back the bowstring. This unusual statuette, elongated and schematically but forcefully rendered, is modeled primarily on the front, portions of the back being virtually flat.

While the source of inspiration for similar Sardinian bronzes is debated, their production appears to have begun as early as 1000 B.C. The presence of small Phoenician figurines brought by Phoenician traders may have supplied some impetus for their production, as might the concurrent developments in bronzeworking on the Italian mainland near Vetulonia. The RISD warrior is a work of the local Nuraghic Culture, which flourished in Sardinia from the 7th through 4th centuries before Christ. Such small bronzes also represent warriors, shepherds, women in various domestic situations, and a variety of animals.

27

CELTO-ETRUSCAN (Certosa Necropolis, Bologna?), ca. 525 B.C.

Situla
Bronze. 10¹¹⁄₁₆ x 8⁵⁄₁₆ (at rim)

Mary B. Jackson Fund. 32.245

Publication: Mitten/RISD, 1975, no. 28.

The bronze situla of the Museum, which is one of the two finest examples known of its kind, is an object from the frontiers of the classical Mediterranean world. These vessels are known in an area extending from the Po Valley of northern Italy in a wide arch which reaches Yugoslavia. They are characteristic therefore only of the northern fringes of the Etruscan domains of Celtic regions.

The style of the three repousse bands of relief on the situla is also characteristic of Celtic rather than the classical Mediterranean taste. It is a style of globules rather than structures, and the bodies of the figures appear to have simply flowed into their poses. The subject matter, however, has been borrowed from Etruscan models. The uppermost band of decoration has two scenes which are typical of Etruscan funeral decoration such as that found in the tomb paintings of Tarquinia. On one side, funeral games are in progress and below one handle we see two boxers competing before a bowl (set on a high stand) and a pair of fire dogs, which together with the small objects (bowls?) piled at either side are apparently the prizes for the winner. A group of four gentlemen in cloaks and stylish caps watches. Beyond the scene of boxing, both to left and right there is a scene of seated musicians and standing figures grouped around cauldrons standing on tripods. Women, identified by the shawls covering their heads, are present at one of these scenes. On the ground beside one is a situla, in shape just like the Providence vessel. In one scene a seated figure (clearly an individual of importance) is added. He is served by a standing cloaked man. In the matching scene there are two seated men holding superbly decorated fans. The scenes of the funeral celebration are enlivened by the presence of birds that perch on the cauldrons and possibly represent favorable omens for the funeral. The Providence situla was reportedly found in a tomb at Bologna and its manufacture as a funeral gift is strongly suggested by the upper band of decoration.

Below the funeral games there is a band of warriors marching with their shields held horizontally and their spears at rest. Their helmets are typically Etruscan. The figures in the lowest frieze depict a line of animals. First come two stags, then two animals without horns, possibly does, and finally two imaginary horned creatures. A running loop pattern completes the decoration above the foot of the vessel.

28

UMBRIAN (Ancarano, province of Perugia?), ca. 450-425 B. C.

Warrior
Bronze. $9^{21}/_{22}$ x $3^{11}/_{32}$. Crest: H. $3^{17}/_{32}$

Mary B. Jackson Fund. 34.011

Provenance: A Castellani; H. Weber; B. d'Hendecourt

Publication: Mitten/RISD, 1975, no. 34.

This statuette eloquently illustrates the difference of approach between Greek and Italic art. Greek art developed unswervingly toward a visually convincing, if not naturalistic, projection of human form in graphic or three-dimensional art. Italic and Etruscan art distorted natural forms, first to create memorable and awesome images, later to experiment with illusionistic imagination. This warrior, almost certainly an image of the Italic war god known to the Romans as Mars, comes from the region east of the Tiber, modern Umbria. He was made during the same generation that witnessed the making of the Parthenon sculptures in Athens and the creation of the Head of a Goddess now in Providence (55.027). But he belongs to a completely alien environment. The anatomical forms have been attenuated and exaggerated so that even in this tiny figure they come to express a towering and irrepressible force. Part of the effect was achieved as well by the towering crest of the god's helmet and by the lance, which should be restored, in his upraised right hand. According to David Mitten, "This statuette is one of the finest examples known of this type of Italic warrior."

ETRUSCAN (Pompeii or Praeneste?), late 4th to mid-3rd century B.C.

Cista

Bronze. 11⅝ x 6⅝ (at lid)

Gift of Mrs. Gustav Radeke. 06.014

Publication: Mitten/RISD, 1975, no. 38.

Often found in female graves at Praeneste (modern Palestrina, about 23 miles southeast of Rome), *cistae* were cylindrical bronze toilet boxes which held a variety of cosmetic needs for the well-to-do lady. Mirrors, perfume flasks, combs, and hairpins were stored in *cistae*. The RISD *cista*, though said to have been found at Pompeii, is undoubtedly of Praenestine manufacture, and consists of a decorated body set on three lion's paws and surmounted by a slightly convex lid. A separately attached handle, fashioned in the form of a Dionysiac couple (an adjoined satyr and maenad), caps the piece.

The engraved decoration around the body of the container represents a unique composition, the significance of which is not wholly clear. Probably modeled on a Greek original (as is much of Etruscan art), the frieze presents at the center a woman, naked except for sandals and a long veil. She gently raises the veil to one side while a kneeling servant adjusts her sandal. Mercury, the messenger god, who is identified by his winged hat and caduceus (a staff surmounted by entwined serpents), stands to her left and faces an interior columned space occupied by a youth and an old man. This enigmatic scene perhaps alludes to an impending marriage. The veiled woman, it appears, is about to be led by Mercury to her youthful bridegroom within the columned space. Given this interpretation, one scholar has suggested that the *cista* itself may have been intended as a wedding gift.

30

ROMAN, ca. 60 B. C.

Portrait of a Man

White marble. 13⅜ x 8⁹⁄₁₆

Museum Appropriation. 25.063

Publication: Ridgway/RISD, 1972, no. 30.

Portrait sculpture was one of the favorite media in Roman art from the period of the Republic through that of the empire. In the Republic we find impressive images of men and women as free-standing statues and as busts. The turning of the head on the RISD portrait suggests that it probably belonged to a statue rather than a bust; a bust would be seen in a more frontal position. The head portrays a man of middle age, almost bald, with facial wrinkles and furrows on his forehead. This so-called verism stands in contrast to the idealistic features in Greek portraiture or the Classicizing portraits from the time of Augustus, following the Republic. It has been suggested that verism in portraiture was related to the Roman custom of taking wax-masks from the face of the deceased. The expression of the RISD portrait, however, is full of will power and does not copy the face of a corpse. He represents rather a man on whom a public honor was bestowed by placing his portrait in a marketplace, a basilica, a library or any other public space. The "veristic" features, typical for this kind of portraiture, which always show men of middle age, are the Republican ideal of a man who has reached an age when he would have assumed leadership and command, either in the military, or in the civil service, or as head of his *familias,* i.e., his clan. Such men are also described in literature of the first century as being rustic and determined, and their ideals are embodied by personalities like the old Cato or Cincinnatus.

31

ROMAN (the villa at the Fondo Bottaro),
ca. A.D. 14-37

Campanian Wall Painting
Fresco and tempera (the latter for
details). 41 x 51½

Museum Appropriation. 38.058.2d

Publication: Winkes/RISD, 1982, no. 2.

From the 2nd century B.C. on, Romans
of the middle and upper classes began
decorating their houses with stucco and
frescoes. First, they imitated a wall
surface that would have been covered
with slabs of colorful stones. Then, from
about 80-30 B.C., the illusion of a vista
into adjacent spaces such as courtyards
with much embellished, yet real, architecture was created. Thereafter, fantastic
architectural compositions are favored.
These are placed before monochrome

backgrounds with little reference to
depth. Finally, during the Fourth
Pompeian Style, this fantastic architecture acquires the illusion of depth and
baroque tendencies.

At the peak of this development,
Mount Vesuvius erupted in A.D. 79 and
covered several towns with lava, thus
preserving an abundance of frescoes.
This fresco comes from the same room,
and possibly the same black wall, as
another in the Museum (38.058.2c). On
the left it creates the illusion of a vista
which reaches into the upper part of a
structure, consisting of a window and a
door supported by an actual column and
a tripod. In the missing center one has to
reconstruct an *aedicula* receding into
space. Here the upper supporting
element is plant-like. Center and side are
bridged by the illusion of a metal frieze
of lotus and palmettes. Across it walks a
bird, while below an eagle appears to be
flying. On top of the window frame
stands a *liknon* (a basket in which a

phallus is hidden under a cloth), which
alludes to the god Dionysus; a horn is
suspended in the window. References to
the god of wine, sex, and drama are
quite common in frescoes, alluding to a
good and happy life. The fantastic
composition combined with the illusion
of depth make this fresco an example of
the emerging Fourth Pompeian Style.

32

ROMAN, 1st or 2nd century A.D.
Probably from the Syro-Palestinian
Coast

Bottle
Marbled glass. 3¼ x 3

Jesse Metcalf Fund. 83.154

As early as the third millennium before
Christ, glass making was developed in
Mesopotamia. Cuneiform texts from
about 1500 B.C. provide recipes for
glass, a craft prized thoughout much of
antiquity. Typically composed of silica,
soda, and lime, glass was first used to
manufacture small objects such as beads
and other jewelry items. Egypt also
established glass factories, best known
during the Amarna period, around 1350
B.C. Abundant examples of Amarna
amulets and core-formed cosmetic
vessels were produced at this time.
Core-formed (or sand-core) containers
were made by applying molten glass
around a core of sand which was then
removed when the vessel had cooled.
With the weakening of the Egyptian
state ca. 1200 B.C., glass production
diminished in Egypt, though it continued
in Mesopotamia.

The ancient core-formed technique for
glass production was still widely used
into the Hellenistic period, though it was
ultimately supplanted in the mid-1st
century B.C. by the revolutionary
invention of glass blowing, a watershed
in the history of glass. Probably developed on the Syro-Palestinian coast along
the Eastern Mediterranean, an area well
known in antiquity for its glass factories,
glass blowing made glass manufacture a
less laborious and therefore less costly
operation. As a result, glass vessels
became available for the general public.
By the mid-1st century A.D. glass
production had quickly spread to Roman
sites. The Roman historian Strabo, a
contemporary of the Emperor Augustus,
mentions Rome as a center for the glass
blowing industry.

The RISD bottle is an exquisite example
of the glass blowing technique. Produced
during the 1st century A.D., not long
after Strabo was writing, the vessel most
likely derives from a Syro-Palestinian
factory. Similar examples, however, are

also known from Roman sites. Its vivid
polychrome and long decorative ribs
testify both to the skill of the 1st century
artisan and a sophisticated market which
demanded colorful glass tableware and
luxury goods. The shape of the bottle,
with its sagging pear-shaped body, flat
base, and tubular neck that subtly
indents at the base, dates the piece to
the 1st or 2nd century A.D. The marbled
appearance of the opaque surface of the
vessel was achieved by picking up chips
of light and dark blue, purple and white
glass which, after reheating, were
swirled about and then inflated like a
balloon from a blowpipe. While the glass
was still hot, a pincer tool was used to
produce the series of eight decorative
ribs around the body of the container.

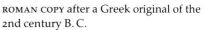

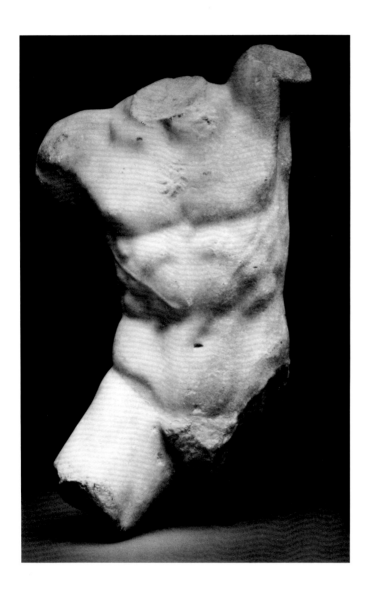

ROMAN COPY after a Greek original of the 2nd century B.C.

Torso of a Fighting Giant
Marble. 21⅜ x 13¹¹⁄₁₆ x 8⅝

Museum Appropriation. 25.064

Publication: Ridgway/RISD, 1972, no. 25.

The contests of heroes and divinities with monsters occupy a large place in Greek mythology and Greek art. In the latter realm these struggles came to symbolize the domination of chaos by the order of civilization and at the same time Greek victories over non-Greek nations. This small struggling figure is identified as a giant (the terrible off-spring of the goddess Earth who attempted to dislodge the gods from Olympus) by the spiral tuft of hair on his chest. It also seems that his left leg was transformed into a snaky appendage (visible on the rear below the left buttock). The dramatic treatment of the musculature and the violent pose of the figure also belong to a scene of combat. The most famous battle of gods and giants is that of the frieze of the Great Altar of Zeus at Pergamon dating from the 2nd century B.C. and today preserved in East Berlin. The Providence figure is probably a Roman copy, possibly at reduced scale, of a similar Hellenistic Greek original.

34

ROMAN COPY after a Greek original of the
5th century B.C.

Male Torso
Marble. 44⅞ x 21½ x 12½

Museum Appropriation. 26.159

Publication: Ridgway/RISD, 1972,
no. 13.

Greek sculptors were frequently called
upon to create statues of victorious
athletes for dedication at the great
international sanctuaries (such as
Olympia) where the dedicator's triumph
had been won. There were sometimes
restrictions on such gifts. At Olympia,
for instance, only three-time winners
were accorded the privilege, and at the
same time other statues were exhibited
which had been ordered from competi-
tors by the judges as a penalty for
cheating. In neither case were the
statues "portraits" in our sense of the
word, but rather figures of idealized
athletes, shown nude as Greek athletes
competed. The athlete's figure in Providence is a faithful copy made under the
Roman Empire (when such figures were
in demand to decorate the splendid
Roman baths and gymnasia) of an
athletic statue from the circle of Poly-
kleitos, the most renowned creator of
such statues of the 5th century. Our
statue displays the logical simplicity of
the Greek conventions for defining male
anatomy. These often exaggerate natural
forms, for example, in the emphasis on
the division between the muscles over
the hip and the leg, but by doing so they
emphasize the power of the body as a
vital machine. The statue is probably to
be restored as an athlete with both arms
upraised securing a victor's fillet on his
head.

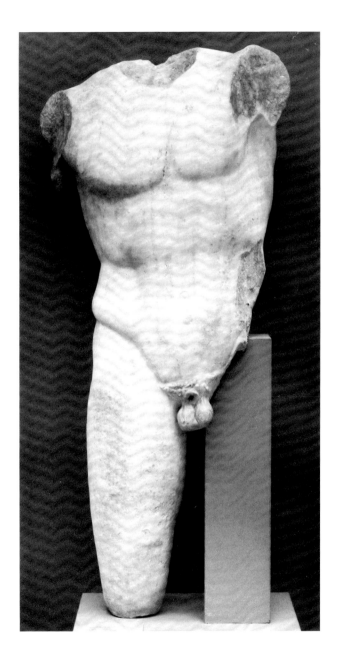

35

ROMAN, first half of the 2nd century
A.D.

Portrait of Augustus
Parian(?) marble. 9³⁄₁₆ x 8 x 6⁷⁄₈

Museum Appropriation. 26.160

Provenance: Probably from Italy

Publication: Ridgway/RISD, 1972,
no. 32.

There had been a long tradition of portraiture on the Italian peninsula before the emperor Augustus initiated the series of imperial portraits. During the Roman Republic, illustrious men had been represented or had had themselves portrayed in a veristic style that stressed the character elements of the face. This style resulted in the production of portraits known for their aged and wrinkled faces. They were often commissioned for private houses.

The change in government from a republic with its senate of nobles to an empire ruled by an emperor, which was established by Augustus in 27 B.C., led to the introduction of new public figures in the Imperial family and a new purpose for portraiture, imperial propaganda. In opposition to the traditional veristic portraits, Augustus favored idealized sculpted versions of himself which stressed his youth and his dignified and calm appearance. The idealization never totally obscured the individuality, for the emperor had to be recognized in his images.

The new imperial portraits were made in vast numbers, and officially sanctioned versions of the images were sent to all regions of the empire. The statues stood in theaters, in market areas, in private homes, and most importantly, in the law courts. Trials could not be conducted without the image of the reigning emperor in place.

The Providence head was designed to be inserted into a separate body, a common portrait technique. The face has a somewhat melancholy aspect which has been achieved by smoothing over all the lines and wrinkles and sharp edges. This type of treatment helps to date the piece to the early 2nd century A.D. and the reign of the emperor Hadrian, when the fondness for this melancholy style was in vogue. Images of popular emperors continued to be made long after the death of the particular ruler. Hadrian commissioned several posthumous portraits of famous men of the late Republic and early Empire for his villa at Tivoli.

36

ROMAN, ca. A.D. 150–160

Portrait of a Man
Tempera (?) on wood. 13½ x 7¾

Mary B. Jackson Fund. 39.025

Provenance: Theodor Graf, Vienna;
Dr. Neudoerfer, Vienna

Publication: Winkes/RISD, 1982, no. 35.

After the Roman conquest of Egypt in 30 B.C., the ancient Egyptian practice of mummification remained in use by many Greek and Roman residents. Additional features, however, were introduced. Especially in the Fayum (in northern Egypt), lifelike painted panels of the deceased in encaustic (using beeswax) or in tempera were inserted in the mummy bandages over the face of the corpse, in place of an idealized Egyptian mask. The custom of covering the face of a mummy with a painted portrait was probably stimulated by the Roman practice of displaying one's family lineage in the form of lifelike painted portraits.

The RISD mummy portrait describes a well-to-do 2nd century Roman citizen of Egypt, dressed in a white tunic with red stripes. In Rome these stripes defined a man of senatorial rank, while in the imperial province of Egypt they were simply an indication of Roman citizenship. The dark lines on the man's fleshy neck mark the turning of his head, a convention in mummy portraits which lasts until the late 3rd century, when figures appear in a full frontal position.

The use of light and shade, as well as the placement of a mass of hair against the highlighted face, suggest a date during the later years of the reign of Antoninus Pius (ca. A.D. 150–160).

Color plate, page 63

37

ROMAN, 2nd century A.D.

Horse Head
Bronze. $6^{11}/_{16}$ x $5^{5}/_{16}$

Museum Appropriation and Special Gift
of Mrs. Gustav Radeke. 27.221

Publication: Mitten/RISD, 1975, no. 59.

The ancient Romans used elaborate couches in their homes for dining, entertaining, and sleeping. Often made of bronze (though Roman literature attests to gold and silver examples), the couches were decorated with bone, bronze, and silver elements, as well as with colored glass inlays. Some Roman couchmakers, several of whose names are recorded, fashioned their couches at such a height that a footstool or even a ladder was necessary to reach them.

The dining couch, known as a *kline*, was equipped with an upward curving headrest at one end and footrest at the other, which are known as *fulcra*. Also serving as armrests for reclining diners, the *fulcra* were embellished with finials in the form of heads of mules, horses, and other animals.

The RISD horse head is a dramatic example of a bronze finial for a *fulcrum*. Full of emotion, the horse twists his head to the right, producing a series of sharp grooves in the flesh behind his jaw. With nostrils flared and lips parted, he seems to be uttering the distinctive whinnying cry of a horse. The corkscrew curls of the mane, and the panther skin, an attribute of the wine-god Dionysus, tied about the horse's chest, contribute to the emotive, Dionysiac quality of the piece. A Dionysiac atmosphere is appropriate to the wine-drinking revelry associated with Roman drinking parties on dining couches.

38

ROMAN, second half of 2nd century A.D.
Said to be from Pamphylia

Pamphylian Sarcophagus
Marble. 55⅜ x 91¾

Museum Appropriation. 21.074

Publication: Ridgway/RISD, 1972, no. 38.

Roman burial practices shifted in the
early 2nd century A.D. from the custom
of cremating the body to burying it
within a coffin. Roman stone coffins,
called sarcophagi, were often elaborately
carved with figured reliefs. During the
reign of the emperor Hadrian (A.D. 117–
138), three dominant forms of carved
sarcophagi (as classified by modern
scholars) were developed in Roman,
Attic, and Asiatic workshops.

Roman sarcophagi, meant to be placed
against the tomb wall or within a niche,
were decorated on only three sides,
while Attic examples, manufactured in
Athens of local Pentelic marble, were
carved on all four sides and typically
illustrated Classical Greek subject

matter. Also sculpted all around were
the Asiatic examples, which were often
framed at the corners to suggest an
architectural structure. The decorative
themes sometimes incorporated scenes
relating to Bacchus, the Roman version
of the savior god, Dionysus. Depicted
with symbols of the four seasons,
Bacchus denoted a god who vanquished
time and therefore death.

The RISD sarcophagus, carved on all
four sides, is framed at the corners by
male figures of the seasons. The architectural quality of these caryatid-like
figures suggests that this is an Asiatic
sarcophagus. The lid, with its projecting
bosses, is also typically Asiatic in form,
and with other details identifies the
coffin as being probably from Pamphylia,
a site on the south coast of Turkey.

The front of the coffin depicts a scene
from the Homeric epic, the *Iliad*. The
slain Hektor, hero of Troy, is dragged
before the crenellated walls of his city by
the beardless Greek hero, Achilles.
Rendered with remarkable vitality, this
is the only such scene to have survived
on an Asiatic sarcophagus, though
drawings indicate that there were other
examples. The scene on the back of the

coffin, of proportions and style wholly
different from the treatment of the front,
illustrates a hunt. Three cupids, aided by
attacking dogs, spear a lion and lioness.
The subject may allude to the deceased
as a hunter, while the epic scene on the
front may associate him with noble
heroes of war.

39

ROMAN, ca. A.D. 210–220

The God Heron
Tempera (?) on wood. 20⅝ x 16¾

Museum Works of Art Fund. 59.030

Publication: Winkes/RISD, 1982, no. 37.

Paintings on wooden panels using tempera (egg to bind pigments) or encaustic (prepared wax mixed with pigments) assumed an importance in antiquity which is today occupied by oil paintings. Few panel paintings have survived, however, except in favorable climates like the Egyptian desert. The rare surviving examples depict portrait busts, such as the Museum's three examples, as opposed to this unusual RISD painting which illustrates the military god Heron. An unusual feature of this painting is its ancient frame. Also noteworthy is the fact that Heron is shown in the act of making a sacrifice as opposed to his usual depiction on horseback.

Heron was popular in Egypt during and after the Greek Hellenistic period. Here he is represented in armor and military mantle with a laurel wreath. His head is surrounded by a *nimbus*. In his left hand he is holding a scroll, while with the right he is pouring something over a flaming altar or incense burner (*thymiaterion*). Behind him walks a small black figure in a white cloak carrying a wreath of roses, possibly a sacrificial servant. On the right and on top of a console is seated a griffin whose paw is resting on a wheel; this is the emblem of Nemesis, the goddess of retribution, who was a favorite among the Roman armies and to whose temple the console alludes. Representations of gods and goddesses making sacrifices exist since the Classical period and are to be understood as a sign of the divine nature of the figure.

In the upper right hand corner is written, "for the sake of Pantophemmios for good," which refers to the donor of this votive panel. Simple outlines, disproportionality of the various parts of the figure and the large eyes convey a rather expressionistic style typical for the beginning of the 3rd century A.D., when this full beard was also in fashion.

40

ROMAN, ca. A.D. 324–337
From the triclinium of the Constantinian
villa at Daphne, near Antioch

Dionysus
Mosaic. 46¼ x 46¼

By exchange with the Worcester Art
Museum. 40.195

Publication: Winkes/RISD, 1982, no. 39.

Colorful floor mosaics were a favorite
aspect of interior decoration of Roman
houses. The mosaics were made from
cubic stones, called *tesserae*, set into
plaster which usually had a preliminary
sketch outlining the main features of the
design. These *tesserae* were cut to size by
the craftsman while setting the mosaic,
and thus could vary slightly in size. The
occasional use of glass *tesserae* is a sign of
a later date.

The subject of the floor mosaic is
usually related to the function of the
room; in this case it was the floor of a
dining room. The entire decoration was
divided into two parts. In one half,
surrounded by decorative patterns,
appeared the framed images of the
mythological followers of the wine-god
Dionysus. The images were turned
toward this tondo with the representation of the god, who faced the
entrance of the room. In the outer half of
the decoration were representations of
the four seasons and a large hunting
scene; the center was occupied by a
fountain. A youthful Dionysus appears
with the traditional long hair and the
green vine leaves and wearing a
panther-skin, the *pardalis*. His head is
crowned by a *mitra*, an attribute for this
god which is found only in the ancient
Near East. Pleasures of the hunt, fullness of life expressed by the seasons,
and representations surrounding the
god of wine serve as suitable decorations
for a dining-room which was owned by
one of the wealthy residents of Daphne,
the most residential quarter of Antioch
in Syria. Excavations have uncovered
many fine mosaics here, and this one,
along with two others in the Museum,
are among the most outstanding mosaics
from the time of Constantine the Great.

41

ROMAN, early 4th century A.D.

Lar
Bronze. 6⅞ x 2¹⁵⁄₁₆

Gift of Mrs. Gustav Radeke. 62.061

Publication: Mitten/RISD, 1975, no. 67.

Worship of ancestors in the form of *lares* was an important aspect of Roman religious life. A special niche called a *lararium* (shrine of the guarding gods of the house and its inhabitants) was reserved in the Roman house for statuettes of the ancestral *genius* of the *paterfamilias* and for a pair of flanking *lares*. Under Augustus (30 B.C. – A.D. 14), the cult for the household *lares* (*familiares*) and those for the state (*compitales*) gained new prominence. At that point emerged two different forms of youthful *lares*, who both wore the same tunic as this *lar*. The quietly standing *lar* was called the *lar familiaris* and the dancing *lar*, the *compitalis*. Soon household *lares* acquired livelier poses, as in this work.

The Providence *lar* is very well preserved; just the fingertips and the thumb of the outstretched hand are missing. He was hollow cast and has some inlay: there are copper stripes on the tunic and the pupils of the eyes would have been silver. In his raised hand was a *rhyton*, while his left held a *patina* to pour a libation. On his head he is wearing a wreath. The windblown drapery is a reflection of the art of the 5th century B.C., but it is here transformed into a stiff, ornamental and unnatural stylization, typical for late Roman art. The Providence *lar* appears to be a rare example of the survival of the cult at a time when Christianity became the state religion.

42

JAPANESE, ca. 1150

Buddha Dainichi Nyorai
Cryptomeria wood. H. 116

Museum Appropriation. 36.015

Provenance: Yamanaka, Kyoto

Publication: *Museum Notes/Bulletin*, RISD,
July 1936, pp. 34–35.

In order to free the imperial throne from
the encroachments of an increasingly
powerful Buddhist clergy, the Japanese
capital in 794 was moved north from
Nara, the scene of that religion's great
early triumphs, to the foot of Mount
Hiei. Here, on the site of the modern city
of Kyoto, a great new city called Heian
Kyo (Capital of Peace and Tranquility)
was constructed, providing an elegant
new setting for both the court and the
bureaus of government. It also served as
the focus of cultural and artistic life in
Japan for almost the next 400 years, and
during this period not only did the main
political, economic and religious
developments of the empire issue from
this metropolis, but its artistic forms
wielded a remarkable authority.

The multitude of surviving monuments from this period reflects a
surprisingly rich and diverse cultural
fabric, one well illustrated from the
perspective of the Buddhist arts. The
introduction of Esoteric Buddhism,
known as Vajrayana ("The Thunderbolt
Vehicle"), expressed the new decentral-
ization of religious power as well as the
enlarged role of ritual which characterized the age. Esoteric Buddhism offered
immense spiritual and material rewards,
and its sects made prominent use of a
complex pantheon and liturgy. One of
these new sects known as Shingon or
True Word, brought by the monk Kukai
from China in the early 9th century,
dominated thought during the early

Heian period, and employed elaborate
magic formulas in its highly metaphysical
teachings. At the center of this new
systematic theology was Dainichi Nyorai
(Sanskrit *Mahavairocana*), the supreme
deity represented by the Museum's
extraordinary mid-12th century example.

The name Dainichi was originally a
solar adjective describing the Buddha,
but in the Shingon sect this name is
applied to the Buddha who is the great
generative force which lies at the center
of all creation, and from whom other
Buddhas emanate. As the Buddha in his
ultimate form of reality, his secret
doctrines were distinguished from those
revealed by the historic Buddha, and
these nearly pantheistic concepts were
incorporated into art, with the result that
Buddhist imagery flourished under
Shingon influence. Most of its temples
were situated away from the capital, and
the monumental RISD Dainichi served as
the chief image of such a temple, one
known as Roku-onji. At least 300 years
ago Roku-onji was destroyed by fire, but
the image was rescued and stored,
dismembered, in the attic of a farmhouse
in the small village of Awago until 1933.

By the late 10th century, the Esoteric
sects were being challenged by less
arduous and more accessible Buddhist
doctrines, and later Shingon sculpture,
like the Museum's example, often
reflects these new attitudes of gentleness
and mercy. Rather than volumetric
unity, the RISD image shows a deliberate
disproportionality and massiveness of
form in both the size of the head and the
elongated arms, qualities fully in
keeping with earlier Heian work. Over
nine feet tall, the solemn sculptural
presentation is flat and static, its
symmetrical, triangular form set upon a
base of widely thrust knees and articulated by a shallow carving of drapery
and jewelry. Although parts of the

sculpture have been restored, notably the forearms, the original was fashioned from the wood of giant Cryptomeria trees in a method known as *kiyose-bori*, whereby the image was carved from several pieces and then fit together, a technique which made possible larger sculptures as well as greater delicacy of expression.

The figure is an aid to devotion whose iconography reflects the Indian source of Buddhism. The *ushnisha* crowning the head represents Enlightenment; the long earlobes, empty of the earrings worn by the historical Buddha during his royal childhood, indicate his vow of poverty; his monastic garment symbolizes detachment from the world. Subtle surface effects concentrate attention on the head, its looming visage imbued with an austere spirituality that is expressed in profoundly human terms. Swollen eyes and sensual lips convey a humane benevolence that is consistent with later Heian work in its calm embodiment of eternal compassion. While many larger Buddha images were often polychromed, here only the upper head, missing its original metal head-dress, and the jeweled arm bands show traces of black pigment, exploiting the subtle qualities of the wood grain as a formal element. Enough remains of the damaged hands to identify the *hokkai-join*, the concentration *mudra* or ritual gesture that is associated with Dainichi. Not present in Indian sculpture, the symbolism of the circular union of two hands represents the universe, the unity of the material and the spiritual. Similar *mudras* are seen in smaller Dainichi images of approximately the same date in the Kogen-ji and Shoraku-ji temples in Shiga prefecture east of Kyoto.

With the rise of radically different aesthetic systems in the 13th century, Japanese artistic energy was no longer primarily directed toward religious symbolism and the canonical restraints of Buddhist imagery. By the late 12th century newer sects clearly had supplanted Shingon and by this time a decline in originality and expressive potency had already long been underway. The RISD Dainichi represents the last phase of the traditional Buddhist arts in Japan, and has preserved within its compelling form the symbolism and spiritual exaltation of a once-dominant force in Japanese culture.

Color plate, page 64

43

JAPANESE, Tosa School, mid-17th century

Genji Monogatari (Tale of Genji)
Ink, light washes and gold on paper.
6½ x 5⅝ (each panel)

Mary B. Jackson, Jesse Metcalf, and
Helen M. Danforth Funds. 82.103.1-2

Provenance: Yamanaka, Kyoto; F.
Baekeland, New York

Publication: *Museum Notes*, RISD, 1983,
p. 14.

Considered the classical text of Japanese
secular literature, the *Tale of Genji* has
served as a rich vehicle of expression
over the centuries for the artists of
Japan. Composed in the early 11th
century by Murasaki Shikibu, a lady-in-
waiting at the imperial court, the story
chronicles the life and manners of the
imperial household and aristocracy
during the Heian period (897–1185).
Centered on the fictional hero Prince
Genji and his amorous intrigues in court
circles, its images gently evoke the
atmosphere of decorum and ceremony
that pervaded this elite society.

The RISD *Genji* is an exquisite
document of aesthetic concerns in 17th
century Japan. Concentrating on the
well-known episodes of the text, the
work unfolds in the form of 54 paintings
alternating with 54 calligraphies. The
paintings represent a continuation of the
earlier *yamato-e* (Japanese painting)
tradition. In a spirit of increasing self-
awareness that extended back to the 10th
century, Japanese artists emphasized
indigenous elements to counteract the
strong influence of China, particularly in
their choice of subject matter and their
formal, decorative approach. It was
during the 17th century that a new surge
of interest in the *Tale of Genji* and *yamato-
e* emerged, led by aesthetically inclined
aristocrats and a prosperous merchant
class. Among painters the *yamato-e*
tradition had been preserved in earlier
periods by the Tosa school, which now
found itself at the vanguard of the
movement.

The RISD *Genji* typifies the taste of the
wealthy classes for personal illustrated
copies in a small format and miniaturistic
style. Normally in a polychrome version,
the story in the early 17th century began
to appear in *hakubyo* or ink outline form.
The delicacy and refinement of *hakubyo* is
readily apparent in the RISD example,
and close parallels are found in *Genji*
albums in the Freer Gallery, Washington
and the Cleveland Museum of Art. The
subtle, economical precision of drawing
and detail are joined in this elegant,
linear style, exemplified by the deft
handling of facial characterizations and
the minutiae of garments and architectural details. Traditional *yamato-e*
conventions such as diagonal walls and
blown-off roofs hark back to the Heian
period, as do the sophisticated contrasts
of complex and blank areas which reinforce the abstract decorative effect
despite an extremely subtle use of
shading. Although the Tosa artists of the
RISD albums remain anonymous, their
visualization of the story stands as a
revealing, intimate portrait of a complex
and highly refined metropolitan culture
– one secular yet inescapably colored by
a Buddhist sense of its own impermanence.

44

JAPANESE, late 17th century

No Robe
Silk with embroidered and stenciled
decoration. L. 55½

Gift of Lucy T. Aldrich. 35.457

Provenance: Collection of Marquis
Mayeda

Publication: *Lucy T. Aldrich Collection of
Japanese Costumes*, RISD, 1937, pl. 2.

No is a Japanese theatrical form that evolved under strong Zen Buddhist influence during the Muromachi period (1333–1568), transforming traditional literary themes with an overlay of metaphysical meanings. Developed in the late 14th century under the direction of Kan'ami Kiyotsugu and his son, Zeami Motokiyo, No is the oldest major theatre art in Japan that is still regularly performed. The culmination of several dance-drama forms, it encompasses a wide variety of techniques and influences that includes both temple and popular entertainments. Without patronage until 1374, when the *shogun* (military dictator) Ashikaga Yoshimitsu attended a performance, the popularity and refinement of No gradually increased, its mature form representing a sophisticated, well-balanced synthesis of dance and mime.

Performed on a bare stage with musicians and only the backdrop of a painted tree, all parts are played by men, and the use of masks is required for female and supernatural roles. Equally important is costume, which, in keeping with the flamboyance of Japan's stage and national dress, has traditionally served as a brilliant vehicle for the expression of aesthetic ideals. This example is one of many from the Museum's superb collection, considered one of the finest outside of Japan, and it illustrates a more naturalistic aspect of No robe design. Longtailed birds, embroidered in blue and white on a soft red ground, spiral gracefully upwards through drifting golden clouds, the robe's floating, dancing effect richly evocative of the identification with nature so often reflected in Japanese textile design. The technique is known as *nuihaku*, a decoration of embroidery combined with gold or silver stenciling known as *surihaku*.

The classical theatrical amusement for the upper classes, No drama took on both religious and aristocratic overtones as it became a kind of morality play in which ethics were taught. The transcendent qualities of robes like this example were instrumental in the presentation of those ideals and attitudes. Drama is not necessarily created in No by realism, but by poetic recollections of both the actors and the chorus, and it is movement, amplified and organized by costume, that acts as a dream-like gloss to the ideas carried by those words.

Color plate, page 65

45

JAPANESE, late 17th – early 18th century

Bugaku Costume
Silk embroidered damask with gold paper and metal ornamentation. L. 101¼

Gift of Lucy T. Aldrich. 37.005a,b,c

Publication: *Lucy T. Aldrich Collection of Japanese Costumes*, RISD, 1937, pl. 43.

When Prince Genji danced the "Waves of the Blue Sea" in the *Genji Monogatari* (Tale of Genji), the classical text of Japanese secular literature written in the early 11th century, the official Japanese court dances known as Bugaku were at their height as a performing art. Ordinarily performed by official court dancers and musicians in palaces, as well as in religious ceremonies in the precincts of shrines and temples, Bugaku also formed an integral part of a nobleman's education during the Heian period (897–1185), becoming so fully integrated into court life that a festival or ceremony rarely occurred without it.

Music and dance were among the first cultural imports from Korea during the 7th and 8th centuries, undoubtedly under the influence of the Confucian precept that musical harmony fostered political harmony, making it indispensable for court functions. Additional dances were added from the Chinese court, and although ritual Confucian music was certainly emulated, other borrowings reflected the cosmopolitanism of the T'ang capital, and even Indian and Southeast Asian forms eventually were incorporated. When these foreign dances were collected and rearranged for the new Heian court in the 9th century, native dances were added and the number of musicians and dancers along with stage and costume were standardized, and have remained so down to the present day.

Both the ceremony and refinement of that court culture are richly evoked by the rare Edo period Bugaku costume preserved in the Museum's collection, a pendant to a similar costume that is one of the treasures of the Kasuga Shrine, the sacred Shinto site at Nara. Consisting of three pieces – robe, vest and helmet – the costume, known as *kasane-shokozu*, features dark blue, salmon and cream as its predominant coloring. The robe *(shitagasane)* with train and reddish sleeve bands is a white damask embroidered with a series of blue lozenges containing flowering *kiri* (paulownia),

which are surrounded by crests and cherry blossom sprays in a symmetrical arrangement. This broad diaper pattern is echoed and condensed in the sleeveless blue vest *(hanpi)*, where flowering *kiri* and multi-colored birds alternate. Completing the ensemble is the helmet *(torikabuto*, literally "bird head piece"), a striking green form whose high peak and upswept apron are brocaded with gold cloud forms; long hanging silk cords with tassels and metal *kiri* ornaments further enhance the formal effect. When the dancers are assembled on stage, with masks and accompanied by percussion and wind instruments, the formal, stylized movement of these colored silks progresses in rhythmic unison, celebrating both the sources and spirit of Japanese court life.

46

TOSHUSAI SHARAKU
Japanese, active 1794–95

Matsumoto Koshiro IV in the Role of Fishmonger Gorobei, 1794
Polychrome woodblock print, with mica background. 14⅜ x 9½

Gift of Mrs. Gustav Radeke. 20.1132

Japanese prints are often referred to as *ukiyo-e* (pictures of the floating world), a term used to evoke the theatres, festivals, brothels, and restaurants that made up the pleasure quarters of Japan's great cities. Prior to the Edo period

(1615–1867), the woodblock print was essentially regarded as a non-artistic medium used mainly for literature and inexpensive Buddhist icons. But from the early 17th century, a new interest in the urban everyday world stimulated an original development in print production, one geared for mass consumption and highly responsive to fluctuating popular tastes, both refined and vulgar. Hundreds of thousands of prints had been produced by the end of the period, and while despised by upper class artists and their patrons, they were exceedingly popular, though deemed expendable, with the classes that consumed them. Traditionally a collaborative effort involving publisher, artist, block-cutter and printer, hundreds or even thousands of impressions were made from each design, ranging in subject from actors and courtesans to nature and literary scenes.

The career of Toshusai Sharaku remains one of the great enigmas in the history of the medium. His entire artistic career spanned only ten months (1794–95), during which time he designed some 150 prints, almost all of them depicting scenes from *kabuki* performances. Few reliable biographical details are known, nor have any juvenilia come to light, so the emergence of his prints fully formed and in a style so distinctively his own makes Sharaku an even more compelling figure. All that can be gleaned from the sources is that he was a No actor in the service of the *daimyo* (feudal lord) of Awa and that his prints were considered unpopular in his time, hardly the case today in Japan and the West, where his works are among the most highly prized of all Japanese prints.

This portrait of Matsumoto Koshiro IV depicts the actor as the fishmonger Gorobei from the play *Katakiuchi Noirai-Banashi* (A Medley of Tales of Revenge), performed at the Kiriza in 1794, which recounts the tale of two courtesans who avenge the death of their father with the aid of Gorobei. Sharaku's portrait discards the usual idealization and replaces it with a probing intensity that successfully evokes the moods of the play. Although somewhat restrained in comparison to his usual work, where exaggeration and satire frequently blossom into outright caricature, Sharaku's graphic approach remains aggressively inventive.

Color plate, page 65

47

OGATA KORIN
Japanese, 1658 – 1716

The Gossipers
From the *Korin Gafu*, 1802 edition
Polychrome woodblock print. 10⅜ x 15

Gift of Mrs. Gustav Radeke. 20.1324

This woodblock print was executed from a series of ink drawings taken from the sketchbook of Ogata Korin, best known as one of Japan's greatest decorative painters. His mature artistic career coincided with the Genroku era (1688–1704), a period in which a new merchant class joined forces with artisans and forged a distinctly urban taste that preferred an art both lavish and diverse in its expression. The enormous wealth of these merchants was freely spent along the restricted lines established by the Tokugawa shogunate, and under the influence of the rich classical heritage of the old capital at Kyoto, an extravagant art emerged, one conscious of the past as well as its own material splendor.

Born into a wealthy family in Kyoto, Korin studied traditional Kano painting under Yamamoto Soken, his father. Under the influence of his predecessor Sotatsu, a celebrated screen painter of the 16th century, Korin's style embraced native traditions in reaching beyond the academic confines of the Kano school, with its strict adherence to Chinese orientation and ink techniques. An artist of far-ranging vision and power, Korin developed a strong sense of sumptuous display, and applied his talents to many media – painting, textile design, pottery, lacquer – while infusing each with an extraordinary decorative sense of space and color.

The sketchbook from which this print was made, known as the *Korin Gafu*, was edited in 1802, long after Korin's lifetime (1658–1716), and demonstrates the extraordinary technical skills of Japanese printmakers. In its intimate, almost humble, glimpse of an elderly pair gossiping beneath a tree, many of the principles characteristic of Korin's screen paintings are clearly evident. His soft, liquid handling of form describes floating figures in the space of the foreground, shapes seemingly arranged at random on the surface of the paper. Their limp forms are contained by broad calligraphic lines quickly and economically set down, a quality even more apparent in the quicksilver stroke of the rakes lying nearby. Outline, however, is completely abandoned in the depiction of the tree, its broad washes a controlled cascade of pale color that evokes the spontaneity of the forces at work in nature. This carefully studied observation of the world is informed with humor and compassion, as well as a mild, playful sense of caricature.

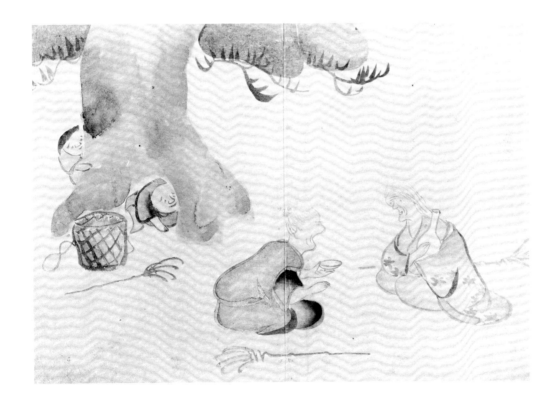

48

CHINESE, Northern Wei dynasty,
first quarter of the 6th century

Court Musicians
Grey clay with polychrome. H. 6⅝

Gift of Mrs. Murray S. Danforth.
34.781–2

Publication: *Bulletin,* RISD, July 1925,
pp. 25–28.

Pottery figurines provide one of the most dramatic reflections of the stylistic change and development that occurred in the non-Buddhist arts of northern China in the late 5th and early 6th centuries. During a time when war and "barbarian" invasions split China into separate spheres, the northern treatment of *ming-ch'i* – objects placed in the tomb for the "use" of the deceased – broke with the previously dominant Han tradition seen in the rare examples excavated from southern sites. In place of bold geometric volumes and mass we see flattened, elongated forms articulated by low relief and incised lines, qualities also seen in figure painting and Buddhist sculpture of the period, and these innovations yielded a grace and elegance strikingly at odds with the sometimes clumsy proportions of the late Han.

These two *ming-ch'i* represent court musicians, their figures painted in flesh tones and dressed in rich red tunics fastened at the waist and trimmed with dark collars and V-necklines. One wears the curious box-like cap characteristic of both courtiers and high military officials during the Northern Wei period, while the other's hair is gathered into a topknot. Standardized facial features were typical whether the figure was male or female, courtier or servant, and the dreamy, beatific smile, elegantly stylized eyebrows, squarish proportions and small nose are all conventional elements in this mode. The angularity of form is offset by the sweeping line of the robes as they flow across the shoulders and arms, merging with bodies in an elegant balance of line and plane.

Examples of *ming-ch'i* from both the Han and Six Dynasties periods often included musicians, and in the typical Northern Wei tomb they were standard along with guardians, camels, and foot and mounted soldiers. Considered necessary and important components of court life, musicians performed both ritual and aesthetic roles in processions, entertainments and ceremonies. The RISD figures have lost their instruments, but similar examples are known with drums, reed pipes, flutes and other wind instruments. Although purely secular in content, the strong facial symmetry and conventionalization evident in these types strongly points to the influence of Buddhist sculpture of the period, and their quiet elegance and introspection can be traced to that source.

49

CHINESE, Northern Wei dynasty, 386–557

Dragon
Grey clay with traces of red pigment.
12½ x 13

Museum Appropriation. 30.005

Provenance: C. T. Loo, New York

Publications: *Bulletin*, RISD, April 1930, pp. 45–46; H. Munsterberg, *Dragons in Chinese Art*, New York, 1972, p. 27, no. 22.

This magnificent Wei dragon is regarded as one of the finest in American collections. The taut, arching back and glowing eyes of this remarkable beast convey, not the expected quiescence of a creature in repose, but the urgent potential of unleashed power. Set firmly upon sturdy flat feet and sinewy haunches, the body is a consistent tension of smooth, muscular curves streaked with red pigment. Beginning with the elongated arc of the neck and chest, these curves surge through the powerful vault of the back to be discharged at the top of the tail. The wing-like shapes at the shoulders and the pointed linear rhythms of the scales along the spine and the horns atop the head suggest an imminent leap into the skies. The wildly animated head, with its deeply sculpted hollows and flat planes, carries an extraordinary mocking grin.

The dragon (*lung*) does not appear in the neolithic art of China, its first appearance dating from the middle of the second millennium B.C. during Shang times. It is thought to derive from Western Asia where dragons in art occurred much earlier, and while its generally fearsome appearance is surprisingly similar in both regions, the Chinese dragon is regarded not as a force of evil but rather as a benevolent and auspicious animal. In Chinese mythology the dragon's symbolic connotations are myriad, but two associations have always been paramount. As a dynastic emblem the dragon symbolized the might and authority of the royal house, and during the later Ming (1368-1644) and Ch'ing (1644-1912) dynasties it was ubiquitous as the dominant animal motif in imperial artistic production. But above all the dragon was seen as a sky emblem in art and literature, inhabiting the clouds and sending rain to the earth to insure the fertility of the fields and a good harvest; without proper veneration, its power was a potentially destructive force capable of bringing floods.

These awesome and sometimes capricious powers of the dragon are best illustrated by legends surrounding early Chinese artists who sought to capture their mysterious force, like the 6th century painter Chang Seng-yu. When he added the eyes to a pair of dragons he had painted on the wall, it is said that thunder and lightning immediately filled the air and the dragons ascended to heaven. The physical appearance of the dragon was also endlessly discussed by both scholars and artists, and the view of the dragon painter Tung Yu offers a fitting description of the qualities found in the RISD sculpture:

"... The male has horns and his body always writhes violently. He has deep-set eyes, wide-open nostrils, a pointed beard and compact scales. The body is strong toward the head and diminishing toward the tail. He is red as fire, grand and beautiful."

50

CHINESE, Northern Wei dynasty, 386–557

Stele
Grey limestone with traces of polychrome. 43¼ x 22

Gift of Manton B. Metcalf. 18.119

Publication: Osvald Sirèn, *Chinese Sculpture from the Fifth to the Fourteenth Century,* London, 1925, vol. II, pl. 137.

The invasions and civil disorders that marked the Six Dynasties period in China were not wholly destructive. Remarkably enough, it was during this period that Chinese culture was stimulated to new creative levels, activated by the nascent fervor of Buddhism and the energy of steppe conquerors. The kingdom of Wei, established in 386 in the northern corner of Shansi province, was founded by one of these nomadic groups, a tribal offshoot of the Tatars known as the T'o-pa, and by the mid-5th century northern China was unified under their banner. In the process of consolidating political power, the T'o-pa Wei became eager followers of Chinese culture, and through intermarriage and a conscious policy of sinification by the ruling house, Chinese language, customs, and dress were encouraged.

This change and innovation is reflected in art as well, for as fervent devotees of Buddhism, a foreign religion recently introduced from India through Central Asia, Wei patrons of Buddhist art helped shape China's artistic heritage during this period. Representative of the new visual form that Buddhism assumed under the Wei is this votive stele in grey limestone. Possibly a substitute for a gilt bronze image, it was placed in a courtyard or temple by followers seeking merit, and traces of paint reveal that it was originally polychromed and perhaps partially gilded.

In the center against a flaming mandorla is the Buddha, seated upon a lion throne indicative of his earthly royal status. Simply attired in monk's robes, he embodies the Buddhist ideal of renunciation. However, the essence of the image is transmitted to the worshiper through *mudras,* ritual gestures of the hands. The left hand is in *varada mudra,* which denotes giving, while the missing right hand was probably extended in the *abhaya mudra,* palm outward and fingers raised, a gesture of dispelling fear. At either side stand Bodhisattvas, more richly attired beings who have gained entry to *nirvana* but choose to remain in the world and help others attain salvation. The figure on the right is Avalokiteshvara (*Kuan-yin* in Chinese), the Lord of Compassion, signified by the lotus bud and *kalasa* (ambrosia bottle) held in his hands; on the opposite flank stands Maitreya, the Buddha of the Future. The mandorla, whose emanations symbolize the illuminating effect of Buddhist doctrine, encompasses all the figures as well as seven Buddhas of the Past, in the ring of the halo.

These shapes and forms are marked by the linear rhythms and elongated proportions characteristic of Wei sculpture, and represent a shift from the plasticity of Indian forms. The Wei preference for low relief modeling and angular form is evident in the square heads and drapery folds, the latter imparting movement to the flat surfaces. By means of these austere formal elements the primary intent of the image as a devotional aid is enhanced and Buddhist doctrine is visualized with a compelling spiritual presence.

51

CHINESE T'ien-Lung Shan, Northern Ch'i
dynasty, 550–577

An Adoring Saint
Sandstone. 23¼ x 16⅜

Mary B. Jackson Fund. 43.187

Publications: The Detroit Institute of
Arts, *Buddhist Art*, October 1942, no. 53;
Sherman Lee in Schwarz/RISD, 1947,
pp. 35–40.

Situated in Shansi province are the 21
cave temples of T'ien-Lung Shan
(Heavenly Dragon Mountain). In both
India and China, Buddhist cave temples
are considered among the great monuments of religious art, their surfaces
carved or painted over the centuries for
devotional purposes. At T'ien-Lung
Shan a soft, gray and tan sandstone is
found that was carved under the
Northern Ch'i dynasty (550–577) as well
as the Sui (589–618) and T'ang (618–906).
Here the Buddhist forms transmitted
from India via the trade and pilgrimage
routes of Central Asia achieved a level of
maturity and assurance not found at
earlier Chinese sites such as Yün-Kang
and Lung-Mên.

The Museum's relief originally
belonged to one of the four caves (I–IV)
datable to the Northern Ch'i period, and
most likely was located to the side of a
niche containing principal figures of the
Buddha and Bodhisattvas. Immediate
parallels to the RISD example are the
well-known examples from Caves II and
III at the Fogg Museum, Harvard
University, and the capabilities of
Chinese relief sculpture are dramatically
presented here.

The constriction and reticence so characteristic of three-dimensional Chinese
works is absent in the RISD relief, as
volume and weight give way to a line
whose movement propels drapery into a
maelstrom of folds and creases. From
this abstraction of angles and curves
emerges the adoring figure, hands
extended and head upturned in a
gesture of offering that evokes both
earlier Indian models and later Christian

examples in the West. As compelling as
its beauty may be, however, the grace
and fervor of the saint draw more from
religious than aesthetic urges, as the
simple act of supplication embodies the
self-giving so central to early Buddhist
doctrine. The transitional style that
emerged under the Northern Ch'i
represents a brief, intense flickering of
the piety and adoration soon to disappear
in the cosmopolitan elegance of T'ang
sculpture.

52

<small>CHINESE</small>, Northern Ch'i Dynasty, 550–557

Head of Buddha
Grey stone. 16 x 10

Gift of Mrs. Gustav Radeke and Mrs. Jesse H. Metcalf. 15.228

The face of this Buddha, round and pleasingly full, tantalizes with the lingering suggestion of a smile. An impression of weight, solidity and mass is effortlessly conveyed by a simplicity of treatment intent on emphasizing the plastic qualities of human form. Economy and gentle restraint in the broad carving of the facial features results in an image whose tenderness and humanity are unmistakable. Contrasting with the smooth, plain surfaces of the face is the ornamental patterning of the coiffure, and the organic swelling of form is everywhere countered by a subtle dominance of design so often found in Chinese sculpture. This delicate balance of naturalism and design is delivered in the straightforward manner that marks much of Buddhist sculpture under the Northern Ch'i dynasty.

When the Northern Ch'i supplanted the Eastern Wei in the north in 550, a different style in sculpture was already evolving in the provinces of Shansi, Hopei, and northeastern Honan. Behind these new developments was more frequent communication with cultures to the west, particularly India, and the emergence of new concepts within Buddhism itself. The increasingly popular appeal of the Pure Land (Ching t'u) sect after the middle of the 6th century created a demand for representations of its supreme Buddha, known as Amitabha, who presided over the Western Paradise. Rather than requiring meditations and austerities to reach this paradise, only a sincere heart was asked, and under the sway of this spirit much Buddhist sculpture took on softer, more sympathetic qualities. More important was the powerful and direct stimulus of Indian sculpture of the Gupta period (320–600), as the often severe geometric and linear style dominant throughout the first half of the 6th century was replaced by a more volumetric approach. Now Chinese sculptors attempted to indicate the presence of the human body under garments, although never approaching the sensuous exuberance and animation of Indian form. In fact,

the essential lessons of the Indian approach to sculpture were so quickly and thoroughly assimilated that it is extremely difficult to point to specific Indian examples as models.

Buddhist sculpture under the Northern Ch'i stood as a distinct entity, free from its predecessors as well as its better known successors created under T'ang patronage. The massive bulk generally associated with Northern Ch'i examples like those of the cave temples at Hsiang-t'ang Shan at Hopei frequently over-shadows the gentler qualities nearly always present, as in this example. The Museum's Buddha is potentially of great importance, and a number of different provenances have been proposed. Szechwan province has been suggested, but on the basis of certain features of carving on the face, it may represent a rare example of the Northern Ch'i style executed in the southern provinces, of which there are no other known examples in American museums.

53

CHINESE, Shansi province,
Sui dynasty, 581–618

Bodhisattva
Grey limestone with traces of
polychrome. H. 39½

Gift of Manton B. Metcalf. 20.192

Publication: Osvald Sirèn, *Chinese
Sculpture from the Fifth to the Fourteenth
Century*, London, 1925, vol. I, p. 82, pl.
303.

The Sui dynasty has an historical and
artistic importance out of proportion to
its relatively short duration. Resistance
by an aristocracy fearful of relinquishing
its nomadic heritage in the face of
increasing sinification at the court led to
the breakup of the Northern Wei
dynasty in 535, and, amidst the struggles
of rival Tatar factions, northern China
again was plunged into political chaos.
Under the energetic leadership of Yang
Chien, a general who claimed Chinese
descent but in all probability was also of
Tatar lineage, the northern throne was
usurped in 581; when Sui armies swept
across the Yangtze in 589 and seized the
Chinese-ruled southern capital, China
was once more united after 400 years of
internal division. As Wen Ti (the
Cultural Emperor), Yang Chien established a dynasty whose political and
artistic achievements would serve as the
foundation for one of the greatest of
Chinese empires, the long-lived T'ang.

Reflective of the new synthesizing
trends that characterized Sui efforts is
Buddhist sculpture, and from the
multiple stylistic trends that marked the
preceding centuries sculptors now
effected a unification of formal elements
that foreshadowed the three-dimensional
explorations of the T'ang. The RISD
Bodhisattva embodies many of these
advances, its imposing figure highly
architectonic in its emphasis on the
columnar shaft of the body, a borrowing
from Northern Ch'i sculpture. Standing
in a long, heavy robe ornamented with
pearl chains looped around buckles, the
low relief modeling and linear articulation of flat surfaces seen in Northern
Wei works have now been replaced by a
tendency toward high relief. This new
solidity and sense of volume is firmly
anchored by the graceful drapery folds
that descend to the ground.

The ornamental adornment of
Bodhisattvas like this example often
tends to encroach upon the body,
obscuring any perceptible organic form,
and what is presented instead is a
cascade of sharp-edged drapery that
charges the surfaces with movement.
Somewhat battered under its high
crown, the oversized head emanates the
compassion and inner tranquility that
commanded high esteem from devotees
of these figures. On the basis of its
material, a soft sandy stone, the northeastern province of Shansi has been
suggested as the place of origin.

54

54

CHINESE, 6th century

Chimera

Grey stone. 20½ x 17

Museum Works of Art. 43.592

Provenance: C. T. Loo, New York

Publication: *Masterpieces of Asian Art in American Collections II*, Asia House, New York, 1970, p. 72, no. 26.

The dynamic properties of Chinese animal sculpture are clearly and efficiently embodied in this small but monumental 6th century stone example. Unlike the gigantic winged lions and chimera that have guarded imperial tombs in the lower Yangtze River Valley since the 5th century, it forsakes the usual elongated, striding form in favor of a bold concentration of power and fiery spirit. Wheeling around to face an unseen adversary, the body's defiant movement ingeniously amplifies the enormous torque generated within the confines of its small circular base. The urgent gaze and gaping mouth promise violence and destruction, yet the embellishment by stylized ornament, such as the appliqué-like feather forms along the spine and winged flanks, tends to transform that impulse into decorative channels. By combining vigorous form with highly animated ornament, the

necessary qualities for combating evil have been skillfully expressed in stone.

The fantastic nature of this impressive chimera is bound up in a complex pedigree that in all likelihood was borrowed by the Chinese, for it reaches back to the ancient Near East and Mesopotamian art. Various fabulous beast combinations in the later art of Babylon, Assyria, Achaemenid Iran and Bactria attest to the vitality and attraction of this mythical beast across Asia. The earliest securely dated example in China is associated with the tomb of Dao I, A. D. 209, near Ya-chou in Szechwan, there seen in its flat, striding pose. The final development can be seen in numerous figures placed at the tombs of the rulers of the Southern dynasties, the Sung (420–79), Ch'i (479–502), Liang (502–57) and Ch'en (557–89) in the region of Nanking and Tan-yang in Kiangsu province. With the fall of these dynasties in the second half of the 6th century, both chimeras and winged lions suddenly disappeared as tomb guardians, ending a spectacular phase in the evolution of Chinese sculpture.

55

CHINESE, T'ang dynasty, 8th century

Ananda

Black granite. H. 8

Gift of Mrs. Gustav Radeke. 17.055

Provenance: R. Meyer Riefstahl

China under the T'ang dynasty (618–906) rivaled the strength and prestige of the earlier Han dynasty. While T'ang armies extended the borders of the empire as far west as Turkestan in Central Asia, the capital of Ch'ang in Shensi, reaping the benefits of an enormous commercial trade, played host to a cosmopolitan populace and grew to what was then known as the greatest city in the world. By about 700, Buddhism enjoyed its widest influence as an organized religion and was a dominant force in Chinese cultural life. These conditions allowed Buddhist sculpture to flourish, and the realistic bent of many T'ang sculptors led to the use of more pliable but perishable materials such as wood, clay, and dry lacquer, with the result that nearly all monumental works have disappeared, many of them destroyed during persecutions of the religion in the 9th century.

Works in stone like the RISD example, however, survive in sufficient numbers to illustrate the main traits and developments of T'ang Buddhist sculpture. This quietly forceful example in polished black granite is most likely a representation of Ananda (*A-nan* in Chinese), the favorite disciple of Shakyamuni Buddha. Fully sculpted in the round, the head almost certainly once belonged to a full-length standing figure, one which would have flanked a central image of the Buddha in a temple. Gone is the elongation seen in the preceding centuries, replaced by the qualities so admired in the metropolitan T'ang style, such as volume and plasticity. Still present are the spiritual qualities of early Buddhist figures, only now they are latent rather than dynamic; no longer the product of linear tension and conventionalized anatomy, they are expressed sensually in ample forms like full lips and heavy-lidded eyes.

As the embodiment of wisdom and devotion, Ananda was often honored in sculptural displays, as a similar poly-chromed figure of the early 8th century

55

in Cave 328 at Tun-huang demonstrates. Black granite of the type used for the RISD head is indigenous to the area around the capital, which together with its stylistic characteristics suggests that the head may have been executed there. Rather than the heroic self-absorption frequently employed to convey the concept of wisdom in other sculptural traditions, the Buddhist canon as expressed here stresses simplicity, self-sacrifice, and devotion as the path to ultimate wisdom.

56

CHINESE, Ch'ing dynasty (1644–1912)

Gourd Flask (pien-hu)
Porcelain with underglaze blue decoration. H. 14½

Bequest of Susan Martin Allien. 35.663

While much of Chinese art experienced fluctuating rates of rise and decline throughout history, porcelain enjoyed a long period of continuous development and production. Persistent experimentation, beginning with the low-fired, unglazed earthenware of the Neolithic period, led to the discovery of white porcelain as early as the T'ang dynasty (618–906), and from the 10th to the end of the 19th century, porcelain wares maintained a universal popularity. Blue-and-white porcelain in particular was in great demand, its rich, distinctive cobalt blue designs the subject of endless pictorial and decorative variations. This ware in a variety of shapes and types was exported in large quantities to Japan, Indonesia, the Philippines and the Near East, ultimately reaching Western Europe in the 17th century.

The center of production was the great pottery town of Ching-te-Chen in the Jao-chou district of the southern province of Kiangsi, established in the early years of the Ming dynasty (late 14th and beginning of the 15th century). Cobalt blue decoration was first developed in the early Yuan period (1260–1368) using native cobalt, but eventually cobalt ores of purer quality were obtained from the Near East and were known in China as *su-ma-ni*, meaning Mohammedan Blue. Mixed with native cobalt to prevent running, this combined pigment resulted in a rich blue which was then painted on the raw white bodies of the vessels dry enough to receive it. After glazing, mainly by dipping, they were fired at high temperatures ranging between 1400 and 1500 degrees centigrade. The new brush-painted decoration gave greater freedom of expression, and designs were copied not only from nature, but from paintings, brocades, and special albums of decorative motifs.

This splendid example features a globular body with flattened sides and short cylindrical neck from which two tubular, scalloped handles emerge to join the body. The cool, bluish-white ground is covered with an all-over floral spray, its contours softly blurring like "ink in snow." Unlike the imperial wares made at Ching-te-Chen for the Ming and Ch'ing emperors, the enormous production for trade, including the Museum's example, did not carry reign marks on the base that help in dating. The dating and identification of this piece depends entirely on stylistic criteria and analogies to dated works, both of which suggest Ch'ing production.

56

57

CHINESE, Ch'ing dynasty, 1735–1796

Ch'i-Fu Robe
Silk tapestry with fur trim. L. 56½

Gift of Lucy T. Aldrich. 35.390

Publication: *Bulletin*, RISD, December 1938, pp. 3–6.

Worn on official or festive occasions, the *ch'i-fu* ("auspicious dress") is usually known as the "Dragon Robe" *(lung-p'ao)*. This was the costume of all in attendance at court or in service to the Manchu imperial government, serving as the official period costume, and it survives in greater numbers than any other form of court attire. The dragon was the supreme symbol of the dynasty, used to decorate all objects worn or used by the imperial household as well as those who represented imperial authority.

The dragon, however, represents only one component of the complex *ch'i-fu* decoration, which symbolized the concept of universal order that was the basis of statecraft in imperial China. These complex decorative systems, ultimately based on Ming period prototypes, were strictly governed by a set of regulations commissioned by the Ch'ien-lung emperor in 1759 and known as the *Huang-ch'ao li-ch'i t'u shih* (Illustrated Catalogue of Ritual Paraphernalia of the Ch'ing Dynasty). This code not only urged resistance to the restoration of native Chinese costume, but also maintained the crucial distinctions of rank and status in official costume worn by each officer, courtier and official, which related directly to that worn by the emperor.

In addition to the five-clawed dragon, the coat of the emperor was decorated with the twelve ancient symbols of imperial authority, which referred to his sacrificial obligations and were restricted to him alone. Yellow was the dynastic color of the Manchu, reserved for the emperor and his chief consort, and this example is particularly fine with its trim of soft grey fur around a yellow field. Symbols for the sun, moon, constellation and mountain at the shoulder, chest and back stand for the four major annual sacrifices made by the emperor. Temporal power is symbolized by the *fu* character (judgment) and axe (power to punish); paired dragons and pheasant denote dominion over the natural world. The five elements of nature – water, metal, fire, plant life and earth – are represented at the back by water weed, libation cups, flame, a plate of millet, and the mountain. Remarkably, this intricate symbolism is complete only when the coat is worn. The human body serves as the world axis, and the neck opening – the gate of heaven or apex of the universe – separates the material world of the coat from the wearer's head, symbolic of the spiritual realm. Together they form a schematic representation of the universe, elegantly linking imperial authority with that of heaven.

58

CHINESE, Ch'ing dynasty, 1821–1850

Ch'ao-Fu Robe
Embroidered silk gauze. L. 55¼

Gift of Mrs. Jesse H. Metcalf. 37.043

The conquest of China in 1644 by a band of nomadic warriors from what is now known as Manchuria brought to the throne a people both culturally and ethnically different from the Chinese. Calling their dynasty Ch'ing (Pure), the Manchu attempted to counter the threat of assimilation by the Chinese through a military and political structure that insured the separation of conqueror and conquered. The Manchu also emphasized the obvious cultural attributes that denote ethnic differences, such as language and custom, but the most visible distinction was in costume. By changing the court attire from the flowing robes and upturned slippers of the sedentary Ming to the riding coats, trousers, and boots of the nomadic steppes, the new rulers established their national dress as symbols of authority that celebrated their origins, although they too were eventually assimilated.

Literally meaning "court robes," *ch'ao-fu* were ceremonial gowns worn for the great state sacrifices and the highest court functions, those conducted by the emperor himself for the well-being of the empire. As the most conservative of Manchu garments introduced into China, they retain many features of pre-conquest costume, and this example clearly reveals the remarkable fusion of the two cultures. The upper part is essentially a hip-length riding coat, and below, the aprons are a vestige of those worn by nomads over other garments, the object being to create a more impressive appearance with formal garments. Another probable vestige of an earlier costume form is the small tab at the lower right of the coat (*jen*), perhaps a closure. Replacing the original animal skins are the costly silks and embroideries of Chinese tradition, and here a rich dark blue silk gauze forms the ground over which the official decoration of Manchu costume is embroidered. The strict distinctions of title, rank, and status in the imperial court were required in metropolitan and provincial administrations as well as military organizations, and this official insignia, whose elaborate iconography represents the Confucian universe, carries both cosmic and political significance.

The *ch'ao-fu* is the garment most commonly depicted in period ancestor portraits, and its use as a burial coat designates it as the rarest type of Ch'ing coat. Its form and decoration demonstrate not only the potency of the costume as a vehicle of political and religious beliefs, but also its ability to convey the luxury, wealth, and separation that marked the upper stratum of Chinese society under the Ch'ing.

59

GANDHARAN, 2nd–3rd century

Head of Buddha
Grey schist. 11⅜ x 6⅞

Helen M. Danforth Fund. 81.211

Provenance: Doris Wiener

Publication: *Museum Notes*, RISD, 1982, pp. 18–19.

When Alexander the Great in 327 B.C. conquered Gandhara, the region northwest of India between the upper Indus valley and the course of the Amu Darya, this ancient area underwent a number of remarkable transformations, particularly in its artistic traditions. With the subsequent assimilation of western Hellenistic influences, Gandharan culture by the Christian era had managed to devise a new visual synthesis in sculpture that eventually appeared at sites from Hadda to Taxila; a formal vocabulary derived from Classical art was adapted to provide a new context for the themes and legends of Buddhism.

Born Siddhartha Gautama in the mid-6th century B.C., the Buddha (Enlightened One) was a prince, apparently from the border of Nepal, who in his lifetime renounced materialism and gained wide renown as an ascetic for his ethical teachings. The ideas developed during his meditations and teachings formed the basis of the enormous appeal of the religion and thought that carried his name throughout most of Asia. More of a reformer of earlier Indian thought than a revolutionary, Buddha preached an alternative to the pain of existence:

"There is a middle path, a path which opens the eyes and bestows understanding, which leads to peace of mind, to the higher wisdom, to full enlightenment. What is that middle path? Verily it is this eight-fold path . . . Right views; Right aspirations; Right speech; Right conduct; Right livelihood; Right effort; Right mindfulness; Right contemplation."

The growing attraction of this message together with the competition of a highly figural Hindu religion necessitated an elaboration of Buddhism. Yet it was the combination of contact with Classical art and indigenous Indian sculptural developments that appears to have stimulated the relatively late development of the Buddha in human form, and the RISD head clearly reflects the Classical traditions that thrived at Gandhara.

While only a fragment of a larger work originally attached to a rock wall, this image subtly asserts the graceful fusion of illusionism and convention that characterizes Gandharan sculpture. The proportions of the face, the fleshy modeling of the neck and cheeks, and the assured precision of the mouth and nose are all reminiscent of Hellenistic representations of Apollo. However, the RISD head could never be mistaken for a Classical work. The iconography of the Buddha – *urna* (tuft of hair between the eyes), *ushnisha* (cranial protuberance indicative of wisdom), the distended ears devoid of earrings (symbolic of his asceticism) – remains intact, reworked but clearly discernible to the devotee, while the elongated eyes and rhythmic brows under a schematic cascade of hair are distinctively Indian in their conception. But it is the tranquil interior expression of the face that still commands attention, a synthesis of Classical form and Buddhist thought that even now conveys the quiet power of transcendence.

60

INDIAN, Bengal, ca. 1100

Vishnu with Lakshmi and Sarasvati
Black chlorite stone. 30¾ x 18¾

Gift of the Sofro Family. 63.060

Provenance: Peter Marks, New York

Under the rule of the Pala and Sena dynasties (730–1203), the sculpture of Bengal in eastern India was, at its finest, the equal to any produced in India. At the end of the 11th century the Palas, great patrons and protectors of Buddhism and many of its holy sites, were eventually forced out of this immensely fertile delta area of the Ganges and the Brahmaputra rivers by the militant Senas. The new ruling family is traditionally remembered for its role in strengthening Brahmanical Hinduism in Bengal, with both Shiva and Vishnu the objects of increased attention in scholarship and literature. Sculpture also played a central role in these devotional cults, and the works of this period represent the last stages of a tradition soon to vanish with the invasion of Turkic Muslims at the end of the 12th century.

Pala and Sena works, in Hindu or Buddhist modes, continued the earlier sculptural traditions of late Gupta art, and it was in that formula that Buddhist art was transmitted from Bengal into Nepal, Tibet, Burma, Thailand, and Indonesia. Early Pala sculpture emphasized a highly detailed "metallic" style which utilized the fine-grained, hard black stone of the region, and the impression of imitation of metalwork is reinforced by the large numbers of small bronzes and gilded metal pieces from the area. This relief fragment shows those same qualities with its emphasis on the precise detail of ornamentation against smooth surfaces, as in the sharp patterns of jewelry and transparent drapery. The old Gupta concerns persist, as in the suggestion of swelling flesh at the belly and the triad formula for the figures, the latter a reflection of a tendency found in the oldest religious texts that emphasizes the worship of deities in groups rather than in isolation.

The power and appeal of the relief becomes evident once its subject matter is clarified. The central figure of Vishnu, the preserver of the universe, is regarded by his followers as the supreme being who strives to save mankind from suffering. Lakshmi, the goddess of good fortune, represents good luck and is often employed to avert evil influences; Sarasvati is known as a river goddess connected with fertility and procreation. In its form, style and functions, this triad reflects a synthesis of Buddhist and Hindu elements that illustrates the often subtle interplay of these two traditions in the history of Indian art.

61

INDIAN, ca. 1400

Shiva Nataraja (King of Dancers)
Bronze. 46½ x 37½

Museum Appropriation. 33.026

Provenance: C. T. Loo, New York

Publications: *Bulletin,* RISD, July 1933, pp. 33–38; Alvan C. Eastman, "A Siva Nataraja in the Museum of the Rhode Island School of Design," *Art in America,* October 1941, pp. 216–221; *Master Bronzes of India,* The Art Institute of Chicago, 1965, no. 58.

Shiva stands with Brahma and Vishnu at the head of the Hindu pantheon, a living god who embodies both the eternal paradoxes of existence and the ineffable absolutes beyond. Infinite and eternal, he reveals himself in an extraordinary array of manifestations, none more dramatic or strangely beautiful in Indian art than his form as King of Dancers – Nataraja. Dance figures prominently in the Shiva myth, from dances on the battlefield and in the cremation ground to those with the Dark Goddess Kali. But as Nataraja, his dance is known as *anandatandava,* the fierce dance of bliss, for Shiva dances the cosmos into and out of existence.

He is creator, destroyer, sustainer, giver of solace, and dispeller of fear (five essential acts called *pancakrityas*). In his dance he dramatizes Hindu conceptions of the universe, where life and death continually generate one another, and the Museum's bronze impressively

defines this cosmic dance, symbolizing the *pancakrityas* by means of attributes, gestures and pose. Whirling through the blazing arch (*tiruvasi*) of the cosmos, the RISD Shiva is a model of dynamic symmetry, its rhythms sustained by an interior movement seen in Indian sculpture that transforms anthropomorphic shapes into superhuman images. The delicate, paradoxical balance of perpetual motion and stasis is brought into focus in the graceful orchestration of arms and legs poised on a vertical axis, their smooth metallic surfaces radiating an unearthly power.

Creation is triggered by the sound of the drum held in the upper right hand, while the opposite hand cradles the flame that destroys all that is created. The lower right hand, with the palm facing the devotee, is in *abhaya mudra,* the gesture of dispelling fear. In one wondrously poetic motion, the left leg sweeps across and into space to hover serenely beneath the left hand, its fingers pointing to the raised foot which is the place of refuge from ignorance and delusion. Triumph over those evils is symbolized by the right foot crushing the infant-shaped Apasmarapurusa, the demon of forgetfulness who grasps a cobra in his hand. Slightly tilted back in calm aloofness, the mask of Shiva's face floats amidst patterned waves of hair that carry a crescent moon and the small figure of the goddess of the Ganges river.

Regulated by a strict hereditary canon of pose and proportion, Shiva's dance of creative energy remained nearly unchanged over the centuries, reaching back to the earliest extant bronze Natarajas from ca. 900, although the intensity and expressiveness of creative imagination shifted perceptibly from piece to piece. The great achievements of bronze sculpture are found in South India, site of the Vijayanagar kingdom (1336–1546) during whose rule the RISD Nataraja was cast, and here artists mastered the necessary techniques for casting complex works using the "lost wax" method. Meant for placement in a temple, the image was conceived as a symbolic manifestation of the godhead, ultimately without and beyond form. On the popular level, however, it was viewed as the god of myth and legend, worshiped as a destroyer of enemies and as a means of deliverance. In his perfection of modeling and restraint, Shiva as King of Dancers conceals and reveals ultimate reality for his devotees.

62

INDIAN, ca. 1585–90

City in a Landscape
Opaque watercolors, gold on paper.
3³/₁₆ x 4

Museum Appropriation. 17.457

In 1572, while on campaign in Gujarat in western India, the Mughal emperor Abu'l Fath Jalal ad-Din Muhammad Akbar (reigned 1556–1605) evidently had his first contact with Europeans. Apart from stimulating his deep interest in other religious systems, this encounter and others that followed were pivotal events in the evolution of Indian painting, for Akbar became acquainted with European paintings, prints and drawings, which were both studied and copied by his artists. The formal presentation in 1580 of an illustrated Bible to Akbar from Jesuit missionaries accelerated this curiosity, although there is evidence that such work was previously known, and during the last two decades of the 16th century elements of the European tradition were conspicuously quoted in Mughal painting.

Part of the process by which these techniques and devices were assimilated into Indian painting is clearly documented by this small, carefully rendered watercolor in the Museum's collection. A copy by an Indian artist, perhaps of a detail of a northern European painting, this work shows the growing concern for naturalism and precise visual observation that made European painting of such interest and value to the Mughals.

Architecturally, it superficially represents a walled Indian city with its towering domes and monumental pointed arch, but closer inspection reveals forms clearly alien to the indigenous building tradition, such as gabled roofs.

Eschewing the flat surface design characteristic of earlier Indian and Persian painting, the architecture is relatively three-dimensional in its effect and imparts a real sense of physical mass in space. Equally successful is the introduction of tonal variations to indicate distance, marked by a distinct atmospheric "bluing" of objects in deep space. These traits, as well as the modeling seen in the rocky outcroppings and topography of the city, are all derived from European techniques. Architectural renditions very similar in treatment and form are deftly inserted into a number of Akbari manuscripts around the year 1590, such as the *Baburnama* and the *Akbarnama* pages now preserved in the Victoria and Albert Museum in London. By the early 17th century Indian artists had completely absorbed these Europeanisms into their own artistic vocabulary, transforming them into distinctly Mughal conventions rather than self-conscious borrowings.

63

INDIAN, ca. 1590

Workmen in a Garden
Right half of a double-page illustration to the *Baburnama* (Memoirs of Babur).
Outline by Basawan, painting by Suraj Gujarati.
Ink, opaque watercolors, gold on paper.
9¹⁵⁄₁₆ x 5⁹⁄₁₆

Museum Acquisition. 17.463

Publications: E. Schroeder in Schwartz/RISD, 1947, p. 75; E. Smart, "Six Folios from a Dispersed Manuscript of the *Babarnama*," *Indian Painting*, London, 1978, p. 116.

Among many of the great military figures of Islamic history, physical prowess and political ruthlessness were frequently tempered by surprisingly keen aesthetic sensibilities. Babur, the Mughal conqueror of India (reigned 1526–30), was typical of this phenomenon, and his memoirs known as the *Baburnama* reveal a remarkably rich and diverse personality. Written as narrative prose in Chagatai Turki, the language of his native Turkestan, it records his campaigns, battles and celebrations as well as vivid descriptions of the flora and fauna he observed as he crossed from Central Asia to India; his detailed accounts disclose an often contemplative nature, one marked by a profound sensitivity to natural beauty. Babur's illustrious grandson Akbar (reigned 1556–1605) later ordered a Persian translation of the text, which was completed and presented to him on November 24, 1589, and it appears that the royal workshop immediately began the illustration of its pages, the incidents to be depicted quite possibly chosen by the emperor himself.

It is to this copy that the RISD page once belonged, and of the approximately 580 folios and 193 paintings executed, only three text folios and 108 paintings survive. At least 50 artists are known to have worked on this manuscript, a perhaps not uncommon number for historical works with their high rate of illustration, and most of the paintings were the work of pairs of artists, one responsible for the outline, the other for the coloring. While this system has periodically been explained as a training process whereby master artists provided designs to be painted by younger apprentices, the collaborative nature of Islamic manuscript production suggests that this method was more likely used to accelerate manufacture. According to one estimate, the entire production of this copy may have taken six months to complete.

The right half of a double-page illustration, one of many in this dispersed manuscript, this page depicts workmen gathering stones and shrubs and is one of three which show Babur engaged in his great love, gardening. He is known to have built numerous gardens in both Samarqand and Kabul, and in the dusty plains of Hindustan, which his memoirs make clear he disliked, the construction of gardens was undoubtedly an attempt to recall the cool, scented air and brilliant flowers of his distant homeland. The urgency of the task at hand is underscored by the rush of figures and water toward the other side of the composition, executed with a relative simplicity and vigor of style that effectively mirrors the spirit of the text. Persian elements linger on in the rock formations with their coral tones, but the composition, palette and naturalism are fully in keeping with the mature imperial style developed under Akbar in the late 16th century. Basawan, who is credited with the outline by a marginal attribution, was one of the great early Mughal painters, and Akbar's biographer Abu'l Fazl singled him out as one "among the forerunners on the high road of art."

64

INDIAN, 16th–17th century

Dagger (khanjar)
Steel blade with ivory hilt. H. 12

Gift of Mrs. Gilman Angier. 83.111

Provenance: Wendy Findlay; Peter Marks, New York

Publications: *Indian and Southeast Asian Ivories*, The Brooklyn Museum, 1982, no. 28; *Museum Notes*, RISD, 1984, p. 11.

A stunning example of technical virtuosity and sculptural invention, this Indian dagger was not merely an ornamental trapping but a necessary and perhaps frequently used weapon. Designed for thrusting in close hand-to-hand combat or hunting, daggers were also greatly favored as royal gifts, often exquisitely jeweled and conferred upon Indian princes and warriors as a sign of high distinction. In the early 17th century, the Englishman Sir Thomas Roe, in his embassy to the Mughal emperor Jahangir (reigned 1605–27), spoke in glowing terms of the richness of the swords and daggers given as presents at court. This attitude is fully confirmed in the decoration of Jahangir's own personal hunting dagger, now preserved in the Salar Jung Museum, Hyderabad, which is studded with diamonds, rubies and emeralds.

Changes in dagger styles and types were fewer than with swords, yet at any given period or locale several different versions were in use. The Museum's example appears to be a *khanjar*, a form extremely popular in India but also known among the Persians and Turks as well. Apt to be more highly decorated than any other knife, *khanjar* hilts became especially rich vehicles for embellishment, and were made of ivory, jade, horn, crystal or other semiprecious materials frequently set with jewels.

Crowned by a highly charged carving of a lion's head, the warm amber patina of the ivory hilt is brilliantly balanced against the cold sinuosity of the recurved steel blade, whose tip is thickened by a rib descending from the vegetal decoration beneath the quillon. An ingenious extension of a second lion's head in steel from the beaded quillon to the pommel of the hilt forms a knuckle guard that echoes the main decorative feature. Similar configurations with dragon heads are seen in a series of 17th century South Indian daggers from the collection of the National Museum, New Delhi.

With the advent of Muslim rule in India, the ancient art of ivory carving underwent changes in the late medieval period. The best examples were produced in Orissa in the eastern part of the country and in Sri Lanka, where with certain minor modifications, careful, meticulously detailed work continued to reflect the old traditions with surprising fidelity up through the 18th century. As the most imposing feature of the dagger, the hilt reflects the exaggerated energy of these carving traditions in its deep undercutting and delicately stylized features, evident from the goggle-eyes and luxuriant mane of the lion down to the minutely rendered decorative panels of the handle. The hilt consists of separate pieces for the head and shaft, and while undoubtedly original, the handle appears to have been repaired at some point. The appropriation of the lion, an ancient symbol of royal authority in India, as the main decorative motif would have made this dagger equally attractive to both Hindu and Muslim rulers. The small inscription on the blade beneath the quillon – the number "835" in Devanagari script – perhaps represents a Rajput inventory number, but the weapon could have been made for a member of any number of ruling elites in 16th and 17th century India. From at least 1100 B.C. India has been renowned for the beauty and strength of its weapons, and this dagger continues the long Indian tradition of casting weaponry in the form of fine art.

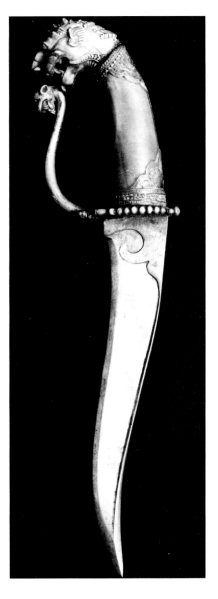

65

INDIAN, 17th century

Lovers in a Pavilion
Ivory. 6⅞ x 5⅜

Helen M. Danforth Fund. 82.038

Provenance: Peter Marks, New York

Publication: *Museum Notes,* RISD, 1982, p. 19.

Originally part of a door that contained at least three other similar panels, this ivory relief evokes in its superb carving the luxury and attention the medium has often commanded in India. The theme of lovers in a pavilion is a common one, particularly in Indian painting, and figures are conventionally placed on a dais underneath an arched opening, as they are here. Sculptural effects, achieved by a deep undercutting that approaches full relief, are balanced with linear form and rich detail to produce an image informed by the intent and effects of painting as well as carving. The laborious and time-consuming process of ivory carving is effectively obscured by the softly rounded curves and silky finish of polished surfaces. Details of costume, architecture, and various objects in the pavilion are thrown into relief by the deep shadows that caress these forms, and the effect is decidedly courtly in its refinement and elegance.

The variety of locations proposed as a place of production for the Museum's ivory reflects the dissemination of similar subject matter, techniques, and media in India during this period. Orissa in eastern India or one of the principalities of western India, perhaps Gujarat, have been suggested, although it is reputed to have originated in Mysore in southern India. However, a series of ivory images of the 17th century from the Deccan, the plateau extending over most of peninsular India, seem to afford the closest parallel. A Deccani female archer in the Los Angeles County Museum of Art presents similar features, with the same attenuated hands and fingers, elongated body proportions, facial features, and finish.

66

INDIAN, Mughal period, dated A.H. 1021/1612–13

Wine Cup of the Emperor Jahangir
Fine-grained green hardstone (quartz and chromian muscovite). 2⅞ x 4¾

Helen M. Danforth Fund. 84.163

Provenance: Sardar Muhammad Yaqub Khan; Amir Sayyid 'Ali Khan (Afghan); Amir of Bukhara; Sir Stephen Courtauld; F. W. W. Bernard, Esq.; Bashir Muhammad

Publications: R. Skelton, "The Relations Between the Chinese and Indian Jade Carving Traditions," *The Westward Influence of the Chinese Arts from the 14th to the 18th Century,* ed. W. Watson, London, 1972, p. 104, fig. 26e; *The Indian Heritage, Court Life and Arts under Mughal Rule,* Victoria and Albert Museum, London, 1982, p. 122, no. 372.

Among the most precious of all Mughal objects are imperial wine cups. This unique example of hardstone carving, apparently the second oldest Mughal-made imperial wine cup in existence, was fashioned from a green hardstone previously thought to be rock crystal stained green.

The decoration is both floral and epigraphic. While a lotus rosette discreetly graces the bottom of the foot in crystalline perfection, the central band of the cup presents eight ogival cartouches, each enclosing a vigorous, naturalistic cluster of flowering plants. Visually, however, the cup is ultimately keyed by two finely executed horizontal bands of Persian verse at the rim and above the foot, their gliding rhythms softening the force of the floral elements. Along with mystical and mythological allusions, the inscriptions state that the cup was ordered by Jahangir in the year 1612–13.

The six couplets in *nasta'liq* script may be read as follows:

A Upper band beneath rim:
This is the cup of water (of life),
nourisher of the soul,
Of King Jahangir (son) of King Akbar,
Who can see from its shadow the dome of heaven.
(It is) the world-displaying cup (*i.e.,* Jamshid's cup showing the events) on the face of the Earth.
Having poured the cup of his munificence over the world
He has caused the fountain of the spirit to flow.
Since this cup was completed at his command
May it be full of the Water of Life for ever.
B Lower band above foot:
May the seven climes be according to his desire;
May his cup be passed around eternally.

Its hijri year is obtained from the imprint "the seventh year of the king's reign."

The cup has an extensive provenance, including rulers of Afghanistan as well as the Amir of Bukhara, that speaks of the fascination an imperial Mughal wine cup held among later ruling elites in the eastern Islamic world. The Mughal dynasty (1526–1858) surpassed both its predecessors and contemporaries in its patronage of carved hardstone objects, valued for their rarity, beauty, and difficulty of carving. No wine cups survive from the reigns of the first three Mughal emperors, but under Jahangir (reigned 1605–27) four examples are known, of which this is the second oldest and one of only two known to have been specifically ordered by the emperor himself. In both form and decoration, it suggests Iranian metal prototypes, yet its decoration is also typical of Indian stone carving and relates to earlier traditions.

Jahangir's cup illustrates the formal and eclectic qualities of the period, but it also powerfully crystallizes Mughal ideology and attitudes. Wine drinking, forbidden by the Qur'an, came to be viewed as a special province of royalty, and, like banqueting, hunting, and polo, the wine cup symbolizes privilege and power. Yet wine was also recognized as a common poetical metaphor for mystical release, and this aspect, underlined by the spiritual connotations of inscription, links imperial concerns fc both divine sanction and personal salvation with political power.

Color plate, page 65

67

INDIAN, ca. 1615-20

Portrait of the Emperor Jahangir
Black ink in pen and brush, heightened
with colored washes, on paper. 6⅛ x 3¼

Gift of Mrs. Gilman Angier. 81.230

Provenance: Terence McInerney

Publication: *Museum Notes*, RISD, 1982,
p. 20.

In Mughal art the patron often played a role equal to or greater than that of the artist, and in the figure of Jahangir (World Seizer), the fourth Mughal emperor and eldest son of Akbar, India found perhaps its most exacting connoisseur. While lacking the political and military skills of his father, he inherited from him an intense curiosity about man and the world, but with a range of interests that were more specific and less far-ranging. During his reign (1605–27) Jahangir reduced the size of the royal ateliers in order to maintain the highest levels of quality and precision, and his artists responded by exhibiting increasing powers of naturalism and observation. Jahangir's pride in their technical abilities was justified when Sir Thomas Roe, King James I's emissary to the Mughal court, was unable to distinguish between an English portrait miniature he had shown the emperor and a copy made by a leading Mughal artist.

Jahangir seems to have been particularly interested in natural history and portraiture, including his own, as the RISD drawing demonstrates. Probably intended as a preparatory sketch, it shows the distinctive realism and intense scrutiny that distinguished Mughal royal portraiture from the conceptual formalism of the related Persian tradition. Facing left in profile, the Emperor stands with his right hand extended and his left grasping a sword, widely-used conventions in Mughal painting. An archer's ring on his right thumb, his *patka* (sash), locket and jewels around his neck, and turban are all carefully indicated. Despite the lofty status of the subject, the facial characterization is both accurate and sensitive; the rolls of flesh under the chin and the wrinkles around the eyes are studied and duly recorded. On the basis of its lively expression and quality of line, it appears that this portrait is a life study, as are two other similar drawings, one in a private collection, the other in the Los Angeles County Museum of Art.

68

INDIAN, Deccan, Golkonda, ca. 1640-50

Reynolds Coverlet
Stenciled, painted and dyed cotton.
106 x 89

Gift of the Glocester Heritage Society.
82.203

Provenance: Chester Reynolds, Jr.,
Rhode Island; Glocester Heritage
Society, Glocester, Rhode Island

Publication: *Museum Notes*, RISD,
1983, p. 13.

This remarkable gift to the Museum has
brought to light a unique and important
addition to a select group of 17th century
Indian painted textiles. Probably used as
a floor covering, the design format is
identical to that of a pile carpet with an
outer border of geometric and floral
motifs enclosing a central field, both of
which are hand painted in mordants, a
complicated and time-consuming dye
process that fixes various colors to cotton
fiber.

The importance of this textile clearly
lies with the contents of the central field,
where myth and imagination collide
with the physical world. Packed almost
to the point of solidity are real and
imagined flora and fauna in multiple
shades of red, brown, blue and green on
a neutral ground. Approximately 425
birds and over 400 animals from the
Indian, Iranian and Chinese worlds
swarm through a thick mass of foliage
and rock forms. Imbued with a bright,
wide-eyed tension that gloriously transforms the entire setting, these creatures
are the sole inhabitants of this fantastic
landscape.

Conspicuous by his absence is man,
his presence intimated only by the inclusion of five architectural motifs in the
lower third of the field. From a distance
the field is not easily deciphered, and
the fertile imagination behind this
design has achieved a scope of vision
and scale that continually astounds with
its majestic sweep and startling swings
of mood. Tempering the exotic flux,
however, are numerous passages of
humorous anecdote and wit that keep
this world earthbound. For every
soaring stag and ecstatic blossom there
lurks a laughing feline or ludicrous
demon, and even animal combats are
defused by sly dragons and grinning
carnivores.

Parallels to the RISD cotton are found
in a small but well-defined group of
cottons from Golkonda which are now
classified as part of the "Early Coromandel Group." Dated to 1640–50, these
works are distinguished by their pile
carpet format and Islamic subject matter
drawn in large part from the painting of
early 17th century Iran. While there are
similarities of size, style and technique
with these examples, the distinctive
composition and subject matter of the
"Reynolds Coverlet" finds no close
analogues among them.

However, another Iranian strain, one
whose roots are traceable back to the
fantastic landscapes of 15th century
Turkman artists in western Iran,
provides an immediate link. In terms of
subject matter and composition there are
striking affinities to the RISD cotton, and
while Turkman themes found their way
into India via Safavid and Mughal art, a
more direct link with Golkonda is established by the Turkman origins of the
ruling Qutb-Shahi dynasty itself. While

more or less compositionally true to its
prototypes, the theme is reworked here
in the contemporary Golkonda style and
supplemented by native additions and
inventions.

The unique character of the "Reynolds
Coverlet" represents a new category for
early Coromandel painted cottons.
Although not overtly Islamic, its features
suggest a wider range of Iranian sources
for Golkonda textile production in the
17th century and reaffirms the extraordinary ability of Golkonda artists to
imaginatively recast disparate sources
into a distinctly Indian vision.

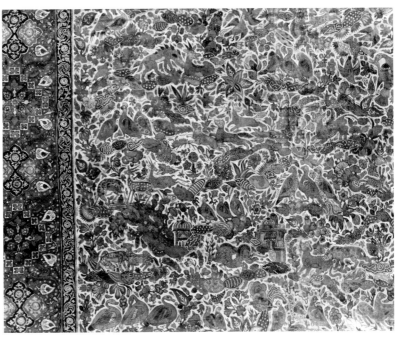

(detail)

69

INDIAN, Mughal, ca. 1650–60
Attributable to Payag

Shah Shuja Hunting Nilgai
Opaque watercolors, gold on paper.
10¼ x 6⅝.

Museum Works of Art Fund. 58.068

Provenance: R. E. Lewis

Publication: E. Smart, "A Recently
Discovered Mughal Hunting Picture by
Payag," *Art History*, December 1979,
p. 396.

This superb Mughal painting belongs to
a select group of royal hunting scenes
executed between 1650 and 1660.
Featuring the emperor Shah Jahan
(reigned 1627–58) or his sons with
retainers engaged in the pursuit of
buffalo, lions, or *nilgai*, the known
pictures of this type include two in the
Padshahnama in the Royal Collection,
Windsor Castle, two in the Chester
Beatty Library, Dublin, and one in the
Keir Collection, with the Museum's
work constituting a sixth example.
Mounted on an 18th century album
page, the painting shows a prince –
identifiable as Shah Shuja, a son of Shah
Jahan – and two companions hunting

nilgai (antelope) at twilight with the aid
of a female decoy. The glow of a brilliant
orange and gold sunset suffuses the
entire landscape in a misty light that
tends to blur forms and obscure details.
The main subjects emerge from this veil,
however, with the characteristic focus
and clarity of Mughal painting, their
presence accentuated by the details of
textiles and the texture of fur.

The dark, moody atmosphere that
pervades this scene is characteristic of
Payag, an artist who began painting
under Akbar (reigned 1556–1605) but is
best known for his numerous works
from the reign of Shah Jahan. In itself a
powerful work, the painting also
provides an important glimpse of a
Mughal prince outside the rigid confines
of formal imperial settings and individual
portraits. Yet it never fully escapes the
celebratory concerns and intentions of
much of the painting done for Mughal
royalty; the elaborate preparations for
the hunt and the entourage, including
an artist, all ensure that the quarry – and
the moment – will not escape and that
the prince will emerge victorious.

70

INDIAN, Golkonda, ca. 1700

Tent Hanging (qanat)
Stenciled, painted and dyed cotton.
80¾ x 115

Gift of Lucy T. Aldrich. 37.010

Provenance: Amber Palace *toshkhana,*
Rajasthan

Publication: V. Murphy in "Textiles,"
*The Indian Heritage, Court Life and Arts
Under Mughal Rule,* Victoria and Albert
Museum, London, 1982, p. 84, no. 211.

Indian luxury textiles, admired and
coveted in the ancient world, scaled ever
greater heights under Muslim rule. A
particularly rich and inventive tradition
was centered in the Deccani sultanate of
Golkonda during the 17th and 18th
centuries, where a spectacular production both for domestic and foreign
markets added to the already fabled
wealth of this diamond-rich kingdom.
The exuberance of line and soft saturated
color that mark this important tent

hanging are characteristic of the best
Golkonda work. Here, three niches with
alternate grounds of red, white, and
purple enclose fantastic flowering trees
and plants with roughly symmetrical
arrangements of branches and blossoms.
This architectural framework encloses
intensely vibrant blossoms and palmettes
in bleeding, polychromed patterns on a
surface thick with wispy tendrils and
darting Chinese cloud forms. The
spandrels and borders separating the
niches are thickly patterned with
scrolling leaf and flower motifs in several
colors on a yellow ground. Borders at
top and bottom are filled with boldly
repeating geometric devices containing
floral arabesques reminiscent of the well-
known *rumal* (cloth used as a towel,
handkerchief or covering) from this area,
and above the upper border is a band of
identical flowering plants, politely
ordered in relation to the turbulence
below.

   The Museum's example is a section
from a larger set, and other sections
from this *qanat* include one niche in the
Textile Museum, Washington, D.C., one
in the Cooper-Hewitt Museum, New
York, and another in the Los Angeles
County Museum. It was formerly in the
Amber Palace *toshkhana* (a storehouse for

furnishings, wardrobe, etc.) and was
perhaps used in the service of the rajas
of Amber, who as vassals of the Mughals
would have maintained their own
scaled-down versions of the enormous
imperial encampments of tents and
enclosures that accompanied the
Mughal emperors in the field. The intox-
icating complexity and beauty of
examples like this demonstrate the
capability of large expanses of decorated
cloth to generate a sense of splendor and
luxury, and it was undoubtedly this
power to alter and transform a setting
that explains much of India's long
fascination with textiles.

Color plate, page 66

71

INDIAN, Rajasthan, early 19th century

Temple Hanging (pichhavai)
Opaque watercolors on cotton. 103 x 84

Helen M. Danforth Fund. 84.020

Provenance: Terence McInerney

Publication: *Museum Notes,* RISD, 1984,
p. 12.

In different periods of Indian history, the pantheon of Hinduism has undergone periodic shifts in structure which reflect changing human needs and values as well as growing powers of comprehension. These changes are manifested in the various forms assumed by the gods, a phenomenon strikingly brought to life by the Museum's early 19th century temple hanging.

Vishnu, the Preserver of the Universe, has often intervened in the affairs of gods and men by adopting human or animal form, and one of these incarnations – Krishna – superseded Vishnu himself among many of his devotees. A devotional sect founded by Vallabhacarya in the late 15th century viewed Krishna as the most perfect manifestation of Vishnu, and in an intense form of worship known as *bhakti,* which calls for a fervent personal attachment to the deity as a means of salvation, Krishna was, as he still is today in this sect, worshiped as the supreme deity. Emphasis is placed on service to one particular image of Krishna known as Sri Nath-ji, the Lord of the Mountain. This form commemorates an incident from the Krishna myth where the god, with the little finger of his left hand, lifted Mt. Govardhan over his head to shield his followers from a rainstorm sent by the god Indra. Based on an actual black stone image brought to the parent temple in Nathadwara in Rajasthan in 1691, this icon is the primary imagery of a *pichhavai,* which is hung behind the statue and acts as a kind of stage set for a variety of ceremonies.

Worship is directed toward a re-enactment of Krishna's youth in Brindaban in the land of Braj, viewed by his followers as the highest plane of existence and the ultimate goal of the soul. With the aid of a *pichhavai,* the image is bathed, clothed and fed by priests in an extraordinary daily ritual. In addition, 24 special festival days are observed, and the RISD hanging represents *Annakut* (mountain of food), which commemorates the feeding of Krishna in his manifestation as god of the mountain as well as celebrating the first fruits of the autumn harvest. Designed to direct the viewer toward eternal Brindaban, pictorial imagery is steeped in metaphorical allusions that coincide with the poems sung at the temple, while continual repetition and the conservatism inherent in religious art have given rise to a highly restricted style. The deep blue image of Sri Nath-ji holds the center against a background whose decoration is inspired by Mughal architectural ornament, and additional images of Krishna, who serve as his proxies, multiply around him. Splendidly two-dimensional in effect, the flat areas of color, including luminescent oranges and lavenders, boost conventions into a higher key. The conceptual thrust is only slightly modified by the inclusion of flanking priests who tend the baskets of food in the foreground, their distinctive facial features naturalistic by comparison but equally set in place as design elements.

Because of the strict format of these paintings they at one time were all assumed to have come from Nathadwara, which has certainly been true in recent times, but it is now clear that they can be attributed to other centers. Attendant figures are given similar treatment in a number of Sri Nath-ji paintings from Kota, the great Rajput painting and drawing center, and on the basis of style are attributed to the reign of Ram Singh II (reigned 1828-66), which provides a tentative date and provenance for the RISD hanging. Rather than simply a static visual aid, a *pichhavai* is a catalyst for a ritual whose whole tenor is congregational, an aspect normally lacking in Hindu temple worship. The devotee shares in the bliss of Krishna by taking part in his sport or play (*lila*), symbolic of the relations between the supreme being and phenomenal creation, and through this adoration the soul proceeds to ultimate bliss.

72

CAMBODIAN, 12th century

Head of a Brahmanical Deity
Grey stone. H. 8½

Museum Appropriation. 31.282

Publication: *Bulletin,* RISD, July 1932,
pp. 44–46.

From its earliest periods and from reign
to reign, the history of Cambodia has
witnessed a continuous alternation
between Buddhism and Hinduism. With
the collapse of the ancient kingdom of
Funan during a period of warfare in the
7th and 8th centuries, the Khmers,
presumably a Cambodian people from
the north, asserted their autonomy and
created within a short time one of the
great civilizations of Asia. Culminating
in the splendid monuments of Angkor,
the center of wealth and culture that
rivaled Augustan Rome in both size and
splendor, Cambodian architectural and
sculptural traditions under the Khmer
devised distinctive interpretations and
modifications of Indian forms, the
ultimate source of religion and art in that
society.

Earlier Cambodian sculpture from the
so-called pre-Khmer period can be
generally divided into two main cate-
gories: works totally dependent on
Indian influence and those showing
indigenous traits, such as the brilliant,
free-standing Harihara from Prasat
Andet, whose plastic volumes border on
the abstract in their sensitivity to
surface. Khmer development of Buddhist and Hindu images in the following
centuries established new types, and by
as early as the 10th century certain traits
were formulated that remained canonical
throughout the history of Khmer
sculpture, as the Museum's 12th century
example demonstrates. A tendency
toward generalization is present in the
treatment of form, the columnar mass
readily apparent under a seemingly
sparse surface articulation that stresses
rigidity. Replacing the sensual respon-
siveness of pre-Khmer statues is a
hieratic severity and formalized
hardness, by this point essentially
formulaic in its details. They include full
lips, long narrow eyes marked by incised
double lines, the horizontal ridge of the
eyebrows and the straight nose with
broad nostrils. The elongated ears,
pierced for earrings, and the *ushnisha* or

cranial protuberance are conventional
signs of holiness. A stylized beard is
indicated on the chin, and its definition,
like that of the hair, is in no sense
naturalistic.

While these individual features melt
into a mask-like effect, ethnic features
are clearly in evidence, and it is known
that the Khmers were in the habit of
deifying their kings. However, the
matted *jatamakuta* coiffure, characteristic
of ascetics, was especially connected
with Shiva, and the presence of the third
eye tends to support that identification.
Whatever its real identity, it clearly
projects the gracious dignity that marks
so much of Cambodian imagery, royal or
divine.

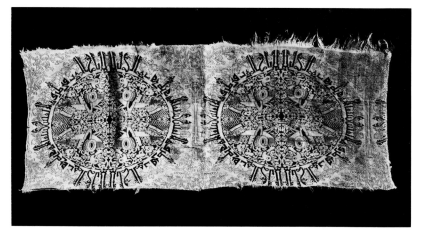

73

74

IRANIAN OR CENTRAL ASIAN, 15th century

Candlestick Finial
Bronze. 5¼ x 4⅞ x 2

Mary B. Jackson Fund. 81.210

Provenance: Spink and Son

Publication: *Museum Notes*, RISD, 1983,
p. 12.

Much of the eastern Islamic world
during the 15th century – Eastern Iran,
Afghanistan and the southern areas of
Soviet Central Asia – came under the
control of the Timurid dynasty (ca. 1375–
1506). Originally nomadic Turkic horsemen, these descendants of Timur
(Tamerlane) so successfully assimilated
the political and cultural traditions of
royal Islamic Iran that they came to be
regarded as the supreme embodiment of
Islamic urban culture in the eastern
Islamic world. Cultural patronage
appears to have been closely linked with
political status in the Timurid house,
and almost all major princes seem to
have been patrons of architecture and
the arts of the book.

Less well known is metal work done
under Timurid patronage, and it has not
survived in large numbers. The rare
known pieces of this type are now in the
possession of the British Museum and
the Hermitage Museum, Leningrad, as
well as two others in private collections
in London and Geneva. The RISD
example is striking for the controlled

73

IRANIAN, Seljuq period, 12th century

Silk Fragment
Silk compound weave. 9½ x 24¼

Museum Acquisition. 36.010

Provenance: Arthur Upham Pope

Publications: *Bulletin*, RISD, October
1937, pp. 74–77; P. Ackerman, *Guide to
the Exhibition of Persian Art*, The Iranian
Institute, New York, 1940, p. 749, no. 20.

The physical nature of the weaving
process made textiles natural vehicles for
Islam's rich decorative repertory, as this
rare Iranian silk fragment so eloquently
demonstrates. Two pairs of birds, set as
mirror images against a coiling vegetal
arabesque on a dark blue ground, are
enclosed by oval medallions. The buff-
colored interstices between these are
filled with brownish symmetrical vegetal
patterns, while separate strands inter-
weave with the stylized *kufic* script
radiating outward from the perimeter of
the medallions. Charged by foliated
vertical shafts, the Arabic inscription
dominates the field with its insistent
admonition: "Be not secure from death
in any place nor at any breath." The RISD
fragment is part of a larger fabric that
was apparently covered with a repeat
pattern of these medallions, and other
pieces are known in American and
European museums. Although the
origins of these fragments are disputed,
they are generally seen as burial silks
and are attributed to the city of Rhages
in western Iran, an important urban
center under the Seljuq dynasty (11th–
13th centuries).

Medieval Iranian silks illustrate the
high level of virtuosity and sophistication
achieved by artisans during this period,
in addition to reflecting important technical advances. However, these developments did not preclude the inclusion of
traditional imagery. The old Iranian
device of heraldic animals within circles
reflects the persistence of pre-Islamic
Iranian themes as well as their adaptation
to new uses. By attaching a proverbial
Arabic inscription along with the characteristic arabesque, the designer has
transformed an old symbol and informed
it with new meaning.

74

torque of its coiled central shaft, which gives way to a pair of opposed dragon heads that majestically expand into free space. The finely worked upturned heads, defiantly thrust heavenward, convey a monumentality and presence far exceeding the work's actual size. On the basis of comparison with other examples, this finial most likely served as a candlestick and was positioned atop a truncated conical base.

Although it appears in numerous media and contexts throughout the history of Islamic art, the meaning of the dragon is still little understood. During the Timurid period dragon heads were common as ornamental features on a series of jade tankards ranging in date from 1456 to 1511, and earlier examples are connected by inscriptions to Ulugh Beg, a grandson of Timur and ruler of Samarqand (reigned 1417–49). Recent scholarship has proposed an astrological meaning for the theme of entwined dragons. In the view of medieval Muslim astrologers, the dragons represented the pseudo-planetary nodes of the moon's orbit, the Arabic *al-jawzahr*, which were regarded as the head and tail of a giant serpent or dragon which affected solar and lunar eclipses. A similar interpretation for these candlesticks would be physically reinforced and animated by the presence of candle flames, perhaps specifically referring to solar eclipses.

75

IRANIAN, Mazandaran, dated Ramadan A.H. 877/February 1473

Cenotaph
Carved wood. 44½ x 46⅜ x 73¼

Museum Appropriation. 18.728

Provenance: H. Kevorkian, New York

Publications: G. Wiet, *Le Caire*, Musée Arabe du Caire, 1933, p. 48, no. 53, pls. XIII–XIV; A. U. Pope, ed., *Survey of Persian Art*, Oxford, 1939, vol. XII, pl. 1472; E. Grube, "Notes on the Decorative Arts of the Timurid Period," *Gurura-jamanjarika* (Studi in Onore Giuseppe Tucci), Naples, 1974, p. 264, fig. 146.

Pride of place in the RISD Islamic collection has long been held by this celebrated cenotaph, one of the rare signed and dated examples of the type in American and European collections. While the most complete sequence of Islamic woodcarving can be traced in Egypt, it is only from the 14th century on that it appears in consistent numbers in Iran, and the Museum's piece demonstrates the technical sophistication reached during the following century.

Nearly all the extant Iranian or Central Asian woodwork from the 15th century is preserved in an architectural context, the majority of it in the form of mosque furniture, and the most important early group surviving is to be found in Turkestan and Samarqand. Comparable in quality and state of preservation to many objects from that group is the RISD example. A cenotaph was customarily placed in a funerary chamber connected with or adjacent to a mosque, serving as a memorial for the deceased whose remains lay elsewhere, often in a chamber below. This particular cenotaph was meant for Taj al-Mulk wa'l-Din Abu'l Qazim, the son of Imam Musa al-Kazim. According to its copious Arabic inscriptions, it was ordered by the Baduspanid Gustaham for the Imamzada Abu'l Qasim in Mazandaran, a region located in northern Iran on the south Caspian littoral. Remarkably, the names of both the craftsmen are also given, Ustad Ahmad *najjar* (carpenter) and Ustad Hasan b. Husayn. The only known comparable work is the monumental cenotaph of Saif al-Din Bakharzi in Bukhara which dates from the late 14th century.

Not immediately apparent to the eye is the juxtaposition of inscriptions with geometric and vegetal ornament. A horizontal frieze of Arabic script flows around the top of the casing and carries the dedicatory inscription, while vertical panels on each face contain sayings of the Prophet Muhammed that exhort all believers to obey and respect God as well as look to the next world, for ". . . life is an hour." It has been suggested that the tops of each of the four corner posts were fashioned to receive candles to be burnt as offerings, but this remains conjectural. The comparative rarity of wood in Iran was undoubtedly a partial reason for its lavish decoration, and carving in relief remained throughout the centuries the most popular and developed wood technique in the Islamic world. However, the brilliance of surface that characterizes this example, particularly its density and overall patterning, is due primarily to the desire to embellish a commemorative object. Another level of meaning can also be proposed, one especially appropriate for a funerary monument but perhaps characteristic of all Islamic decoration: by covering all sides with deeply cut designs and pattern, the dematerialization of the surface is suggested, implying the fleeting impermanence of the physical world. The decoration would then function as a visualization of what the inscriptions proclaim – the reality of God alone is all that ultimately remains for man.

75

76

IRANIAN, Safavid dynasty, ca. 1535

Resting Camel
Brown and black ink on paper. 1¾ x 2⅜

Museum Acquisition. 17.420

Publication: Schwarz/RISD, 1947, p. 66, fig. 2.

One of the tangible fruits of political unification in 1501 under Shah Isma'il Safavi was the occurrence of yet another florescence of the arts in the history of Iran. Directly related to the administrative joining of eastern and western Iran was a parallel process in the arts of the book. The refined classicism of Timurid painting was animated by the inherent dynamism and emotion of Turkman art, and the synthesis that resulted dominated painting and drawing throughout the course of the century. Even provincial centers, noted for their variety in the previous century, now came almost completely under the sway of this new metropolitan style in vogue at the Safavid court. Its influence and attraction for patrons at rival courts are underscored by its role as a formative element in the development of both Mughal and Ottoman court painting.

The diminutive camel in the Museum's collection exquisitely illustrates the characteristic strengths and capabilities of Safavid artists. Clearly the work of a major royal artist, the camel is shown saddled and kneeling to be mounted, drawn in brownish ink and washes, with black accents in the wrinkles of the neck and harness perhaps added by pen. The convincing delineation and

76

amplification of the powerful volumes of the body results from the complementary effect of shadows and soft textures of fur on the swelling line so often prominent in Safavid draughtsmanship. This close observation of anatomical structure and proportion suggests a study from life rather than the copying based on drawn models which was central to much of previous artistic practice and education in Iran.

Although a similar unpublished drawing of a camel, attributable to the 15th century and now in the Topkapi Saray Library in Istanbul (H. 2153, F. 50b), conceivably could have served as a model, the insightful depiction of physical reality shown here clearly argues against such an interpretation. The fineness of scale and precise execution seen in this example are characteristic of the classical tradition of Persian manuscript illustration, but the sensitive observation that dominates this witty and subtle rendering signals the new importance of naturalism in the visual arts of Iran.

77

IRANIAN, Safavid dynasty, second half of the 16th century

Riders in a Landscape
Silk compound weave. 12¼ x 28½

Museum Appropriation. 36.011

Provenance: Arthur Upham Pope

Publications: A. U. Pope, ed., *Survey of Persian Art*, Oxford, 1938–9, vol. III, p. 2092, note 1; P. Ackerman, *Guide to the Exhibition of Persian Art*, The Iranian Institute, New York, 1940, p. 442, no. 11.

One of the treasures of the Museum's Islamic collection is this rare fragment of a figured silk from Iran, a brilliant grafting of the developments of Safavid court painting onto a woven structure. A pair of addorsed horsemen stands in the clearing of a thickly forested landscape, each with a groom tending to his resplendent yellow mount. Both riders and horses, elegantly inflated with the knowledge of their own magnificence, are ablaze in a glow of reds and yellows against a rich dark blue background. Details of garments, like the folds of the turban wrapped around the characteristic Safavid baton, are carefully and precisely delineated in dark lines to articulate the force of color. The extravagant heraldic display of these figural groups is matched by the lush leaves and flowers surrounding them, their gentle lyricism sharply punctuated by bare, jagged branches.

Figural textiles such as this one are undoubtedly the result of collaborations between court painters and weaving workshops. During the 16th century in

77

Iran, textile design and production flourished not only at the royal capitals but also at provincial centers that supplied the court, often working from cartoons or stencils provided by the artists of the shah. Under Shah Tahmasp (reigned 1524–76) Safavid painters synthesized eastern and western Iranian painting to create a figural vocabulary that was reflective of the luxury and refinement of court life. The figural type found in the RISD piece, formulated at the capital of Tabriz, was carried on in textiles in a number of weaving centers until the end of the century. The city of Kashan in western Iran, formerly a leading center of ceramic production, achieved great prominence at this time as a producer of textiles and carpets for the court, and has been suggested as the place of manufacture for the cloth of which this is a fragment. The only other known piece is in the collection of Mrs. W. H. Moore in the Yale University Art Gallery.

78

TURKISH, Ottoman dynasty, 18th century
Tomb Cover
Silk compound weave. 36¼ x 26
Museum Works of Art Fund. 46.504
Provenance: Old Paris, New York

It would be difficult to overestimate the enormous role that textiles have historically played in Islamic culture. Regardless of whether the social context was royal, religious, urban, or tribal, textiles were necessary for furnishing identification, protection and decoration. Silk textile production in Turkey under the Ottoman dynasty (1299–1924) enjoyed an unusually long and distinguished history, and the traditional association of luxury fabrics with Muslim religious practices was responsible for the creation of powerfully hypnotic designs like this large fragment of a tomb cover.

Over a deep green ground move animated bands of white calligraphy, their elegant verticality further amplified by the angles of a chevron pattern that encloses them within its alternating widths. The four different repeating Arabic inscriptions – the wide bands in *thuluth jali*, the narrow ones in *thuluth* –

do not name the deceased but instead present orthodox statements of faith, including the *shahada* ("There is no god but God; Muhammad is the Prophet of God") along with phrases praising God and the Prophet. Normally draped over the symbolic sarcophagi found in Ottoman mausolea, their unique design perhaps served as an imitative reference to the triangular grave markers that often graced the place of burial.

Silk fabric was for centuries a vital and dominant element in Turkey's far-flung economic network. A number of Ottoman archival documents have provided valuable information on the silk industry, especially its center, the city of Bursa, and through the establishment of influential trade guilds high artistic and qualitative standards were rigorously upheld. The result of these practices can be seen in the RISD piece, and covers of this type appear to have been woven without any major variation over a period of several hundred years. On the basis of its condition and greater width than 16th and 17th century examples, the Museum's fragment, like a similar piece in the Musée Historique des Tissus in Lyon, is datable to the 18th century.

78

79

MELANESIAN, New Ireland, ca. 1890

Malanggan Mask
Painted, carved wood; plant pith.
32½ x 8½ x 11½

Museum Works of Art. 43.184

Provenance: E. Segaredakis, New York;
Speyer collection, Berlin

Publications: *Museum Notes*, RISD,
May 1943; R. Linton, P. Wingert,
R. D'Harnoncourt, *Arts of the South Seas*,
Museum of Modern Art, New York,
1946, p. 161.

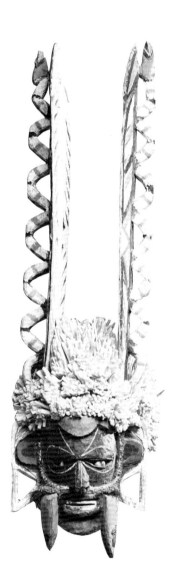

In New Ireland, part of the Bismarck Archipelago to the east of New Guinea, the old material culture, now almost completely vanished, has been preserved in objects like this ceremonial mask. The main context for much of the artistic production in the northern districts of the island was a series of important memorial rites known as *malanggan*. The visual appearance of objects made for the *malanggan* festival reflects not only the requirements of ritual but also the manner in which an artist created the object.

After a formal expression of sorrow, subsequent *malanggan* rites were typically joyous occasions, incorporating social purposes such as the initiation and circumcision of boys, so that while deceased members of the clan were honored, the clan was also renewed. The design for each particular sculpture was the property of each clan, and consisted of representational and symbolic forms used to construct figures, friezes, and even entire mythical scenes involving powerful spirits in zoomorphic and anthropomorphic form. At the climax of the ceremony, the sculptures were put on display, the community gathering to mourn and honor its deceased ancestors. After use in the ceremony, the masks were either burned or allowed to decay, with the individual designs retained only in the memory of the clan headman. When a design was needed again for new rites, it was recreated by the headman directing the carving and painting, the means of transmission essentially conceptual rather than visual.

The forms of these masks are often combined with profuse, elaborate surface designs, a synthesis that produced complex sculptural creations endowed with the appearance of nervous movement and tension. This highly stylized formal organization so typical of Melanesian works was based on a careful construction of diverse materials. The face of the Museum's example is of cut and polished wood, which was painted with a dark brown tint to give the surface a copper tinge. Eye sections, lips, and the ground of the beard are clay applications, designed to hold inlaid eyes and a stubbly beard, the latter composed of seed structures. The pale yellow of the hair consists of plant pith, while below hang the remains of long silky whiskers of dry roots, which originally drooped over the tusk-like mandible projections. Apart from the grimacing mouth, the most compelling feature is the eyes, made of turbot shells of green and golden brown that gleam with dark intensity. The combination of human forms with other symbols, like the snake and bird representations on the vertical appendages, often refer to a legend or event associated with an ancestor, and this desire to combine the physical with the mythological resulted in a highly ornate elaboration. The ultimate power of the mask lies in this ability to transform the face and present to both the wearer and the viewer a different vision of human personality.

80

MEXICAN, Veracruz, ca. 600–900

Palma
Volcanic stone. H. 26⅞

Mary B. Jackson Fund. 43.194

Provenance: Pierre Matisse, New York

Publication: Schwarz/RISD, 1947, pp. 83–90, illus. p. 82.

The modern name *palma* refers to a variety of tall, thin stones flaring at the top, usually carved with a variety of figural and non-figural decoration, and thought to originate in the region of Veracruz on the Gulf coast of Mexico. Belonging to a style of sculpture formerly called "Totonac," an ethnic term now regarded as irrelevant, *palmas* are connected to a group of functional forms – including yokes and *hachas* (figural blades) – that are believed to be associated with an ancient ritual ball-game.

The existence of ball-games in Meso-america from the time of the Spanish conquest is known from early colonial accounts, but these descriptions are of little use in reconstructing the rules of play or the significance of the game in its Preconquest form. The evidence of the Tajin ball-game reliefs has given rise to the theory that *palmas* were worn by players or were stone replicas of a game accessory originally made of a lighter and more perishable material. Ball players in the reliefs wear items resembling *palmas* in front of yokes that are placed around their waists. While it is hard to believe that heavy stone objects such as these were designed to be worn by participants in a game, archaeologists do not rule out the possibility, although a ceremonial signi-ficance for the *palma* is also proposed.

This example, carved in a porous volcanic stone, has a broad triangular base, its underside concave as if to fit a yoke, and rises to a fan-shaped finial. The subject matter of *palmas* ranges from birds, animals, and human beings to inanimate objects such as bundles of spears or arrows. Here, a human face silently emerges from the density of ornamentation covering the shaft, its oddly soft contours and blank eyes dominated by a gaping mouth. The characteristic scrollwork and other design elements are cut to varying depths, creating the effect of an agitated geometric surface broken by the smooth, organic form of the face.

A nearly identical *palma* is in the Dehesa collection, and the arbitrary simplification and unorthodox arrange-ment of ornament in both these tall examples suggests a later stage of development. Recent iconographic studies of the Tajin reliefs have seen reflected in the game the conception of complementary forces posed as opposites in a dualistic universe. The sculptural qualities of the *palma* – the contrast of light and shade, geometry and natu-ralism – may echo that dualistic conception.

81

MEXICAN, Aztec, 15th century

Monkey
Volcanic stone. 14 x 10½ x 9¾

Mary B. Jackson Fund. 43.545

Provenance: Pierre Matisse, New York

Publication: Schwarz/RISD, 1947, pp. 83–90.

The term "Aztec" is used in a general sense to describe all the peoples who lived in the valley of Mexico in the 14th and 15th centuries. Although there is a relative wealth of textual sources in native and Spanish languages for this last major pre-Hispanic civilization of Mexico, only the bare outlines of Aztec religion are known. Their religion was one of the most complex polytheistic systems known, with the pantheon containing over 200 named deities, each capable of appearing in multiple forms. Although this pantheon of deities was largely anthropomorphic, most of the gods possessed an animal spirit identity *(nahualli)* into which they sometimes transformed themselves.

Free-standing, three-dimensional stone images like this example do not exist in quantity prior to the Postclassic period (1200–1521), but during this period a new tradition emerged, centering on representations of deities, humans, and animals. While seldom completely shedding an appearance of cubic or columnar mass, a new sense of observation is evident in the convex surfaces and naturalistic details that breaks with the severe, architectonic conceptualization of earlier sculpture. The clear emotional tone of Aztec animal sculpture has its roots in a view of the natural world that was highly animate: the earth was sometimes described as a part-serpent, part-amphibian creature, while the green surface of the earth was metaphorically represented by the feathered serpent. Because animals are prominent in mythology and deity symbolism and are represented without elaborate imagery, it is thought that examples like this may have been placed next to deity images in shrines and temples. Human and animal identities are fused in this sensitive rendering of a seated monkey with earrings, feet crossed and knees upraised in a pose known from contemporary human portrayals. The pitted stone surfaces of the body swell and sag beneath a hunched back as the mask of the face confronts the viewer, both alive and inanimate in its vibrant conventionalization.

One of the two principal calendrical systems of the Aztecs was a 260-day divinatory calendar of 13 numbers and 20 days. The 20 days were represented by signs, such as the monkey, and every person was given the name of the day on which he was born, as were the gods. Each day sign carried favorable, unfavorable or indifferent associations, which were also conveyed by related gods, directions, and colors. The monkey day sign *(ozomatli)* was ruled by Xochipilli-Macuilxochitl, the god of music, dance, and festivals. Aztec males born under the monkey sign were thought to be of good disposition, happy and gregarious, and likely to become musicians, dancers, and craftsmen.

82

NORTHWEST COAST, British Columbia, ca. 1830

Portrait Mask
Painted, carved wood; abalone shell.
8¼ x 7¾

Jesse Metcalf Fund. 45.089

Provenance: Heeramaneck Galleries, New York

Publication: Evan M. Maurer, *The Native American Heritage: A Survey of North American Indian Art*, The Art Institute of Chicago, 1977, p. 304, no. 473.

The part of the North American continent known as the Northwest Coast comprises the coastal strip of Alaska south of Yakutat Bay, the west coast of Canada, and the northern coast of the state of Washington. This richly endowed area, with its tremendous forests, teeming river valleys, and rugged Pacific coastline, provided not only an easy abundance of food and materials for the peoples who inhabited it, but also gave rise to a distinctive system of values and beliefs. Northwest Coast Indians developed elaborate rituals centered around feasts, economic rivalries, and the performance of tribal

legends. A key concept in much of this activity was social rank. Its expression, whether through totem poles or the *potlatch* feast, usually had as its intention self-glorification and display of wealth, the latter often of enormous proportions due to strategic tribal control of fur and fishing areas. Yet despite this seemingly secular, humanistic viewpoint, the natural world was still explained by the supernatural; animate and inanimate objects were thought to be controlled by spirits who, if properly influenced by the shaman or medicine man, would favorably influence the course of events.

The objects used in these tribal ceremonies were integral to their influence and success, and wooden masks vividly demonstrate the power and imagination of Indian carvers. Wood carving was the primary art of the Northwest Coast, and masks were made of a great variety of woods – Douglas fir, cedar, Sitka spruce, and adler – depending on construction and purpose. Mechanical devices were sometimes incorporated that opened the mask to reveal inner designs, often representing the spirit of the outer personification. Supplemented by natural and imported materials used for decorative elaboration, these masks were frequently used by costumed dancers in dramatic performances of family or creation myths, some repre-

senting spirits or religious deities, while others were caricatures or, perhaps like this example, portraits. While abstraction and convention are prominent features in Northwest Coast masks, there is an even greater preoccupation with the control of three-dimensional form. Regardless of a mask's degree of stylization or recombination of parts, proportion and conventions are manipulated to avoid obscuring the natural subject, whether human or animal.

The sensitivity and realistic modeling of this mask seems to indicate the work of the Tlingit, a people particularly noted for their portrait masks. The labret in the pierced lower lip identifies the mask as female, either a portrait of a clan dignitary or the representation of a shamanistic female spirit. The muscular features of the face are encased in the warm, polished patina of a dark brown grained wood, its broad, subtle surfaces conveying an interior presence. Here, the clear concern for underlying bone structure is symptomatic of a more general interest in revealing an inner state, and in the spare carving of these penetrating eyes and firmly set mouth, the essence of personality is presented to the onlooker.

83

NIGERIAN, Benin, 17th century

Royal Ancestor Portrait
Bronze or brass with tin. $9\frac{5}{8}$ x $7\frac{1}{2}$

Gift of Lucy T. Aldrich. 39.054

Publications: *Bronzes and Ivories from the Old Kingdom of Benin*, Knoedler and Company, New York, Nov. 25 – Dec. 14, 1935, no. 5; *Museum Notes*, RISD, Winter 1955, p. 12.

The fame of Benin, located on the edges of the delta of the Niger River, rests on the works of traditional art produced over the last 600–700 years at the capital, Benin City. At its height, the kingdom extended some 500 miles west into Dahomey and to the Niger in the east. For the Edo inhabitants, political organization centered on the king and his court, and it was the *oba*, or king, who was both the temporal and spiritual ruler of his subjects. The Portuguese "discovery" of Benin in 1485 seems to have occurred at the height of Benin's political power, and the impact of European contact can be seen in terms of religious conversion, assistance in warfare, and the introduction of European goods, including guns and supplies of brass. Originally used to cast cannon, this brass acted as a catalyst on Benin art, as it increased the supplies used in the production of bronze sculpture, the supreme material expression of Benin ideals.

When a king succeeded to the throne on the death of his predecessor, an altar was ordered where the deceased ancestor could be worshiped. Objects for this altar were carved and cast, including bronze heads in memory of the deceased, and in openings at the top of these heads were placed carved ivory tusks which leaned against the wall at the back of the altar. Unfortunately, no work of art from Benin can be securely dated before 1897, the date of a British punitive expedition that resulted in the looting of Benin artifacts. When the first Benin bronze heads were produced is uncertain; while the early 14th century is usually suggested, the practice of making memorial heads in wood and clay seems to have existed some 400 years before that date.

It is thought that the Edo learned the art of bronze casting from the state of Ife, where an exquisitely refined naturalism was practiced that remained unparalleled in the history of African figural sculpture. Benin smiths, however, struck a distinctively independent path, casting the human head in a powerfully stylized view of physical form. Apart from its function as a mark of rank, the high collar of coral beads nearly engulfs the head, shaping the entire piece into a squat, cylindrical shaft, its hieratic, machine-like presence stated in remarkably simple terms. Facial and decorative features are efficiently reduced to formal essences that ornament smooth planar surfaces. These heads acted as effective symbolic expressions of a concept central to Benin life: man's activities on earth are subject to ancestral will. The living *oba*, acting as a priest before the shrine, performed the role of an intermediary between the deceased and the living, and the head served as a vehicle for that exchange by combining memorial and communicative functions in starkly conventionalized form.

84

ATTRIBUTED TO LIPPO MEMMI
Italian, ca. 1285–1361

Mary Magdalen
Tempera and gold leaf on panel.
18¾ x 9

Museum Appropriation. 21.250

Publication: Michael Mallory, "An Altarpiece by Lippo Memmi Reconsidered," *Metropolitan Museum Journal,* vol. 9, 1974, pp. 187–202.

This panel, with its flat gold leaf background and a figure subtly modeled in pastel tones, dates from the beginnings of the Italian Renaissance in the 14th century. Following the example of Giotto and Duccio, Italian painters of this period were finding a more naturalistic style through volume, light and perspective. Lippo Memmi, to whom this panel is attributed, painted in Siena between 1317 and 1356. Although he worked at first with his father, Lippo's mature painting shows the influence of his more famous brother-in-law Simone Martini. Simone's work is characterized by rhythmic relationships, using the elongated and elegant proportions associated with the Gothic style in France to create fluid and weightless volumes. Lippo followed Simone's interest in graceful lines, but produced compositions that were slightly more formal and figures that were less animated and naturalistic.

The Museum's panel portrays Mary Magdalen carrying her ointment jar. This subject and the panel's size suggest that it was once part of a larger altarpiece, most likely a polyptych which incorporated subjects such as the Virgin and Child, saints, and religious narratives, which were combined in carved wooden frameworks. It has been proposed that seven large paintings attributed to Lippo Memmi are the main panels for an altarpiece depicting the Virgin and saints. The flattened tops of these panels suggest that Lippo's altarpiece may also have had another register. Citing the evidence of measurements and gold punchwork patterns, as well as similarities of coloring and composition, Mallory has suggested that a group of five smaller panels including the RISD Magdalen were probably painted for the altarpiece by Lippo and his assistants. Together, the two registers show a program of saints that relate to the Franciscan order, making it possible to speculate that the altarpiece was made for the Franciscan church in Colle di Val d'Elsa, near Siena, where two of the large panels were documented in a 19th century inventory.

Color plate, page 66

85

ITALIAN, last quarter of the 15th century

The Entombment of Christ
Terracotta. 56 x 72 x 19

Gift of Mrs. Jesse H. Metcalf. 12.253

Publication: *Bulletin*, RISD, vol. I,
no. 3, 1913, pp. 1–3.

This terracotta *Entombment* from the niche of a chapel combines the sculptural technique of high relief with figures which are modeled almost in the round. The group would have originally been fully painted, although few touches are left other than in some areas where dark paint seems to have soaked into the baked clay. The identity of the sculptor, probably of the late 15th century, is unknown.

In traditional series of scenes of the Passion of Christ, the Entombment is the fourth Station of the Cross. The two full-length figures – Joseph of Arimathea, who begged Pilate for Christ's body after the Crucifixion, and Nicodemus, who assisted him in preparing it for burial – are holding Christ's body suspended in a shroud.

The Virgin, Mary Magdalen, and the other mourning figures not mentioned in the Gospels were often included in representations of the Entombment as far back as the 14th century, when artists combined the scene with the iconography of the Lamentation. The choice of seven figures to surround Christ is surely symbolic. Seven is the number of charity and the Seven Sorrows of the Virgin, as well as the Seven Gifts of the Holy Spirit, which were received by the Apostles after Christ's resurrection.

The greatest influence upon this group probably stems from the Florentine sculptor Donatello, in particular the works that Donatello executed at Padua between 1444 and 1453. Among the sculpture that Donatello completed during his nine-year stay is a relief of the Entombment on the back of his high altar for the church of Sant'Antonio. The figures and the composition of the Museum's sculptural group are quite similar to Donatello's prototype, and provide the basis for its date of execution.

Donatello's modifications of this originally Byzantine subject – the drapery which falls in natural folds, revealing the rounded forms of the figures, and the calculated symmetry of the composition – reflect the renaissance of classical sculpture and rhetoric. The individualized expressions of grief, as opposed to the Byzantine and Medieval stereotypical depiction of emotions, are the result of emerging humanistic concerns. The artist of the Museum's group has been influenced by these specific qualities of Donatello's sculpture; but the *Entombment* sculptor's more restrained depiction and the modeling suggest that the work is by a provincial artist, perhaps from Cremona or Mantua, rather than by a Paduan master who might have studied directly with Donatello.

86

JACOPO SANSOVINO
Florentine, 1486–1570

Venetian Nobleman, ca. 1560
Terracotta. 29½ x 23 x 12

Museum Works of Art Fund. 54.167

Provenance: von Schwabach, Berlin

Publication: John Pope-Hennessy,
"The Relations between Florentine and
Venetian Sculpture in the Sixteenth
Century," in *Florence and Venice:
Comparisons and Relations,* Florence,
1979–80, pp. 323–335.

Like many of the humanistic minds of
the Italian Renaissance, Jacopo Sansovino expressed his creative brilliance
in many ways. Trained in Florence as a
sculptor, Jacopo Tatti, surnamed Il
Sansovino after his master Andrea
Sansovino, moved back and forth
between sculptural and architectural
projects in that city and Rome. After the
Sack of Rome in 1527, Jacopo settled in
Venice and became the *Proto dei Procura-
tori di Supra* or Chief Architect for this
cosmopolitan center.

   The Museum's terracotta bust of an
unidentified Venetian nobleman clearly
demonstrates aspects of Sansovino's art
and the artistic milieu of the Venetian
High Renaissance. This work is a *modello*
for a marble bust in the Victoria and
Albert Museum, and is freer in expression and more intense in its portrayal of
the sitter's personality. Only decades
before, the portrait bust was more often
than not a public affirmation in which
the person portrayed appeared as he
wished to be, not as he was. Sansovino
brought sculpture closer to painting by
approaching the portrait as a record of a
specific physiognomy and a specific
personality. In this work, the furrowed
brow, concentrated gaze, and weight
and dignity of the pose add a presence
to the subject new to Venetian sculpture.
In his sculptural portraits, Sansovino is
credited with incorporating the richness
and complexity to be found in portraits
by Titian. John Pope-Hennessy has
described this terracotta as ". . . a sort of
inquisition in which the sitter is asked
and answers questions about himself."

Color plate, page 67

87

LEANDRO BASSANO
Italian, 1557–1622

Adoration of the Shepherds, ca. 1592–1594
Signed in black: Leander. A. Ponte
Bass.is Fac.at
Oil on canvas. 41 x 66

Bequest of Lyra Brown Nickerson,
by exchange. 81.093.

Provenance: Thomas Agnew and Sons,
London, 1981

Publication: *Museum Notes,* RISD, 1982,
pp. 22–27.

Leandro was a third-generation painter
of the Dal Ponte family, who took the
name Bassano from their home town
some 30 miles northwest of Venice. The
workshop, which dominated local
artistic production, was established
shortly before 1500. About 1540 Jacopo
Dal Ponte, the more talented of the
founder's two sons, returned from a
sojourn in Venice and took over the
parental shop. During the next five
decades, Jacopo developed a style that
combined vignettes of peasant life with
grand religious subjects. Paintings by
Jacopo Bassano were so popular that a
large workshop developed, staffed
primarily by his four sons.

Leandro Bassano gained much of his
artistic training in his father's active
workshop during the 1580's. The theme
of the Adoration of the Shepherds,
which by its very nature combines the
realities of everyday activities with the
divine, was a hallmark of the Bassano
workshop, and Leandro undoubtedly
copied and assisted on paintings of this
subject produced by his father and older
brother Francesco. The Museum's
Adoration of the Shepherds, however, is
believed to have been painted soon after
the deaths of both Jacopo and Francesco
in 1592. The nocturnal setting is a tribute
to his father's great *Adoration* in S.
Giorgio Maggiore in Venice, yet Leandro
expanded the composition and intensified the details. Around the Holy Family
gather humble peasants awaiting salvation, each made individual by a feeling
of exact detail. Leandro sculpts the
figures in a dramatic play of deep
shadows highlighted with incandescent
passages of intense color. As they
assemble around the Christ Child in the
foreground, an angel announces the
miracle to shepherds in the distance.

Much of the beauty of this *Adoration*
stems from the magical light given off by
the Christ Child, a glow that reflects
across the figures and unifies the image.
The candle held by a boy at the base of
the column and the glowing cinder
kindled by another boy on the right
cannot compete with the magnificent
nimbus surrounding Christ. This
concern with light (two other sources are
the angel and the setting sun in the far
right) is typical of the Bassano family
and of late 16th century proto-Baroque
colorism in Venice.

Color plate, page 67

88

FRANCESCO VANNI
Italian, 1563/5–1610

*The Virgin and Child Appearing to
Saint Francis of Assisi,* 1599
Oil on canvas. 104¾ x 72

Corporation Membership Dues Fund.
57.227

Provenance: Nôtre-Dame-des-Anges,
Chapelle des Lucquois, Lyon, 1785;
Claude Tolozan d'Amaranthe, 1801;
Cardinal Fesch, 1845; St. Thomas
Clavering

Publication: *Museum Notes/Bulletin,* RISD,
December 1958, pp. 4–8.

In 1599, when Francesco Vanni painted
*The Virgin and Child Appearing to St.
Francis of Assisi,* the influence of Federico
Barocci had spread throughout central
Italy and above all to Siena and the
paintings of Vanni. The Museum's
painting of St. Francis receiving the
Christ Child from the Virgin has a long
history. The work was originally commissioned in 1599 by the Franciscan
Cardinal Bonvisi as an altarpiece for a
monastery chapel in Lyon, France.
Before the French Revolution, the
painting was removed from the Chapel
and sold, eventually appearing at
auction in Rome. It remained in private
hands until it was purchased by the
Museum in 1957.

St. Francis was a favorite subject in
religious painting in this period. While
his stigmatization is probably most
familiar, his vision of the Virgin Mary
with the Christ Child began to appear in
art towards the end of the 16th century.
In the version of the legend painted by
Vanni, Saint Francis returns one night to
a particularly beautiful place in the forest
to pray. Miraculously, the Virgin and
Child appear in a blaze of light. Mary
places the Child in the Saint's arms,
where he is loved and embraced until
dawn. The aged friar meditating on a
skull, symbol of mortality, does not
appear in the original source for the
story, the *Fioretti.* In a strict interpretation
of the text, an unbeliever would be
watching from a hiding place in the
distance.

Painted in subtly modulated, somewhat Mannerist colors, Vanni imbues
the scene with an unearthly quality. To
these elusive tones the artist adds a
radiant light to evoke a supernatural

apparition. The result is a painting that
captures all the mysticism and human
tenderness of the Franciscan legend.
Vanni's pride in his work is demonstrated
by the fact that he made a drawing after
the painting, now in the Victoria and
Albert Museum, London, which Vanni
gave to Cornelis Galle to engrave and
publish as a print.

89

GIUSEPPE CESARI, called Cavaliere
d'Arpino
Italian, 1568–1640

Perseus and Andromeda
Oil on slate. 27¾ x 21⅝

Anonymous gift. 57.167

Provenance: Duchesse de Berry, Venice;
Julius Weitzner, London; private
collection, Providence

Publication: Herwarth Röttgen, ed., *Il
Cavalier d'Arpino*, Rome, 1973, pp. 39,
78–79, cat. no. 10.

Giuseppe Cesari, known as the Cavaliere
d'Arpino, was one of the major late
Mannerist painters in Rome. During the
Roman building campaign of Pope Paul
V, Cesari completed many of the monumental frescoes and mosaics in the
interiors of these buildings and super-
vised the decoration of others. In
addition to this large-scale work in
Rome, Cesari and the painters in his
workshop produced many paintings of a
smaller format. He found an extremely
receptive market for these works in
Rome and frequently repeated his most
popular subjects.

The *Perseus and Andromeda* in the
Museum's collection is one of the finest
of these small paintings by Cesari.
Although quite a few versions of this
subject exist that are attributed to Cesari
and his workshop, this is his first formu-
lation and the only known version that
bears an authentic signature. Although
no details of the specific commission for
this painting are known, it can be dated
to 1592–93, when Cesari was at the
height of his career.

The story of Perseus and Andromeda
in Ovid's *Metamorphoses* was extremely
popular during the 16th and early 17th
centuries. As described by Ovid,
Perseus sees Andromeda chained to a
rock above the sea. She is doomed to
become the victim of a ferocious dragon,
as punishment for her mother's foolish
bragging. Perseus gallantly offers to slay
the dragon in exchange for Andromeda's
hand in marriage.

Many aspects of this tale contributed
to its great appeal for Mannerist artists.
Foremost, it provided an opportunity
to display one's virtuosity in painting
the female nude. The theme of the
bound woman, with its connotations of
voyeurism and vulnerability, was
extremely popular, as were the depiction
of anthropomorphic monsters and the
motif of a severed head, here that of
Medusa who had been slain by Perseus.

A key concept of Mannerist art was
the freedom of the artist to borrow,
manipulate, and recreate compositions
and motifs from other works of art. This
idea was directly related to the increased
use of prints as a means of publishing
artists' paintings. In this fashion, Cesari
took his composition from an engraving
by Goltzius (1583) and a wood engraving
by Bernard Salomon for the texts of Ovid
(1557). Rather than duplicate either of
these, he played with the design by
reversing figures and by changing relationships of scale between them.

90

ALESSANDRO MAGNASCO
Italian, 1667–1749

Arsenal in a Ruined Basilica, ca. 1711–20
Oil on canvas. 57¾ x 84½

Museum Works of Art, Georgianna
Sayles Aldrich, Mary B. Jackson, Edgar
J. Lownes, Walter H. Kimball, Jesse
Metcalf, Museum Gifts and Museum
Membership Dues. 63.061

Provenance: G. Cramer Gallery,
The Hague

Publication: B. Geiger, *Magnasco*,
Bergamo, 1949, pp. 104–106.

Alessandro Magnasco's paintings
occupy an interesting position in the
development of Italian Baroque art.
Magnasco, who was born in Genoa in
1667, combined Baroque compositional
design with the flickering calligraphy of
Jacques Callot and the tempestuous
romanticism of Salvator Rosa. His large,
often crowded scenes evoke a mysterious
grandeur that seems removed from the
"golden age" of North Italian painting.

Arsenal in a Ruined Basilica, thought to
have been painted in Milan between
1711 and 1720, may be part of a group of
three large works. Two other views of
populated ruins are in the Conte Fausto
Lechi Collection, Calvisano (Brescia). All
three works share related architectural
elements; the spaces between the tiny,
sketchy figures and the monumentalized
ruins are in each case filled with an
assortment of instruments of battle and
camp life. All these accessories cluster at
the bases of the piers of the once magnificent structure that now supports the
occasional cannon, drum, or broadside
posted to a column. Magnasco painted
these forms in a rapid, almost nervous
brushstroke, passages of which sparkle
with magical light effects and visually tie
the work together. The artist's fascination
with monumental ruins, and the inter-
mingling of myriad genre details with
fantastic pictorial invention, link
Magnasco with the later inventions of
Guardi, Piranesi, and Canaletto.

91

92

91

GIOVANNI BATTISTA TIEPOLO
Italian, 1696–1770

The Angel of Fame, ca. 1750
Fresco, mounted on canvas. 130¼ x 78

Museum Appropriation. 32.246

Provenance: H. Gonse, Paris

Publications: Pompeo Molmenti, *Tiepolo, La Vie et l'Oeuvre du Peintre*, Paris, 1911, p. 198; Antonio Morassi, *The Paintings of Giovanni Battista Tiepolo*, Greenwich, Connecticut, 1962, p. 45.

Among 18th century Italian painters, Giovanni Battista Tiepolo quickly rose to a pre-eminent position in the art of his time. Tiepolo's work lavishly enlivened the major palaces of Venice and other important European courts, for he was primarily in demand as a designer and painter of great decorative cycles. The Museum's ceiling fresco representing *The Angel of Fame* most probably comes from one such cycle in the Palazzo Labia in Venice, ca. 1750, painted at the height of the artist's career. While the main salon featured the story of Antony and Cleopatra, small rooms throughout the palace contained decorated ceilings and may have been the original location for the Museum's fresco.

Tiepolo's mastery is seen best in his ceiling frescoes. This medium, in which paint is applied to wet plaster, was most appropriate for the grand manner which required images covering vast spaces. Tiepolo's fame rests on his ability to enliven classically composed images with a rapid, vigorous brushstroke. Intensely fresh and exuberant, the artist's monumental figures soar into a grand Baroque world of illusionistic space and silvery light. A cool palette that emphasized Tiepolo's interest in luminosity became the artist's hallmark, as the tones reflect the light on figures, clouds, and architectural enframement.

The Museum's panel personifies Fame. Dramatically foreshortened, she carries her most familiar attribute, the trumpet, in her left hand. In her right is the laurel branch, symbol of the victor's crown, an appropriate accessory to Fame. Although the final execution of this work may have been by Tiepolo's son Domenico or another member of his studio, it nevertheless embodies not only the master's design, but also his powerful and typically Venetian combination of brilliant draughtsmanship and fresh, exuberant colors, all on a monumental scale.

Color plate, page 68

92

FRANCESCO GUARDI
Italian, 1712–1793

The Scuola di San Marco with the Loggia Erected for the Benediction of Pope Pius VI, May 19, 1782
Oil on canvas. 15¼ x 12¾

Gift of Mrs. Murray S. Danforth. 53.115

Publication: Ross Watson, "Guardi and the Visit of Pius VI to Venice in 1782," *Report and Studies in the History of Art*, Washington, 1968, pp. 115–132.

Francesco Guardi's *Scuola di San Marco with the Loggia Erected for the Benediction of Pope Pius VI, May 19, 1782*, commemorates the pontiff's visit to Venice in that year. Not since the Peace of Venice was concluded in 1177 had a Pope been received in this Italian city. Pius VI stands out as the most distinguished visitor to Venice of the 18th century, though his stay was intended as a five-day respite on a return journey to Rome from Vienna.

In spite of the request that His Holiness be received with a minimum of ceremony and as a simple priest, the *Signoria* of Venice planned official entertainment with four major events culminating in a Papal Benediction on a specially built loggia erected in the Scuola di San Marco outside the Church of SS. Giovanni e Paolo. To commemorate the Papal visit, Pietro Edwards, Inspector of Fine Arts for the city, commissioned

Francesco Guardi to paint the four major ecclesiastical ceremonies. Guardi received the commission two days after the Pope's departure, so his information for the views most likely depended on eyewitness accounts from various observers and sketches the artist made of the locales after the events took place. The painting at the Museum is from one such study.

Two sets of four paintings resulted from the commission; seven paintings are today spread around the world in public and private collections (one is believed destroyed). The significance of the Papal visit created a demand for additional versions of the Papal Benediction, the most public of the events. Five oil sketches are known today of the loggia as it looked after the Pope's departure, the most noteworthy being in Providence and at the National Gallery of Art, Washington.

Guardi's painting of the site is more than documentation. Enveloped in a glistening atmosphere, tourists dot the space that days before held thousands. We follow their movement deep into the structure and rest at the niche above which the Pope delivered his benediction. Within this small painting, the artist has captured the majesty of the event without actually showing it, evocatively depicting the locale and its curious inhabitants.

93

TILMAN RIEMENSCHNEIDER
German, 1460–1531

Pietà, ca. 1505–1515
Lindenwood. 18 x 15 x 5½

Museum Works of Art Fund. 59.128

Provenance: Bayerische National Museum, Munich

Publications: Hubert Schrade, *Tilman Riemenschneider*, Heidelberg, 1927, vol. II, p. 41, no. 328; Justus Bier/RISD, 1960, no. 3.

Intensely devotional images were an intrinsic part of German Renaissance art. Traditional Gothic subjects, handled in a manner which emphasized their great emotional appeal, continued to be produced alongside the progressively "Italianate" images by artists such as Albrecht Dürer. Perhaps most moving for the devout of this era was the representation of the Pietà, the dead Christ mourned by the Virgin Mary.

This fine example of the subject is by the mature Riemenschneider, and incorporates the same intricacy of detail in hands and faces as is found in his great Creglingen Altarpiece of the same period. In this small sculpture, Christ's broken, limp body is held up by Mary for the viewer's contemplation, in counterbalance to the Virgin's sorrowful expression and her animated drapery, which swoops and curls in intense Gothic curves. An emphasis on the patterning of light and shadow rather than linear definitions also associates this sculpture with the Creglingen Altarpiece.

Riemenschneider's workshop is known to have produced many examples of this subject. The Museum's *Pietà* holds a unique place in our current understanding of this artist's production. Long considered to be by the hand of Riemenschneider, the Museum's work is small enough to have been carved without assistance. It may in fact be a model figure, copied on a large scale by assistants in Riemenschneider's workshop. One such copy is now in the Church of St. Anne, in Obernburg, Germany.

93

94

BENEDIKT DREYER

German, ca. 1485–1555

Christ in the House of Simon, ca. 1515–1525
Wood with polychrome. 22½ x 24 x 4⅞

Helen M. Danforth Fund. 49.067

Provenance: Figdor, Vienna; Bondy
collection; Blumka Gallery, New York

Publication: Gert von der Osten and
Horst Vey, *Painting and Sculpture in
Germany and the Netherlands 1500–1600*,
New York, 1969, pp. 51–52, plate 37.

This fine wooden sculpture is one of a
scattering of parts from the once
complete altar in the parish church in
Lendersdorf, Germany. This fragment
helped secure the inclusion of the altarpiece stylistically into Benedikt Dreyer's
oeuvre. After much research, the Lendersdorfer altar is now indisputably
accepted as the work of this Lüneburg-
Lübecker wood sculptor, though its
exact date has yet to be determined. The
parish church of St. Michael, for which it
was carved, was completed in 1510. In
1734, the altar was moved to another
part of the church. It was severely
damaged in 1843. Twice repaired at the
end of the 19th century, the Museum's
relief was probably removed at the time
of restoration, as a known copy of the
RISD portion was carved by the man
who did the overall restoration.

Only the middle portion of the
Lendersdorfer altar has been reconstructed. Central to the composition is a
figure of St. Michael preparing to weigh
souls as two angels sound the Last
Judgment. (These angels, or copies, are
in the collection of the Wadsworth
Atheneum in Hartford.) Above, Christ
sits in majesty, as the Virgin Mary and
St. John pose as intercessors. Below are
the souls of the Blessed and the Damned,

some being led to Heaven while others
are dragged to Hell. The Museum's
Christ in the House of Simon was probably
grouped with scenes of Mary showing
the Christ Child to Joachim and Anna,
and of Christ as the Gardener. Their
location in the overall altar composition
has yet to be determined.

Benedikt Dreyer's unique vision is
clear in the Museum's relief. First, there
is a distinct differentiation in the figures
according to their spiritual status. The
tenderness and warmth of the idealized
Christ and Mary Magdalen contrasts
sharply with the vivid characterization
of the fat man picking his teeth, the
inquisitive Simon the Pharisee with his
bald, squarish head, and Martha, Mary's
sister, aloof and with her hands calmly
folded on her stomach. Dreyer's sharp
angularity and simplification of forms
create a solid substructure that firmly
supports the details of face and gesture
that vividly tell the story. To complete
the reality of details, Dreyer found his
inspiration in contemporary everyday
life; the three figures behind the table
are in 16th century German dress.

95

GEORG VISCHER
German, ca. 1520–1592

Fertility
Bronze. H. 23¾

Museum Appropriation and Friends.
20.139

Provenance: W. G. Parsons, Rome

Publications: *Bulletin*, RISD, July 1925,
pp. 28–31; E. F. Bange, *Die deutschen
Bronzestatuetten des 16. Jarhunderts*,
Berlin, 1949, p. 122.

The importance of Nuremberg in the
history of early Renaissance bronze
sculpture is due in large part to the
Vischer family, who were active in
Nuremberg from 1453–1554, and
operated the most significant bronze
foundry in Germany during that period.
While the identity of the workshop as a
whole is much more clearly defined than
the work of individuals within the shop,
attributions of works to specific family
members have been attempted.

When the Museum acquired this
bronze figure in 1920, it was attributed to
Peter Vischer the Younger, the best-
known member of the Vischer family,
born in 1487. The sculpture was
identified as *Eve*, a common Renaissance
subject for the depiction of the female
nude. More recently, scholars have
considered this work closer to the hand
of Georg Vischer. Georg, the eldest son
of Hans Vischer, was born about 1520.
His participation in workshop activities
is first mentioned in 1540. A signed and
dated work from 1554 is the last-known
product of the Vischer foundry. The
Museum's bronze is therefore likely to
be from the second quarter of the 16th
century.

This nude woman is now thought to
be a personification of Fertility rather
than a representation of Eve. In her right
hand she holds a branch with a nut,
while her left gently squeezes her breast
– a gesture which, like the nut, is a
symbol of fecundity. Her form and pose,
with fluid curves and graceful contrapposto, offer a sharp contrast to many
female figures conceived in the Vischer
workshop, which recall more Gothic

ideals of human form. The Museum's
Fertility clearly reflects Italianate models
of classical, ideal beauty in its elongated
slenderness, soft modeling of facial
details, and cascading hair. Interestingly,
the Vischer *Fertility* recalls Italian Renaissance forms at about the same time as
the Vischers' contemporary in Nuremberg, Albrecht Dürer, was creating his
own more robust proportional ideals of
beauty.

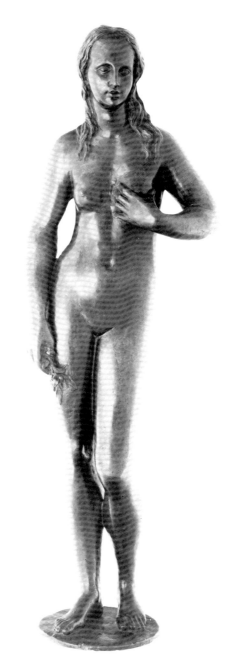

96

MASTER OF THE PROVIDENCE CRUCIFIXION
Utrecht, active ca. 1450–1460

The Crucifixion with Two Thieves
Oil on panel. 27$^5/_{16}$ x 18$^7/_8$

Georgianna Aldrich, Mary B. Jackson,
Jesse Metcalf, Edgar J. Lownes, Walter
H. Kimball, Helen M. Danforth Funds
and Corporation Membership Funds.
61.080

Publications: *Museum Notes/Bulletin*,
RISD, May 1962, pp. 1–40; K. G. Boon,
"Een Utrechtse schilder uit de 15de
eeuw: de Meester van de Boom van
Jesse in de Buurkerk," *Oud Holland*,
LXXVI, 1962, pp. 51–60.

Among the most noteworthy regional schools of Netherlandish painting during the mid-15th century was Utrecht. Out of the artistic production of the city, a few significant works of art have survived, including the important *Crucifixion with Two Thieves*, an intensely expressive painting acquired by the Museum in 1961. The research for this acquisition identified a previously unrecognized hand in mid-15th century Utrecht painting, now designated the Master of the Providence Crucifixion.

The Utrecht school, while possessing characteristics of its own, was subject to the cross-currents of outside influences. Unlike Bruges, the center of Flemish artistic production at this time, Utrecht was slightly provincial and its artists were essentially eclectic. The strongest artistic influence was that of Jan van Eyck; the task of sustaining the Eyckian tradition in the northern Netherlands fell to Utrecht, and one of its more accomplished practitioners was the artist of the Providence Crucifixion.

Iconographic elements such as the two equestrian figures holding a single lance directly quote van Eyck's *The Crucifixion and Last Judgment* in the Metropolitan Museum of Art. A sharp-rising background with the Holy City on a plateau beyond, often repeated by Utrecht artists, is a compositional device invented by van Eyck. Lastly, the figural types, which mix caricatured faces with portrait-like individuals, come directly out of the Eyckian vocabulary.

The Museum's panel has been identified with six other stylistically similar works believed to have been produced by the same workshop, if not the same hand. Through its association with these works scattered in collections around the world, the Providence Crucifixion has been dated between 1450–1460. These works are termed the Soudenbalch Group and include four illuminated manuscripts, a triptych in the Centraal Museum in Utrecht, and a fresco of the *Tree of Jesse*, also in Utrecht. The most common stylistic bond in these six works, including the large paintings, is the miniaturist technique, which is, again, a close connection with van Eyck.

97

FLEMISH, early 16th century

Madonna and Child with St. Barbara and St. Catherine
Oil on panel. 36 x 34¼

Museum Works of Art. 58.196

Provenance: Sir Lawrence Kennard, Bt.; Christie's, London, Nov. 12, 1957; T. P. Grange, London, 1958

Publication: H. Pauwels, "Een nieuwe Toeschrijving aan Ambrosius Benson," *Fédération des Cercles d'Archéologie et d'Histoire de Belgique. Annales,* 1974, pp. 291–296.

This anonymous panel painting of the *Madonna and Child with St. Barbara and St. Catherine* exhibits an unusually rich iconographic and stylistic history. It combines two Italian sources in the image of the *Madonna del latte* usually associated with the Milanese painter Bernardino de' Conti and the figures of saints related to works by Bernardino Luini and Giovanni Antonio Boltraffio. The influence of these Lombard artists, all followers of Leonardo, can be seen particularly in the soft modeling and delicate facial features of the women. But the Northern European origins of the work are ultimately conveyed in the masterfully painted details of clothing and architecture, as well as the inscription in Dutch on the hem of St. Catherine's robe.

This eclectic combination of Italian and Flemish elements was common in Antwerp in the early decades of the 16th century, and formerly this panel was attributed to Quentin Matsys and Ambrosius Benson, influential northern artists who were familiar with the work of their contemporaries in Italy. While close examination suggests that the RISD painting is not by either hand, there are two other unattributed Flemish works (Walker Art Gallery, Liverpool, and Mittelrhein-Museum, Koblenz), produced at this same period, which are related to it. Significantly, these variants each include the figure of St. Joseph picking fruit in the background and small angels holding the canopy over the Virgin's head, iconographic elements related to the angel bearing the bowl of fruit in the RISD work.

The figure of the angel was only recently discovered after restoration of the panel removed layers of overpaint,

probably added to the painting in the 19th century when it was damaged in a fire while in the Kennard collection. Some of the stylistic inconsistencies, such as the awkward handling of St. Catherine's cuff or differences in facial modeling of the female figures and the angel, further suggest that some passages in the painting may be by a different hand. However, the overall coherence of the composition, its beautifully rendered details of texture and color, and its awareness of Italian Renaissance painting have resulted in a work that is both visually delightful and historically important.

98

HENDRICK GOLTZIUS
Dutch, 1558–1617

Christ on the Cold Stone, 1602
Monogrammed and dated, HG Ao 1602.
Oil on copper. 18¾ x 13½

Museum Purchase. 61.006

Provenance: Jacob Matham, 1603; Rudolf II, Prague, 1603; Dresden dealer, May, 1891; S. Hartveld, Antwerp, 1928; D. Splitter, Antwerp, 1933; Christie's, London, Nov. 25, 1956, lot 144; Spitzer and private collection, England; Arcade Gallery, London

Publication: E. K. J. Reznicek, "Het begin van Goltzius' loopbaan als schilder," *Oud Holland,* 1960, p. 35ff., ill. no. 2.

Hendrick Goltzius is best known for his virtuoso engravings and chiaroscuro woodcuts, among the most brilliant achievements of later Dutch Mannerism. Karel van Mander, the artist who was Goltzius's friend in Haarlem and who wrote a long biography of him, says that in 1600, at the age of 40, the artist ended a brilliant engraving career and turned his attention to painting for the remainder of his life; the RISD work is Goltzius's first extant painting and is dated 1602. It

was engraved by his stepson and pupil Jacob Matham, from whom it was bought for the great collector, Rudolf II of Prague.

The subject of the painting can be linked to two themes common in Christian iconography. The first depicts Christ, flanked by two angels, prone on the Stone of Unction where he was prepared for burial. Such scenes symbolize the Eucharist, or the transubstantiation of Christ's flesh and blood into consecrated bread and wine: the stone bearing Christ's body represents the altar tablet upon which the bread and wine are presented. The second theme incorporated here is that of Ecce Homo, when, after the Flagellation, the suffering Christ is shown to the people. Wearing the crown of thorns and holding instruments of the Flagellation crossed over his chest, Christ waits for the executioners to take him to the cross. The bucket of vinegar, the broken reed, and the scourges scattered about the foreground are further reminders of the Flagellation.

Stylistically, the painting is fully mannerist in its coloring, lighting, and modeling of the figures, as well as in its debt to the Flemish artist Bartholomaeus Spranger.

99

JOACHIM WTEWAEL
Dutch, 1566–1638

The Marriage of Peleus and Thetis, 1610
Signed and dated, Joachim wte wael fecit Anno 1610.
Oil on panel. 43 x 65

Mary B. Jackson Fund. 62.058

Provenance: Auction, J. Bergoen, Nov. 4, 1789, The Hague; Count Serge Ignatieff; V. M. Vasiliev; Benisovich, New York

Publication: C. M. A. A. Lindeman, *J. A. Wtewael,* Utrecht, 1929, pp. 115–116.

In this major example of later Dutch Mannerist painting, Joachim Wtewael has depicted a dramatic moment in the wedding feast of Peleus and Thetis. Hercules and the immortal Olympians have assembled in celebration; the newlyweds, seated behind the table, are being served by Mercury, while Apollo sings the future deeds of their unborn son, Achilles, in the Trojan War. Eris (Discord), who was not invited, appears at the upper left of center, about to throw down a golden apple inscribed "For the fairest." This act will ultimately lead to the Trojan War.

This painting, which is related to a number of paintings and drawings of the same subject by the artist, typifies late Dutch Mannerism in several respects: the *horror vacui* of its crowded, dynamic composition; the complicated poses, glowing skin, and exaggerated muscularity of the figures; the placement of the subject itself far in the background and at a diagonal, with an emphasis on secondary activities; extreme contrasts in scale, ranging from distant vignettes to large, foreshortened foreground figures, in rear view, which act as framing devices; dramatic effects of color and light and shadow; and the naturalism of the still-life and genre details.

Dutch Mannerism at the turn of the century was concentrated in two cities, Utrecht and Haarlem; Wtewael was a prolific painter and draughtsman in Utrecht who also became deeply involved in the politics of the time, particularly the war of independence from Spain and the conflict between Protestants and Roman Catholics.

Color plate, page 69

98

100

SALOMON VAN RUYSDAEL
Dutch, ca. 1602–1670

The Ferryboat, 1645
Signed and dated, S.vR. 1645
Oil on canvas. 38½ x 56¾

Museum Appropriation. 33.204

Provenance: John Nugent; Mervyn,
Viscount Powerscourt; Mrs. Louis
Raphael, London

Publication: Wolfgang Stechow, *Salomon
van Ruysdael*, Berlin, 1938, p. 108.

Salomon van Ruysdael was one of the
major creators of what we think of as the
typical 17th century Dutch landscape: a
low horizon, massive clouds towering
into the sky, a few trees on a bank, a
clutch of houses, and a canal or harbor
leading into the background. The artist
adds here a ferryboat, filled to over-
flowing with peasant travelers and even
a child relieving himself over the side.

   This is one of Salomon's most magis-
terial canvases, in which the tight,
restless calligraphy of the foliage
complements the monumental diagonal
wedge of clouds into the background,
echoed by the canal below. The Dutch
were a society dominated by a prosperous mercantile middle class that
wanted many paintings of many
different subjects, and they were a very
new country that survived by trading
throughout the world and by encouraging waves of immigration from all
over Europe. Perhaps as a result of this
openness, their fundamental contribution to European art is their obsession
with recording the physical world, their
passion for documenting even the
smallest or most trivial phenomena of
daily life, and this documentation, by
major artists on a major scale, is
exemplified by this powerful canvas
from the middle years of the 17th
century.

Color plate, page 69

99

100

101

FRENCH, Burgundian, ca. 1106–1112

Saint Peter from the Third Abbey Church of Saint Peter and Saint Paul, Cluny

Limestone with traces of gesso and polychrome. 29 x 17 x 10

Museum Appropriation. 20.254

Provenance: Thiebault-Sisson, Paris; Durlacher Brothers, New York

Publications: Stephen K. Sher, *The Renaissance of the Twelfth Century*, Providence, 1969, pp. 24–28; Kathryn McCauley, *St. Peter from Cluny: A Medieval Puzzle*, Providence, 1974.

When it was purchased by the Museum in 1920, this limestone sculptural fragment was identified only as a Romanesque figure of St. Peter. In the 1930's, the scholar Kenneth Conant related it to the sculptural fragments he

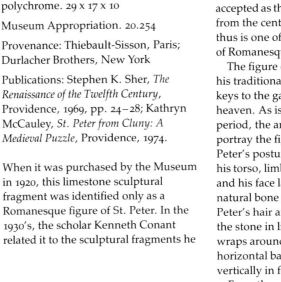

was finding in his excavations of the great abbey church of Cluny III in Burgundy, which for 400 years was the largest church structure in Christendom. After much scholarly debate and research, the Museum's St. Peter is now accepted as the finest fragment remaining from the central portal of this abbey, and thus is one of the most important pieces of Romanesque sculpture in America.

The figure of St. Peter is identified by his traditional attribute – he holds the keys to the gates of the kingdom of heaven. As is typical of the Romanesque period, the artist has made no attempt to portray the figure naturalistically. St. Peter's posture is hunched and twisted; his torso, limbs and fingers are elongated; and his face lacks any suggestion of natural bone structure. The details of St. Peter's hair and beard are incised into the stone in linear patterns, and drapery wraps around his body in decorative horizontal bands instead of falling vertically in folds affected by gravity.

From the unfinished back and hunched-over posture, it is evident that the RISD St. Peter was intended as part of an architectural relief positioned above eye level. Such reliefs were the primary decoration for church portals. The great portals with their programs of sculptural relief provided a transition, both physically and spiritually, for visitors – from the church exterior and everyday life, to the symbolic heaven on earth of the church interior. These programs often centered on a depiction of the Last Judgment, with Christ in Majesty surrounded by a mandorla of light, reminding the entering faithful of their own mortality.

The excavations at Cluny uncovered several fragments from the portal reliefs that make it possible to identify a general style for Cluny sculpture. The Museum's St. Peter shows elements of this style, such as facial features, hair, and the pleating of its costume. Drawings and written descriptions of the portal at Cluny while the abbey was still standing document that four figures, including a St. Peter, occupied the spandrels above the arch of the tympanum of the portal. These descriptions and the scientific comparison of stone samples from known Cluny sculpture support the identification of the Museum's sculpture as having once been a part of the decoration of the great church.

102

FRENCH, late 13th – early 14th century

Diptych with Scenes of the Nativity, Crucifixion and Last Judgment
Ivory with traces of polychromy.
Each leaf 9½ x 5¼

Museum Appropriation. 22.201 a–b

Provenance: Alfred Maudsley Collection; Durlacher Brothers, 1922

Publications: R. Koechlin, *Les ivoires gothiques français*, Paris, 1924, vol. I, pp. 180–182, vol. II, p. 148; *Transformations of the Court Style*, Providence, 1977, pp. 60–61.

Devotional objects in ivory for both the church and the court enjoyed an increased popularity throughout the 13th and early 14th centuries. Their production centered in the Ile de France, and as precious objects of trade, ivories spread throughout the Christian world, disseminating a new French international style. Gothic ivories borrowed their subjects primarily from illustrated manuscripts, yet found inspiration in new developments in architectural forms and decorative sculpture. They also exploited the more traditional forms of ivory relief from the earlier Byzantine and Romanesque carvers, particularly the diptych. The subjects represented were generally conservative as well, focusing on events in the life of the Virgin, the life of Christ, and the Passion.

The diptych at the Museum is one example of a type *à frise d'arcature*, distinguished by the elaborate carvings of the framing arcades. Unusual in this example is the compartmentalization of the scenes depicted, with multiple events combined within one framework.

Beginning at the bottom left within the framed niche are the Annunciation to the Virgin, the Nativity, and the Annunciation to the Shepherds. Continuing across to the right side is the Adoration of the Magi. In the upper register, beginning at the left, are the Crucifixion and the Coronation of the Virgin (again set into one compartment), and the Last Judgment on the right, complete with a register of the souls of mankind rising up at the judgment.

The artist's passion for embellishment is most pronounced in the trefoil arches decorated with crocketed gables and grapevines which make up the enframing arches. Within this structure, each vignette is delicately carved with much detail and elaboration. The patterning of the angels' and doves' feathers, the weave of the Infant's cradle and the ornamentation of Christ's throne reveal a sensitivity of observation found only in the finest extant examples of Gothic ivory reliefs.

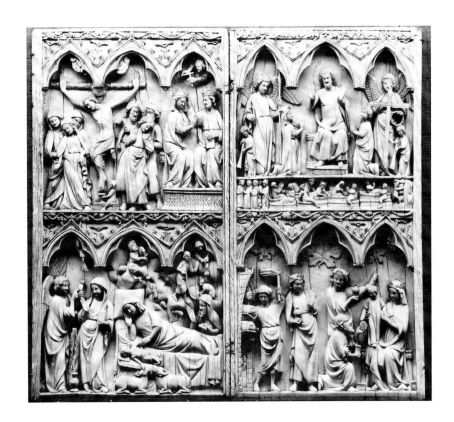

103

FRENCH, ca. 1500

Saint Roch
Wood with polychromy. 41½ x 21¾ x 10

Museum Appropriation. 21.398

Provenance: Durlacher Brothers, New York

Publication: *Bulletin*, RISD, vol. XI, no. 3, 1923, pp. 31–32.

French sculpture at the end of the 15th and beginning of the 16th century was in a state of transition. From its deeply rooted traditions as ecclesiastical architectural decoration, aspects of late Gothic style coexisted with new forms of the Italian Renaissance. To the north, artists generally continued to produce work that concentrated on Gothic linearity, while the robust and challenging forms of Sansovino and Michelangelo were spreading across central and northern Italy. In central France, in the region of Paris and the Loire valley, a style emerged dated "circa 1500" that expressed the mixing of the currents of northern tradition and southern innovation in three-dimensional form.

The Museum's *St. Roch* characterizes typical wooden sculpture of this period, probably produced in the area around Paris. Within this work is a growing sense of the body and a new idealized quality of individual human expression, combined with the linear perfection of Late Gothic altar figures. While St. Roch's pilgrim's cape twists and folds in elegant S-curves that reveal the artist's interest in line, he stands in a pose of pronounced contrapposto, an Italian gesture of shifting body weight. There is a solidity to the figure, enlivened by the line of the drapery and the sweetness of the individualized expression.

The character of *St. Roch* was popular at this time as a protector of the sick. This Christian saint, born in southern France in 1293, used his wealth to ease the suffering caused by the great plague of that era. On his return from a pilgrimage to Rome, Roch contracted the disease and was left to die in the countryside. Through the attention of his faithful dog, who daily brought him bread, Roch recovered and returned to his native Montpellier. The saint's efforts to cure the sick were popularized throughout Europe during the 15th century, with numerous representations produced as both a devotional figure and as intercessor with the Virgin on behalf of the faithful, who hoped to be spared infection. The Museum's sculpture is a typical depiction, including his pilgrim's cape and hat decorated with cross keys and shells, his staff (now missing), the gesture that reveals his infected thigh, and his faithful dog with a loaf of bread in his mouth.

103

104

104

SÉBASTIEN BOURDON
French, 1616–1671

Landscape With a Mill
Oil on canvas. 33⅞ x 41⅜

Mary B. Jackson Fund. 51.506

Provenance: Kean Brown Osborn, 1853; F. Smith Bucknole, 1935; Sir George Leon; Mrs. Warwick Bryant, Windlesham Moor, 1959

Publication: Pierre Rosenberg, *France in the Golden Age,* The Metropolitan Museum of Art, New York, 1982, pp. 230–231.

Sébastien Bourdon, like many artists of the period, traveled extensively throughout his native France, Germany, and most importantly, Italy. While studying in Italy, Bourdon produced a large number of *bambocciate,* or genre paintings of peasant life in the streets of Rome. After contact with the work of Poussin in Paris, Bourdon's canvases assumed a more regularized, geometric composition, painted in brighter, more vibrant colors. In 1652–53, Bourdon was the court painter to Queen Christina of Sweden, producing numerous official portraits.

Landscape with a Mill was probably painted late in the artist's career, perhaps after 1658. It is one of a few pure landscapes he produced, and owes less to outside sources than much of his earlier *oeuvre*. Bourdon combines here Poussin's rational structure of orderly, receding compositional planes with his own evocative sense of color. Bourdon's originality lies in his incorporation of these two diverse modes of 17th century French painting: the classical with the natural, the ideal with the real.

Color plate, page 70

105

GABRIEL-JACQUES DE SAINT-AUBIN
French, 1724–1780

Le Lever du Jour
Indistinctly signed, lower right.
Oil on canvas. 18 x 40¾

Museum Appropriation. 38.147

Provenance: Henri Pannier, Paris

Publication: Emile Dacier, "Gabriel de Saint-Aubin," *Revue de l'art ancien et moderne,* January 1912, pp. 13–15.

Gabriel-Jacques de Saint-Aubin is considered to be one of the finest draughtsmen of the 18th century. As a pupil of Jeaurat and Boucher, Saint-Aubin entered the competition for the prestigious Prix de Rome three times, but failed each time to win the chance to study there. Little known during his lifetime, he taught and exhibited at the Académie de Saint-Luc in Paris, where he lived throughout his life. Saint-Aubin is best remembered today for his many illustrations and drawings in the margins of Salon *livrets,* guides to Paris, and sales catalogues that capture the spirit of 18th century life in the French capital.

The Museum's painting, intended as a work to be hung over a door and viewed from below, is less typical of Saint-Aubin's interests in illustration than in decorative painting using allegorical themes. The mythological subject, fleshy eroticism, and loose, fluid handling owe a conspicuous debt to his teacher Boucher. The work has traditionally been interpreted as the passing of night into day, personified here by Night, crowned by the morning star, surrendering herself metaphorically to the god of Day, who awakens to begin his westward journey across the sky. The subject, however, may be a synthesis of myths, suggesting also Diana's embrace of Endymion. For the 18th century artist, it is the most common cycle of nature transformed and glorified by two voluptuous figures embracing at dawn.

105

106

HUBERT ROBERT
French, 1733–1808

Architectural Fantasy, ca. 1765–70
Oil on canvas. 45 x 58

Museum Appropriation. 37.104

Provenance: Mrs. T. Morris Murray,
Boston

Publications: M. Charles Sterling,
Exposition Hubert Robert, Musée de
l'Orangerie, Paris, 1933, no. 23; D. Daly,
"A Painting by Hubert Robert," RISD,
October 1937, pp. 72–74.

During the first decades of the 18th
century, numerous important Roman
ruins were discovered and excavated,
including the copious finds at Herculaneum and Pompeii. From throughout
Europe, artists and humanists, as well as
the wealthy and curious, flocked to Italy,
while at the same time antique marbles
were unearthed and transported back to
foreign courts. In 1754, the young

Hubert Robert accompanied the son of
his father's employer, the Marquis de
Stainville, on just such a cultural
pilgrimage from France to Italy.

As a talented artist, Robert obtained
permission to study at the French
Academy in Rome, an important center
for the reawakening interest in antiquity
and archaeological discovery. At the
French Academy, Robert studied under
Giovanni Panini and befriended
Giovanni Battista Piranesi and Jean-
Honoré Fragonard. Together they
sketched the Italian landscape in all its
variety, from the decayed monuments of
the Roman Empire to Renaissance
gardens and Baroque palaces. Robert
returned to France in 1765, was admitted
to the Academy, and quickly rose to
prominence as the leading exponent of
historical landscape painting, adopting
the nickname "Robert des Ruines."

At his most typical, Robert drew upon
the appeal of the antique, yet exaggerated
his original sources by rearranging and
distorting them. Often the real and the
imaginary are combined into evocative
suggestions of the arcadian past. In the
RISD painting, Robert brings together
architectural details not found in one

specific building, in order to create a
pastiche of abundant decoration. This
canvas can be directly related to two
compositions from 1768 and 1769, one at
Barnard Castle, Bowes Museum, and
one in the Musée, Dunkirk, which was
exhibited in the Salon of 1769.

Dominating the scene is a coffered
arched bridge that doubles as an
approach to the palace entrance. Winged
Victories soar in the spandrels, giving
the bridge more the character of a
triumphal arch. The forms of the palace
façade take on the guise of a triumphal
arch as well, complete with victory
flames. Robert's imaginary building is a
vehicle for sculptural elaboration as well,
and allows the artist to demonstrate his
knowledge of antique sculpture.
Numerous recognizable statues can be
seen here, including the *Laocoön* group
centered over the palace entrance, the
Apollo Belvedere and a statue of Aphrodite
in niches near the central arch, and the
two monumental horses flanking the
bridge, drawn from the bronze horses
above the central portal of St. Mark's in
Venice.

107

JEAN-BAPTISTE-CAMILLE COROT
French, 1796–1875

Honfleur, le vieux bassin, ca. 1822-25
Signed at lower right: Corot; incised to
right of signature: Honfleur
Oil on canvas. 11¾ x 16¾

Museum Works of Art. 43.007

Provenance: Alfred Forgeron, 1890;
Edouard Napoléon César Edmond
Mortier, Duc de Trévise; M. Knoedler,
1942–43

Publication: Alfred Robaut, *L'Oeuvre de
Corot,* vol. 2, Paris, 1905, cat. no. 35.

Honfleur is one of Corot's earliest paintings, executed before his first trip to Italy in 1825. Corot began what little formal training he had in 1822. He studied briefly with his contemporary Achille-Etna Michallon, who in 1817 had been the first winner of the French Academy's newly established Prix de Rome for historical landscape. Michallon died suddenly, and Corot continued his studies with Michallon's teacher, the neoclassical painter Jean-Victor Bertin. *Honfleur* reflects this classical training in the hard-edged clarity of its forms and in the rather restrained application of paint.

Honfleur, however, is not an historical landscape. Although later in his career Corot would experiment with this genre, his first efforts, and ultimately the subjects that interested him the most, were the natural landscape free of narrative detail. Even before his trip to Italy, Corot was painting out of doors, as Michallon had encouraged him to do. Although *Honfleur* exhibits the freshness of a scene observed from nature, it is

ultimately a student work and an experiment in perspective. In Corot's painting of the same subject of ca. 1830 (Robaut, cat. no. 223) the volumes of docks, houses, and ships are more skillfully and convincingly treated, reflecting the lessons he had learned during his three-year sojourn in Italy.

The *Honfleur* of ca. 1822–25 does, however, contain elements which remain important for Corot's later work and for 19th century painting as a whole. The artist's interest in geometric shapes is already in evidence here. Corot's lifelong preference for softly subdued color can be seen even in this early work with its variety of earth tones mixed with white. And the direct observation of nature evident in *Honfleur* becomes the dominating feature of 19th century landscape painting, culminating in the art of the Impressionists.

108

THOMAS COUTURE
French, 1815–1879

Romans of the Decadence, ca. 1847
Oil on canvas. 16⅞ x 26½

Mary B. Jackson Fund. 54.004

Provenance: Sydney W. Winslow, Jr.;
Charles A. Ditmas, Jr.

Publication: *Enrollment of the Volunteers:
Thomas Couture and the Painting of
History,* Museum of Fine Arts,
Springfield, Mass., 1980, p. 92.

The RISD *Romans of the Decadence* is a
working-scale preparatory oil sketch for
the monumental painting of this subject,
showing the aftermath of a Roman orgy,
now in the Musée du Louvre, Paris. The
Romans caused a sensation when
Couture exhibited it at the Salon of 1847,
and was awarded a Medal of the First
Class. Its success was largely due to the
correlation of Couture's artistic aims
with those of the French government
and critics in 1847. By mid-century the
innovations of both classicism and
romanticism seemed tired, and the

grand tradition of French history
painting doomed to the anecdotal
tableaux of Gérôme and Delaroche. With
the *Romans* Couture sought to restore
the classical tradition of history painting
and its relevance to contemporary
events. His painting was a conscious
fusion of the art of the old masters
(especially Veronese, Raphael, and
Poussin) and more recent French artists
like David and Géricault. Like his
predecessors, Couture wanted to convey
a moral message of contemporary social
significance. The result was a work
which sought to be all things to all
people: the epitome of *juste milieu*
painting.

The source of the painting is a passage
from Juvenal: "More damaging than any
enemy, luxury has rushed upon us and
avenges the enslaved world" (6. 292–
293). The use of a classical source links
the painting to the neo-classical tradition
of David, as does the frieze-like distri-
bution of figures across a shallow stage-
set space. However, Couture's use of a
range of warm colors has its roots in the
romanticism of his teachers Gros and
Delaroche.

The most striking aspect of the
Romans, however, is the way in which it
departs from the traditions Couture

attempted to emulate. Instead of depicting a noble moment from antiquity to
serve as an example for contemporary
life as David would have done, Couture
chose a scene of decadence and moral
depravity. Although the picture is
classically balanced and there are focal
points like the central reclining courtesan
(who is contrasted with the upright
statue of the noble Germanicus directly
above her), there is no climactic moment
or action to which the figures respond.
This lack of narrative structure was a
radical departure from the academic
tradition Couture sought to restore and
surpass.

Precisely because of its eclectic nature,
the *Romans of the Decadence* lent itself to
multiple contemporary interpretations.
The decadent Romans of late antiquity
were thought by critics variously to
symbolize the French aristocracy in 1789
and the corruptions of the July Monarchy
of Couture's own day. Thus, in terms of
both style and content Couture's intention of creating *juste milieu* painting was
achieved.

109

EUGENE DELACROIX
French, 1798–1863

Arabes en Voyage (Arabs Traveling), 1855
Signed lower left: Eug. Delacroix 1855
Oil on canvas. 21¼ x 25½

Museum Appropriation. 35.786

Provenance: Prince Anatolii Demidoff, 1856 (?); Baron Michel de Trétaigne, ca. 1870; Baron Nathaniel de Rothschild, 1872; Baron Dr. Henri de Rothschild, ca. 1901; Georges Bernheim, 1933; Martin Birnbaum, 1935

Publication: *Journal d'Eugène Delacroix*, April 5, 1832 and February 1, 1856; Alfred Robaut, *L'Oeuvre Complet d'Eugène Delacroix*, Paris, 1855, p. 341, no. 1277.

In 1832 the Count de Mornay was sent by the King of France, Louis Philippe, to conclude a treaty with the Sultan of Morocco, whose lands bordered on the new French territory of Algeria. The young painter Delacroix, then 34, was invited to travel as the Count's companion on this long and difficult journey, which brought their suite through Spain, Morocco and Algiers. Orientalism had played an important role in Delacroix's work of the previous decade. The *Massacre of Chios* (1824, Louvre) and orgiastic *Death of Sardanapalus* (1827, Louvre) showed the artist's interest in the exotic Orient, inspired, respectively, by the grim realities of contemporary history and by contemporary romantic literature. Delacroix's voyage to North Africa, however, enabled him to support this interest with the concrete detail of observed fact. Throughout his travels, the artist filled his sketchbooks and diaries with observations of Arab life that would provide him with ideas and motifs for the remainder of his career. In North Africa Delacroix discovered the contemporary heirs of antiquity, and the heroic subject matter of the Ecole translated into a modern idiom that lacked the drabness of contemporary Parisian life. To a friend in Paris he wrote, "You would suppose you were in Rome or Athens without the Atticism, but with the mantles, the togas, and a thousand antique traits."

The RISD canvas, painted 23 years after Delacroix's journey, gives evidence of the longevity of the impressions gathered by him in North Africa. The painting is a loose adaptation of a passage recorded in his *Journal* on April 5, 1832, when his entourage, returning from Meknes to Tangier, passed a valley "stretching back as far as the eye can see," and encountered an Arab family and a female rider whose horse was pulled aside by a groom as the French party passed. Delacroix's *Arabes en voyage* translates this momentary occurrence into a grandiose conception that expands conventional notions of heroic landscape and narrative composition. By virtue of the dramatic diagonal descent of the figures down the mountainous desert pass, and the sweep of the valley and sky before them, Delacroix translates an exotic genre into a composition reminiscent of Rubens's royal pageants. The luminous coloring and bold brushwork contribute to this effect, and are in marked contrast to the subdued color and handling of contemporary academic painting. The distance of this subject from the grim reality of mid-19th century Paris nevertheless distinguishes Delacroix's painting from the work of mid-century Realists such as Courbet. This scene possesses the authority of observed fact, unlike Delacroix's earlier Byronic fantasies, yet it remains ultimately a subject that appeals to the imagination, and hence is Romantic in inspiration and appeal.

Delacroix's *Journal* dated February 1, 1856, mentions a painting, *Arabes en voyage*, acquired by Prince Demidoff, which has long been accepted to be the canvas now at RISD.

Color plate, page 70

110

EDOUARD MANET
French, 1832–1883

Le Repos, ca. 1870
Signed at lower right of print in
background: Manet
Oil on canvas. 58¼ x 43¾

Bequest of Mrs. Edith Stuyvesant
Vanderbilt Gerry. 59.027

Provenance: Durand-Ruel, 1872;
Théodore Duret, 1880; Galerie Georges
Petit, 1894; Jean-Baptiste Fauré, 1894;
Durand-Ruel, 1895; George Vanderbilt,
1898; Mrs. Edith Stuyvesant Vanderbilt
Gerry

Publication: *Manet, 1832–1883*, Grand
Palais, Paris, and The Metropolitan
Museum of Art, New York, 1983,
cat. no. 121.

Le Repos is the second of many paintings
of Berthe Morisot that Manet executed
during his career. Berthe first posed for
Manet in 1868 as one of three figures in
The Balcony (Musée d'Orsay, Galerie du
Jeu de Paume, Paris). During the summer of 1870 Manet began this painting,
in which Berthe is the sole subject. The
portrait was exhibited at the Salon of
1873.

Berthe Morisot was a distinguished
painter in her own right. She greatly
admired Manet's work, and after
meeting the artist through their mutual
friend Fantin-Latour in 1867, benefited
from Manet's suggestions and criticism
of her own painting. In 1874 Berthe
Morisot participated in the first Impressionist exhibition. She would become
the wife of Manet's brother Eugène.

Le Repos is Manet's most intimate
portrait of his friend and colleague.
Berthe Morisot lounges casually on a
couch, but her expression is pensive,
suggesting an inner tension that is in
fact revealed in her letters to friends and
family. Recent examination of this
painting under ultraviolet light shows
that Manet significantly reworked the
figure to achieve this unique combination
of physical relaxation and mental
activity. The intimate nature of the
portrait is further achieved by Manet's
handling of paint. Loose brushstrokes
define Berthe's white dress as well as the
chair and the print in the background.
Berthe's face and hair are treated softly,
enhancing her very human expression.
Manet would experiment further with
both the single figure in a reclining pose
and with increasingly loosened brushstroke during the 1870's in such paintings
as the *Portrait of Stéphane Mallarmé* of
1876 (Musée d'Orsay, Galerie du Jeu de
Paume, Paris).

In *Le Repos* Manet also creates a
charming picture of contemporary
Parisian life, a theme which occupied
him throughout his career. Berthe is
fashionably dressed, and poses on a
plum-colored couch that was in her own
studio. The print on the wall above her
head is a triptych woodblock print by
the Japanese artist Kuniyoshi. Japanese
art was very much in vogue in Paris by
the mid-19th century, and this print may
have been owned by Manet. In this way,
Manet creates both an intimate portrait
of a close friend and an enduring
glimpse of 19th century Paris.

Color plate, page 71

111

EDGAR DEGAS
French, 1834–1917

La Savoisienne, 1873
Signed, upper left: Degas
Oil on canvas. 24⅛ x 18⅛

Museum Appropriation. 23.072

Provenance: Durand-Ruel

Publication: Paul-André Lemoisne,
Degas et son oeuvre, vol. II, Paris, 1946,
cat. no. 333.

La Savoisienne is Degas's portrait of a
young peasant girl from the province of
Savoie. Neither the identity of the sitter
nor the circumstances of the portrait are
known; nevertheless the work occupies
a pivotal place within the artist's *oeuvre*.

Degas is best known for his depictions
of contemporary Parisian life – ballerinas,
the race track, the opera. He was also a
prolific and brilliant portraitist. Degas
began his career, however, within the
established academic tradition. After a
brief apprenticeship at the Ecole des
Beaux-Arts in Paris and extended trips to
Italy, Degas began in 1865 to submit
history paintings to the annual French
Salons. Degas ceased this activity after
1870, however; his interest permanently
shifted to the realism of Manet and the
emerging younger Impressionists.

La Savoisienne is, then, a relatively
early realist work by Degas. It combines
aspects of the artist's never-forgotten
formal training and his new-found
freedom of subject matter and interpretation. This painting, with its
wonderfully restrained handling of line,
reminds us that Degas always considered
draughtsmanship of primary importance. His inspiration was Ingres, whom
he had once met while a student at the
Ecole des Beaux-Arts, and who had
advised him always to "draw lines . . .
from memory or from nature." The
graceful symmetry of the girl's pose and
the gentle play of the ovals of her face,
headdress, and wide blouse collar owe
much to the portrait tradition established
by Ingres.

Despite his allegiance to past art,
Degas by 1873 was committed to the
depiction of contemporary life. *La
Savoisienne* is unusual in that its subject
is a peasant – Degas is almost exclusively
a recorder of urban life – but the directly
observed quality of this portrait is
typical. It is a portrait of an individual,
not an anonymous representative of her
class like the peasants of Bouguereau.

Although Degas never shared his
fellow Impressionists' views on the
value of painting *en plein air*, he was
certainly in accord with their technique
of using loose brushstrokes to create a
naturalistic visual effect. *La Savoisienne* is
restrained in comparison to some of the
artist's later works, especially those in
pastel, but the loose treatment of the
whites of the girl's blouse and particularly
her headdress anticipate the costumes of
his ballet dancers of the later 1870's and
80's.

112

JEAN-LEON GEROME
French, 1824–1904

Woman Washing at the Well (Moorish Bath),
ca. 1874
Signed at lower right: J. L. Gérôme;
inscribed "à ma fille Madeleine"
Oil on canvas. 32³⁄₁₆ x 25¾

Membership Fund. 66.280

Provenance: Madeleine Masson, née
Gérôme; Georges Masson; French and
Co.

Publication: *Jean-Léon Gérôme (1824–
1904): Paintings and Drawings,* Dayton
Art Institute, 1972, cat. no. 45.

Moorish Bath is a preparatory oil sketch
for the now lost final version of Gérôme's
painting. Such pictures as the *Moorish
Bath* resulted from Gérôme's extensive
travels in Egypt and the Near East and
were especially popular with the French
public. The exotic and often violent
nature of these foreign lands captivated
the imagination of many earlier 19th
century French artists such as Delacroix
and Ingres. Much more than his
predecessors, however, Gérôme focused
on the everyday customs and opulence
which accompanied this "barbarism."

Gérôme painted many versions of the
Moorish Bath, a young woman at her
toilette assisted by a servant. The
example in the Museum of Fine Arts,
Boston, is only one of many related
works by the artist. It was a theme that
allowed Gérôme to display his
considerable talent in painting the
female nude. That the artist himself
considered this the most important
aspect of his painting is revealed in the
RISD canvas, where only the nude is
fully finished. As a strong advocate of
his own academic training with its
emphasis on drawing from life, Gérôme
employed models to pose for him in his
Paris studio, where he reconstructed his
exotic vision.

The finished version of this painting is
known to us through an engraving
(Edward Strahan, ed., *A Collection of the
Works of J. L. Gérôme,* vol. 1, New York,
1883, pl. 3). The completed painting
retained all the essential components of
the sketch, but details were added such
as an intricately patterned tile floor and
more strongly pronounced shafts of light
which illuminated the bather. The most
striking change was the bather's head.
In the sketch she gazes into her wash
basin, unconscious of our existence, but
in the finished painting she turned to
look out at the viewer.

Gérôme's *Moorish Bath* reveals his
customary working method of setting
down his first thoughts for a painting in
an oil sketch. Gérôme never sold these
initial experiments, but often gave them
to friends and family. The carefully and
smoothly finished nude in this painting
stands in sharp contrast to the roughly
painted servant and surroundings; such
detail would be more resolved in the
artist's completed paintings.

113

CLAUDE MONET
French, 1840–1926

Le Bassin d'Argenteuil, 1874
Signed, lower left: Claude Monet
Oil on canvas. 21¾ x 29¼

Anonymous gift. 42.219

Provenance: Comte de Rasty, 1880; Alexandre Rosenberg, 1898; Gaston Bernheim de Villers, 1919; M. Knoedler, 1928; Carroll Carstairs Gallery, 1936; Mrs. Murray S. Danforth, 1938

Publication: Daniel Wildenstein, *Claude Monet: biographie et catalogue raisonné*, vol. I, Lausanne/Paris, 1974, cat. no. 325.

Claude Monet's *Le Bassin d'Argenteuil* depicts one of the artist's favorite subjects from the 1870's: sailboats on the Seine at Argenteuil. Monet lived at Argenteuil, a suburb of Paris, from 1871 to 1878. At that time the town was a center for pleasure boating and sailing competitions. Monet and the artist friends who visited him at Argenteuil – particularly Manet, Renoir and Sisley – made the town their artistic center as well. Monet's numerous paintings of Argenteuil reflect both his lifelong interest in landscape and his predilection at that time for scenes of contemporary life.

The basin of the river depicted in this painting was repeatedly painted by Monet. Here the Seine was at its widest and most of the boat races took place. On the banks of the river were tree-lined promenades, one of which can be seen in the background of the painting.

Monet's painting of the 1870's has often been described as belonging to the "classic" phase of Impressionism, a period in which Monet developed the formal properties of brushstroke and color that were so radical in their time. Monet had painted landscapes in the 1860's, but, as can be seen in *Le Bassin d'Argenteuil*, he became increasingly interested in painting the more ephemeral aspects of nature, especially the effects of light, color, and motion on land and on water. In *Le Bassin* the small broken brushstrokes loaded with bright, intermingled colors give the scene its vibrancy and convey the shifting visual sensations always found in nature. The man-made elements in the painting – the sailboats and the house in the background – are composed of larger strokes of pure white with dashes of red, and create a subtle contrast to Monet's treatment of the natural environment in which they rest.

Of Monet's many paintings of the Seine at Argenteuil, the most closely related is *Le Pont d'Argenteuil* of 1874 in the Musée du Louvre, Paris. In this painting brushwork and color are more controlled, but the disposition of the boats in the foreground is very similar. The RISD *Bassin d'Argenteuil* is in fact one of the most populated of Monet's scenes of Argenteuil from the summer of 1874; other paintings show less emphasis on sailing and more on the river itself. However, in 1875 Monet turned again to boating scenes. He was not yet ready to abandon the happy combination of man's activity in the landscape for pure landscape, as he was increasingly to do in the 1880's and 1890's.

Color plate, page 72

114

JAMES-JACQUES-JOSEPH TISSOT
French, 1836–1902

Ces Dames des Chars (The Circus),
1883–1885
Signed lower right: J. J. Tissot
Oil on canvas. 57½ x 39⅝

Gift of Walter Lowry. 58.186

Provenance: Julius Weitzner

Publication: *James Jacques Joseph Tissot: A Retrospective, 1836–1902*, Museum of Art, RISD, and Art Gallery of Ontario, 1968, cat. no. 36.

Tissot's *Ces Dames des Chars*, also called *The Circus*, is one of a series of at least 18 paintings depicting different types of Parisian women which the artist executed between 1883 and 1885. The paintings were exhibited first in Paris in 1885, and in London the following year. Tissot was well-known for his depictions of society women, but this series was his last major attempt at the *genre*: he spent the rest of his career working primarily on biblical illustrations.

Precedents for series like Tissot's "La Femme à Paris" existed in contemporary literature and popular illustration. Tissot was unique, however, in transforming his idea into a series of large-scale, individual paintings. Tissot also included women from all classes of society in his series, unlike the illustrated magazines which concentrated on women of fashion.

The woman as circus performer is a recurring theme in Tissot's work. In *Ces Dames des Chars* the subject is the women who ride the chariots at the Hippodrome d'Alma in Paris. Related paintings in the series are *The Amateur Circus* (Boston, Museum of Fine Arts) and *The Tightrope Dancer* (present whereabouts unknown). *Ces Dames des Chars* contains many elements characteristic of the series as a whole, but taken to further extremes. We are spectators, seated perhaps in the first row of the hippodrome. The viewer's vantage point is low, and the chariots seem almost to bear down upon us. Any feeling of intimacy is counteracted, however, by the stiff poses and frozen expressions of the women as they circle the ring. The spectator's physical proximity and psychological distance from those women creates a dynamic tension that permeates the painting.

Other compositional irregularities contribute to the unsettling effect of *Ces Dames des Chars* on the viewer. Tissot deliberately cuts off our view of the horses, giving the painting a snapshot-like quality that reveals his interest in both photography and the compositional methods of Degas. Tissot combines his style of painting, a highly detailed brand of realism, with bright, even opulent color, and feathery but tightly controlled brushstrokes. The effect is an all-over patterning reminiscent of Japanese art. The realism, combined with the almost anti-realistic unconventionality of composition found in *Ces Dames des Chars*, characterizes much of Tissot's work.

115

CLAUDE MONET
French, 1840–1926

La Seine à Giverny, 1885
Signed lower right: Claude Monet 85
Oil on canvas. 25½ x 39½

Museum Appropriation, by exchange.
44.541

Provenance: Potter Palmer; Wildenstein

Publication: Daniel Wildenstein, *Claude Monet: biographie et catalogue raisonné*, vol. II, Lausanne, 1979, cat. no. 1007.

Claude Monet settled at Giverny in Normandy in 1883. Although an inveterate traveler, Monet lived there until his death in 1926, constantly expanding his studio space and planning and planting his extensive gardens. Giverny and its environs served as an endless source of inspiration for Monet, and he painted the landscape in every season and under all weather conditions.

La Seine à Giverny, dated 1885, is an early work from the Giverny period. Monet's first paintings of Giverny were all of the Seine, which he had already painted frequently at other locations such as Argenteuil. The river was always a fresh subject for Monet, who once said, "I have painted the Seine all my life . . . I have never been bored with it: to me it is always different."

Although painted in the first few years of his residence there, *La Seine à Giverny* already reflects significant changes in Monet's painting style from the 1870's. In this painting Monet is less interested in accurately transcribing – however freely – the phenomena of nature, and more in exploring the subtle relationships of color and tone. The muted and varied blending of the blues and greens of foliage, water and sky are the true subject of this painting. In the 1880's Monet also became more interested in capturing the reflection of the landscape in the water. This two-dimensional imagery occupies a prominent place in *La Seine à Giverny*, especially when compared to its treatment in RISD's *Le Bassin d'Argenteuil* of 1874.

Monet experimented copiously with these new interests, and as usual repeatedly selected the same site. At least two paintings of the same view of the Seine, also from 1885, are known, one in a private American collection, and one in the Musée Marmottan, Paris. The artist chose a similar view again in 1897 for his series *Morning on the Seine*. Although he had always worked in a serial manner, in the late 1880's and 1890's Monet first systematically pursued the idea of creating specific series of paintings of the same subject at various times of day. *La Seine à Giverny* is a precursor to this later important development in Monet's art.

116

116

PAUL CEZANNE
French, 1839–1906

Le Jas de Bouffan, 1887–1888
Oil on canvas. 25¾ x 31⅞

Museum Appropriation. 33.053

Provenance: Ambroise Vollard; Paul
Rosenberg; Max Kapferer; Galerie
Zborowski

Publications: Lionello Venturi, *Cézanne,
Son Art, Son Oeuvre,* vol. 1, Paris, 1936,
no. 463; *Exposition Cézanne,* Pavillon de
Vendôme, Aix-en-Provence, 1961, cat.
no. 50.

Le Jas de Bouffan depicts the country
property of that name outside Aix-en-
Provence, bought by Cézanne's father in
1859. The farm buildings and the
distinctive grove of chestnut trees at the
Jas de Bouffan provided a constant
subject for Cézanne. The Provençal
countryside, including nearby Mont
Sainte-Victoire, remained Cézanne's
principal source of inspiration for
landscape painting throughout his
career.

Cézanne rarely signed or dated his
works. *Le Jas de Bouffan,* dated 1885–87
by Venturi, has recently been given the
slightly later date 1887–88 by John
Rewald. The painting is a mature work
by Cézanne, and shows both his debt to
the Impressionists and his independence
of them.

When he studied in Paris during the
1860's Cézanne met Monet, Renoir and
Pissarro. He participated in the Salon
des Réfusés in 1863 and in the first
Impressionist exhibition in 1874. It was
to the painting style of Pissarro that
Cézanne was most drawn. The light
palette and feathery brushstrokes of the
foliage in *Le Jas de Bouffan* owe much to
Pissarro's example. But as this painting
also demonstrates, the more Cézanne
painted, the less he would ally himself
with Impressionist goals. He continued
to use dark colors to outline objects such
as tree trunks and building contours,
giving forms the physical definition that
the Impressionists were attempting to
dissolve. Most significantly, Cézanne
used Impressionist techniques to create
wholly un-Impressionistic works. The
elements in this landscape are constructed of horizontal, vertical or
diagonal patches of color, which in turn
form faceted planes. The effect of this
architectonic painting structure is a
massive, timeless landscape very different from the fleeting images captured
by Monet and Pissarro. *Le Jas de Bouffan*
is unusual in Cézanne's *oeuvre* in that
the pale greens of the foliage suggest a
particular season, early spring. But the
artist makes no attempt to record
ephemeral light effects, movement, or
fugitive weather conditions in this
landscape.

117

AUGUSTE RODIN
French, 1840–1917

Balzac, 1893
Signed and inscribed on base: Rodin
orig./Alexis Rudier, Fondeur, Paris
Bronze. 50¼ x 20½ x 24¾

Museum Associates and donations from
Museum Members. 66.057

Provenance: Parke-Bernet, Sale 2420,
May 23–24, 1966

Publication: *Bulletin,* RISD, May 1966,
pp. 1–23.

In 1891 the Société des Gens de Lettres
commissioned Auguste Rodin to create a
monument commemorating Honoré de
Balzac (1799–1850), the great French
naturalist writer and the Société's
second president. Rodin worked on this
project for seven years before arriving at
the final version of his *Balzac* in 1898,
which, although highly controversial at
the time, is now seen to occupy a pivotal
place in the history of modern sculpture.

Although Rodin made many preparatory studies, the RISD *Balzac* is his first
fully conceived and executed idea for the
final sculpture. This *Balzac* is one of
three of the same size cast in bronze in
1893; the other casts now belong to the
Art Institute of Chicago and the Los
Angeles County Museum of Art.

The *Balzac* of 1893 was the result of
extensive research on the part of Rodin.
The sculptor was already familiar with
Balzac's works; he set about to discover
the man himself. Rodin looked at photographs and graphic reproductions of
famous portraits of Balzac, and he knew
of at least one portrait bust of the author,
done by David d'Angers in 1844. Rodin
also traveled to Balzac's native province
of Touraine to make models of facial and
physical types which resembled his
subject.

The adoption of a standing full-length
pose was necessitated by the terms of
the commission (the monument was
intended for the Place du Palais Royal in
Paris). Otherwise, the conception of the
sculpture was initially left to Rodin,
whose concern at this stage was to
immortalize his subject as realistically as
possible. The sculptor daringly chose to
represent Balzac both middle-aged and
nude. The novelist stands firmly with
legs apart and arms crossed in a pose
that has been variously described as that
of an athlete and an orator. This combination of physical and mental strength is

also found in the head, whose tilt and facial expression suggest both introspection and self-confidence. In spite of Rodin's unidealized modeling of Balzac's heavy physique, the figure assumes heroic proportions. The muscular crossed arms resting above Balzac's massive stomach minimize his actual girth. The face, although wrinkled, remains alert and forceful. Rodin creates a superb portrait of one of France's national heroes.

The Société des Gens de Lettres thought otherwise. They rejected both this 1893 version of *Balzac* and the one Rodin produced in 1898 as unsuitable for public display. The 1898 version, a fully-robed, much less physical but no less brilliant conception of Balzac, was never even cast in bronze during Rodin's lifetime.

Color plate, page 72

118

117

118

PAUL CEZANNE
French, 1839–1906

Au Bord d'une Rivière, 1904–05
Oil on canvas. 23¾ x 29

Special Museum Reserve Fund. 43.255

Provenance: Ambroise Vollard; Durand-Ruel, 1939

Publications: Lionello Venturi, *Cézanne, Son Art, Son Oeuvre*, vol. II, Paris, 1936, no. 769; *Cézanne, the Late Work*, Museum of Modern Art, New York, 1978, no. 85, p. 288.

Au Bord d'une Rivière is a late landscape by Cézanne, painted only a year or two before his death in 1906. The location of this scene of a river and the houses on its banks is not known, but may well be the environs of Fontainebleau, where Cézanne worked in 1904. A watercolor sketch entitled *La Seine aux Environs de Paris*, first related to this painting by Venturi, would seem to corroborate the general location of the motif.

Cézanne's late paintings, especially the works after 1900, show significant changes in style from anything he had done before. *Au Bord d'une Rivière* is characteristic of these changes. This painting lacks the three-dimensional architectonic structure of the artist's earlier landscapes. While four basic planes can be determined – the empty foreground, the river, the bank with houses across the river, and the sky – the only structural indication of depth is the curved wall at the far right of the painting. Distances are established not only by line but by the gradual diminution in scale and by the color modulations of the patches which compose the scene.

Brushstroke and color thus become the structural determinants and the expressive forces in *Au Bord d'une Rivière*. In earlier landscapes like RISD's *Le Jas de Bouffan* of 1887–88, Cézanne combined small, feathery brushstrokes with larger planes of color. But in this late work, Cézanne uses only broad, densely packed vertical strokes to construct the landscape. The inclusion of passages of more animated diagonal strokes – in the center foreground and in the sky – gives the painting its expressive energy. One can also see in these tightly constructed, abstracted facets of color, and in the ambiguity of planar and three-dimensional space, an important precedent for the Cubist style that would be developed by Picasso and Braque in the following years.

Color plate, page 73

119

PABLO PICASSO
French (b. Spain), 1881–1973

The Diners, 1901
Signed in blue: Picasso
Oil on cardboard. 19 x 25

Bequest of George Pierce Metcalf. 57.237

Provenance: André Lefèvre, Paris;
Galerie Balay et Carré, Paris; Carroll
Carstairs Gallery, New York, 1957

Publication: Pierre Daix, Georges
Boudaille and Joan Rosselet, *Picasso, The
Blue and Rose Periods, 1900–1906*,
Greenwich, Connecticut, 1966, no. V.66,
pp. 42, 45, 158, 184.

Pablo Picasso's second visit to Paris and true artistic debut occurred in 1901 when he shared an exhibition with a fellow Spanish artist at the important Galeries Vollard. The Museum's *Diners*, perhaps titled *Drinkers* or *Brasserie*, may have been among the 60 works by Picasso in the show. It is a prime example of his style and subject matter during the summer of 1901.

Picasso's youthful disenchantment with modern life in increasingly industrialized and separatist Barcelona found support in *fin-de-siècle* Paris in the work of artists such as Henri de Toulouse-Lautrec and Jean Louis Forain. Like Toulouse-Lautrec, Picasso often recorded his impressions of the Parisian *demi-monde* in makeshift or portable media, using oil on cardboard for the *Diners*. The *Diners* recalls Toulouse-Lautrec's couple at a table, *A la Mie* (1891, Boston, Museum of Fine Arts), in which value and hue contrasts between the man and woman convey their detachment from one another. The ultimate source for the subject, however, is Degas's well-known *Absinthe Drinkers* (1876, Louvre), with which the *Diners* shares its asymmetrical composition and the sharply rising table dominating the foreground.

In his interpretation of the motif, Picasso focuses on the individual's isolation in the midst of Paris's abundant pleasures. Rendered in somber tones and restrained brushwork, the male protagonist rests his chin on his hand and his elbow on the table, withdrawn in what would become an autograph pose during Picasso's imminent Blue Period. A female companion leans toward the man, overwhelming him with her expansive hat and slash of red lipstick. Picasso defines her costume, the food and the café décor in extravagantly applied and colored paint. Strident pinks, reds, oranges and yellows convey the garishness of Parisian nightlife and may reflect the novelty of electric lighting in contrast to the gaslighting Picasso was accustomed to in Barcelona. Anticipating Matisse and the Fauves, his coloristic freedom is surprising for an artist who would renounce color increasingly over the next years as he approached the monochrome Cubist palette.

The *Diners* once belonged to André Lefèvre, who became a major collector of Cubism under the guidance of the progressive German art dealer D. H. Kahnweiler.

120

PABLO PICASSO
French (b. Spain), 1881–1973

Woman Reading A Book, 1911–1912
Signed on verso: Picasso
Oil on canvas. 16¾ x 10

Museum Works of Art Fund. 51.094

Provenance: Wilhelm Uhde, Paris, 1912–1914; Drouot, Paris, May 30, 1921, *Wilhelm Uhde Collection*, cat. no. 50; Alphonse Kann, Saint-Germain-en-Laye; Carroll Carstairs Gallery, New York, 1951

Publication: Pierre Daix and Joan Rosselet, *Picasso, The Cubist Years, 1907–1916. A Catalogue Raisonné of the Paintings and Related Works*, London, 1979, p. 265.

Cubism radically challenged ideas that had been central to painting since the Renaissance. Based in Paris, and influenced by Cézanne and African sculpture, Pablo Picasso and Georges Braque began in 1908 to paint the geometrically simplified landscapes that earned the title Cubist. The two artists rapidly dispensed with conventional figure/ground relationships, consistent light sources, and one-point perspective, instead exploiting their freedom as painters to fragment and rearrange the appearance of the subject. Toward the end of 1912, this "analysis" of the subject yielded a "synthetic" phase of Cubism accompanied by a shift in medium from painting to collage. During the next two years, pictorial considerations – flatness, shape, color – increasingly dictated composition. Picasso and Braque, with Juan Gris after 1911, effected the essential Cubist advances by the out-break of World War I in 1914. Though they themselves never completely discarded subject matter drawn from external reality, the Cubist artists paved the way for the 20th century break-through to abstraction.

The complex relief of shaded planar facets constituting the Museum's *Woman Reading a Book* is characteristic of "high" analytical Cubism of 1910–12. Picasso abstracts a traditional portrait formula into a pyramidal concentration of light and graphic activity. "Keys" such as the woman's stylized eyes, nose, and wavy hair just above the center of the canvas enable the viewer to identify the subject. Below, a drinking glass, the scroll of an armchair, and several views of a book can be distinguished.

Daix groups *Woman Reading a Book* with works executed during the spring of 1911. Presumably he does so because of the rather staccato linear framework and the independence of modeling from this structure. Also, the painting lacks the stenciled lettering Picasso and Braque frequently applied to affirm the flat surface of their pictures beginning in early 1912. Records belonging to the first owner of the painting, the progressive German collector Wilhelm Uhde, however, date it 1912. The blue color of the armchair on the left side of the canvas agrees with this later dating, since in 1912 Picasso began to introduce touches of color to animate the neutral brown and greys typical of the analytical Cubist palette.

121

RAYMOND DUCHAMP-VILLON
French, 1876–1918

Seated Woman, 1914, cast 1915
Signed on base: R. Duchamp-Villon
Inscribed on back of base: Roman Bronze
Works, NY
Bronze with applied gold-washed
patina. 28 x 8 x 9½

Mary B. Jackson Fund and Membership
Dues. 67.089

Provenance: John Quinn, New York,
1915–1927; Spingarn Collection, New
York; Parke-Bernet, Sale no. 2539, April
5, 1967

Publication: Daniel Robbins, "The *Femme
Assise* by Raymond Duchamp-Villon,"
Yale University Art Gallery Bulletin,
Winter 1983, pp. 22–30.

Considered by many to be the most
important Cubist sculptor, Raymond
Duchamp-Villon died in World War I
after a career of barely 20 years.
Duchamp-Villon and his older and
younger brothers, Jacques Villon and
Marcel Duchamp, formed the nucleus of
the Puteaux Group of Cubist artists,
named for the Parisian suburb where the
group convened. An alternative to the
"Montmartre" Cubism of Picasso and
Braque, the Puteaux Group addressed
issues of the modern industrialized
world more directly.

Like many members of the group,
most notably Fernand Léger, Duchamp-
Villon focused in particular on the
machine's relationship to and effect on
man and nature. His development of
this theme climaxed in 1914 with two
works, the masterful, metamorphic
animal/machine, *The Large Horse*
(Hirshhorn Museum, Washington,
D. C.), and the present *Seated Woman.*
The *Seated Woman* is representative of
pervasive "robot" imagery appearing
internationally before and after World
War I in the work of Boccioni, Epstein,
Archipenko, Schlemmer, and Léger.
More than any of these artists, Duchamp-
Villon celebrated the association
between efficient machine forms and
classical formal ideals, balancing
smooth, "machine-turned" conical and
ovoid shapes of limbs, torso, and head
in a delicate contrapposto. Specific links
can be drawn to the rather complex
seated pose of Michelangelo's San
Lorenzo *Virgin.* A more immediate,
though general, source is the work of
the powerful 20th century classicist,
Aristide Maillol.

The present gilt-washed bronze cast is
the second of three (Yale University Art
Gallery, New Haven, and Ludwig
Collection, Cologne) made from the
original plaster, now lost. Under the
sponsorship of John Quinn, a key
American collector of avant-garde art in
the early 20th century and devoted
patron of Duchamp-Villon, the
Museum's and the Cologne pieces were
cast by the lost wax method in the
United States. Both were gilded
according to Duchamp-Villon's wishes.
The Museum owns a drawing (67.090) of
the sculpture that may have accompanied
instructions for Quinn sent by the artist
from France (New York Public Library).
After World War II, the Louis Carré
Gallery cast eight posthumous bronzes
without gilding from a second plaster
cast (Philadelphia Museum of Art).

Color plate, page 73

122

GEORGES BRAQUE
French, 1882–1963

Still Life, 1918
Signed on verso: G. Braque '18
Oil on canvas. 18¼ x 28¾

Mary B. Jackson Fund. 48.248

Provenance: Galerie Georges Moos,
Geneva; Theodore Schempp, New York,
1948

Georges Braque joined the French army in 1914, bringing to an end his close friendship with Pablo Picasso and the five-year collaboration that had spawned Cubism. When Braque returned to painting in 1917 after recovering from a severe wound, he was eager to catch up with advances made by Picasso and by Juan Gris, who had remained in Paris during the war. At the same time Braque began to break conclusively with Picasso both personally and artistically.

Painted in 1918, the Museum's *Still Life* exemplifies the transitional character of Braque's post-war work. The unusual composition, in which a large diamond set against a neutral ground contains a traditional Cubist still life, is one Braque favored between 1917 and 1919. Though neither as frequently nor as prominently, both Picasso and Gris had explored diamond and skewed rectangular shapes in a similar manner since 1915. These experiments accompanied general concern for the autonomous and therefore highly abstract work of art along the lines of the "picture object" promoted by Albert Gleizes and Jean Metzinger in their influential essay, *Du Cubisme,* 1912. The diamond format, it seems, provided a unifying formal transition between the elemental rectangular shape of the canvas and the complex Cubist patterning on its surface. These issues had repercussions in the Netherlands in Mondrian's well-known "lozenges" or diamond-shaped canvases, also begun during World War I.

Within and across the diamond Braque applies paint in a manner that has little to do with Picasso or any other artist. The fairly coherent fruitbowl motif, the broad brushwork, and the green, orange, gold, brown, and black color scheme herald the reasonably legible yet richly colored and fluidly painted still-life compositions that would dominate Braque's art over the next 40 years.

The Kröller-Müller Museum in Otterlo, the Netherlands, owns two other important diamond paintings by Braque. Related paintings bearing eccentric geometric shapes including lemons, almonds, or octagons can be found in the United States in the collections of the Philadelphia Museum of Art, the Norton Simon Foundation, Los Angeles, and Mr. and Mrs. Joseph Pulitzer, Jr., St. Louis.

123

HENRI MATISSE
French, 1869–1954

The Green Pumpkin, ca. 1920
Signed lower right: Henri Matisse
Oil on canvas. 30½ x 24½

Anonymous gift. 57.037

Provenance: Flechtheim, Berlin, ca. 1920;
Meirowsky, Switzerland (acquired from
Flechtheim); Mayer, Geneva, 1954

Publications: Adolph Basler, *Henri
Matisse,* Leipzig, 1924, n.p.; John
Elderfield, *Matisse in the Collection of the
Museum of Modern Art,* Museum of
Modern Art, New York, 1978, pp. 200–
201.

Many artists and poets, notably
Bonnard, Delaunay, Gris, Boccioni,
Mallarmé, and Rilke, touched upon
window themes in the early part of the
20th century. The motif held special,
lifelong fascination for Matisse, who
explained, " . . . for me space is one
unity from the horizon right to the
interior of my workroom . . . the wall
with the window does not create two
different worlds." Matisse affirmed this
view in numerous interior scenes
featuring windows. Also related are his
studio pictures and many other paintings
in which his own paintings figure prominently as motifs.

A window, centered on the vertical
axis of the painting, occupies the entire
upper half of the Museum's *Green
Pumpkin.* Consistent with his preference
for partial or cut-off views, Matisse
depicts most of the window, but omits
the encasement along its upper and side
edges so that both window and painting
share a single frame. By literally
equating window and pictorial space in
this way, Matisse compensates for the
unusually continuous naturalistic
drawing and spatial construction of the
image. Boldly drawn ribs with dense
blue-green paint make the pumpkin an
unusually plastic entity for an artist
known above all for brilliant, dema-
terializing color. Outside the window,
Matisse paints trees, shrubbery, and
clouds in a more open and animated,
but quite descriptive, graphic shorthand.
Some coloristic freedom is evident in the
irregularly shaped areas of flat, opaque
color which mark out highlights and
shadow on the window sill, not in
differing value but in contrasting hues of
red, blue, and yellow. The overall palette
of the picture, however, if not entirely
subdued, contains a good deal of black
and is more conventionally earthy than
Matisse's norm.

The conservative character of the
Green Pumpkin links it to works executed
in the early 1920's. The painting shows
the same view as another important
picture in the Museum of Modern Art,
the *Blue Window,* ca. 1911–13, which
looks out from Matisse's bedroom on to
his studio at his suburban home in Issy a
few miles southwest of Paris. However,
Matisse has abandoned the flattened
and relatively monochromatic space that
had been inspired by synthetic Cubism,
in favor of a more naturalistic palette
and a more volumetric treatment of
form, suggesting a retrenchment from
the increasing abstraction of his work in
the pre-World War I period. Adolf
Basler, who published *The Green Pumpkin*
in 1924, dated it 1920, which is currently
accepted as its date of execution.

124

JOHN SINGLETON COPLEY
American, 1738-1815

Governor Moses Gill, 1764
Oil on canvas. 49¾ x 39½

Jesse Metcalf Fund. 07.117

Rebecca Boylston Gill, ca. 1773
Oil on canvas. 49¾ x 39½

Gift of Isaac C. Bates, William Gammell,
Henry D. Sharpe, Elizabeth Z. Shepard,
D. B. Updike, George Wetmore, and
Mrs. Gustav Radeke. 07.120

Provenance: Mary Barron (White) Pratt,
Boston, 1873; Robert M. Pratt, 1907

Publications: Barbara Neville Parker
and Anne Bolling Wheeler, *John Singleton
Copley, American Portraits in Oil, Pastel
and Miniature*, Boston, 1938, pp. 82–84;
Jules David Prown, *John Singleton Copley*,
vol. I, Cambridge, 1966, pp. 38–39, 215,
plate 128, and pp. 89, 215, plate 326.

As the foremost portrait painter in
colonial America, John Singleton Copley
recorded the likenesses of the elite of
New England and New York society
from the early 1750's until his departure
for England in 1774. The Museum is
fortunate in having four portraits by this
master, spanning the most fruitful
period of his artistic production in
America, and offering an interesting
insight into Copley's development.

In 1764, Moses Gill, the 33-year-old
future Governor of Massachusetts,
commissioned paintings of himself and
his wife Sarah Prince Gill. Nine years
later, in 1773, after the death of Sarah,
Moses married Rebecca Boylston. Her
portrait by Copley is believed to date
from that year. These husband and wife
pendant portraits thus illustrate two
phases of the artist's *oeuvre*.

Governor Moses Gill was painted at a
time when Copley's position as *the*
colonial portrait artist was at its height.
Because of Copley's limited training and
limited contact with European art, primarily through prints and copies, a
certain unevenness is evident in his
work of this period, yet it is this very
directness of observation without artifice
that makes his images of the patriot
leaders of pre-Revolutionary America so
forthright in characterization.

By 1773, when *Rebecca Boylston Gill* is
believed to have been painted, Copley
had received the accolades of Sir Joshua
Reynolds and the Society of Artists in
London, and had traveled to New York.
His painting style was by now richer,
more subtle, and notably more complex
and sophisticated. Rebecca Boylston Gill
is depicted in the most fashionable
costume and setting, and attention is
paid to the smallest details of lace and
embroidery, with a greater sense of
richness achieved throughout. In
marked contrast to her husband's earlier
surroundings, Rebecca Boylston Gill
stands before a landscape accented by a
Doric column and a distant mountain
vista.

Color plate, page 74

125

GILBERT STUART
American, 1755–1828

Portrait of Sarah Cutler Dunn,
ca. 1809–15
Oil on wood panel. 27¾ x 22¾

Museum Appropriation. 31.273

Provenance: Sarah Cutler Dunn, 1815;
Sarah Cutler Dunn Sargent, 1825; Mary
Turner Sargent Burgess, 1868; Thomas
Burgess, 1890; Nathan Matthews, 1898;
Mary M. Burgess, 1912; Alexander
Manlius Burgess, 1914

Publication: Mandel/RISD, 1977,
pp. 108–09.

Born in Rhode Island and trained in
Europe, Gilbert Stuart came to Boston
from Washington, D.C., in 1805, living
there until his death. As the famous
portraitist of George Washington, he
was naturally much sought after by the
local gentry to execute their family
portraits. Sarah Cutler Dunn and her
husband Samuel were no exception.
Samuel Dunn was from a Providence
family, though he moved to Boston in

1785 where he lived the life of a sea
captain turned merchant.

In the Museum's portrait, Sarah Dunn
is presented in a manner befitting the
wife of a well-to-do Bostonian. It is Mrs.
Dunn's costume, in particular her
French Empire ringlets, starched lace
ruff and "India Shawl," that places her
portrait in the first decades of the 19th
century. The fact that both husband and
wife portraits were painted on panel also
narrows the period of their production,
for Jefferson's Embargo of 1809 prevented
the importation of canvas from England,
forcing Stuart to use wooden panels as
the support.

It is believed that Stuart painted
roughly 800 portraits after his return
from study in England, many of them in
Boston. There was, therefore, considerable pressure to do a summary job in
order to get on to the next commission.
With *Sarah Cutler Dunn,* for example,
Stuart eliminated any suggestion of the
sitter's arms or hands. Yet despite its
summary treatment, by focusing on the
face the artist has captured the character
of a woman of fortitude as well as
fashion.

126

THOMAS COLE
American, 1801–1848

Landscape With Tree Trunks, 1828
Signed and dated lower center: T. Cole
1828 Boston
Oil on canvas. 26 x 32¼

Walter H. Kimball Fund. 30.063

Provenance: William F. Carey, 1841; H.S.
Speed, Boston, 1930

Publication: Mandel/RISD, 1977, no. 1.

Recent study of the correspondence
between Cole and one of his most
important patrons, Daniel Wadsworth,
has revealed that this work was painted
in Boston during the summer of 1828.
Cole, in an attempt to raise money for a
trip to Europe to study Old Master
painting, held a public exhibition at the
Boston Athenaeum of his ambitious
biblical paintings, including *The Expulsion from the Garden of Eden,* 1827–28
(Museum of Fine Arts, Boston). But
Cole's turn toward pure landscape
painting in the RISD work marks an
important commitment to the depiction
of the American wilderness.

This scene, while an imaginary
composition, is probably based on
sketches that Cole had made in the
White Mountains the previous summer.
The tiny figure of an Indian, standing on
the rocky outcropping in the center of
the painting, gestures dramatically
toward the mountain peak in the
distance. The shape of this rugged peak
suggests that of Mount Chocorua in
New Hampshire, an important site in
Indian legend and the setting for Cole's
Scene from "The Last of the Mohicans" of
1827, based on the James Fenimore
Cooper novel. The inclusion of the
Indian, the blasted tree trunk, and
stormy skies in the RISD landscape draws
attention to the dramatic changes that
were occurring in the American
wilderness, changes wrought by nature
and also by the white man. This theme,
of central importance throughout Cole's
work, also served as a subject for many
Hudson River School painters in the
following decades.

125

127

FITZ HUGH LANE
American, 1804–1865

View of Little Good Harbor Beach,
Cape Ann, 1847
Oil on canvas. 26 x 30

Jesse Metcalf Fund. 38.068

Provenance: The artist, 1848; Robert B.
Campbell, Boston, 1938

Publication: Mandel/RISD, 1977,
pp. 148–50.

View of Little Good Harbor Beach, Cape Ann
was painted in 1847, the last year of Fitz
Hugh Lane's involvement with his own
lithographic firm of Lane and Scott. An
early transitional work, this painting's
precise compositional forms and sharp
contrast of luminous distance with the
shadowed foreground are more characteristic of printmaking than painting.
These contrasts hint at the possibility
that Lane was acquainted with the work
of the English marine painter Robert
Salmon, who came to Boston in 1828.
Lane exhibited *Little Good Harbor Beach* in
1848 at the Boston Athenaeum, where he
had shown paintings since 1841 and
where he would have had the opportunity to see exhibited not only the
works of Salmon, but also Dutch 17th
century painting, to which this work is
clearly indebted.

The view is of Cape Ann, Massachusetts, near Gloucester, where Lane had
grown up. He moved back to Gloucester
in the winter of 1847 after his sojourn in
Boston, although the Museum's painting was probably based on sketches
made at Little Good Harbor in the spring
or fall of 1846. Lane enlivens this scene
of everyday activity with a precise attention to detail. Out of this keen observation, a full narrative of the day is
presented. Yet there is an unsettling,
unnatural stillness in the scene. Each of
the figures in the painting, with the
exception of the cart driver and the man
pushing away from the shore at the
right, stands facing the far distance as if
magnetized by its spiritual light. It is in
part this quality of intensified observation
that causes Lane to be associated with
the "luminists."

126

127

128

Chocorua Peak, 1855
Oil on canvas. 41 x 60⅛

Gift of the Rhode Island Art Association.
52.104

Provenance: The artist, 1855; the Rhode
Island Art Association

Publications: Ellen Lawrence, ed., *To
Look on Nature, European and American
Landscape 1800–1874,* Providence, 1972,
pp. 81–82; Mandel/RISD, 1977, pp. 31–
34.

Durand spent the summer of 1855 in the
White Mountains of New Hampshire,
staying in North Conway, near Mount
Chocorua. *Chocorua Peak* is a direct result
of this visit, and is based on a drawing
dated August 22, 1855, currently in the
collection of the New-York Historical
Society. A guide book of 1860 containing
a very similar engraving illustrating the
peak of Chocorua describes it as the
sharpest in the area with the exception
of Mount Adams, saying that "there is
no other summit from which the preci-
pices are so sheer and sweep down such
cycloidal curves." Durand concentrates
on the summit itself; the total absence of
human or animal life is unusual for him
at this point in his career. Even the
depiction of individual trees–so much a
part of Durand's *oeuvre*–is reduced to
two bare-branched silhouettes pointing toward the peak from the left
foreground.

The same year that he executed
Chocorua Peak, Durand published his
famous "Letters on Landscape Painting"
in *The Crayon.* In these letters he
encouraged the young art student to
work directly from nature and to concentrate on "his native resources," that is,
"the scenery of his 'own green forest
land.'" He then outlined procedures for
the beginning artist, stressing the
importance of drawing "with scrupulous
fidelity" first and then moving on to
"palette and brushes." Durand's
adherence to his own advice is particularly clear in *Chocorua Peak,* where the
variations in the mountain's contours
are noted as carefully as veins in an
anatomical drawing. In the early 1850's it
was Durand's usual procedure to
prepare on-the-spot drawings for the
middle ground and distance of his views
and then combine these with a foreground based on his stock of tree
studies.

At the time that *Chocorua Peak* was
painted, Durand was probably the best-
known living American landscape artist;
thus it is not surprising that he should
have been asked to participate in the
Rhode Island Art Association's September 1855 exhibition. Durand must have
prepared the painting quickly in order
for it to be ready for the showing, and
the Art Association must have purchased
the picture out of the exhibition.
Chocorua Peak was placed on loan to the
Museum as early as 1878, the year after
the Rhode Island School of Design was
founded. It formally entered the permanent collection in 1952, almost a century
after it had made its first appearance in
Providence.

129

THOMAS CRAWFORD
American, 1813–1857

Morning Star, 1856
Marble. 59 x 21 x 23

Gift of Mrs. C. Oliver Iselin. 42.299

Publication: Sylvia E. Crane,
White Silence, Miami, 1972, p. 456.

The Museum's marble *Morning Star*
dates from late in Thomas Crawford's
abbreviated career. Crawford's efforts as
a professional sculptor began with his
arrival in Rome from New York in 1835.
By 1856, when *Morning Star* was carved,
Crawford had an international reputation
as a "Grecian genius" and the "sculptor
laureate" of American artists working in
Rome. As the first American sculptor to
settle in Italy, Crawford quickly became
the most dedicated of American Neo-
classicists.

Thomas Crawford made his initial
impact on American and specifically
Bostonian taste with the execution of the
first nude male figure shown in America.
Yet unlike the sensation that would be
caused by Hiram Powers's *Greek Slave* in
1847, Crawford cloaked his *Orpheus and
Cerberus* of 1843 (Museum of Fine Arts,
Boston) with the piety of Victorian senti-
mentality, and it was received with great
enthusiasm. Numerous commissions
soon followed, including the decoration
of the Senate and House of Representa-
tives in Washington, D.C. Crawford's
Progress of Civilization for the Senate
pediment, his *Armed Freedom* atop the
dome of the Capitol, and the bronze
doors of the Senate and House of Repre-
sentatives buildings dominated the last
decade of his career.

While his Washington commissions
occupied much of Crawford's attention,
numerous other works were produced
during this period. *Morning Star,* carved
in Rome in 1856, is one of many allegorical subjects he executed at mid-century.
Represented here is a personification of
the planet Venus as she rises ahead of
the sun. The figure strides forward,
animated by the wind-blown toga which
leaves one shoulder bare. With her left
hand she draws a drapery over her
head, caught by the wind, and seems to
rise out of the very marble she is made
from.

130

WILLIAM MORRIS HUNT
American, 1824–1879

The Violet Girl, 1856
Signed and dated at lower right:
Wm. M. Hunt 1856
Oil on canvas. 39½ x 32⅛

Gift of Mrs. S. Foster Damon. 72.177

Provenance: The artist, 1857;
James Davis, Boston, 1879; Henry
Winsor, Boston, 1894; Mrs. Edmund M.
Wheelwright, Boston, 1924

Publication: Mandel/RISD, 1977, no. 72.

Begun in 1851 in Paris, where the young
artist was studying with the academic
painter Thomas Couture, *The Violet Girl*
was not completed until Hunt returned
to the United States in 1856. When the
painting was first exhibited in a Couture-
like sketch state at the Paris Universal
Exposition of 1855, it was admired for
the "delicious harmonies" of color, and
indeed, it is Hunt's treatment of color,
the deep resonant hues of red, blue, and
violet placed against the white background wall, which is the visual strength
of this work. The silhouetted single
figure also suggests the influence of
Jean-François Millet, whose simple,
everyday genre subjects were popular
paintings at the Paris salons of the
1850's.

Hunt put a few finishing touches on
the painting before it was exhibited to
the American public at the National
Academy in New York in 1857, and the
work quickly proved to be popular in
this country as well. It was one of six of
Hunt's paintings that were copied as
lithographic prints the following year.

With paintings like *The Violet Girl*
Hunt established an American taste for
more freely painted, close-valued,
simple figure subjects derived from the
French Barbizon school. As Hunt
became a successful painter and established teacher in Boston in the 1860's
and 1870's his interest in European art
had an important influence on a number
of other prominent 19th century
painters, including John LaFarge,
Eastman Johnson, and Winslow Homer.

131

EASTMAN JOHNSON
American, 1824–1906

Sugaring Off, ca. 1861–66
Oil on canvas. 52¾ x 96½

Jesse Metcalf Fund. 45.050

Provenance: Mrs. Eastman Johnson, 1907; W. B. Cogswell; Misses F. Pearl and Elizabeth Browning, 1940; Curt Valentin Gallery, 1945

Publication: Mandel/RISD, 1977, pp. 158–63.

Eastman Johnson was born and raised in Maine; hence the event depicted by this painting, which occurs every spring when the maple syrup is tapped from the trees, was an integral part of his life. It is not surprising that he should select a subject for one of his monumental genre paintings of American life from these childhood memories. Johnson's particular interest in portraying a typically New England scene between the years 1861 and 1866 was undoubtedly spurred by the Civil War, which encouraged Americans to think in terms of their national and regional identity. It seems likely that the pressures of the war led the artist's thoughts to the relatively undisturbed community scenes of sugaring off which he had known in his youth and which persisted in the North despite the strain of war. While numerous sketches and studies were produced on this subject, with the Museum's version the largest, a final version was never realized.

Johnson conceived of this scene as a contemporary document, but, having recently studied in Düsseldorf at the time when Emmanuel Leutze was producing *Washington Crossing the Delaware*, he had been directly exposed to the academic methods involved in preparing a monumental work. Since he viewed his *Sugaring Off* as much more than a popular illustration, it was natural that he should attempt to model his work on the discipline and goals of this highest form of narrative art. Johnson's yearly visits to Maine in the early 1860's for on-the-spot sketches of the maple-sugaring process and of the people who performed it were an appropriate preparatory procedure for producing a commemoration of any great historical event. So, too, Johnson's use of a rapid, free stroke for these preparatory sketches showed his familiarity with French academic methods as transmitted through his teacher, Thomas Couture.

Surely the most striking features of the Museum's *Sugaring Off* are its large size and the great freedom and airiness of both its composition and paint application. The picture remained in this state in Johnson's studio for at least 40 years, until his death, because he was never able to interest a prospective patron in a monumental finished work on such a theme. Johnson's lack of financial success with this genre painting based on the ambitious procedures of history painting did not, however, lead him to modify his methods in future depictions of everyday life.

132

MARTIN JOHNSON HEADE
American, 1819–1904

Brazilian Forest, 1864
Oil on canvas. 20¹/₁₆ x 16

Gift of Mr. and Mrs. C. Richard
Steedman. 68.052

Provenance: The artist, 1865; Governor
Henry Lippitt, Providence, 1866

Publication: Mandel/RISD, 1977, pp. 38–41.

Brazilian Forest was painted in London
shortly after Heade arrived there from
Brazil in June 1864. The picture is based
on material from the first of his several
trips to Brazil, Nicaragua, and Colombia.
Although his principal concern in the
area was with a project centering on
local species of hummingbirds to be
depicted in oil and later in chromolitho-
graphs, *Brazilian Forest* indicates that
Heade had botanical interests as well.
The painting is an accurate, realistic
representation of a truly extraordinary
botanical wonder, the South American
rain forest. The canvas is dense with
jungle vegetation, the most remarkable
of which is the delicate, feather-leafed
tree fern occupying the center. A hunter
is present at the right with his rifle and
dog, but he is no more than a picturesque
detail.

If Heade painted the *Brazilian Forest* as
part of a series of "Forest Studies of
South America," as his own inscription
on the back of the painting indicates, he
must have intended it to serve as part of
a project at once educational, topo-
graphic, and decorative. He was one of
the first American artists to travel to
South America, although he was preceded by Frederick E. Church, who
became Heade's good friend in the late
1850's, just after Church's own return
from that part of the world.

Church's painting of Cotopaxi, the
Ecuadoran volcano, was executed just a
year earlier than Heade's *Brazilian Forest*.
Heade may well have seen Church
working on it in his studio and thus
have been further inspired to make the
trip himself. Unlike Church, however,
Heade's view of South America is not
heroic, panoramic, or implicitly religious.
His work is a microscopic analysis of the
country itself, its trees, its minerals, its
flowers and birds, rather than a cinematic
presentation of volcanic wonders. In
Brazilian Forest Heade ignores dramatic
incident in order to better provide his
viewer with the direct experience of the
humid, airless, tree-tangled forest.

133

JOHN SINGER SARGENT
American, 1856–1925

A Boating Party, ca. 1889
Oil on canvas. 34⅝ x 36⅜

Gift of Mrs. Houghton P. Metcalf in
memory of her husband Houghton P.
Metcalf. 78.086

Provenance: Estate of the artist, 1925;
M. Knoedler, New York, 1925; E. A.
Milch, New York; Horatio Seymour
Rubens, New York, 1926; Victor Spark,
New York, 1942; Scott and Fowles, New
York; Mr. and Mrs. Houghton P.
Metcalf, Providence, 1948

Publication: Mandel/RISD, 1977, pp. 179–182.

Sargent captured here the leisure activities of his companions in *A Boating Party*,
set at Fladbury Rectory on the River
Avon, England, where the artist joined
several members of his family late in the
summer of 1889. Visits to the Worcester-
shire countryside had become a habit

132

133

with Sargent since his arrival in London in 1885. In this work, Sargent portrayed his sister Violet (in a black fur cape), the artist Paul Helleu, and Alice Guérin, Helleu's wife.

Sargent was encouraged by his Fladbury setting to reexamine the possibilities of the river scene, although he had been frustrated in past summers by the logistics of painting from a boat on the water. Initial work on *A Boating Party* could have been done from a conveyance like the *bâteau atelier* which Sargent had previously employed. This "floating studio" was probably based on one that Claude Monet had devised in the 1870's to overcome the difficulties of painting river scenes. However, the variety of interests and results in this painting and the sharp cropping of the punt in the lower right corner suggest that he may have begun work outdoors, then continued it in the studio with the aid of photographs.

In terms of style, *A Boating Party* suggests the recurring influence of Monet, as well as an interpretation of Impressionism that parallels the late works of Edouard Manet. Like Manet,

Sargent shows an interest in retaining flat local color and natural, relaxed poses, while interpreting water and landscape with the broken brushstrokes and close contrasts used by the Impressionists generally. While he does not achieve an Impressionist unification of the picture plane, Sargent demonstrates his reliance on Monet in quotations from the latter's recent paintings of the period just before *A Boating Party*. The work, which captures a *dolce far niente* mood that was favored in some of Sargent's holiday watercolors, was most likely considered unresolved by the artist. It was left unsigned and never publicly exhibited during Sargent's lifetime.

134

JOHN WHITE ALEXANDER
American, 1856–1915

The Blue Bowl, 1898
Oil on canvas. 48 x 36

Jesse Metcalf Fund. 04.141

Provenance: The artist, 1898

Publication: Mandel/RISD, 1977, pp. 193–196.

The Blue Bowl presents a quintessentially Art Nouveau subject and composition. It was executed in Paris, after Alexander and his wife, presumably the model in *The Blue Bowl*, had been living there for about eight years. Alexander was among the best known American artists working in Paris, and would have been aware of the group of Belgian Symbolists known as Les XX. The Brussels school of Art Nouveau is known to have been strongly influenced by the work of the English artist Aubrey Beardsley, whose illustration *The Peacock Skirt* is very close to *The Blue Bowl* in the pose of its main figure – shoulder and back to the viewer and head and hair shown in profile – and the amount of space and attention given to her skirts. Alexander would have had an opportunity to become familiar with Beardsley's work firsthand while he lived in England in the late 1880's. Interestingly, Alexander has captured some of the texture so evident in Beardsley's "stippled or dotted manner" by painting his picture on a heavy-grained canvas.

134

135

WINSLOW HOMER
American, 1836–1910

On a Lee Shore, 1900
Oil on canvas. 39 x 39

Jesse Metcalf Fund. 01.003

Provenance: The artist; M. O'Brien and Son, Chicago, 1900; Frank W. Gunsaulus, Chicago, 1900; M. Knoedler, New York, 1901

Publication: Mandel/RISD, 1977, pp. 79–84.

In a letter of August 1900, written just a month before he painted *On a Lee Shore,* Winslow Homer complained that his "work of the past two or three years has been mostly in watercolors" and that "for the last two months" he has "not painted – too many people about this place." But by October of that year, *On a Lee Shore* was completed and Homer began work on two other stormy seascapes, *Eastern Point, Prout's Neck,* and *West Point, Prout's Neck* (Sterling and Francine Clark Art Institute). Homer termed *On a Lee Shore* "a very excellent painting" almost immediately upon its completion; it was the Museum's first purchase with the Jesse H. Metcalf Fund, which was established in the same year that the canvas was painted.

On a Lee Shore, which was painted near the end of Homer's career, summarizes many of his best qualities as an artist. Like most of the shore paintings done at his home in Prout's Neck, a rocky peninsula south of Portland, Maine, this large oil painting has a limited palette, where sky, sea, and land continually merge and are redefined by changing effects of the weather and the force of the sea. More progressive in style than many of the other seascapes from this period, *On a Lee Shore* demonstrates Homer's awareness of European modernism and the Japanese print, with its asymmetrical composition and contrast of the solid forms of the rocks and the fluidity of the water.

Color plate, page 75

136

MARY CASSATT
American, 1844–1926

Simone in a Larged Plumed Hat, ca. 1903
Oil on canvas. 25 x 25

Gift of Mrs. Murray S. Danforth. 60.095

Provenance: F. Dupré, Paris; Joseph Katz, Baltimore; Hirschl and Adler Galleries, 1959

Publication: Mandel/RISD, 1977, no. 58.

The calm atmosphere evoked by Mary Cassatt's paintings tends to obscure the tenacity of her vision with respect to her own style. Forced to live abroad in order to complete her art education and to perfect her technique, Cassatt brought with her to Paris the preference for realism found in the paintings of her native Philadelphia. Although clashing with the tenets of the Academy, her views found a favorable response among those French painters who were themselves at odds with the Academy. In 1879 she became one of the few women, and the only American, to exhibit with the Impressionists.

Like Degas, Mary Cassatt deliberately limited herself to certain familiar subjects: family, friends, and the comfortable rituals of domestic life, thus allowing full exploration of these themes. By 1901 when she began a series of pastel portraits of little girls posed against plain backgrounds, the precise draughtsmanship of earlier work was giving way to softer effects; firmness of line and contour no longer characterized her work. One of these pastels, *Head of Simone in a Large Plumed Hat* in the collection of the San Diego Museum, may well have served as a preparatory piece for the RISD painting. The wide, scribbled chalk strokes are echoed in the canvas, where they enliven the surface but do not contain form through linear contours, in the manner of academic painting.

Working with a limited palette, usually with one bright color – blue in this instance – Cassatt painted children of the Oise countryside where her summer home, Château de Beaufresne, was located. Simone appears at least 20 times, often in beribboned or feathered bonnets, in a group of portraits done in pencil, oil, and pastel. Her round face, small nose, bright eyes, and Cupid's-bow mouth are the features typically favored by the artist. Cassatt was not interested in depicting the energy of childhood, but preferred to portray well-behaved girls of four or five years old, who were able to pose for extended periods. Partial to hats, she frequently painted children in hats intended for adults. The arms and shoulders are suggested here, rather than defined; there is a hint of a frame or windowsill at the left.

Like most portraits executed by Cassatt, this one was not commissioned. The child's pensive expression, together with the cool tones of the paint, evoke the quiet atmosphere characteristic of Cassatt, who said that her most important work lay in studies of childhood and infancy.

137

JOHN SINGER SARGENT
American, 1856–1925

Señor Manuel Garcia, 1905
Oil on canvas. 54⅜ x 38

Museum Appropriation. 19.141

Provenance: Copley Gallery, Boston

Publications: M.S. McKinlay, RISD, vol. VII, no. 4, 1919, p. 38; C.M. Mount, "Carolus Duran and the Development of Sargent," *Art Quarterly,* 1963, vol. XXVI, pp. 385–417.

Counted among the finest portraits in the collection of the Museum is *Señor Manuel Garcia* by the American expatriate John Singer Sargent. Born in Florence, Sargent studied first in Rome, then at the Accademia in Florence, eventually entering the studio of Carolus-Duran in Paris. From Carolus-Duran the artist received a solid technical training. By the 1880's Sargent had established himself as one of the more celebrated and sought-after painters of European and American society, for individual and group portraits as well as landscapes and *plein-air* studies.

Garcia is represented here at age 100. The painting was commissioned in 1905 as a gift for the celebrated musician's 101st birthday, by "20 international learned societies and 800 individuals sharing in the expense." Garcia's character and achievements – as a professor at the Royal Academy of Music in London, author of a treatise on the human voice, and inventor of the Laryngoscope, which was a medical aid in the study of the vocal cords – are captured in Sargent's masterful depiction of his head and hands. Garcia sits erect and alert, his head brilliantly set off against the dark background and suit of clothes, a man of commanding confidence and experience.

A charcoal study of Garcia's head, now in the collection of the Montclair Art Museum, most likely is a preparatory study for the Museum's painting and may also give a clue to how Sargent painted his elderly subject. It has been suggested by Charles Mount that Sargent often used photography in the painting process, and photographs exist of Sargent seated in his studio in the same position as the subject of the Museum's portrait. He may in fact have used his own torso, or at least his trouser legs in the photograph, to compose the lower portion of the portrait of Garcia, thus keeping his sittings to a minimum.

138

GEORGE BELLOWS
American, 1882–1925

Rain on the River, 1908
Signed lower left: Geo Bellows
Oil on canvas. 32³/₁₆ x 38³/₁₆

Jesse Metcalf Fund. 15.063

Provenance: The artist, 1915

Publication: Mandel/RISD, 1977, no. 96.

Bellows's windswept scene of Riverside Park in New York is a masterfully painted landscape, rich in tonal harmonies of gray, white and black. Natural forms, such as the rocky ledge in the foreground, are not depicted in realistic detail, but rather recreated in the density and immediacy of Bellows's vigorous brush strokes. Other compositional elements, such as the asymmetrical diagonal of the railroad tracks and the calligraphic handling of trees, suggest the influence of Japanese art.

As a member of the Ash Can School, Bellows was primarily interested in creating a specifically American art that reflected the reality of modern urbanism. Like Robert Henri, George Luks and John Sloan, Bellows sought to do this through his choice of subject matter. In cityscapes of New York, drawn from scenes of middle- and working-class life, the Ash Can School artists rejected the elitist, European standards of abstract painting and instead focused on the

recognizable features of urban America. The importance of such subjects for the development of American modernism had been suggested only a few years earlier by the critic Sadakichi Hartmann. His "Plea for the picturesqueness of New York" is almost an exact description of Bellows's painting:

"A picture genuinely American in spirit is afforded by Riverside Park. Old towering trees stretch their branches toward the Hudson. Almost touching their trunks the trains on the railroad rush by. On the water, heavily loaded canal boats pass on slowly, and now and then a white river steamboat glides on by majestically, while the clouds change the chiaroscuro effects at every gust of wind."

139

FRANK W. BENSON
American, 1862–1951

Summer, 1909
Oil on canvas. 36⅜ x 44⅜

Bequest of Isaac C. Bates. 13.912

Provenance: The artist, 1910

Publication: Mandel/RISD, 1977, pp. 206–209.

Frank Benson was a founder of the Ten American Painters, a group involved in what has been termed "a kind of academy of American Impressionism." He began his career as a mural painter, executing *The Seasons,* 1897, for the Great Hall of the main building of the Library of Congress, Washington, D.C. (The Museum owns two studies for the *Spring* and *Autumn* sections of this mural program.) *Summer* also recalls Benson's mural project. While this painting could be termed a landscape with figures, it is in fact organized on the same principles as the Library of Congress murals. Like the murals placed high above the viewer, Benson slightly distorted his figures in *Summer* and flattened their spatial setting, thus focusing attention on the women's faces. *Summer* might be considered a quintessential example of American Impressionism, and yet it remains basically a *plein-air* picture, more in the tradition of American outdoor portraiture associated with Winslow Homer. Benson did indeed base his painting completely on reality. He used his family as models and painted the whole scene outdoors, most likely on North Haven Island in Penobscot Bay, Maine, where he summered. His growing preoccupation with the problems of natural light eventually turned him from the academic figure painter he had been in the 1890's to a landscape painter of sportsmen in the Canadian wilds in the second decade of the 20th century, again in the manner of Winslow Homer.

139

140

140

PAUL MANSHIP
American, 1885–1966

Dancer and Gazelles, 1916
Bronze. 32½ x 33 x 10

Museum Appropriation. 17.363

Provenance: The artist

Publication: Edwin Murtha, *Paul Manship*, New York, 1957, no. 85, plate 17.

Paul Manship is recognized today as the master of the "Style Conscious" manner, marked by economy of form, clarity of outline, and elegance of surface. This style, popular in America during the first decades of the century, continued the international spirit begun by late 19th century painters by applying it to sculptural form. Often the subjects of this international "moderne" were muscular athletes and heroes of both the recent and archaic past.

After several years at art schools in St. Paul, Philadelphia, and New York, Manship attended the American Academy in Rome from 1909 to 1912. During his stay in Europe, Manship traveled extensively, finding particular inspiration in Archaic Greek sculpture extant in both Greece and Italy. The simplicity and directness of 5th and 6th century B. C. Archaic and Severe Style sculpture appealed to the young artist and affected his entire production after his return from abroad.

Along with the aesthetic awareness of ancient Mediterranean three-dimensional form, Manship was inspired by Asian subjects. The motif of this work, a woman flanked by two deer, is derived from classical Indian painting. In *ragamala* illustration, *todi ragini*, one image in a larger cycle of 36 images of men and women, is represented as a lady in a forest holding either a garland or a stringed instrument, sometimes dancing, and always accompanied by two deer or black buck. For the Museum's bronze *Dancer and Gazelles*, Manship thus drew upon Indian painting for its theme and Archaic Greek sculpture for its style.

Other casts of *Dancer and Gazelles*, in an edition of 12, are in public and private collections, including the Metropolitan Museum of Art, the Art Institute of Chicago, and the National Museum of American Art. The most popular of all the Manship commissions is the *Prometheus Fountain* at Rockefeller Center in New York City.

141

ROBERT HENRI
American, 1865–1929

Mary with the Red Ribbon, 1926
Signed lower left: Robert Henri
Oil on canvas. 24 x 20

Walter H. Kimball Fund. 32.002

Provenance: The artist, 1926; Macbeth Gallery, New York, 1928

Publication: Mandel/RISD, 1977, pp. 138–39.

Robert Henri was a member of The Eight, the first American artists to aim programmatically at founding a native style that reflected the American experience. Later known as the Ash Can School, these artists rebelled against academic norms and produced a style of painting that emphasized the individuality of the artist. Their subjects were the tenement streets of New York and the people who inhabited them, though their images were more a celebration of street life than a condemnation of social ills.

In his teaching at the Art Students League, Henri emphasized the importance of working in large masses which have "fine shapes" and "fine colors." Although this advice was first written in 1915, Henri continued to follow it throughout his career, as can be seen in the simple shapes and brilliant colors of *Mary with the Red Ribbon*. Henri's own notes on the picture dwell on color; he describes the background as "warm dark brownish," the hair ribbons as "Red O," the apron as "soiled white," and Mary's water-blue eyes as "blue grey." The picture was painted in Ireland, where the Henris summered between 1924 and 1928.

Always encouraging students at the Art Students League to work with great speed – "have your energies alert, up and active" and "finish up as quickly as you can" – Henri increased this emphasis on quickness towards the end of his life to the point that he "could seize the expression of a child in a half-hour."

141

142

CHARLES SHEELER
American, 1881–1965

Yankee Clipper, 1939
Signed: Sheeler 1939.
Oil on canvas. 24 x 28

Jesse Metcalf Fund and Mary B.
Jackson Fund. 41.006

Provenance: Downtown Gallery, New
York

Publication: "Power: A Portfolio by
Charles Sheeler," *Fortune* Magazine,
December 1940, pp. 73–83.

Fortune Magazine commissioned the Museum's *Yankee Clipper* along with four other major paintings by Charles Sheeler for a portfolio on the theme of Power which appeared in the December 1940 issue. The magazine sent Sheeler all around the country to experience first-hand, and to make his own photographic studies of, the most up-to-date manifestations of "power." Sheeler ultimately painted a huge suspended propeller in a Tennessee River hydroelectric plant (private collection), a steam turbine at the Brooklyn-Edison power plant (The Butler Institute of American Art, Youngstown, Ohio), Boulder Dam in Colorado (collection of Mrs. John D. Rockefeller III), and locomotive engine wheels (Smith College Art Museum), as well as the RISD picture. The Museum's painting represents a cowled 1500-horsepower Wright Cyclone engine in the wing of a Boeing Yankee Clipper.

Christened by Eleanor Roosevelt in a widely publicized ceremony, March 3, 1939, this long-range "flying boat" was introduced by Pan Am for the first regular non-stop transatlantic passenger service.

The preface to *Fortune*'s portfolio reflected the interests of its high-level management audience, in particular a faith in technology and industry as the solution to the Great Depression:

"[Sheeler] shows [the instruments of power] for what they truly are: not strange, inhuman masses of material but exquisite manifestations of human reason. As the artists of the Renaissance reflected life by picturing the human body, so the modern American artist reflects life through engine forms such as these; forms that are more deeply human than the muscles of a torso because they trace the firm pattern of the human mind as it seeks to use co-operatively the limitless power of nature."

The commission for the Power portfolio was probably prompted by paintings Sheeler made from his own highly acclaimed photographs documenting Ford's River Rouge plant in Dearborn, Michigan (1927).

The relationship between Sheeler's paintings and photographs had become a close and unusual one over the course of the 1930's. On the one hand he belonged to the circle of avant-garde photographers connected with Alfred Steiglitz's 291 Gallery in New York, where his photographs were considered original works of art. Yet he often used the very same photographs as studies, though not exact models, for his "precisionist" paintings. Such a source in photography is suggested in the cropped and close-up view of the *Yankee Clipper.* The hard, clean edges and the finely graded tonal transitions, capturing the sheen of the metallic surfaces, reflect a photographic aesthetic as well. So does the stasis of the image in spite of the enormous potential motion of the propeller.

Duchampian everyday, non-art subjects, and above all, constructionist geometric order, also reinforced Sheeler's fascination with mechanical themes. He explained, "I had come to feel that a picture could have incorporated in it the structural design implied in abstraction and be presented in a wholly realistic manner."

143

JACKSON POLLOCK
American, 1913–1956

Magic Lantern, 1947
Signed lower center and on verso:
Pollock 47
Oil, oil based enamels, aluminum paint
and tacks. 43 1/16 x 21 7/8

Gift of Peggy Guggenheim. 54.005

Publication: Francis Valentine O'Connor
and Eugene Victor Thaw, eds., *Jackson
Pollock: A Catalogue Raisonné of Paintings,
Drawings and Other Works*, New Haven
and London, 1978, vol. I, no. 172.

Magic Lantern is one of the earliest of
Jackson Pollock's poured paintings. This
series, executed between 1947 and 1950,
is the most famous of the great mid-20th
century American paintings that established New York as the center of the
avant-garde for the first time. Labeled
Abstract Expressionism, the new
painting featured expansive, wall-scale
formats, gestural techniques, and new
surface emphasis achieved through
"fields" of color, or of graphic pattern
functioning as color in Pollock's case.
Other artists associated with the movement include Willem de Kooning,
Robert Motherwell, Barnett Newman,
Mark Rothko, and Clyfford Still.

Inspired initially by the automatist
drawing of surrealists André Masson
and Joan Miró and by Hans Hofmann's
experimental handling, Pollock began to
pour and spatter paint onto his canvases
in 1943. Only in 1947, however, in
paintings like *Magic Lantern* did he gain
the control of the technique that resulted
in his most highly original work. Pollock
activated the entire surface of the canvas
in a skein of looping and pulsing linear
configurations poured one on top of
another. Freed from any traditional
boundary function, the poured lines
constantly change direction and never
cluster enough to create a static or
graspable focus. In *Magic Lantern*,
Pollock dematerializes the image further
by introducing shimmering aluminum
paint.

That he was not yet wholly comfortable
with such pure opticality, however, is
suggested by the tacks he affixed to the
painting. Like the combs, buttons, keys
and even cigarettes found in other works
of 1947, these tactile accents permit a
reassuring, albeit contrived, physical
reading of surface. The paint itself in
Magic Lantern is denser, less penetrable
than the open skeins of later works.
Here the pourings are slow and thick,
appearing to bleed and even curdle at
points. Also striking is the rather
intimate size and vertical format of the
work in contrast to the wall-size, lateral
formats Pollock would increasingly
favor.

Magic Lantern was given to the
Museum by Peggy Guggenheim, who
helped launch Pollock's career during
the 1940's at her Art of This Century
Gallery in New York.

Color plate, page 76

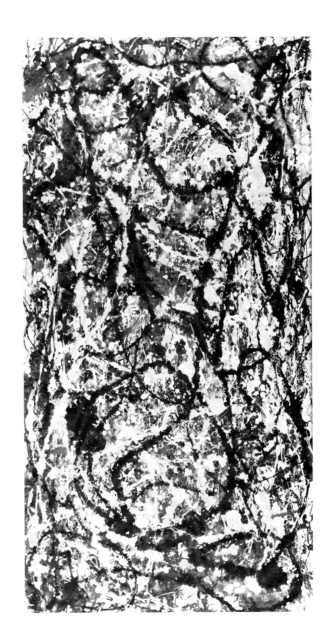

144

JOSEPH CORNELL
American, 1903–1972

Untitled (White Sand Fountain),
ca. 1949–1952
Signed on back: Joseph Cornell
Mixed media, glass, sand, wood.
12¼ x 8½ x 4⅝

Helen M. Danforth Fund. 81.006

Provenance: Family of the artist (?);
Allan Stone Gallery

Publications: Joseph Cornell papers,
Archives of American Art, Smithsonian
Institution, gift of Elizabeth C. Benton,
n.p.; *Museum Notes*, RISD, 1983, pp. 27–
28, ill.

Joseph Cornell was one of a small group
of American artists who exhibited with
the Surrealists. All of Cornell's work,
following the pivotal experience of Max
Ernst's Surrealist collage-novel, *La
Femme 100 têtes*, in 1931, can be tied to
Surrealist and Dada montage techniques
that developed unexpected or dis-
oriented juxtapositions. The box
construction, Cornell's best known and
almost exclusive art form during the
1940's and 1950's, relates especially to
Marcel Duchamp's Readymades and
Kurt Schwitters's Merz constructions,
both of which sometimes involved
boxes. The Cornell box reveals its
assembled contents to the viewer
through an open, often glassed front.
This proscenium, or stage-like means of
presentation, links the boxes to the cage
and game board constructions of
another Surrealist, Alberto Giacometti.
Like Giacometti's pieces, Cornell's boxes
are small enough to be object-like and
therefore to exist in the viewer's space,
yet they remain distinctly apart by virtue
of their framed quality.

Though Cornell concentrated on
evoking different states of mind, he
avoided the often brutal, nightmarish
content of Surrealism. Instead, fascinated
by the passage of time, he focused on
memory rather than dream. A sort of
Victorian nostalgia is reflected in many
of his found objects, which include star
charts, marbles, children's building
blocks, postage stamps, clay pipes,
stuffed birds, and reproductions of
works of art. These he assembled
according to certain recurring themes or
structures in his art such as soap bubble
sets, observatories, aviaries, dovecotes.

Cornell's reference to time is most
explicit in "sand fountains" like the
Museum's box. Not to be confused with
his related horizontal "sand boxes," the
upright sand fountains feature single
broken glasses filled and surrounded by
sand. Besides the obvious hourglass and
erosion associations, nostalgic details
such as the yellowed paper, weathered
wood, and blue tinted glass relate the
work to the *trompe-l'oeil* still lifes of 19th
century American bric-a-brac painted by
William Harnett and John Peto. The *Sand
Fountain* might also be considered a
modern parallel to the 17th century
Dutch *memento mori.* In this respect the
"poetry" of Cornell's sand fountains is
similar to certain aspects of Baroque or
Romantic works. On the other hand,
lacking the grotto-like encrustation,
seashells, and added objects that
complicate other works in this series, the
Museum's piece demonstrates a clarity
of structure characteristic of Cornell's
grid-like dovecote series.

Cornell himself must have appreciated
this unusually comprehensive expression
of his concerns. In the artist's notes from
June 13 and 14, 1952, he almost certainly
refers to the Museum's box since it is the
only sand fountain known so far that
contains a turquoise glass with a spiral
stem:

> ". . . listening to Brahms Violin
> Concerto – painting Colombier
> wooden balls – finding more broken
> glass fragments for sand fts. – the
> turquoise spiral one working out that
> day to a beautiful perfection – speedy,
> effective revision from stagnant
> materials . . . although better day than
> many with the turquoise glass sand ft.
> working out all in a day – revision of
> box done for 3 yrs. or so. Masterwork/
> Magnificent/Inspiration."

145

ELLSWORTH KELLY
American, b. 1923

Pole, 1957
Oil on canvas. 80 x 50½

The Albert Pilavin Collection of
20th Century American Art. 68.053

Provenance: Robert Fraser, London;
Parke-Bernet Galleries, Sale no. 2653,
Feb. 15, 1968, cat. no. 115

Publication: *Museum Notes,* RISD,
May 1969, pp. 21-23.

Ellsworth Kelly belongs to the "second
generation" of avant-garde American
painters, dubbed "post-painterly
abstractionists" by the critic Clement
Greenberg. Seeking to extend optical
sensations generated by the "color
fields" of Barnett Newman, Clyfford
Still, and Mark Rothko, artists of the late
1950's and 1960's reacted against the
distinctly personal, gestural application
of paint practiced by the Abstract
Expressionists. In order to isolate pure
color sensations, Kenneth Noland,
Morris Louis, and Jules Olitski down-
played the physical action of painting
and the physical texture of the paint
itself through various staining and
spraying techniques. Kelly, on the other
hand, developed an anonymous, almost
mechanical precision of contour and
unmodulated color, the most extreme
form of "hard-edge" abstraction
explored in varying degrees by Frank
Stella, Al Held and others. Cursive,
though hard-edged, delineation of large
areas of flat color reflects a European
link, specifically to Joseph Albers and
late Matisse, that distinguishes Kelly
from his American contemporaries.

Responding in part to the coloristic
flicker or "popping" occurring in Mondrian's grid structures, where black lines
intersect on a white ground, Kelly began
to conceive of black and white as color in
a series of paintings executed between
1954 and 1957. Like all of Kelly's abstrac-
tions, the black and white paintings
derive ultimately from the artist's experience of specific natural phenomena.
Kelly has described a bus ride on Staten
Island in 1954 when he was struck by
moving shadows falling across an open
paperback book on his lap. He traced
many of the shapes, later transcribing
them to a permanent sourcebook of
imagery for his paintings.

The title of the Museum's painting,
Pole, probably refers to the shadow of a
telephone or street light pole from the
bus ride. The diptych composition, a
constant in his black and white pictures
from this period, derives from the
bilateral symmetry of the paperback
source. Kelly even physically divided
some of the paintings, though not *Pole,*
into two separate canvas panels. The
bowed pages of the paperback surely
prompted the introduction of curves into
the series and into Kelly's art in general
following several years of severely
rectilinear abstraction.

Like most of the black and white
paintings, *Pole* is, in Kelly's words, a
"night" picture in which, contrary to
perceptual custom, white serves as
figure and black as ground. Capitalizing
on the tendencies of white to expand
and black to contract, Kelly makes the
two large, curving white shapes billow
out, seemingly smothering the black
between them and in the corners of the
picture. Typically, he establishes subtle
ambiguities that prohibit a straightforward reading of the image. Cut off
along the edges of the canvas, the white
shapes cannot be read as complete
figures. A similar catch is the single
straight vertical line which bisects the
upper edge, and which, because it sets
up a neutral relationship between black
and white, encourages a more traditional
reading of black as figure in this part of
the canvas.

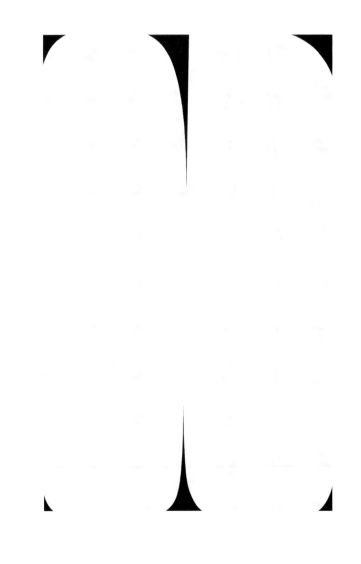

146

WAYNE THIEBAUD
American, b. 1920

Wimbledon Trophy, 1968
Signed lower left: Thiebaud, 68
Oil on canvas. 24 x 18⅛

The Albert Pilavin Collection of
20th Century American Art. 69.041

Provenance: Allan Stone Gallery, New
York

Publication: *Museum Notes,* RISD,
May 1969, pp. 39–42.

Wayne Thiebaud's *Wimbledon Trophy* was commissioned by a magazine under circumstances very similar to those surrounding the *Yankee Clipper* painted by Charles Sheeler for *Fortune. Sports Illustrated* sent Wayne Thiebaud to England to do a series of paintings on the Wimbledon tennis tournament. The Museum's *Trophy* appeared in the June 24, 1968 issue of the magazine with three other paintings: *Tennis Ball* (Richard Gangle, New York), *Outer Courts* (Allan Stone, New York), and *Girl Toweling Off* (Tony Bernuth Cook, Greenwich, Connecticut). In 1968–69, *Sports Illustrated* commissioned several such series from American and European artists with the choice of sport left up to the individual artist. Thiebaud selected tennis, a sport he played himself. Other series included Mel Ramos on surfing (March 17, 1969) and Richard Estes on hockey (November 3, 1969).

Thiebaud was associated with the Pop movement during the 1960's. Like many Pop artists, Thiebaud had trained commercially, and adopted techniques of commercial illustration in his own monumental art. He drew his well-known cafeteria display subjects from popular American culture. Richly impasted paint surfaces, however, situate the Northern California artist outside Pop and more directly in the San Francisco Bay Area tradition of Abstract Expressionist figurative painting. Begun by Richard Diebenkorn, David Park, and Elmer Bischoff in the early 1950's, this "painterly realism" has been continued by artists as diverse as Thiebaud and the ceramist Robert Arneson.

The emblematic *Wimbledon Trophy* demonstrates Thiebaud's bold and flattening illustrator's silhouetting and characteristically wide range of intense color accents. He describes the silver trophy and the Union Jack flag it rests on in the same "luscious," fatty paint impasto he developed to perfection in his paintings of frosted pastries. This touch reflects the ironic "Funk" attitudes toward sacred institutions and traditions pervasive in Northern California during the mid-1960's.

Color plate, page 76

147

CY TWOMBLY
American, b. 1929

Untitled, 1968
Signed on verso: Twombly '68
Oil and crayon on canvas. 79 x 103

The Albert Pilavin Collection of
20th Century American Art. 69.060

Provenance: Leo Castelli, New York

Publication: *Museum Notes*, RISD,
May 1969, pp. 42-45.

Though he may be considered a "second generation" American abstract painter, Cy Twombly responded to Abstract Expressionism very differently from his "post-painterly" contemporaries. Little interested in the "color field," Twombly focuses on drawing as a gestural process. He often marks out informal geometric figures including mathematical and linguistic symbols, which read as conceptual, though hermetic, "signs." Deployed in and against a painted ground, this "handwriting" fluctuates between elegant calligraphy and aggressive graffiti-like scrawling. The typically large scale of his canvases amplifies the physical and the ambiguous rhetorical dimensions of Twombly's work.

Around 1967 Twombly began to develop a dark palette of greens, blues, and greys, to which "blackboard" paintings like the Museum's work belong. He claimed that the resemblance of his pictures to blackboards was unintentional, and that he merely wished to devise a new kind of black and white painting. The apparent process of drawing, erasing, and redrawing generates richly complex value runs of grey. Twombly allows the white wax crayon that "masquerades as chalk" to mix with the dark grey oil ground and to drip down the canvas. Resulting irregularities of tactility and modulation in the painted surface spawn new drawing. This exploitation of accident recalls the work of the Swiss painter Paul Klee, as does Twombly's interest in extracting order from disorder and vice versa. Twombly's awareness of European art developed in Rome where he has lived and worked since 1957.

Drawn heart shapes such as those in the Museum's picture first appeared in Twombly's work in 1959. Sometimes indistinguishable from erotic scribblings of breasts and buttocks, the hearts generally evoke love associations in themes such as *Leda*. From 1967 to 1972 Twombly used hearts along with figure eights or infinity symbols, rhomboids and other secondary geometric shapes. Inspired by the drawings of Leonardo da Vinci, in particular the powerful *Deluge* series, Twombly became fascinated with the abstraction of motion during this period. While at least one painting (1967, Stephen Mazoh) emulates Leonardo's expressive, continuous spiraling quite directly, most of Twombly's work involves the discrete figures mentioned above. Generally, the more stable the figure, the more agitated the line defining it becomes. In the case of a painting at the Museum of Modern Art (1969), Twombly bends simple rectangles into arching planes, literally "throwing them into perspective." In the RISD picture the artist suggests motion more typically through the multiple superimpositions or redrawings of the hearts and their diagonal orientation.

148

148

ROBERT WILSON
American, b. 1941

Stalin Chairs, 1977
Lead draped over fiberglass armature.
33 x 61 x 61 (each)

The Albert Pilavin Collection of
20th Century American Art.
83.151.1–2

Provenance: Marian Goodman Gallery,
New York

Publication: *Museum Notes*, RISD,
1983, no. 2.

Robert Wilson has earned an international reputation as a theatrical
innovator, visual artist, video artist,
writer, and performer. His drawings
serve as storyboards or scripts for his
often non-verbal narrative theatrical
productions. Props designed for particular productions are sometimes later
translated into permanent materials to
become eloquent sculptural presences.

A pair of draped chairs appeared in
The Life and Times of Joseph Stalin, the 1973
opera which lasted 12 hours. Rather than
presenting a political or historical
situation, the production focused on the
single pivotal moment in the life of a
person, or Everyman. In this case, it was
the death of Stalin's first wife that
transformed him. In the middle of the
fourth act, the central moment of the
opera both in time and meaning, two
Stalins appear seated in draped chairs–
the character prior to the turning point
in his life and the new, changed man.
These cloth-draped stage props were the
genesis of the sculpture, *Stalin Chairs*.

Wilson chose to cover fiberglass forms
with sheets of lead because of the
material's ability to drape and fold. With
time the surface of the lead oxidizes into
a rich mottled patina. The brooding
quality of these objects, their anthropomorphic character, and their monumental presence express a narrative
content beyond that of ordinary
furniture.

149

149

WIFREDO LAM
Cuban, 1902–1982

Le Présent Eternel, 1944
Mixed media on jute. 85¹/₁₆ x 77

Nancy Sayles Day Collection of
Latin American Art. 66.154

Provenance: Patricia K. Matisse,
New York; Pierre Matisse Gallery,
New York, 1966

Publication: Patrick Waldberg, *Totems et
Tabous: Lam, Matta, Penalba*, Musée d'Art
Moderne de la Ville de Paris, Paris, 1968.

Le Présent Eternel provides an excellent
cross-section of the often overlooked
complexity in the painting of Wifredo
Lam. It was executed in the 1940's, a
period of great innovation for the artist,
when he painted the canvases that gave
him international recognition, such as
his best-known work, *The Jungle* (1943,
Museum of Modern Art, New York).

Lam was born in Cuba in 1902 and
exemplified the ethnic heterogeneity of
the island: he had Chinese, Spanish, and
African ancestry. In 1924 he left Cuba to
study art in Spain. He established an
acquaintance with Picasso in Paris
(1939–1940), and joined the Surrealists
just before the Nazi invasion of France.
From 1941 to 1952 he resettled in Cuba.

The often mentioned influence of
Picasso becomes evident in the spatial
organization and some formal configurations of *Le Présent Eternel*. The face of the
figure to the left, for example, appears to
derive from Picasso's horse-headed
creatures. Lam's primary and consistent
sources of inspiration were the Cuban
landscape and the Afro-Cuban cultures
he experienced "from within" in the
1940's. Afro-Cuban symbols were the
most obvious elements in his complex
perception of the primitive. In *Le Présent
Eternel*, the little head placed in a dish,
held by the central figure, represents
Eleguá, the God of Crossroads. The
hand and arrows on the upper right
corner, against a background of palm
leaves, stand for Shangó, God of Justice,
who hurls thunderbolts down to earth
from his natural habitat – the palm tree.
Several paintings and drawings of the
period 1942–1948 are also based on three
subjects, such as *The Wedding* or *La Noce*
(1947, National Galerie, Staatliche
Museen, West Berlin). The use of three
figures stems from Lam's interest in
Oriental philosophies: three stands for
Tao, the ultimate source of all things,
existing as the constant interaction
between the two complementary cosmic
forces – Yin and Yang.

A preparatory drawing for this painting, *La Belle Hélène*, is in the Helena
Benitez Collection, Saarbrücken.

150

FERNANDO BOTERO
Colombian, b. 1932

La Familia Pinzón, 1965
Oil on canvas. 68¾ x 68¾

Nancy Sayles Day Collection of
Latin American Art. 66.271

Provenance: The artist, 1966

Publications: Cynthia Jaffee McCabe,
Fernando Botero, Washington, D.C., 1979,
p. 100; Carter Ratcliff, *Botero*, New York,
1980, pp. 51, 59, 61, 64, 69.

Fernando Botero's art creates a world
where conventional form has gone awry;
where people and the environment they
inhabit, both natural and manmade, are
gigantic. Born in Colombia in 1932,
Botero studied art in Madrid at the
Academy San Fernando before traveling
to France and then on to Italy. While in
Italy, Botero studied the frescoes of
Giotto and Piero della Francesca, and the
canvases of Uccello and Masaccio. In
1960 Botero moved to New York City
where he lived until 1971; he currently
lives in Paris. Botero's rise to popularity
as an artist coincides with the Museum's
purchase of *La Familia Pinzón* in 1966, the
year of his first one-man museum exhibition at the Milwaukee Art Center.
Botero rapidly became an international
success and continues as a force in
contemporary realist painting.

La Familia Pinzón characterizes
Botero's wit, as he portrays the "typical"
mid-1960's urban Colombian family.
Though their ages may span 30 years, all
the members of this clan look alike,
including the trusty dog. They seem the
picture of health and prosperity in the
world Botero has created – full of
innocence and good will – and yet on
another level these caricatures become
disturbing, almost threatening, in their
grotesque fullness.

The Museum's painting holds an
important position in the development
of Botero's style. Considered to be his
earliest fully developed work, *La Familia
Pinzón* is the first work where all objects
in the composition successfully operate
in their own space. It is this self-
sufficiency of form that gives these
images a power and presence that is
Botero's hallmark.

Color plate, page 77

150

151

ITALIAN, Venice, 1499

Hypnerotomachia Poliphili
Book illustrated with woodcuts. 11½ x 8⅙ (book)

Museum Works of Art. 51.509

Publication: Joyce Nalewajk, *The Illustrated Book*, RISD, 1980, no. 38.

The *Hypnerotomachia Poliphili*, published by Aldus Manutius in 1499, is acclaimed by numerous critics as the epitome of the Renaissance illustrated book. The design of the book as a whole – its typography, woodcut illustrations, and general layout – reveals a harmony of proportion that characterizes the best artistic achievements of its age. The still-unattributed woodcuts, which the most recent scholarship places within the circle of Mantegna, have a clarity and refined beauty quite advanced for 15th century book illustration.

Since the introduction of printing in Italy in 1465, the printed book had met strong resistance from humanist circles, whose members tended to prefer the more precious art of illuminated manuscripts. Aldus Manutius made great progress in breaking down such prejudice by publishing scholarly, well-printed octavo editions of the classics which proved extremely popular. But whereas the Greek and Latin texts were gradually accepted in printed form, printed illustrations were still associated with vulgar, popular works.

The illustrations of the *Hypnerotomachia Poliphili*, depicting art objects and scenes from antiquity, used what was considered to be a "medieval" medium – the woodcut – to present classical subject matter. In the text, written by Francesco Colonna, the same sort of fusion occurs. Poliphilus, in quest of his beloved Polia, falls asleep and dreams of wandering through antiquity; classical subject matter is presented within the format of medieval romance. At its date of publication, the *Hypnerotomachia Poliphili* was viewed as a confrontation between the classical and the medieval, an awkward clashing of opposed forces, yet the book actually bridged the gap between classical and vernacular literature.

152

LUCA CAMBIASO
Italian, 1527–1585

The Descent from the Cross, ca. 1570
Pen and iron gall ink with brown wash;
traces of red chalk smudging on corners.
16½ x 11⁵⁄₁₆

Purchased and presented by Miss Ellen
D. Sharpe. 50.298

Provenance: Sir Peter Lely, London,
1618–80; Sir Robert Witt, London;
Matthiesen, London, 1950

Publication: Johnson/RISD, 1983, no. 4.

Luca Cambiaso, better known as a
draughtsman than as a painter, was
perhaps the most significant artist of
Genoa of the late 1500's. The greatest
period of his draughtsmanship occurred
at the end of his career when he evolved
the highly simplified, cubistic style
characteristic of the drawing illustrated
here. A powerful and rapid graphic
shorthand, it reflects the artist's use of
crude models made of clay or wax as
prototypes of abstract form. Revolutionary in the 16th century, it remains
modern to the 20th.

There are at least ten drawings of *The
Deposition* attributed with various
degrees of certainty to Cambiaso. All
have been linked to his painting of the
same subject (Church of S. Chiaro sopra
il Bisagno), though it is difficult to chart
their progression to the finished work.
One of these (Louvre) is nearly identical
to the RISD sheet in mood, moment, and
treatment. Upon closer examination,
however, this second work appears to be
a school piece, a repetition by the artist's
workshop of the RISD original.

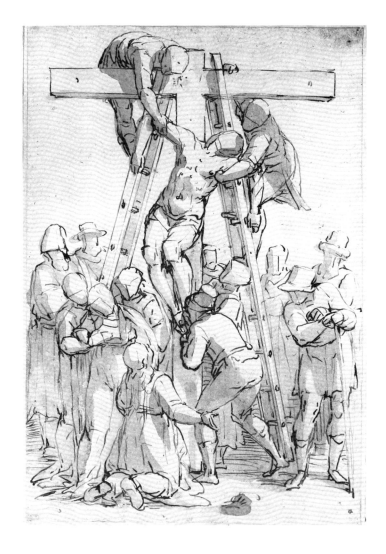

153

GIOVANNI BENEDETTO CASTIGLIONE
Italian, ca. 1600/10–1663/65

Christ on the Cross Adored by Angels, ca. 1650's
Brush and brown and red-brown paint with blue, white, and red touches on laid paper. 15 x 10⅜

Gift of Mr. Henry D. Sharpe. 50.300

Provenance: Colnaghi, London

Publication: Johnson/RISD, 1983, no. 11.

In addition to his status as a major exponent of the Baroque style in painting, Castiglione was an influential graphic artist during all phases of his varied career. A master technician, he was the virtual inventor of the monotype and the brush drawing. His brush drawings, like this work, reflect the influence of Rubens and Van Dyck, whose small oil sketches are said to have provided the inspiration for the technique. Castiglione is further credited with introducing Rembrandt's style,

particularly in printmaking, into Italy.

The example of Van Dyck may have dictated this depiction of the Crucifixion as a devotional image rather than an historical event. It became one of Castiglione's most popular compositions throughout the 1650's, generating numerous studio versions and copies, as well as the artist's own variations on the theme. Only one other known drawing (Windsor Castle) limits the composition to the crucified Christ and adoring angels. This suggests that they represent an early stage in the development of the iconography.

It was perhaps this newness of the subject in the artist's mind that accounts for the freshness and sincerity of the drawing. The intensity of religious feeling is characteristic of Castiglione's late work. So, too, is its direct communication through the nervous energy of his brushstrokes, making of the RISD drawing a moving personal image.

Color plate, page 78

154

GIOVANNI BATTISTA TIEPOLO
Italian, 1696–1770

Head of an Old Man
Inscribed on verso at bottom right in pen and brown ink: 1961 x rs; and in another hand in pencil: 443
Red chalk heightened with white on blue "Venezianer" paper. 9¼ x 7½

Museum Works of Art. 48.427

Provenance: Bossi-Beyerlen, Stuttgart, 1882; Dr. Hans Wendland, Lugano, 1927; Philip Hofer, Cambridge

Publication: Johnson/RISD, 1983, no. 18.

Of the approximately 1500 extant chalk drawings attributed to the Tiepolo family, many can be related to paintings, primarily by Giovanni Battista, before 1770. The greatest concentration appears to fall within the 1740's and 50's, and is largely associated with the great fresco cycles at the Scuola del Carmine and at Würzburg. Specifically, they represent

153

154

close, but not impeccable guides to that day's fresco work.

No painted piece has yet been found for which this drawing may have been a study. There can be no question, however, that it is the hand of Giambattista at work here. Both the sureness and firmness of outline and the fast pace and spontaneity of its placement on the page are hallmarks of the elder Tiepolo's style.

The close relationship of this head to other chalk studies confirms the attribution to Giambattista and, further, places it in the decade of the 1750's. It bears a particular similarity of type and technique to a series of three drawings of an old man's head seen from different angles in the Correr Museum, a *Head of an Old Man* in the Princeton Art Museum, and one at the Achenbach Foundation, all datable to this period.

155

FRANCISCO JOSE DE GOYA Y LUCIENTES
Spanish, 1746–1828

El Agarrotado (The Garroted Man), ca. 1778–1780
Etching and burnishing. 13 x 8½

Mary B. Jackson Fund. 81.041

Provenance: Ernest Brown and Phillips, London, 1919; Colnaghi, London, 1921; Museum of Fine Arts, Boston, from whom purchased

Publication: *Museum Notes*, RISD, 1981, p. 24.

Of the three greatest printmakers in the history of the medium, Dürer, Rembrandt, and Goya, the prints of Goya have been the most difficult to assess. This is primarily due to the relative rarity of sheets printed by him or under his supervision.

The RISD *Garroted Man* is a rare example of a work conceived and printed by Goya himself. After completing an apparently unique proof impression in blue (Metropolitan Museum), Goya printed a very small edition. Three other editions would follow, all posthumous: one in 1830, and two published by the Calcografia in Madrid in 1868 and 1928. The RISD sheet bears all the hallmarks of the first edition: a fine, clear, clean-wiped impression showing strong plate-polishing scratches in the unworked areas, on a heavy, absorbent, laid paper.

The *Garroted Man* is an early work, and has been called Goya's first major statement as an artist. Despite its considerable impact, the precise subject matter remains somewhat obscure. Strangulation by the garrot, an iron collar fastened around the neck, was considered the privilege of the nobleman convicted of a civil crime. It was said to be an easy, though slow, death. Goya's figure, his costume, context, and accoutrements, closely reflect period accounts of aristocratic executions by garroting. Questions of who the figure is and what his misdeed was remain unanswered. However, the profound sympathy with which Goya has drawn the figure ultimately speaks to broader issues of the great loneliness of death and the meaning of the pain man inflicts upon man.

A preparatory drawing for the print (British Museum) was transferred to the plate by tracing the design with a stylus, a procedure Goya would rarely use again.

155

156

JAN GOSSAERT called Mabuse
Flemish, 1478–1532

Adam and Eve, ca. 1525
Black chalk on two sheets of paper
joined horizontally; a large irregularly
shaped loss repaired at right. 22¾ x 30¾

Walter H. Kimball Fund. 48.425

Provenance: Acquired by the Albertina,
Vienna, 1908; reverted to Archduke
Friedrich after World War I; sold by
Archduke Friedrich to Viennese collector
Czeczowicka; sale, Vienna, May 12,
1930, lot 102; Oscar C. Bondy, Vienna; in
1938, Bondy's collection confiscated; in
1945, the drawing returned to Bondy's
widow, Mrs. Elizabeth Bondy, New
York; purchased from Mrs. Bondy in
1948

Publications: H. Schwarz, "Jan Gossaert's
Adam and Eve Drawings," *Gazette des
Beaux Arts*, VIᵉ Series, vol. 42, September
1953, pp. 157, 160–63, 166; Johnson/RISD,
1983, no. 72.

Dutch and German artists of the early
16th century introduced an interpretation
of the Temptation based explicitly on
carnal knowledge. It was, moreover, a
theme associated with the power of
woman over man symbolized by the
sexual act. Specifically, woman's nature
was seen as the more sensual, capable of
subverting the natural spirituality of
man to lust. The drawing illustrated here
is among the boldest and earliest representations of its kind in Renaissance art.

Gossaert was a pioneer of the Renaissance style in the North, and proponent
of the new Italian interest in the human
form. He produced nine Adam and Eve
drawings – out of a total extant drawing
oeuvre of 20 – in which this subject is
employed as a powerful vehicle of form.
The RISD drawing is close in style to a
painting of the same subject (Jagdschloss
Grünewald, Berlin) which appears to
date slightly later than the drawing, and
may, in fact, be a copy after a lost
original. It is likely the drawing served
as a *modello* to be submitted to a patron
for approval. It has also been suggested
as a study for a painting on glass, or
copy record of a painting about to leave
the artist's studio.

It is interesting to note that Gossaert
drew upon several earlier sources for his
design of the figures. Adam's lower
body is based on that of Adam in
Michelangelo's *Creation* on the Sistine
Ceiling, and on the ancient sculpture,
the *Spinario*. Eve's lower body is derived
from Dürer's engraving, the *St. John
Chrysostom*, and the serpent from a
Dürer woodcut of about 1505. Gossaert's
erotic approach to the theme was
anticipated, and probably inspired, by
Dürer's pupil, Hans Baldung Grien.

157

REMBRANDT HARMENSZ VAN RIJN
Dutch, 1606–1669

Landscape
Verso drawing of trees and plank fence. Pen and bistre ink, brown wash; black chalk on verso. 5¾ x 10¼

Jesse Metcalf and Mary B. Jackson Funds. 49.134

Provenance: Friedrich, August II of Saxony

Publication: Johnson/RISD, 1983, pp. 179–182.

There are many reasons why Rembrandt turned away from his imaginary, High Baroque landscapes of the 1630's to the more specific, even identifiable views of the countryside around Amsterdam in the 1640's and 1650's. Such landscapes became more and more popular throughout the Netherlands at the middle of the century; in fact, it was in the late 40's that the crucial transition was made to an emphasis on the most dramatic aspect of the Dutch landscape, the sky, in the work of Simon de Vlieger, Jan van de Cappelle, and Aelbert Cuyp. In addition, there was a vogue for Arcadian subjects in Holland and throughout Europe at this time – shepherds and shepherdesses (or young sophisticates dressed up as such) – a fashion that Rembrandt responds to, satirizes, and deepens in meaning and relevance. There was also an explosion of popular demand for the etching, a specialty of Rembrandt's and a medium beautifully suited to capturing the flat polderland, canals, and seascapes that characterize the country. Most importantly, perhaps, Rembrandt's interest in the Dutch landscape – high, flat, and broad – goes hand in hand with the "High Renaissance" transformation of his work after 1640, frontal, direct, and centralized.

In the RISD drawing, reminiscent of his etching from about 1650, *Landscape with a Milkman*, the pen gouges out the shore of the canal, the banks of the dike, the bridge, the farmhouse embedded among trees. This powerful simplification intensifies the emotional presence of the two men standing by the bridge and on top of the dike, like surveyor's markers defining the distance. As Egbert Haverkamp-Begemann has pointed out (Chicago, 1969), the drawing of the same scene in the British Museum (Benesch 832) may well have been executed a few years earlier; at the least, its softer forms, the almost tangible moisture in its atmosphere, are very different in character from this drawing and are closer to the chalk sketch on the verso, where the artist captures the fullness and softness of foliage in a copse of trees.

Rembrandt's quick definition of major forms, outlined in straight strokes of a broad-nibbed pen and filled in with splashes of brown wash, was soon popular among the members of his circle and characterizes the drawing styles of such prolific draughtsmen as Pieter de With, Philips Koninck, Roelandt Roghman, and Abraham Furnerius.

158

159

JOHN ROBERT COZENS
British, 1752–1799

*Lake Nemi with a Distant View of Genzano
and Monte Circeo*
Blue, green, and grey wash with pencil
underdrawing. 14⅝ x 20¹⁵⁄₁₆

Anonymous gift. 70.118.19

Provenance: Sotheby's, London,
February 1960; Fine Arts Society, London

Publication: Cormack/RISD, 1972, no. 21.

Cozens's scene of Lake Nemi typifies the
formula for the British travel view in the
late 18th century: it is Italian, it is large in
size, it is picturesque in the subtle
rendering of atmosphere and in the
careful framing and silhouetting of
components, and it is majestic and
monumental – especially in contrast to
the diminutive figures at middle ground.

The work also characterizes the transformations in watercolor painting by this
time. Throughout the 18th century, as
drawings became more collectible and
oil paintings more expensive, the watercolor began to usurp the place of the oil
on the Salon wall. As here, they grow
increasingly large in scale, concentrating
on broad effects rather than on detail or
the articulation of parts. In *Lake Nemi*,
drawing as such is minimal, and edge
and outline are de-emphasized. Instead,
Cozens's major concern is with tonality,
opacity, and soft atmospheric effects, the
usual province of oils. Although Cozens
occasionally experimented with the
bright colors and transparency that are
the inherent virtues of the watercolor
medium, his finished watercolors are
typically treated in this more conventional, oil-oriented manner.

158

RICHARD WILSON
British, 1714–1782

The Capucins at Genzano, 1754
Signed in crayon on border at lower left:
R. Wilson f. 1754; and in crayon at lower
right: No. 15; inscribed in ink at bottom
center: Capucins at Genzano
Black chalk and stump heightened with
white on faded blue paper. 11⁵⁄₁₆ x 16⅝

Anonymous gift. 70.118.60

Provenance: Earls of Dartmouth, by
family descent; Christie's, January 29,
1954; Agnew's, London

Publications: Cormack/RISD, 1972, no. 7;
H. Solkin, *Richard Wilson, The Landscape
of Reaction*, The Tate Gallery, London,
1982, no. 47.

The year 1969 marked the beginning of a
series of gifts from a single private
collection of English watercolors dating
from the late 17th through the 19th
centuries. The Museum's watercolors
from this donor range from topographical
views with their debt to the Dutch tradition to romanticized versions of the
landscape borrowed from Italian paintings, and from tightly controlled images
to naturalism and freedom of technique.
Virtually every major master of the
medium is represented in this superb
collection, one of the finest in the
country.

This drawing is one of a series Wilson
executed in Rome in 1754 for the second
Earl of Dartmouth. The most important
set of Wilson drawings known, there are
25 extant, and these were rediscovered
only in 1948 in a cupboard at Patshull
House. At least 43 others, however, had
been lost in the intervening century and
a half, since documentation at Dartmouth
places the original number at 68.

In a style that blends romantic atmosphere with topographical accuracy, the
drawing depicts Lake Nemi southeast of
Rome from the terrace of a Capuchin
monastery. In the background is the
Palazzo Cesarini, near the town of
Genzano, and the Mediterranean. It was
a view much beloved by English artists
and the RISD Museum possesses several
works, most notably by J. R. Cozens, of
similar scenes. Wilson himself produced
many versions, one an oil painting
executed in the 1760's (Metropolitan
Museum) and probably based on this
drawing.

A preliminary study for the right side
of the RISD work appears in Wilson's
sketchbook of 1754. Apparently, he
wanted to determine the placement of
the angled terrace in relation to the
distant buildings before beginning the
final design here; in the oil version, this
relationship is once again slightly shifted
to the right. It is likely that the RISD
sheet, too, was begun *in situ* as was
Wilson's wont, contributing to the light-
filled intensity of the scene.

JOSEPH MALLORD WILLIAM TURNER
British, 1775–1851

The Arch of Old Abbey, Evesham, 1793
Signed and dated in black ink in lower
left: W Turner. 1793
Blue and grey wash, watercolor, and
black ink over pencil on off-white paper.
8½ x 10¹⁵/₁₆

Anonymous gift. 69.154.60

Provenance: Mrs. Worthington Sale;
Montague Guest, 1910; C. Morland
Agnew; C. Gerald Agnew; Agnew's,
London

Publication: Cormack/RISD, 1972, no. 46.

Not yet 20 when he executed this
watercolor, Turner displays here his own
beginnings in the topographical
landscape tradition of Edward Dayes.
This is apparent not only in the care
given to accuracy and detail in the scene,
but in the way Turner uses the watercolor
medium: the delicate strokes depicting
the architecture and cloudy sky, the
monochrome underpainting and pale-
ness of the washes applied over it, and
the slanting light cutting across the arch
all reveal the influence of Dayes. Nonetheless, there is a good bit of Turner in it
as well. Although it suggests nothing of
the loosely painted and brightly colored
technique for which the artist became
known, the vigor with which the surface
is attacked, a certain crudeness about the
handling, and the interest in atmospheric
effect are quintessentially Turner.

This watercolor and a companion
piece were executed after drawings done
on the spot during the summer of 1793
in the vicinity of Hereford. Many of
these images were engraved for the
antiquarian study on Evesham published
by William Tindal in 1794. Despite the
fact that much of Turner's work was
destined for the engraver's plate at this
time, the RISD work was not among
them. Instead, the prototype used for
the Arch in the Evesham publication
seems to represent a move away from
topographical fact toward a more
personal, romantic, and mature vision:
space has been condensed, detail
generalized, and the arch contrasted
dramatically with the distant town in
size and handling.

159

160

161

161

THOMAS GIRTIN
British, 1775–1802

Valle Crucis Abbey, 1798–9
Signed in brown ink in lower left corner:
T. Girtin
Watercolor and brown ink over pencil on
cream paper, laid down. 6⅞ x 10¹³⁄₁₆

Anonymous gift. 71.153.5

Provenance: Ackland; G. W. Harvey-
Samuel; Fine Arts Society, London

Publications: Thomas Girtin and David
Loshak, *The Art of Thomas Girtin*,
London, 1954, p. 174; Cormack/RISD,
1972, no. 42.

The fragmentary depiction of the site in
this work makes it difficult to link
absolutely with Valle Crucis Abbey. The
Abbey appears frequently in Girtin's
work, the first time in 1793–4, reflecting
a predominant concern with topographical accuracy. In contrast, the series of
works to which the RISD drawing
probably belongs are more personal and
intimate. They were executed following
a trip to North Wales in the summer of
1798, where the artist made on-the-spot
sketches for them.

Despite the demeanor of the figure,
restricted foreground space, and use of
slanting light – all classical conventions –
the drawing strikes a clear note of
romantic solitude. Specifically, it relates
to work of J. R. Cozens, which Girtin
was then copying at the home of Dr.
Monro. Rich accents of color applied in
spots instead of strokes, the use of
architecture for atmosphere rather than
record, and even the handling of the
watercolor medium strongly suggest
Cozens. The emotional intensity of the
scene is Girtin's own, and characterizes
him as an early progenitor of the
Romantic movement in Britain.

162

162

THOMAS ROWLANDSON
British, 1756–1827

A Meeting of Cognoscenti
Pen and brown and black ink, watercolor
over pencil. 9⁵/₁₆ x 14¼

Gift of Mrs. Gustav Radeke. 20.504

Provenance: Dame Charlotte de Bathe

This drawing, formerly called *After Dinner*, has been retitled according to that of a nearly identical sheet recently on the London art market (present whereabouts unknown). The existence of two such exact drawings by Rowlandson is not uncommon: the artist was well known for copying his own works years after he had completed the original. As his *oeuvre* lacks a clear-cut stylistic development, it is difficult to determine which of these two works is the "original." It is abundantly clear, however, that the RISD drawing is the finer. Line is sure and firm here, color is of an extraordinary delicacy, a certain degree of clarifying detail is introduced, and the general effect is one of lightness and elegance.

Though independently wealthy, Rowlandson was the victim of a gambling habit, and frequently turned to the production of caricatures to support it. While this in part determined the great numbers of these works by his hand, they are rarely insincere, and have been both popular and memorable. This drawing depicts eleven periwigged gentlemen, each of dramatically different character, engaged in after-dinner conversation; some are bored, some impassioned, and some officious. Surrounding them are the trappings of 18th century aristocratic society, especially in the form of *objets d'art*. Even these are animate, and seem to mock the *cognoscenti* below. It is not with the bitterness of a Gillray, or the moral invective of a Daumier, however, that Rowlandson characterizes the scene. Instead, the tone is one of lively charm and gentle wit that distinguishes Rowlandson from his caricaturist colleagues.

163

WILLIAM BLAKE
British, 1757–1827

St. Paul Preaching at Athens, 1803
Signed in pen in lower left: Wm. B.,
1803.
Watercolor and pen. 18 x 12¼

Gift of the Estate of Mrs. Gustav Radeke.
31.280

Provenance: Thomas Butts; H. G. Bohn;
Mrs. de Putron; B. G. Windus

Publication: David Bindman, *William
Blake, His Art and Times*, New Haven,
1982, no. 75.

Thomas Butts was one of a very few lifetime patrons of the eccentric genius, William Blake. Beginning in 1799, he commissioned both paintings and watercolors from Blake with sources in the Bible and great literature. *St. Paul Preaching at Athens*, based on the Acts of the Apostles, is one of over 100 watercolors executed for an illustrated Bible planned by Butts. The drawing was delivered to him in 1803 with a letter from Blake in which the latter spoke of its "great forwardness" and his satisfaction with his "improvement."

Nevertheless, it is somewhat stiffer than most of Blake's work from this time, perhaps because it was a subject to which the artist was not naturally inclined. Commensurate with this is the hieratic composition in which St. Paul, raised upon a platform, addresses the viewer directly in strict frontality. Around him are reduced figures representing the generations of humanity – man, woman, young, old, troubled, trusting. From him emanate the rays of truth and enlightenment, illuminating each face in turn. In color, form, and gravity, the drawing relates to the great Early Christian manuscript pages much beloved by the artist.

163

164

GEORGE CHINNERY
British, 1774–1852

Sunset
Watercolor and ink. 4½ x 6½

Anonymous gift. 73.204.6

Provenance: Agnew's, London

Publication: *Museum Notes*, RISD, 1980, p. 28.

British artists not only developed the study of landscapes in watercolor as a separate genre but were the first to examine light and atmosphere in a sustained manner, an interest that was resumed in the 19th century by French artists. Many were the first to record distant and unknown territories. George Chinnery was fascinated by the exotic. He spent the greater part of his artistic career first in India from 1802 to 1825 and then in Canton and Macao until his death. *Sunset* dates from his Indian period. It is an intimate scene of a ruined temple with figures sitting or standing in water. Colors range from golden shades to mauves and browns with touches of brown ink. Chinnery has used a fluid, loose technique in the rendering of forms, and the pigment has been applied to wet paper, lending a subtlety to the contours. While his portraits in oil tend toward a flashy bravura, his watercolors, like this one, show a quiet sense of time and place.

165

PETER DE WINT
British, 1784–1849

The Lock Gate, ca. 1810–15
Watercolor and sepia over pencil. 11⁷⁄₁₆ x 18⅛

Anonymous gift. 70.118.26

Provenance: Fine Arts Society, London

Publication: Cormack/RISD, 1972, no. 68.

De Wint's style is characterized by an original sense of composition, lively, rapid technique, and brilliant *chiaroscuro* effects. Although his work is difficult to date, this drawing is tentatively ascribed to the period 1810–15, shortly after the artist became a student at the Royal Academy and an Associate of the Old

164

165

Water Colour Society. It shares with work of these years a particular feeling for mass and a certain crudity of touch.

If this work is, in fact, a product of this period, it anticipates the directness of vision – without classical convention or Romantic inflection – of early realist artists like Constable. The open gate, however, with the river placed at a sharp right angle to the picture plane, lends considerable tension to this otherwise realist image. A radical motif, it pulls the viewer's eye to the distant background where it meets only the wall of the river bank, a subtle, sunlit patch of watercolor pigment.

166

JOSEPH MALLORD WILLIAM TURNER
British, 1775–1851

Rainbow: Osterspey and Feltzen on the Rhine, ca. 1819–25
Signed in black ink in lower right:
J. M. W. Turner RAPP.
Blue and brown washes heightened with white on light brown paper, laid down.
7⅜ x 11½

Anonymous gift. 71.153.2

Provenance: W. B. Cooke, 1822; J. Slegg, 1823; B. G. Windus, Tottenham, 1852; A. C. Pilkington; Fine Arts Society, London

Publications: Cormack/RISD, 1972, no. 50; Galerie Nationale du Grand Palais, *J. M. W. Turner*, Paris, 1984, no. 139.

In 1817, Turner completed a trip along the Rhine during which he produced a large number of sketches. From these, 51 finished Rhine views were executed and presented to Turner's patron, Walter Fawkes, and 36 others were intended for use in a book on Rhine views between Cologne and Mainz. Although the book never came to fruition, Turner completed at least three of the images around 1819: *Ehrenbreitstein* (Bury Art Gallery & Fogg Art Museum), *Neuwied* (National Gallery of Scotland), and *Osterspey and Feltzen*.

As in the case of *Ehrenbreitstein*, however, there is a second view of *Osterspey and Feltzen* (Stanford University Museum of Art), making it unclear which work was actually intended for publication. It was not at all unusual for Turner, and other British artists of travel views, to produce multiple versions on commission, occasionally altering details according to whim or request. The RISD sheet, in fact, includes a dog in the foreground not found in the Stanford version. Both are dependent on a sketch in the British Museum which may be the original drawing done *in situ*.

The scene is characteristic of Turner's views both in watercolor and oil ca. 1819–25, in its emphasis on a low, widely-spreading design, picturesque detail picked out with the brush, and diminutive genre activity in the foreground. In terms of paint handling, it is likely that the RISD drawing is the later of the two. Its brighter color, more heavily worked surface, and greater variety of touch suggest a date closer to the concerns of 1825 than 1819.

Color plate, page 79

166

167

WILLIAM BLAKE
British, 1757–1827

The Book of Job, 1825
Book illustrated with 21 engravings,
artist's proofs. 17½ x 12 (book); 16¾ x
10¾ (plates)

Gift of Mrs. Jane Bradley in memory of
Charles Bradley. 22.298

Provenance: John Linnell, Plymouth,
England

Publication: Joyce Nalewajk, *The
Illustrated Book*, RISD, 1980, no. 47.

William Blake, poet, painter, and one of
the greatest original illustrators in both
technique and artistic conception, was
forced to earn his livelihood making
reproductive engravings for books. Even
in that venture he had financial difficulty:
his writings contain hostile remarks
about the great publishers of the time,
Boydell, Macklin and Bower, who
refused to supply sufficient commissions.
Despite his early influence on
Palmer, Calvert, and Linnell, it was not
until later in the century with Ruskin,
Rossetti, and the 1874 reprint of his *Book
of Job* that Blake's genius was fully
recognized.

   The Job theme had occupied Blake
since the 1790's, when he made an
engraving of Job and his friends.
Around 1818–20, he made a set of
watercolors illustrating the Book of Job
for his friend Thomas Butts, and another
for his artist friend John Linnell in 1821.
Linnell commissioned Blake to engrave
the book. The engravings date from 1823
to 1825, and the book was published in
1825 in an edition of 315 copies. Blake's
extended involvement with the writings
of the Old Testament, whose philosophy
was totally at odds with his own,
resulted in a book which qualifies for
Roger Chastel's definition: "One does
not illustrate a book, one extends it."

168

DAVID COX
British, 1783–1859

The Hayfield, 1833
Signed in ink in lower left corner: David
Cox, 1833
Watercolor. 13⅞ x 19⅞

Anonymous gift. 71.153.24

Provenance: John Platt; Mrs. G. P. St.
George, Ledsham Hall; Christie's,
London, 1946; Brigadier T. Robbins;
Christie's, London, 1946; Agnew's,
London, 1955

Publication: Cormack/RISD, 1972, no. 73.

The Hayfield was one of Cox's favorite
subjects, and many variations exist both
in watercolor and oil. Ours is particularly
close to one of 1832 now in the
Birmingham Museum and Art Gallery.
Both are entirely characteristic of Cox's
middle period when he had abandoned
a somewhat dry and conventional
manner in favor of a loose and "impressionistic"
technique. This style, as well
as an abiding interest in atmospheric
effects over form or structure, places him
in the forefront of these developments in
the 19th century, long before the French.

   A number of British artists were
exploring similar interests at about this
time, and none more systematically than
Turner. It is Constable, however, to
whom one should look for Cox's
primary influence in works such as
these. This is reflected not only in Cox's
choice and interpretation of subject, but
in his watercolor technique: an image
built up in bright colors by short,
flickering brushstrokes laid one on top of
the other, resulting in a remarkably fresh
and breezy picture.

Color plate, page 79

167

169

JOHN SELL COTMAN
British, 1782–1842

Rochester Castle
Watercolor in flour paste medium,
pencil, pen and red-brown ink. 8⅜ x
12⅛

Anonymous gift. 69.154.7

Provenance: J. P. Heseltine; Palser
Gallery; R. F. Goldschmidt; Sir George F.
Davies; Agnew's, London

Publication: Cormack/RISD, 1972, no. 87.

This drawing by Cotman is a relatively
late one, probably executed some time
around his final move to London in
1834. It describes Rochester Castle, with
Rochester Cathedral to the left. Cotman
is documented as having visited
Rochester in 1825 and 1839, though its
closeness to London would have
allowed a trip at any period. A very
similar work entitled *Castle on a Hill*
(whereabouts unknown) bears a date of
1830, and another variant (British
Museum) appears to date from the same
era.

As was common to so many British
watercolors of the early 19th century,
Rochester Castle is particularly interesting
for its experimental technique. The
vibrant colors result from a unique flour
paste medium the artist was making
around 1830, and again in 1835. Although
obviously more opaque than watercolor,
it still allowed the paper to show
through, and created a texture which
could be manipulated like oil paint.
Cotman frequently dragged a dry brush
through the tacky pigment to create a
patterned or speckled effect along otherwise broad passages. The flexibility of
this invention initiated a final period of
creativity in Cotman's work, bringing to
a close the somewhat formulaic quality
of his middle period with newly sensitive and imaginative landscape images.

168

169

170

SAMUEL PROUT
British, 1783–1852

St. Andrew's, Brunswick
Signed in ink in lower left: Prout
Watercolor with pen and ink. 16½ x 10½

Anonymous gift. 70.118.36

Provenance: Agnew's, London, 1958

Publication: Cormack/RISD, 1972, no. 113.

Formerly called a view of Cologne, Würzburg, or Braunschweig, this drawing can now be securely identified as Brunswick, with St. Andrew's Cathedral in the background. A preliminary version of the watercolor exists, in pencil (Fogg Art Museum), on which the artist has inscribed the location.

It is ironic that the work has defied correct identification, since, like most of Prout's work, it has been drawn with careful detail and great topographical accuracy. Prout was a virtuoso draughtsman, and like his compatriot Cox, produced a number of drawing manuals for beginners. It was this aspect of his *oeuvre* that also won the praise and approval of the influential critic, John Ruskin. Prout rarely tested his hand, however, at other than architectural drawings, and this work is an example of his particular love of medieval cityscapes. His characteristic broken touch is especially sympathetic to the rendering of these slightly crumbled structures, with figures added not for narrative, but to enhance the picturesque quality of the scene.

Prout's talent as a colorist has frequently been overlooked, though it is this that gives to *Brunswick* a lively sparkle and dynamic charm. The unmuddied, almost opaque clarity of color, not a usual feature of the watercolor medium, further places him in the mainstream of mid-19th century formal concerns. It was at this time that color took on primary importance to the creation of a work of art, and was often unrelated to mere descriptive function. Prout's use of a bright and intense palette links him closely to the British avant-garde of the 1850's, the Pre-Raphaelites.

171

SAMUEL JACKSON
British, 1794–1869

Entrance to Cheddar Cliffs, Somerset
Signed in ink in lower right corner:
S. Jackson
Watercolor, brown ink and blue wash.
9¼ x 7½

Anonymous gift. 71.153.30

Provenance: Walker's Galleries, London

Publication: Cormack/RISD, 1972, no. 94.

Along with William James Müller, Jackson was the founding member of the Bristol School, one of a number of regional centers of watercolor painting throughout England in the 18th and 19th centuries. These artists tended to concentrate their interests on the significant monuments of their home locale, and evolved pervasive regional styles relatively untouched by the first waves of modernism.

Characteristic of this, *Entrance to Cheddar Cliffs* combines the emphasis on subtly modulated blue washes of the 18th century with the hint of new

171

170

developments found in 19th century treatises on watercolor painting: in this case, the scrubbing and scratching of the finished surface that was most frequently recommended to expand the range of watercolor technique, as in David Cox's *Treatise on Landscape Painting and Effect* of 1813. Equally suggestive of Cox is the view of nature as a tamed presence in peaceful coexistance with humanity. Nonetheless, in the sheer cliffs which loom over the village is the suggestion of a more hostile vision, as seen in Jackson's great contemporary, Turner.

172

ROGER FENTON
British, 1819-1869

Still Life, ca. 1860
Albumen print. 17¼ x 21¾

Jesse Metcalf Fund. 80.097

Provenance: Daniel Wolf, New York

Publication: *Museum Notes,* RISD, 1981, p. 26.

Roger Fenton, a true pioneer in photography, probably became aware of the new medium very shortly after its invention, ca. 1839. Fenton's earliest successful work began in 1851, and was primarily documentary; his Crimean War photographs of 1855, the first extensive photographic documents of war, are the works by which he is best known. Upon his return from the Crimea, Fenton produced large-format prints intended mainly for exhibition or personal record; little of this work was marketed, and none was printed in great numbers. From this point until his abandonment of photography in 1862, scenes of the landscape and architecture of Great Britain, and to a lesser extent, still-life, dominated his work.

The RISD photograph seems to date from about 1860, and is one of the most ambitious of Fenton's relatively rare still lifes; this particular image may, in fact, be unique. Contemporary photography, especially in England, was alternately influencing and being influenced by late Romantic painting. Fenton's picture, with its languid lines and slightly funereal associations, partakes of this moody milieu. Specifically, his balanced and classicizing composition and acute concern for texture share striking affinities with French still-life painters of the 1840's, especially Philippe Rousseau. Interestingly, Rousseau was an early enthusiast of photography and a member of the Société française de Photographie.

172

173

EDWARD LEAR
British, 1812-1888

Garf Harbor, Malta, 1866
Inscribed in brown ink in lower right:
Rocks near Garf Hasan./Malta/10-11-am./
30 Jany 1866; pen notations in English &
Greek throughout; numbered in black
ink in lower right: (37)
Pen, red-brown ink, watercolor, and
body color heightened with white on
buff paper. 15 x 21¹/₁₆

Anonymous gift. 69.154.57

Provenance: Agnew's, London

Publication: Cormack/RISD, 1972, no.
118.

The second half of the 1860's saw Lear in
various parts of the Continent, including
Rome, Corfu, southern France, Egypt,
and Malta. Plagued by illness – especially
respiratory ailments – since childhood,
Lear took to his trips not only in the
service of the British travel view, but to
improve his health in dry, warm
climates.

Lear had been in Malta in 1862, and
again in December 1865–April 1866,
where he executed this drawing.
According to his notations directly on
the work, it was set down in an hour.
Lear was a master of the quick, on-the-
spot sketch, to be completed later in the
studio; in fact, most of his drawings, like
this one, bear color inscriptions to guide
the artist in his subsequent re-workings.
As a result, much of his work combines
an uncanny and refreshing spontaneity
suggesting a momentary impression –
very important to Lear and to the 19th
century in general – with the reflective,
timeless quality of a studio piece.

There is more at work here, however.
In 1850, at the age of 38 and burdened by
a feeling of inadequacy, Lear decided to
enter the Royal Academy School as a
pupil. In addition, he apprenticed
himself to the Pre-Raphaelite painter
Holman Hunt in order to learn "serious"
painting in the form of oil technique.
Besides his own keen eye for transient
atmospheric effects, *Garf Harbor* reflects
the bold composition and careful detail
espoused by the Pre-Raphaelites and
their champion, Ruskin. Ruskin would
never have approved of a final influence
on Lear's vision: the dramatic chiaroscuro
contrasts, without mediating half-tone,
of photography, which inevitably
affected most late 19th century travel
views.

174

JULIA MARGARET CAMERON
British (b. India), 1815–1879

The Astronomer (Sir John Herschel), 1867
Albumen print. 13¾ x 10⅜

Bequest of Lyra Brown Nickerson,
by exchange. 82.008

Provenance: Daniel Wolf, New York

Publication: *Museum Notes,* RISD, 1982,
p. 35.

"My revered, beloved friend said of this
portrait that it was the finest he had ever
beheld, that it beat hollow everything he
had ever seen in photography." So
wrote Julia Margaret Cameron on a close
variant of this composition, quoting her
"beloved friend" of 33 years and subject
of these portraits, Sir John Herschel
(1792–1871). Herschel had, in fact, introduced Cameron to photography shortly
after its invention in 1839, and contributed invaluably to its development; this
included the critical discovery of photographic fixative, sodium thiosulfite
("hypo"), the invention of the cyanotype
(blueprint), and even the coining of
much of the technical language of
photography. Cameron herself did not
turn to photography until 1863, at the
age of 48, but in the 15 years until her
death, produced an enormous body of
work that is remarkable in its modernity
and power, and which changed the
course of photography.

The Herschel portraits were produced
in Collingwood, the subject's home, in
April 1867, at the photographer's
request. While it seems likely that
several exposures were made at this
time, only three others in addition to
this one have been located. The series
comprises Cameron's most successful
and best-known works, which remain
among the most remarkable portraits in
the history of the art. It is this image that
is, perhaps, the most otherworldly of the
four, emphasizing through manipula-
tions of light Herschel's ghostly countenance. Swathed in shadow, eyes
turned heavenward and barely registered
on film, Herschel's head reminds us of
Cameron's reference to him as her "high
priest," and symbolizes his own activities as an astronomer.

173

175

SIR EDWARD COLEY BURNE-JONES
British, 1833–1898

The Four Prophets, ca. 1877
Pencil. 5 x 16 (each panel)

Gift of Mrs. Gustav Radeke. 20.244

It has recently been confirmed that
Burne-Jones's drawings of *The Four
Prophets* – Isaiah, Jeremiah, Ezekiel, and
Daniel – are cartoons for stained glass,
specifically the figures of the Prophets in
the north wall at the west end of Jesus
College Chapel, Cambridge, executed in
1877. This was a significant commission
for Burne-Jones, including several other
glass panels for figures from the Old and
New Testaments.

Burne-Jones himself acknowledged
that he felt more comfortable in the
preparation of applied or decorative art
than he did at his easel. Stained glass
cartoons were among the very first
works he produced, and in fact, the first
commission he obtained, in 1857. At this
point he was a religious man, having
studied church history since the age of
16 and theology at Oxford with the
intention of becoming a clergyman.
Although he would finally consider
himself an agnostic, a scholarly understanding of the Bible and a love of
medieval art remained with him
throughout his life.

The rigid frontality of these figures,
broken only by a single bent knee, and
their richly articulated robes reflect his
familiarity with High Gothic cathedral
sculpture. This is married in the fluidity
of line, treatment of facial type, and
developed musculature to another
critical influence on Burne-Jones's
oeuvre: the 15th century Italian artists,
most notably Botticelli. Despite the
obvious impact of these periods, Burne-
Jones evolved his own unique style,
characterized by virtuoso draughtsmanship and an exquisite, almost effeminate
gentleness of mood. This tends to
characterize equally the important group
of avant-garde artists which he helped to
found, the Pre-Raphaelite Brotherhood,
so named for the Italian primitives.
Burne-Jones's later work, however, such
as this drawing, reflects a hardening of
the typically flowing Pre-Raphaelite line
and attenuated handling of the Pre-
Raphaelite type.

174

175

176

176

NICOLAS POUSSIN
French, 1594–1665

Moses Driving the Shepherds from the Well,
ca. 1647
Pen and brown ink, brown wash over
traces of black chalk on discolored white
paper, laid down. 6½ x 6⅜

Anonymous gift. 59.020

Provenance: Guillaume Hubert (?),
Paris; Thomas Hudson, London; Sir
Thomas Lawrence, London; Marquis
Philippe de Chennevières, Paris and
Bellevue; Teodor de Wyzewa, Paris;
Hôtel Drouot, February 21–22, 1919,
Paris; Maurice Marignane, Paris; H. M.
Calmann

Publication: Johnson/RISD, 1983, no. 33.

This Poussin drawing is one of several
preparatory studies for the now-
destroyed painting of *Moses Driving the
Shepherds from the Well.* It treats a passage
in the life of Moses from Exodus 11:16,
and would ultimately appear – with
alterations – in the right half of the final
composition. Here, Moses is shown
dominating a triangular configuration of
three figures in a frozen but dynamic
pinwheel effect.

In evolving the figures in this group,
Poussin had recourse to many of his
favorite motifs from earlier art. The most
direct are found in Poussin's beloved
Roman reliefs and Raphael: scenes from
the column of Trajan for the figure of
Moses and the falling shepherd, and the
nearly trampled soldier in Raphael's
Expulsion of Heliodorus for the prostrate
figure beneath Moses's legs. Each of
these figures is also found in the variety
of studies for Poussin's paintings of *The
Rape of the Sabines* of ca. 1633–37, themselves traceable to Giovanni da Bologna's
sculpture of the same subject. They thus
serve as a valuable tool for dating for the
second half of Poussin's career. Further
thematic and formal references to works
of the 1640's such as *Rebecca and Eliezer at
the Well* and *The Finding of Moses* point to
a date in the mid-40's, and this coincides
with our understanding of Poussin's
drawing technique at this period.

Interestingly, a finished drawing of
the entire composition exists, of uncertain attribution (Windsor Castle), with
the RISD group represented unchanged.
It is possible that it was produced by a
member of Poussin's studio from
separate studies such as this, pieced
together to form a whole.

177

177

HUBERT ROBERT
French, 1733–1808

Antique Ruins With Figures
Pen and black ink, brown ink, brown and black washes over graphite with touches of watercolor, heightened with white. 22⅜ x 28⁹⁄₁₆

Museum Appropriation. 38.152

Provenance: Acquired by exchange from Richard S. Owen, Paris

Publication: Johnson/RISD, 1983, no. 46.

Robert's pen and wash studies are largely architectural *capricci*, scenes in which disparate and sometimes imaginary monuments are brought together in unique combinations. Robert became the most important artist working in this genre, one largely circumscribed within the 18th century and a characteristic taste of the period. The RISD work unites fragments of monumental Greek and Egyptian architecture and artifacts. None of these can be identified, and are comminglings of Robert's imagination with actual memories of his stay in Italy. The great scale of this sheet indicates that it was intended to hang like an easel painting on a collector's wall.

It is difficult to assign a precise meaning to the work, and particularly to the prominence of the startled figures in the foreground and the snake. The associations summoned up by this group are clear enough: the youth and beauty of the trio of figures vs. the snake as the Christian symbol of evil and temptation and ancient symbol of death. It is primarily, however, the topical rediscovery of decaying remnants of ancient civilizations by new ones that Robert hoped to suggest.

The RISD drawing was probably executed sometime between Robert's return to France from Italy in 1765, and 1778, the date after which his drawing production decreased. Two other drawings can be related to it: one (in the Metropolitan Museum) is similar in intention, size, medium, and feeling; the other (whereabouts unknown) is a small-scale duplicate with all the hallmarks of a first thought, thereby suggesting that Robert used earlier studies in the creation of these impressive and ambitious works.

178

JEAN-AUGUSTE-DOMINIQUE INGRES
French, 1780–1867

Portrait of Thomas-Charles Naudet, 1806
Signed in pencil at right: Ingres fecit/in Roma/.1806
Pencil on cream-colored wove paper. 9½ x 7

Museum Appropriation. 29.087

Provenance: Thomas Charles Naudet; Naudet family; Hôtel Drouot, Paris, March 9, 1918, no. 181; Henry Lapauze; Hôtel Drouot, Paris, June 21, 1929, no. 20; to Martin Birnbaum for the Museum

Publication: Champa/RISD, 1975, no. 42.

This drawing represents the landscape painter Thomas-Charles Naudet (1773–1810) during his residence in Rome in 1806. Naudet had recently become fast friends with Ingres, also arrived in Rome in 1806. It has been said that Ingres executed this portrait for Naudet to thank him for carrying to Paris certain of Ingres's works.

Although a youthful work – Ingres was still a student – the *Naudet* constitutes the typical and consummate formula for Ingres's portrait drawings. Naudet is presented in a presumably characteristic pose, pencil in hand and sketchpad balanced on his knee. He is affectionately characterized as a bit of a *galante*, dashing, attractive, with a rather amused expression on his face. Ingres is also attentive to the details of Naudet's apparel, from the stand-up collar to the tassels on his boots. Form is realized in a continuous hermetic contour. Ingres heightens this effect by contrast in the whisper-thin touches used to suggest a setting of hummock and grass, and with incredibly subtle tonal variations throughout. An engraving of the work exists by Caroline Naudet, dated 1808, clearly indicating the sitter's justified respect for Ingres's genius here.

178

179

JEAN-AUGUSTE-DOMINIQUE INGRES
French, 1780-1867

Portrait of an Ecclesiastic, Cardinal de Latil,
ca. 1825–27
Signed in pencil in lower left corner:
Ingres Del.
Pencil heightened with white on white
paper, now yellowed. 12¾ x 9½

Gift of Mrs. Murray S. Danforth. 42.073

Provenance: Jean-Léon Gérôme until
1904; Mme. Gérôme

Publication: Champa/RISD, 1975, no. 43.

Jean-Baptiste-Marie-Ann-Antoine de
Latil (1761–1839) was Bishop of Amyclée
(1816), Chartres (1821), Archbishop of
Rheims (1824), and finally, Cardinal
(1826). On the occasion of Latil's conse-
cration of Charles X at Rheims in 1825,
Ingres was commissioned to make
portraits of both, as well as a frontispiece,
to be engraved for a commemorative
publication. The definitive drawing in
wash for the portrait of Latil is now in
the Louvre. Other studies for the
portrait are at Montauban and at
Angers.

In beginning his portrait, Ingres seems
to have resurrected his earlier etching
(1816) of Monseigneur Gabriel Cortois de
Pressigny (1745–1823), Bishop of
Besançon. The three-quarter length
representation of Latil, with his biretta
clutched by the fingers of his left hand
and papers in his right, standing in front
of a table, is identical to the portraits of
Pressigny. So, too, is the episcopal garb
– collar, mantle, gown and pectoral
cross. In fact, this drawing was once
thought to be a portrait of Pressigny, but
subsequent research based on style and
comparisons with other Latil portraits
rules this out. Though Ingres's interpretation of Latil is predictably lively and
sensitive, its closeness to others of his
type is indicative of the portrait formulae
Ingres evolved. A certain remoteness
about the figure of Latil confirms this,
and indicates an official portrait
commission.

180

J.B. GUSTAVE LE GRAY
French, 1820–1882

Ships Leaving Harbor (Napoleon III's Fleet
at Le Havre?), ca. 1856–1857
Albumen print. 12¼ 15⅞

Bequest of Lyra Brown Nickerson, by
exchange. 83.035

Provenance: Janet Lehr, New York

Publication: *Museum Notes,* RISD, 1982,
p. 32.

Gustave Le Gray is among the most
accomplished and elusive figures in the
history of early photography. Like
several other early photographers, he
began his artistic career as a painter in
the studio of Paul Delaroche. By 1848,
eight years after the announcement of
the discovery of photography, he
abandoned his brushes to open a photographic portrait studio in Paris. Attracted
specifically to the complex and manipula-
tive potential of photographic chemistry,
he became one of its most brilliant
students. At a time when the sharply-
detailed glass plate negative and mirror-
surfaced daguerreotype were at their
height, he believed that the future of
photography lay with paper. Inexplica-
bly, Le Gray left Paris for Egypt around
1859, and was last heard from as a
photographer in the World's Fair in
London (1862) and Paris (1867).

The Museum's photograph is a rare
and stunning example of the seascapes
for which Le Gray is best known.
According to Eugenia Parry Janis, these
were executed between 1856 and 1859
along the Normandy and Mediterranean
coasts, and number only between 20 and
30 single images, a minute percentage of
Le Gray's total *oeuvre.* Janis has suggested
that ours captures a send-off given a
fleet of Napoleon III's ships at the harbor
of Le Havre. This would place it early in
this period, when Le Gray is recorded at
the port in 1856–7. More than this,
however, it is a romantic and vital
analogue of the ocean, etched out of the
forms created by intense contrasts of

179

light and dark, bathed throughout in the artist's characteristic rich brown tones, and rhythmically dotted by the passage of ships past the jetty out to sea. It is possible that there are only two other printings of this image, one in a private collection in New York, the other in Paris. This underscores the rarity of much early photography, not fully exploited as a reproducible medium until the 1860's when expanded patronage and improved technology made it feasible.

181

NADAR (Gaspard-Félix Tournachon)
French, 1820-1910

Death-Bed Portrait (the Russian Countess Shuvalov?), 1861
Nadar's red rubber stamp on image in lower right corner; dated 1861 on silver plaque on front of case
Albumen print in ebony case with silver hinges and hardware. 8⅝ x 7⅛ (image); 17⅛ x 15 x 2 (case)

Bequest of Lyra Brown Nickerson, by exchange. 82.009

Provenance: Ken and Jenny Jacobsen, Great Bardfield, England

Publication: *Museum Notes,* RISD, 1982, p. 34.

Nadar – journalist, caricaturist, and aeronaut – opened his photographic portrait studio in Paris in 1853. By the end of the decade, it had attracted virtually the entire artistic and political intelligentsia of Second Empire France, and it is these images by which Nadar is best known.

It is the intense examination of the human spirit at its most critical moment, death, that is the underlying subject of the Museum's portrait, presumed to be of the Russian Countess Shuvalov. In the early years of photography, the death-bed portrait was a widely-practiced genre, the final opportunity to capture the likeness of a loved one, and a dramatic conclusion to the long artistic tradition of *memento mori.* It was, in addition, much more than this: the portrait was not infrequently rubbed or stored with the ashes of the deceased, a powerful testimony to the belief in the magical and shamanistic potential of photography at the moment of its invention. In our portrait, Nadar has adjusted his usual dramatic style to create an image of great gentleness: edges are registered out-of-focus, details softened, and stark light-dark contrasts all but eliminated. Focus is steadily fixed upon the Countess's head as she contemplates the cross weighting her chest; she awaits death, eyes half-lowered, in total, but peaceful, resignation. Perhaps the death of the artist's own adored mother only the year before, leaving him devastated and desolate for some years to come, was a factor in the making of this moving image of aged womanhood.

180

181

EDOUARD MANET
French, 1832-1883

Mlle V. in the Costume of an Espada, 1862
Signed in watercolor in lower right
corner: Manet
Pencil, ink, and watercolor on tracing (?)
paper, laid down. 11⅞ x 8¹⁵⁄₁₆

Gift of Mrs. Gustav Radeke. 21.483

Provenance: Dr. Gustav Radeke,
Providence

Publications: Champa/RISD, 1975,
no. 47; Metropolitan Museum of Art
(and others), *Manet*, New York, 1983,
no. 34.

Mlle V. represents Manet's favorite
model in the 1860's, Victorine Meurent,
dressed as a bullfighter. Drawn after the
painting of the same subject (Metropolitan Museum of Art, New York), it was
made in apparent preparation for an
etching published in October 1862. The
reticence of subject matter here is characteristic of Manet, for whom subject was
used largely as a vehicle for virtuoso
passages of color and brushwork.
Equally characteristic is the borrowing of
motifs from works by other artists, in
this case from Goya's *Tauromaquia* series,
for Manet's background figures.

The precision with which many details
of the oil are reproduced suggests that
the preliminary pencil drawing underlying the watercolor was traced from a
photograph, or with the aid of an optical
device. Since the direction of the initial
pencil hatching runs counter to Manet's
usual stroke, it is possible that the
tracing was executed on the reverse side
of the paper. On one hand, this would
allow for the ultimate righting of the
image if the watercolor were then used
in the etching process; in fact, the
surface of the drawing seems to bear the
incised contours of the tracing stylus as
Manet transferred his drawing directly
onto the copper plate. On the other
hand, by obscuring the initial tracing
Manet was freer to deviate from it in the
watercolor phase. To be sure, the
watercolor deviates considerably from
the oil, most noticeably in its abandonment of hue and value contrast. More
importantly, however, Manet extends
and rationalizes the very idiosyncratic
spatial construction of the oil.

183

HONORE DAUMIER
French, 1808–1879

Don Quixote and Sancho Panza, ca 1865–67
Signed in ink in lower left corner: h. Daumier
Watercolor, pen and ink, and crayon on white paper. 5⅝ x 10¾

Gift of Mrs. Murray S. Danforth. 42.208

Provenance: Van der Hoewen; Blot, Paris; Bernheim Jeune et Cie, Paris; Knoedler, New York; Harald Lettström, Stockholm; César de Hauke, New York

Publication: Champa/RISD, 1975, no. 9.

No theme recurs in Daumier's artistic production with more frequency than that of Don Quixote and Sancho Panza. Cervantes's novel remained the artist's most beloved book, and throughout his life, he read from it often. It is difficult to determine the specific reasons for its appeal to Daumier. It was, however, a popular subject throughout the century, appearing as a symbol of the libertarian-humanitarian political milieu of which Daumier was a part. It is equally tempting to read into its characters Daumier's recognition of self in their humility, and idealism triumphant over cynicism.

The Providence sheet is almost identical in format to two other watercolors (Lemaire Collection, Paris, and the de Schauensee Collection, Pennsylvania) and an unfinished oil (anonymous collection, Zurich). In addition, a fourth work – a charcoal and wash drawing in the Metropolitan Museum – has been cited as an initial exploration toward the Providence watercolor. The Providence and Lemaire compositions are almost exactly the same size and are identical in format. Such nearly exact repetitions are not uncommon in Daumier's *oeuvre*. Particularly in the 1860's when he received little income from lithographic work, the artist frequently made several finished versions of a subject in hopes of selling them. The Providence version was probably regarded as the definitive one by the artist, as it is the only one signed in full, and his intention to sell it explains its relatively high degree of finish.

The repetitions were facilitated by means of a tracing process, though each replica differed in subtle yet definite ways from the original version. Only the basic outlines were traced, and the details of form then freely filled in. This is apparent in the Providence work, particularly in the figure of Sancho, which, rather than a rote imitation, bears the evidence of repeated reworkings and scrapings. Appropriate to the iconography, this figure in general is treated much more heavily in line and tone than that of the Don. As both move into the barren landscape, Sancho is heavy and immutable on his plodding mule, while the wiry Quixote bends forward with nervous energy on his equally lively mount, Rosinante.

184

EDGAR DEGAS
French, 1834–1917

Dancer with a Bouquet, ca. 1877–1880
Signed in pastel in lower left corner:
Degas
Pastel and black chalk over monotype,
and gouache on paper. 15⅞ x 19⅞ (2½
strip added to bottom)

Gift of Mrs. Murray S. Danforth. 42.213

Provenance: Durand-Ruel, Paris; Prince
de Wagram, Paris

Publications: Champa/RISD, 1975, no. 13;
Museum Notes, RISD, 1981, pp. 28–31.

Degas became fascinated with the ballet
as a subject for his work around 1872,
and it is this theme that we most closely
associate with his work. As with the
racecourse, the second most prominent
theme in Degas's work, the ballet was a
vehicle through which the artist could
investigate the phenomena of suspended
motion and constrained form. In addition, the theater provided the opportunity for unusual vistas that lent
themselves to unique compositions and

dramatic lighting effects. Each of these
factors is at work here, as the spectator
occupies a space in the opera box behind
the woman with the fan.

Technically, this is one of Degas's
most experimental works. It began as a
monotype, frequently employed as a
base for his pastels during the period
1874–93. His use of the monotype base
has been convincingly explained as a
means to loosen his hand and predeter-
mine a sketchlike freshness in the
finished work, a direction in which he
was not automatically inclined. It was,
as well, a convenient way of laying into
the composition a basic range of light
and dark tones much the way the old
masters had in underpainting, and as
Degas himself had been taught to
compose. As here, his typical procedure
in this process was the printing of a
strong, pure monotype impression – a
proof as it were (Frelinghuysen Collection) – followed by a faintly printed,
thickly pastelled work represented by
the *Dancer with a Bouquet*. Then, a
counterproof was taken of the first
impression (whereabouts unknown; see
Lemoisne, *Degas et son oeuvre*, Paris,
1946, number 515 bis), on which a trial
run of the pastel overdrawing was
made.

Upon completion of the monotype
here, Degas reworked the impression
with chalks and constructed the setting,
including the *corps* of dancers behind.
He may have planned the spectator
figure from the start, leaving wide and
uneven margins around the monotype
base, though some time elapsed before
her introduction into the composition.
This motif had been "tested" shortly
after the printing of the *Dancer's* base in
a monotype entitled *The Jet Earring*, and
the entire motif, with the open fan, in a
lithograph of ca. 1880, *Woman with a Fan*.
The latter also included an extended
foreground, whose success probably
encouraged Degas to add the 2½" strip
to the bottom margin of his drawing.

Degas's compulsive alterations to his
own images, sometimes over a period of
decades, is legend. *Dancer* appears to
have been in process, from the first
printing of the monotype to the attached
bottom strip, from ca. 1877 to ca. 1880.
Nonetheless, the work betrays nothing
of its lengthy permutations, remaining,
instead, an image of the perfectly
captured instant.

Color plate, page 80

185

EDGAR DEGAS
French, 1834–1917

Before the Race, ca. 1879
Signed in pastel in lower right corner:
Degas
Pastel, gouache, and black chalk on
cardboard. 22¼ x 25¾

Gift of Mrs. Murray S. Danforth. 42.214

Provenance: Mme. Montandon, Paris;
Hector Brame, Paris; César de Hauke,
New York

Publication: Champa/RISD, 1975, no. 14.

The racetrack as a subject intermittently occupied Degas's attention during most of his mature life as an artist. It provided him with a ready opportunity to study the interaction of form and movement, a primary pictorial concern throughout his career. Like his canvases of dancers, those of the races represent the artist's interest in capturing the suggestive patterns of arrested motion. In *Before the Race*, this interest results in the momentarily frozen movements of the horses and jockeys. It also determines the seeming informalities of the composition, such as the figure at the extreme right who is cut off by the frame and the low fence which interrupts a traditionally more open foreground.

The subject of *Before the Race* represents the racers' procession to the starting line. The predominantly profile arrangement of the jockeys and their horses is a convention learned from the English sporting print. The compositional structure is further built upon three horizontals: the fence, the frieze-like disposition of the jockeys' heads, and the horizon line. These elements reiterate and reinforce each other and establish a stabilizing and rhythmic contrast to the curves of the horses'

forms and the prominent vertical strokes of the ground. Across the scene, the jockeys' caps produce a pattern of punctuation marks which recreate, in a sense, the syncopated movement of the horses.

Before the Race is one of several close variants of the theme. The first of these seems to be the *Jockeys at Epsom* of 1862 (present whereabouts unknown). Particularly similar to the Providence work are the Louvre's *Course de Gentlemen*, also of ca. 1862, and the much later *Les Courses* of ca. 1885 (Sam Salz Collection, New York). In general, the relationship of these three works seems to be one of progression toward greater condensation of structure and enlarged vision. In refining the experiments of the Louvre picture and preparing the way for the Salz picture, the Providence work forms a bridge between the two.

186

CAMILLE PISSARRO
French, 1830–1903

Woman with a Wheelbarrow, ca. 1882
Signed in gouache in lower left corner:
C. Pissarro
Gouache, pastel, and black crayon over
drypoint. 9⅞ x 6¾

Gift of Mrs. Gustav Radeke. 23.037

Provenance: Frederick Keppel, New
York

Publications: Champa/RISD, 1975, no. 58;
Museum of Fine Arts (and others),
Pissarro, Boston, 1980, no. 176.

Woman with a Wheelbarrow is an unusual drawing in that Pissarro has used gouache, pastel, and black crayon over a drypoint print made in 1882. The work, however, is not uncharacteristic of Pissarro at this time: the decade of the 1880's was dominated by a return to figural motifs, and Pissarro had occasionally heightened prints with pastel since 1879, a practice he would continue until the 1890's. The composition itself is nearly the same as a gouache of 1892, though that work, typical of its later date, is more loosely structured.

There are several reasons why Pissarro would have chosen to draw over a finished print. At a time when he desperately needed money, Pissarro could easily have sold this kind of work due to its inexpensive price and rapid execution. More important, he had grown increasingly friendly with Degas, whose *oeuvre* at this point was dominated by pastels over monotype. Not coincidentally, Pissarro had learned print-making under Degas's tutelage just a few years earlier, and concomitantly stepped up his drawing production. There is reason to believe, however, that this particular print, as such, was regarded by Pissarro as neither finished nor satisfactory. Pissarro usually reworked a printing plate through several states toward ever greater complexity. The first pull was a simple and skeletal matrix that merely tested the basic compositional format. The print beneath the pastel in this work seems to be that of a first state. Moreover, it bears a long scratch along the entire length of the right side which apparently could not be burnished out. Rather than dispose of the print, Pissarro may have decided to use it as the foundation of a new work of art.

Despite the great beauty of the work and the pre-existing drypoint guidelines, Pissarro seems to have encountered further difficulties with the development of the pastel overdrawing. It has been heavily reworked – more so than most Pissarro pastels – toward denser layers of texture and color. He has also applied gouache, the only time it appears in a work of this type, which, while extending the range of color and texture, restores a sense of surface flatness. As a final touch, Pissarro added a purple border around the drawing, intending to complement the color pattern within and define the whole as a decorative unit.

187

FELIX BUHOT
French, 1847–1898

Westminster Bridge, 1884
Signed in pencil below image: Félix
Buhot/épreuve d'artiste; Buhot stamp in
red ink below image
Etching, drypoint, aquatint, roulette,
and spit bite. 11¼ x 15¹¹⁄₁₆ (plate mark)

Gift of the Charles Z. Offin Fund. 83.020

Provenance: Childs Gallery, Boston

Publication: *Museum Notes*, RISD, 1983,
p. 34.

Félix Buhot was a central figure in innovative printmaking in the 1870's and 1880's, primarily known for original prints of his native rural Normandy and street scenes of Paris and London. *Westminster Bridge*, a painterly study of atmospheric effects, was issued at the peak of Buhot's main period of creativity, 1874–1885.

In a letter to a friend some years after one of several trips to London, Buhot recalled "living in the shadows of the towers of the Old Westminster Abbey . . . and, just around the corner . . . the quays and intense activity. How beautiful it is, especially with the tender misty autumnal skies of this land." Made following a visit to London in 1883, *Westminster Bridge* portrays the "intense activity" on the south bank of the Thames looking across the bridge at Big Ben and the Houses of Parliament, both shrouded in mist. The variety of conveyances, and the people from all walks of life, impart the hustle and bustle of a romantic metropolis, as Buhot would later describe it.

Buhot inked this impression *au chiffon*, "with a rag," in order to create by plate tone his palpable London fog. He has then pierced the dense air by wiping small areas clean, thereby lighting his street lamps. A unique feature of his graphic work is his so-called "symphonic margins," which extend by association the atmosphere of the central image. This etching is the sixth of eight states, and is signed in pencil along with the inscription, "épreuve d'artiste." Buhot wrote in an article in 1884 that by the latter term he meant that he not only pulled the proof himself, but that it marked the termination of the plate. As his final seal of approval, he also stamped this sheet in red with his large owl stamp (Lugt 977), further indicating that this print was a special impression. A lithograph of 1892 (Bourcard-Goodfriend 184) shows Buhot repeating the central image of this etching.

EDGAR DEGAS
French, 1834–1917

Six Friends, ca. 1885
Signed in charcoal in lower left corner:
Degas
Pastel and black chalk on grey paper,
now yellowed. 45¼ x 28

Museum Appropriation. 31.320

Provenance: Jacques-Emile Blanche,
Paris; Durand-Ruel, New York

Publications: Walter Sickert, "Degas,"
Burlington Magazine, November 1917, p.
184; *Museum Notes*, RISD, May 1953, p. 4;
Champa/RISD, 1975, no. 14.

Approximately one-fifth of Degas's total
artistic output was portraiture. It
comprised the bulk of his youthful production, as well as his earliest important
works. After the artist reached the age of
50, however, portraiture made up less
than ten percent of his production. This
decreased interest in the genre has been
ascribed to Degas's failing eyesight and
to his move at this time toward greater
compositional abstraction and generalization, neither of which could accom-
modate the acuity of vision Degas
demanded of himself in portraiture.

Six Friends is possibly the most complicated portrait of Degas's career, if only
for the fact that no other portrait in the
artist's *oeuvre* contains as many figures.
From foreground to background, the
artist has represented Albert Boulanger-
Cavé, the Minister of Arts under Louis
Philippe; the painters Henri Gervex and
Jacques-Emile Blanche; the writers
Daniel Halévy and his father Ludovic;
and the English painter Walter Sickert,
who stands apart from the group on the
left. On the right, the figures form a
tightly-knit compositional unit of
contrasting axes. By alternating the
planar orientation of the figures, Degas
has made each appear isolated and
distinct, while creating a daring rhythm
of overlaps and asymmetries. Sickert,
the foreigner, is placed outside the main
figure as a balancing element, and a
comparison is implied between him and
the Frenchman of similar age, Blanche,
in their back-to-back alignment. Each
figure is emotionally unaware of the
others, while all are similarly trance-like,
and a pervasive feeling of timelessness
overtakes the group.

Degas's accomplished use of pastels in
large, serious works such as this was
singularly responsible for the revival of
the medium in the late 19th century.
Interestingly, both Daniel Halévy and
Blanche recorded the circumstances of
its execution, if in slightly varying forms.
Halévy asserted that the sitters were
assembled at the entrance to the chalet
in Dieppe belonging to Blanche.
Blanche, however, recalled that it was in
his studio at the chalet that the picture
was made. He added, "Ludovic pointed
out to Degas that the collar of my
overcoat was half-turned-up, and was
proceeding to turn it down. Degas called
out, 'Leave it. It's fine.' Halévy shrugged
his shoulders and said, 'Degas is always
seeking the accidental.'" It is probably
Blanche's account that is the more
accurate; not only was Degas in eternal
search for the calculated accident, he
disdained working out-of-doors,
viewing a work as the result of lengthy
permutation and premeditation.

Color plate, page 81

189

GEORGES-PIERRE SEURAT
French 1859–1891

A la Gaité Rochechouart (Café-concert), ca. 1887–88
Conté crayon with white heightening on Ingres paper. 21 x 9¼

Gift of Mrs. Murray S. Danforth. 42.210

Provenance: Félix Fénéon, Paris; César de Hauke, New York

Publications: J. H. Rubin, "Seurat and Theory: The Near-Identical Drawings of the Café-Concert," *Gazette des Beaux-Arts*, October 1970, pp. 237–46; Champa/ RISD, 1975, no. 73.

During the period of 1887–88, Seurat executed several drawings of Paris night life revolving around the café concert. Seven of these drawings are known, all similar in size, technique, and conception. One of these (Fogg Museum, Cambridge) is virtually identical to the RISD drawing.

The subject of the indoor café scene had a long tradition in 19th century French art. The idea was probably first explored in depth by Daumier, after which it regularly appeared in popular journals and illustrations. It was also a favorite subject of Manet and, especially, Degas. The latter in particular was a hero of Seurat's, and undoubtedly constituted the primary influence on this aspect of Seurat's career. Like Degas, Seurat was largely concerned here with the effects of artificial light on the scene, and its power to distort form and evoke atmosphere.

Unlike any of his predecessors, however, Seurat was overwhelmingly involved with the development of a tight and structured composition based on theoretical idioms. The principle informing the *Café-concert* is that of the golden section, a geometric theorem ultimately guiding the placement of each object and figure within the scene. To a large extent this determines the very deliberate, almost static, appearance of the composition. Equally striking is Seurat's dramatic use of technique. By applying the side of his conté crayon to a heavily toothed paper, Seurat achieves a vibrating surface pattern of pits and ridges of pigment. Over this he plays highly contrasted accents of bright light and deep shadow. The resulting liveliness and drama are practically the real subjects of the drawing, subsuming the intricacies of the golden section and even the figures themselves.

190

VINCENT VAN GOGH
French (b. The Netherlands), 1853–1890

View of Arles, May 1888
Signed in pen and ink in lower left
corner: Vue d'Arles/Vincent; verso,
drawing in pencil of the drawbridge at
Arles.
Pencil, India ink with reed pen and
wash on white paper. 17 x 21½

Gift of Mrs. Murray S. Danforth.
42.212a, b

Provenance: Mrs. J. van Gogh-Bonger,
Amsterdam; H. Freudenberg,
Nikolassee, Germany; Galerie Paul
Cassirer, Berlin

Publication: Ronald Pickvance, *Van Gogh
in Arles*, Metropolitan Museum of Art,
New York, 1984, no. 26.

The *View of Arles* drawing can be dated
May 1888 on the basis of a letter Vincent
wrote to his brother Theo. He also
included a sketch of the drawing,
indicating the three distinct areas of
color – violet, yellow, and blue – that
had impressed him at the site. In a
slightly later letter to the painter Emile
Bernard, Vincent further refers to the
finished painting for which this drawing
is a study, again indicating the brilliant
effects of color. Vincent had moved to
Arles in 1888 specifically to study the
qualities of intense color caused by the
bright sunlight of southern France.
While there, he would take up residence
with Paul Gauguin, and before the year
was out, cut off a piece of his ear
following an altercation with him.

In his letter to Theo, Vincent talked
about his difficulties with his subject. "If
the meadow does not get mowed, I'd
like to do this study again, for the
subject was very beautiful, and I had
some trouble getting the composition."
By comparing the drawing with the
finished painting and the sketch
included in this letter, it is clear that
Vincent conceived the composition as a
series of rather distinct parallel bands.
The wedge of shape receding from the
foreground is the result of the artist's
oblique viewpoint, as well as his reliance
on a "perspective frame" used by him
since 1882, and which was set up in front
of the motif.

The lively surface pattern of the
drawing is primarily due to the artist's
manipulation of graphic technique.
Vincent began to experiment with the
Japanese reed pen only upon his move
to Arles, which, he said, put him in
mind of a Japanese village. The wide
range of strokes from small circles and
long lines to dots and dashes is characteristic of Vincent's drawings from the
Arles period to his death, and variations
in ink are suggestive of a wide range of
color. They further support the dynamic
perspectival rush into the distance.
Small dots of ink dramatically decrease
in size and intensity towards the
horizon, implying the distance between
the town and the viewer and effectively
conveying the impression of a field
shimmering in light. Vincent may also
have had recourse to a photograph. This
would similarly distort the foreground,
reflected in the artist's crude and oversized pen strokes in this area, as well as
rendering the village in the distance a
sparkling and delicate jewel. Vincent
would build upon the qualities first
tested in this drawing: in the final two
years of his career, a variegated reed pen
technique would dominate his work, as
would vertiginous kinds of perspective
renderings.

191

PAUL CEZANNE
French, 1839–1906

The Card Player, ca. 1890
Pencil and watercolor on white paper.
19¹⁄₁₆ x 14¼

Gift of Mrs. Murray S. Danforth. 42.211

Provenance: Ambroise Vollard, Paris;
Jacques Seligmann, Paris

Publication: Champa/RISD, 1975, no. 5.

In the autumn of 1890, following a six-
month sojourn in Switzerland, Cézanne
began his important series of *Card
Players*. Based on the local peasantry in
his native Aix, Cézanne completed five
variations of the multi-figural composition in oil, as well as at least 15 studies in
various media of individual figures.

The figure in the Providence drawing
is found in a pencil sketch in the Hono-
lulu Academy of Arts, and in two of the
definitive oils, those in the Barnes Foundation and the Metropolitan Museum of
Art. It is directly related to the latter, and
until recently was considered to be a
preliminary study for it. However, due
to its greater simplification and flatness
and widely differing viewpoint, this
sheet is now thought to have been
drawn after the Metropolitan canvas. In
fact, it more likely served as one of
several "transition" studies to the next in
the series of completed oils, that in the
Pellerin Collection, Paris. Both reveal
(for the first time in the painted version)
an emphasis on broad forms blocked in
by roughened contour, the suppression
of three-dimensional modeling and
coherent patterns of chiaroscuro, and a
lively surface flicker determined by
subtle hue and value modulations. The
last, in particular, announces the sensitive and abstract "proto-cubist" works
that would dominate his *oeuvre* hence-
forth, especially in watercolor.

In this sheet, Cézanne dramatically
varies his pencil strokes in thickness,
length, tone, and gesture, suggesting his
growing disinterest in representational
style and his love of pure drawing as
such. A certain abstract rhythm is
introduced through repeated curving
contour lines played against angular

strengthenings and soft diagonal
hatchings. Although the application of
color is kept to a relative minimum, the
fluctuations of graphic marks introduce
a definite polychromy and force the
areas of white paper between them to
emerge as volumetric forms. In this way,
Cézanne creates an image of great richness and evocative power through the
most simplified and reduced means.

192

192

HENRI DE TOULOUSE-LAUTREC
French, 1864–1901

Yvette Guilbert Taking a Curtain Call, 1894
Stamped in lower left with the artist's
monogram
Black crayon, watercolor, and oil with
white heightening on tracing paper
mounted on cardboard; upper right
corner of sheet replaced. 16⅜ x 9

Gift of Mrs. Murray S. Danforth. 35.540

Provenance: Alfred Walter Heymel,
Paris; Galeries Lévêques, Barbazanges,
Paris; Marcel Guérin, Paris

Publications: Fritz Novotny, "Drawings
of Yvette Guilbert by Toulouse-Lautrec,"
Burlington Magazine, June 1949, pp. 161–
63; Champa/RISD, 1975, no. 78.

The entertainer Yvette Guilbert was one
of Toulouse-Lautrec's favorite models,
and appeared as a subject in his work
from 1893 on. The RISD drawing is a
study for one of 16 lithographs Lautrec
prepared in 1894 as illustrations to
Gustave Geoffroy's book on Guilbert.
Called the French Series, it was followed
in 1898 by a second set of Guilbert illustrations, the English Series.

Fittingly, *Yvette Guilbert Taking a
Curtain Call* appeared as the final image
of the French set, and Toulouse-Lautrec
gave considerable thought to its creation. At least two other works are related
to it. The first (Louvre, Paris) is a pencil
and chalk sketch of the singer in a similar pose in which the artist, ostensibly
working on the spot, attempted to
capture his initial impression. The
second (Toulouse-Lautrec Museum,
Albi) is nearly identical to the RISD work,
and is probably a copy. In fact, it has
been suggested that it represents a
photographic projection of the drawing
heightened in oil.

Characteristically, Toulouse-Lautrec
was not interested in a simple transcrip-
tion of the figure or scene. Instead, with
a highly individual style of rapid lines
and broad shapes, he concentrates on
the idiosyncracies of Guilbert's form,
face, and movement. The artist's sure
hand and profound insight, however,
raise the drawing above the level of
simple caricature, as well as distin-
guishing it from the exceedingly elegant
productions of his closest colleagues in
type, Grasset and Chéret.

193

193

HENRI DE TOULOUSE-LAUTREC
French, 1864–1901

*Professional Skating Beauty – Edouard
Dujardin and Liane de Lancy at the Palais de
Glace*, ca. 1896
Signed in black crayon in lower right
with the artist's monogram
Blue and black crayon, black wash,
heightened with white on light brown
paper. 28½ x 22½

Gift of Mrs. Murray S. Danforth. 35.541

Provenance: Maurice Joyant, Paris; A. M.
Proux, Paris; Hugo Perls, Berlin; César
de Hauke, New York; Jacques Seligmann,
New York and Paris

Publication: Champa/RISD, 1975, no. 79.

This drawing is a study for a lithograph
that appeared on the back cover of the
January 18, 1896 issue of the popular
journal, *Le Rire*. It represents one of the
most fashionable spots in late 19th
century Paris, the Palais de Glace, a
skating rink on the Champs Elysées. An
earlier sketch also exists (Toulouse-
Lautrec Museum, Albi) in which the
figures are shown in nearly identical
poses to those here, but without the
development of the background.

Toulouse-Lautrec's drawing style in
this work – the use of strong, elegant
contours and subordination of three-
dimensional modeling to the two-
dimensional picture plane – constitutes a
relatively brief interlude in his career. It
places him in the midst of the Art
Nouveau movement whose leading
practitioners, such as Alphonse Mucha,
similarly exploited outline for maximum
decorative effect and abandoned all hint
of chiaroscuro. Unlike Mucha, however,
Lautrec would never abandon an idiosyncratic, angular line for the fluidity of
arabesque, the characteristic Art
Nouveau component. Nor would he lose
his interest in personality. Typically,
Dujardin and de Lancy are highly
individual beings whose appearance and
psychology are brilliantly captured in a
manner on the edge of caricature.

194

AUGUSTE RENOIR
French, 1841–1919

Children Playing with a Ball, 1898
Lithograph in 9 colors. 31⁷⁄₁₆ x 24⁷⁄₁₆
(sheet)

Gift of Peter G. Scotese. 82.301.3

Publication: *Museum Notes*, RISD, 1983,
p. 35.

Renoir began printmaking late in his
artistic career. In fact, between 1889 and
about 1912, he produced only 59 prints;
however, he mastered a number of
techniques, infusing many of his plates
with the voluptuous forms and bright
colors for which he is renowned.

Renoir was fortunate to have Auguste
Clot as his printer. Especially expert at
printing in colors, Clot produced the
only state (although the number of
colors varied from impression to impression) of *Children Playing with a Ball*, in an
edition of 200. In the present example,
nine colors were used: yellow, a regular
pink and a fleshy pink, ochre, terra-cotta,
green, blue, black, and grey. As many as
ten colors, as well as black, have been
observed in other impressions. Here, the
three primary colors dominate the
composition.

Renoir turned to lithography only in
1897. Produced in the following year,
Children Playing with a Ball is considered
by many to be his finest graphic work.
According to Roger-Marx (1951), it was
inspired by an earlier pastel. In their
carefree abandon, the children represent
Renoir's instinctive ability to recreate
natural forms, not via *plein air* observation, but by the manipulation of color,
mass, and movement. Along with his
contemporaries, Pissarro and Degas,
Renoir had an approach that stressed
experimentation in various media over
elaboration of technique in one medium.

194

195

196

PABLO PICASSO
French (b. Spain), 1881–1973

Standing Nude, 1906
Signed in pencil in lower left corner:
Picasso
Black crayon on cream paper. 24¹³⁄₁₆ x
18¹⁄₁₆

Gift of Mrs. Murray S. Danforth. 43.011

Provenance: Gertrude and Leo Stein,
Paris; Leo Stein, Florence; Pierre
Matisse, New York, 1937

Publication: Champa/RISD, 1975, no. 56.

Executed in Paris in the fall of 1906,
Standing Nude reflects both in subject
and style the experimental work that led
up to Picasso's critical breakthrough of
Les Demoiselles d'Avignon. Specifically, it
relates to the images of female nudes the
artist executed during his prolific
summer at Gosol (Spain) in which even
and unbroken contours defined classically proportioned figures. The greater
sculptural quality of the RISD *Nude*,
however, her inactivity and resolutely
frontal relationship to the viewer,
suggest a push beyond the Gosol work.
More importantly, the range of drawing
technique revealed in the *Nude* signals a
liberation from Picasso's classicism, and
a broadening of stylistic options.

Standing Nude, in fact, consists of a
series of oppositions between two styles
of drawing: the fine, light crayon line
with which the figure was laid out, and
the subsequent soft rubbing which
models the contours into shapes; these
large areas of modeling as opposed to
areas of untouched paper surrounded by
linear contour; and the angular, dark-
valued drawing of the face contrasted
with the delicate and fluid emergence of
the body.

At least two other drawings bear a
close relationship to the RISD work: a
pastel version (location unknown,
Zervos, I, 357) executed after this
drawing, in which the stylistic conflict is
incidental to a plethora of long strokes of
colored crayon; and a *Reclining Nude* in
the Cone Collection, Baltimore Museum
of Art, in which the oppositions persist
and which appears to have been executed virtually as a horizontal pendant
to the RISD work.

195

HENRI DE TOULOUSE-LAUTREC
French, 1864–1901

Circus Equestrian, 1899
Signed in black crayon in upper and
lower right corners with artist's
monogram; stamped in lower left corner
with artist's monogram
Black, blue, orange, and green crayon
with grey wash on white paper. 19¼ x
12⅜

Gift of Mrs. Murray S. Danforth. 34.003

Provenance: Maurice Joyant, Paris;
Knoedler, New York

Publication: Champa/RISD, 1975, no. 80.

From March 17 to May 20, 1899, Toulouse-
Lautrec admitted himself to a clinic
outside Paris in an attempt to cure himself of alcoholism. During this time, he
poured his artistic energies into a series
of scenes of the circus, and produced 39
large and accomplished drawings. All of
them, of course, were done from
memory, some from as much as ten
years previous when he was a frequent
visitor to the Cirque Fernando. It is not
necessarily ironic that Toulouse-Lautrec
should have turned to the circus as a
subject at this point in his life. Despite
the real but superficial gaiety of these
scenes, Lautrec identified with the
frequently unstable and itinerant lifestyle of the circus performers, and their
freakish status in society.

In fact, this drawing is as much about
contrasts and tensions as it is about the
circus: the gossamer figure precariously
seated on her rock-like mount; wispy
touches of crayon that define her
costume as opposed to the uncharacter-
istically wooden contours of the horse;
and bold passages of black set against
the white of the paper without mediating
half-tone. Most noticeable is the insta-
bility of the composition as a whole.
Perspective is skewed to turn the circus
ring into an ellipse, pushing the entire
scene up and forward, and distorting the
size of the animal's body and that of the
ringmaster. Nonetheless, it is Toulouse-
Lautrec's genius that these inconsistencies, conscious or not, ultimately impart
to the work its great dynamic energies.

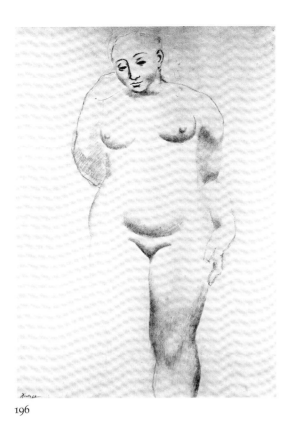

196   197

197

RAYMOND DUCHAMP-VILLON
French, 1876–1918

Seated Woman, ca. 1913
Charcoal on white paper. 17 x 10

Mary B. Jackson Fund and Membership
Dues. 67.090

Provenance: John Quinn, New York,
1914; Arthur B. Spingarn, New York,
1927

Publication: Champa/RISD, 1975, no. 28.

The charcoal studies by the sculptor
Duchamp-Villon were never exhibited
during his lifetime. Barely preserved by
the artist, they attest to his involvement
with the medium of drawing as a private
enterprise and almost totally as a means
of developing sculptural ideas. *Seated
Woman* undoubtedly served as the final
study for the slightly larger sculpture of
the same subject first exhibited in plaster
at the Galerie André Groult in April
1914. The Museum also possesses one of
two casts (entry no. 121 in this Handbook)
in gilded bronze (the other in the Sidney
Schönberg Collection, St. Louis) made
under John Quinn's instructions at the
Roman Bronze Works, New York, in
1915.

The figure in the drawing was first
laid in as an abstract grouping of oval
shapes. The artist is said to have used a
wooden mannequin as his model, which
would have encouraged such a beginning. Over this, however, as in the
sculpture, Duchamp-Villon has begun to
explore the breakdown of volume and
mass characteristic of analytical Cubism
with which both he and his brothers
were involved. Form is created only by
light or its absence, indicated by
hatchings, that serves the Cubist principle and predicts the chiaroscuro
patterns in the final sculpture. Ultimately, this work – as well as the contemporaneous efforts of Jacques Villon
and Marcel Duchamp – is concerned
with the rediscovery of equilibrium
within Cubist dissolution of traditional
form.

Interestingly, Duchamp-Villon's sculpture of *Seated Woman* appears to have
served as the model for another of his
contemporaries, Fernand Léger, in his
Seated Female Nude (private collection) of
the same year (1913).

198

HENRI MATISSE
French, 1869–1954

Untitled, 1951
Initialed in pencil in lower left corner:
HM
Pen and brown ink. 10⅝ x 8¼

Gift of Mr. and Mrs. Barnet Fain. 83.164

Provenance: Pierre Matisse Gallery, New
York; Museum of Modern Art Lending
Services, New York, 1956

Publication: *Museum Notes,* RISD, 1984,
p. 34.

Matisse began his important series of
cut-paper pieces in 1943, at 74 years of
age, while recuperating from a serious
operation. These works, built only of
pure color and the cut edge, are of the
most extraordinary simplicity. Nonetheless, they were implicit even in Matisse's
earliest work, where intensity of palette
and a love of linear arabesque first
appear. The latter was further reinforced
in Matisse's approach to sculpture, in
which outer contour, or profile, was at
least as important as internal modeling.

This drawing is one of a series from a
sketchbook generally related to *The
Parakeet and the Siren.* The sketchbook is
now broken up and dispersed, although
it has been reproduced in limited edition
by the Maison France, Nice (n.d.). More
notably, this sketchbook also served as
preparatory work to Matisse's important
group of cut-paper works of 1952, *The
Blue Nudes.* The Museum's figure, in the
curve of the right leg and tilt of the head,
is especially close to *The Seated Blue
Nude, No. 2* (private collection). It must
be observed, however, that these works
move toward ever-increasing abstraction;
our sketch, an apparent first thought,
would logically relate best to the earliest
numbers in the group.

The sketchbook itself shows this same
progression toward ultimate simplicity
and abstraction. It has been said that
Matisse tirelessly observed the pose on
successive days and from hour to hour,
recording the subtlest of changes in a
new drawing. It seems clear as well that
Matisse's hand moved unguided on the
page while he kept his sight fixed on the
model. Matisse's love of the female body
clearly emerges. So, too, does his
basically sculptural approach to the
sheet, that of taking the blank page and
winding through it a simple contour that
molds form without de-emphasis of the
space inside or out.

198

199

199

THOMAS EAKINS
American, 1844–1916

Baseball Players Practicing, 1875
Signed and dated in watercolor at center
left: Eakins/75
Watercolor and pencil on paper. 10³⁄₁₆ x
12⅛

Jesse Metcalf and Walter H. Kimball
Funds. 36.172

Provenance: Mr. Herbert E. Thompson,
Boston; Mrs. Herbert E. Thompson,
Waltham

Publication: Carmalt/RISD, 1972, no. 11.

Although Eakins was a devoted sports-
man, this is his only known depiction of
the game of baseball. It may be that as
baseball made the transition from
"national pastime" to a competitive club
sport, the artist lost interest.

This charming and popular sheet
combines Eakins's two primary artistic
concerns throughout his career: the
"facts," as he referred to his adherence
to Realism, and a fascination with
momentary effects of light and shade.
The baseball club represented is the
Philadelphia Athletes, easily identified
by their carefully specified uniforms.
Even the players can be identified: the
batter, Wes Fisler, first baseman of the
team, and the catcher, John Clapp. Only
a few spectators are shown in and
around the grandstand, suggesting a
practice session rather than an official
game.

The figures are shown in full afternoon
sunlight, as suggested by their carefully
delineated shadows and the bright
highlights which bounce off their
uniforms. Colors are intense, shifting,
and translucent, an "impressionist"
effect Eakins may have encountered and
absorbed during his stay in Paris at the
end of the 1860's. While in Paris,
however, he was the pupil of the arch
academician, Jean-Léon Gérôme. It is
the latter's attention to detail and tight
contour which Eakins marries to
Impressionist phenomenology and the
American naturalist tradition to create
his own unique style.

200

EASTMAN JOHNSON
American, 1825–1906

Child in Bed, ca. 1875
Charcoal and crayon. 19⅝ x 15¹⁵⁄₁₆

Gift of the Museum Associates. 80.074

Provenance: Albert Rosenthal, New
York, 1945; Knoedler, New York;
Chapellier Galleries, New York; private
collection, Virginia; Childs Gallery,
Boston

Publication: *Museum Notes/Bulletin*, RISD,
1980, pp. 28–29.

Unlike Johnson's usual depiction of
children, *Child In Bed* is a work in which
personal concerns are more important
than description or anecdote. The subject is probably the artist's daughter,
born in 1870; more than that, it is a
portrait of isolation and malaise. The
little figure develops a nearly uncanny

presence as the detail builds from the
shadows around her to the crescendo of
her head.

Johnson began his career as a portraitist, and after 1880, completed it as such.
This drawing is closely linked to stylistic
developments in the mid-1870's.
Throughout the decade, Johnson's
works grew increasingly mood-oriented,
and it was to Rembrandt as much as to
the French Impressionists that he looked
for his feathery technique and dramatic
chiaroscuro. The rich and varied layers
of charcoal in our drawing, worked up
rapidly to an opaque black, stumped or
strengthened in crayon, and scratched
out to uncover the white of the paper,
were characteristic of Johnson's charcoal
technique throughout his life. The
drama with which he manipulated the
medium, particularly evident here, is
credited with having generated a revival
of charcoal drawing in America in the
last quarter of the 19th century.

200

201

WINSLOW HOMER
American, 1836–1910

Waiting for the Start, 1889
Signed in watercolor in lower left corner:
Homer 1889
Watercolor over pencil. 13½ x 19¼

Gift of Jesse Metcalf. 94.005.

Provenance: Purchased directly from the
artist by the donor (?)

The decade of the 1880's is frequently
considered one of Homer's best periods,
particularly for watercolors, and is
certainly one of his most prolific. The
first years of the decade, spent in
England, saw a shift in his work toward
dramatic subject matter and aggressive
technique. After his move to Prout's
Neck, Maine in 1883, he adopted his
characteristic content: the relationship of
humanity to nature, both at play or
sport, and in a struggle for survival.

Waiting for the Start is part of a loose
series of works based on hunting life in
the Adirondack Mountains. It reveals
Homer at a rare relaxed moment, at
peace with a subdued nature. A group
of hunting dogs is shown adrift on a
quiet pond in a square-nosed punt. In
the midst of them is their master, barely
visible at the bow of the boat. The
wooded shores provide an exceptional
vision of New England foliage in fall,
and demonstrate Homer's skill in
capturing their range of color. In fact, it
might be said that despite the charm of
this scene, the real subject of the work is
Homer's watercolor technique. Not only
does he prove himself a master colorist,
but a virtuoso technician, attacking the
sheet with rapid, rather dry strokes that
function both descriptively and decora-
tively. Detail is abandoned to assure an
image of maximum directness and
simplicity.

Homer's interest in the decorative
impact of his work, in color and brushstroke as pure form, and in nature at a
specific point in time link him to similar
concerns among the avant-garde in
France. It is likely, in fact, that Homer
came in contact with the work of the
young Impressionists while in France 20
years earlier. Equally important,
however, if not more so, is Homer's own
native realism, his truth to vision.

Color plate, page 81

201

202

MAXFIELD PARRISH
American, 1870–1966

Cowboys, Hot Springs, Arizona, 1902
Signed and inscribed (artist's hand?) in
pencil on verso: Maxfield Parrish/Hot
Springs, Arizona
Oil mixed in places with melted wax on
cardboard, mounted on wood. 17 x 14³⁄₁₆

Gift of the Estate of Mrs. Gustav Radeke.
31.082.

Provenance: *The Century Magazine* (?),
New York

Publication: Carmalt/RISD, 1972, no. 21.

Parrish is best known for his elegant and
simplified poster designs. He was also
an illustrator of children's books,
murals, and general advertisements,
and became popular during the 1920's
and 30's through calendars, cards, and
prints.

Executed in Arizona where the artist
was recovering from tuberculosis, this
drawing was one of a series that illustrated an article on "The Great
Southwest" in *The Century Magazine* of
May 1902. Parrish had learned oil technique only the year before, after his ink
had frozen on a sketching trip through
the Adirondacks. The newness of the
technique for Parrish accounts for the
unorthodox combination of media as
well as the painstaking and subtle glazes
of oil.

The aesthetic of the work is strictly
linked to the artist's experience in
poster-making: color is clear and
unmuddied, composition is based on the
premise of broad shape, and brushstroke
is virtually invisible. Interestingly, it may
also be attributed to the "models" from
which Parrish worked. The sharpness of
the silhouetted shapes results from his
use of cut-outs to lay out the design,
some of which he was in the habit of
retaining in the final work. Natural
details such as rocks were based on
pebbles the artist found in his backyard.
For lighting effects, he would frequently
illuminate from behind, recreating the
eeriness of the 19th century diorama.
Despite the eccentric nature of these
techniques, Parrish has created a work
of real impact, and one that in its
abstract simplicity has ties to the
contemporary realist movement.

202

203

203

MARY CASSATT
American, 1844–1926

Antoinette's Caress, ca. 1906
Signed in pastel in lower right corner:
Mary Cassatt
Pastel. 30 x 24½

Gift of Mrs. Houghton P. Metcalf, Sr., in
loving memory of her husband. 82.115

Provenance: Scott and Fowles, New
York; Mrs. J. Cameron Bradley; Parke-
Bernet, New York, 1947

Publications: Adelyn Breeskin, *Mary
Cassatt, A Catalogue Raisonné of the Oils,
Pastels, Watercolors, and Drawings*,
Washington, D.C., 1970, no. 484;
Museum Notes, RISD, 1982, p. 36.

Mary Cassatt, the American Impressionist, became one of only two artists
Degas claimed as pupils. She was the
only American invited to exhibit with
the French Impressionists, and she
belonged to a small group of young
women (Berthe Morisot, Eva Gonzales)
within the larger Impressionist movement. Cassatt's "mother and child"
theme is closely associated with her art,
as is the ballet and horse racing with
Degas's. Within this body of work,
Antoinette's Caress assumes a vital position. Its large size literally commands
attention. The after-the-bath theme was
a favorite one of the artist, and the
contrast between the reality-bound
mother and dreamy-eyed aura of the
little girl particularly draws the viewer
into the work.

Cassatt also used Antoinette as a
subject in two oil paintings, *Antoinette
Holding Her Child by Both Hands*, 1901
(Karen Carter Lindley, Fort Worth,
Texas) and *Antoinette at Her Dressing
Table*, 1909 (private collection, Chicago).
The Museum's pastel is more closely
related to five drypoints executed ca.
1910 (Breeskin 209, 210, 211, 212, and
213).

Antoinette's Caress is dated ca. 1906.
Some of Cassatt's late work is marked by
her discordant and harsh use of color,
but the RISD pastel does not share this.
Much of the importance of the work
derives from the strength of Cassatt's
drawing, the freedom and rhythm of her
pastel technique, and her mastery of
color.

Color plate, page 82

204

EDWARD HOPPER
American, 1882–1967

Night Shadows, 1921
Inscribed in pencil below image: To Dick
and Nell Magee
Etching and drypoint before steel-facing.
6¹⁵⁄₁₆ x 8¼ (plate mark)

Gift of The Koffler Family Foundation,
Mr. and Mrs. Gilman Angier, Houghton
P. Metcalf, Jr., Mr. and Mrs. Norman
Bolotow, Mr. and Mrs. C. George Taylor,
and Bequest of Lyra Brown Nickerson,
by exchange. 83.003

Provenance: Dick and Nell Magee, New
York; David A. Tunick, New York

Publication: *Museum Notes*, RISD, 1983,
p. 37.

Edward Hopper is arguably the greatest
American "realist" painter of the 20th
century. Through his early forties,
however, he made his living as an
illustrator, and was better known as a
printmaker than a painter. At this early
period, Hopper associated with The
Eight and later, the Ash Can School –
painters of "unretouched" American
urban and rural life. He was introduced
to etching in 1915, and produced all but
two of his works in this medium by 1923.

Our work features a New York street
corner, a common theme in Hopper's
oeuvre. A thematically similar work, his
1913 painting *New York Corner* in the
Museum of Modern Art, had been
acclaimed at its first exhibition as "a
perfect visualization of New York
atmosphere." A comparison of these
two compositions, however, demonstrates momentous changes over the
eight-year period. The painting is a
straightforward view from the opposite
curb, with street lamp, of generalized
figures walking along both fronts of a
corner store. In the etching, this
commonplace American image has been
stood on end. One is forced to look
steeply down at an oblique angle at a
radically changed scene. It is night, and
a starkly toned figure plods across the
pavement. The sidewalk and the store-
front are cut in half by the diagonal of
the shadow cast by a street lamp. Both
nighttime and solitary figures are persistent themes in Hopper's compositions,
implying both loneliness and a possible
preference by the artist for quiet and
solitude.

As here, Hopper preferred a stark
white paper and a jet black ink that he
got from England for his etchings. The
RISD impression, signed in pencil, was
pulled before the steel-facing of the plate
and the *New Republic* edition, and was
most likely printed by Hopper himself in
1921. The print bears a further pencil
inscription, "To Dick and Nell Magee,"
who were friends and neighbors of the
artist.

205

ANDRE KERTESZ
American (b. Austria-Hungary),
b. 1894

Portrait of Jean, 1930
Signed in pencil below image: A. Kertész
Paris
Silver print. 8⁹⁄₁₆ x 6³⁄₁₆ (image)

Gift of Mr. and Mrs. Edwin Jaffe. 81.101

Provenance: Sander Gallery,
Washington, D. C.

Publication: *Museum Notes*, RISD, 1982,
p. 36.

Kertész is known for his candid scenes
of everyday life taken with a small-format
camera. He began taking photographs in
Austria-Hungary in 1912, although it
was not until 1925 that he left his
business to pursue photography full-
time in Paris. He was an innovator of the
genre now known as photojournalism.

Portrait of Jean is a photograph of the
young Jean Ducrot. Both Jean and his
son, Nicholas, have served Kertész as
editor and publisher, Jean in Paris in the
1920's and 1930's, before the artist settled
permanently in the United States in
1936. Another Kertész photo of Jean
Ducrot has been published: *Jean A.
Ducrot and Bubu*, 1928 (*André Kertész:
Sixty Years of Photography*, p. 94).

Here we have a figure who was
intimately known to the photographer
and who gazes straight out at us; nonetheless, he defies our precise understanding. As we move from his face, his
figure is enveloped by the rich textures
of his tweed suit, captured in soft focus.
These textures contrast with areas of
sharp focus, as in the breast pocket
handkerchief, making this incidental
detail a focal point, and adding a quality
of tension. This element of tension
prevails in the spirit of the subject as
well; he is here younger-looking than in
the earlier photograph, yet seemingly
aware beyond his years. It is a compelling
image, arrested in transition between
directness and mystery, hard and soft,
and suspended in time.

204

206

AARON SISKIND
American, b. 1903

Untitled from *Harlem Document*,
ca. 1932–1940
Silver print. 9½ x 8⁷⁄₁₆

Gift of Matrix Publications Inc. and
Alpha Partners. 83.031.48

Provenance: From the artist

Publication: Ann Banks, ed., *Harlem
Document, Photographs 1932–1940: Aaron
Siskind*, Providence, 1981, p. 72.

Aaron Siskind was perhaps the first white photographer to document life in Harlem between the Wars. This was a period of great complexity for this community. The cultural richness of the 1920's known as the Harlem Renaissance was followed by the deprivations of the Depression at its most extreme. Harlem, its tenements, its energies, its night life, was not unknown to artists at this time, and this, combined with the impetus from government-sponsored projects, propelled them to record conditions there.

Siskind had been photographing independently in Harlem since 1932. In 1936, he and a number of members of the Photo League were approached by the writer Michael Carter to bring together a body of work on Harlem. Though a book was compiled, it was never published. Four years later, Siskind and Carter, along with Max Yavno, embarked on another Harlem-related project, *The Most Crowded Block*. World War II intervened and the project was never completed. The recent publication in book and portfolio of Siskind's *Harlem Document* is the first time these two groups of works have been brought together and presented as such.

The photograph illustrated here, while atypical of the work for which Siskind is now best known, is characteristic of one aspect of the *Harlem Document*: that of the pathos and innocence of life he found there. To be sure, the artist also observed its joys and pleasures, making of the *Document* a balanced and even-handed presentation. Equally remarkable, it is a work of great political and aesthetic unselfconsciousness, betraying nothing of an outsider's status or the polemicist's proselytizing.

205

206

207

208

FREDERICK SOMMER
American (b. Italy), b. 1905

Untitled (Figure in Cut Paper), ca. 1965
Signed in pencil on verso: Frederick Sommer
Silver print. 13¼ x 8¾

Purchased with the aid of funds from the National Endowment for the Arts. 73.179

Provenance: Light Gallery, New York

Frederick Sommer began his career as an architect, turning to painting and drawing in the 1930's. Meetings with the great photographers Alfred Steiglitz in 1935 and Edward Weston in 1936 proved decisive in converting him to photography. He retained his respect particularly for Weston, purchasing an 8 x 10 view camera and painstakingly preserving the purity of the original contact print made from a large negative. Although Sommer still makes prints slowly and infrequently – part of the Weston legacy – his work has grown increasingly personal in effect and content.

Early on, Sommer was attracted by Cubism and Surrealism, some of whose leading practitioners, such as Max Ernst, became close friends. *Figure in Cut Paper,* from a series of works executed around 1965, seems to reflect the influence of Bruguière. Unlike Bruguière, however, Sommer does not restrict himself to inanimate forms which laconically emerge from the surface of the paper. Instead, he arranges sheets of paper cut into sharp-edged forms in front of his camera, and places the nude figure in and around them. Later, he might draw or paint on the negative, or "smoke" shapes onto it that further obscure the distinction between reality and surreality. Ultimately, the subject of these works revolves around this distinction. In formal terms, the images are more closely connected to the Cubist aesthetic in their subtle relationships of tone, dimension, and light.

207

HARRY CALLAHAN
American, b. 1912

Eleanor, ca. 1947
Signed in pencil below image at right: Harry Callahan
Silver print. 4½ x 3¼ (image); 6½ x 4½ (sheet)

Gift of Mr. and Mrs. Gilman Angier. 78.040

Callahan began photography as a hobbyist in 1938 while an employee of the Chrysler Motor Parts Corporation in Michigan. Only slowly did his work begin to take shape. He himself dates his first successful photographs to 1941, and his complete commitment to photography to 1944-45. His earliest and most persistent inspiration was his wife, Eleanor, the subject of much of his work through the 1950's. As subject, Eleanor takes many forms: as individual portraiture, as symbol of universal womanhood, as vehicle for the study of light and shape. In the image illustrated here, as in Callahan's best portraits, all three are combined.

In a style with links to Weston and Cunningham, Callahan presents Eleanor's head in strict frontality, pushed to the surface plane of the paper. Mediating half-tone is nearly eliminated in favor of stark contrasts of black and white that flatten volumes into planes, emphasize contours, and eliminate details. The geometric simplicity which results is nearly classical in its purity. As Eleanor's face emerges from fragments of crossed arms and hands, however, the photograph can take on a kind of surrealistic suggestiveness. It is this ability to render an image on so many diverse levels, perfectly balanced between strict formalism and objective naturalism, that accounts for its great significance.

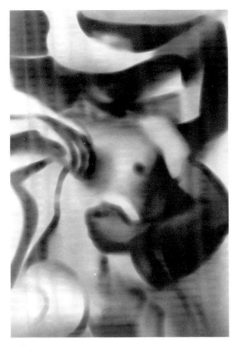

208

209

209

JIM DINE
American, b. 1936

This Sweet Sweet Baby, 1970–71
Mixed media and collage. 60 x 39¾

Purchased with the aid of funds from
the National Endowment for the Arts.
71.070

Provenance: Sonnabend Gallery, New
York

Publication: *Museum Notes*, RISD, 1980,
p. 30.

In this drawing, protruding collage
elements and motifs such as words and
numbers provoke a highly-charged dia-
logue with the viewer. This "theatrical"
aspect, as well as the inclusion of
mechanically-produced images and
"throw-away" objects, and the artist's
way of isolating and monumentalizing
banal subject matter, show Dine's
connection to Pop Art. However, Dine's
affinities with Abstract Expressionism
are explicit in his sensuous handling of
materials. The drawing's lush surface
literally reveals its means of creation, by
the inclusion of a cloth used to rub the
charcoal.

Dine's motifs are as personal as their
treatment. The heart, forming the
nucleus of the drawing and reappearing
in various states of metamorphosis
throughout, is his best-known motif,
simultaneously his most private (referring to his wife) and universal. Sensual
and artistic pleasure are closely entwined
in the work; the printed collage elements
of vegetables may refer to his assertion
that the act of drawing is as enjoyable as
eating a good meal. Compositional elements are numbered as though catalogued; the inconsistency of this
notational system seduces the viewer
into examining all areas of the drawing.
Number 35, the words *This Sweet Sweet
Baby*, may be either a subjective reference
or a purely formal statement. Number
18, a pound note, refers to his 1966–69
London sojourn.

The drawing was begun in 1970, the
year of his first Whitney retrospective
and a period of reflection in his work
(Castleman, 1976, p. 37). The drawing's
heroic scale and daring formal concerns
mark its importance as a statement
summarizing a crucial segment of Dine's
career.

210

JAMES ROSENQUIST
American, b. 1933

Cliff Hanger, 1975
Signed in pencil in lower right corner:
James Rosenquist 1975; inscribed in
pencil, lower left corner: Cliff Hanger.
Acrylic, photolithography, and string on
paper. 35½ x 72⅝ (irregular)

Albert Pilavin Collection of 20th Century
American Art and funds from the
National Endowment for the Arts.
81.060

Provenance: Leo Castelli Gallery, New
York

Publication: *Museum Notes,* RISD, 1981, p.
25.

This work belongs to a series of drawings
executed by the artist for an exhibition in
1976 at Gallery A in Sydney, Australia.
The tripartite arrangement of the forms
against relatively open expanses of
paper characterizes much of Rosenquist's
oeuvre from this period. A diagonal
formed of two ladders and tire treads
extends upwards from the lower left
corner and establishes a directional pattern for the assorted images. An oval-
shaped photolithograph of a suburban
bungalow is fastened at right angles to
the tire tracks and tilts precariously
downwards. A ladder and stenciled tire
intersect in the center of the paper and
reinforce the impression of speed out of
control. The third segment of the
composition contains rainbow-like horizontal layers of color and a large silver
circle which is accompanied by a
penciled label identifying it as a "wreck-
ing ball." The ball has slipped its rope
and has smashed into a wall of colors,
splintering it and even crumpling the
paper. The presence of this agent of
destruction alongside the crumpled
paper injects a decidedly ominous note
into the composition and contrasts
sharply with the festive palette employed
by the artist.

In his works of the 1970's, Rosenquist re-uses elements of his earlier
vocabulary in conjunction with new
non-objective forms and within a context
which appears to be more grim and fore-
boding. Yet the bright colors and title of
Cliff Hanger suggest that this spirit of
danger is mixed with a certain degree of
humor and offhandedness.

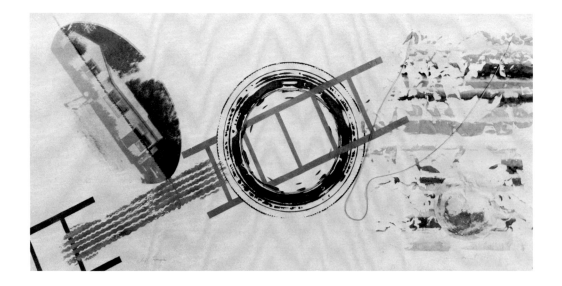

211

EGYPTIAN, Coptic or late antique style, 4th–5th century

Tunic Ornament
Tapestry weave, linen warp, wool and linen weft. 3 x 3

Gift of Mrs. Jesse H. Metcalf. 16.396

The late antique period in Egypt, from the 3rd to the 7th century, encompasses the end of the Roman empire and early Byzantine period. This style, which is sometimes called Coptic, combines Greek, Roman, and Egyptian motifs with early Christian symbols. The term Coptic refers specifically to the indigenous Egyptians, as opposed to foreign invaders or settlers. Existing textiles and other decorative arts show evidence of many diverse styles, influences, and levels of sophistication where pagan and Christian art forms coexisted for long periods of time. For example, images in pictorial tapestries range from elegant figures from Classical mythology to naive depictions of Christian symbols to abstract plant and animal forms. Textile fragments, preserved by the dry desert climate, have been recovered by treasure hunters from gravesites where they were found in abundance. The lack of scientific discovery, in addition to the diversity of styles, makes it impossible to date the textiles precisely. Textile fragments in museum collections range from small pieces used for garment ornaments to large curtains and wall hangings.

The main form of decorative weaving of the period was tapestry, a method where the weaver used colored wefts to completely cover the warp threads, which were held under tension on the loom. A separate weft was used to weave each color area; thus the design was created as the weaving progressed as a part of the structure of textile, rather than being applied after it was woven.

Coptic tunics were woven primarily of linen, bleached in the sun and usually spun to a fine or medium thread. Wool, which is much easier to dye than linen, was woven into colorful tapestry inserts for cuff, neckline, and shoulder bands, and for round and square ornaments on the shoulders and along the hem.

This small tunic ornament, woven of fine linen and wool, probably represents a Christian saint with a nimbus or halo. The finely drawn figure and the grapevine border carry over from the Classical tradition. It probably dates after 330, when Constantine I made Constantinople the capital of the eastern Roman empire and established Christianity as one of the major religions.

212

GREEK, ca. 1600

Dalmatic
Silk brocade with gold braid. 54 x 26

Museum Appropriation. 28.008

Publication: R. Riefstahl, "Greek Orthodox Vestments and Ecclesiastical Fabrics," *The Art Bulletin*, December 1932, pp. 368–372.

After the conquest of Constantinople in 1453, the Eastern Orthodox communities survived under the Ottoman empire as a religious unit made up of Greeks, Serbians, Bulgarians, and Rumanians. Although not as commonly used in the Eastern Church as it was in the Roman Catholic, this dalmatic (or sukkos) was almost certainly made by Greek workmen, although it clearly incorporates Turkish, Persian, and Greek elements, a practice characteristic of Turkish imperial art of the 16th century.

Taken as a whole, the fabric corresponds technically to the Turkish "Brussa" brocades of the 16th and 17th centuries, but it is unique among Anatolian silks because of its figuration. While not rare in Shiite Persia, figurative representation was strictly avoided in Sunnite Turkey. Only a fabric destined for the use of the Christian community might have that type of decoration which would have been avoided by the Turks themselves.

Christ is the central figure in a drop repeat and is represented as seated on a throne with a curved back. The design on the front of the seat seems to be a simplified rendering of the small turned wood balusters frequently decorating the seats of Christ or the Virgin in Byzantine icons. He is surrounded by symbols of the four evangelists: in the upper left is the eagle of St. John, in the upper right the angel of St. Matthew, in the lower left the ox of St. Luke, and in the lower right the lion of St. Mark. Christ thus surrounded by four symbols is found frequently in Cappadocian frescoes and corresponds exactly to the type common in Byzantine icons. In Christ's features is an attempt to render the severe expression of the Pantokrator: the eyebrows are raised, the pupils set high within the orbits, and the mouth turned downward at the corners. On either side of his head are two typically Turkish flowers, the rosebud and the carnation, well known from the Brussa fabrics.

213

TURKISH, Istanbul, 17th century

Velvet Cushion Cover
Silk and cotton satin weave, silk
supplementary weft, silk cut pile. 43 x 23

Gift of Mrs. Gustav Radeke. 16.003

The Ottoman empire existed from 1299
until the establishment of the Republic
of Turkey in 1923. The classical period of
the Ottoman empire was during the
century following the reign of Suleyman
the Magnificent (reigned 1520–66). At its
peak, the empire included Western Asia,
Northern Africa, the Balkan Peninsula, and Hungary. An important
aesthetic contribution of Ottoman court
art was the development of intricate
continuous patterning in textiles,
ceramics, and architecture.

Magnificent silks were used as wall
hangings, tent linings, and cushion and
floor covers ornamented on a majestic
scale. This velvet cushion cover with the
large scale repeated pattern, which is
related to the lotus blossoms of ancient
Egypt and China, was designed by an
artist and woven in a court manufactory.
Such Turkish velvets were also popular
in Europe as vestments and wall
coverings for the Church. It is difficult to
distinguish between some Italian and
Turkish textiles of the 16th and 17th
centuries, since design ideas were
borrowed and traded back and forth.
Floral motifs, especially tulips and
carnations originally from Persia, reflect
the popularity and enjoyment of
gardens by the nobility of both Europe
and the Near East. Many basic designs
were used over long periods of time and
appear in endless variations; thus, it is
difficult to date the textiles precisely.

This velvet has striking contrasts of
color and texture; the sheen of the ivory
colored satin foundation weave contrasts
with the softness and intense color of
the deep red and chartreuse cut pile.
The pile is employed to create an architectural framework of large palmette or
carnation-shaped compartments filled
with small flowers. The scale, colors,
textures, and continuous pattern have
all been combined to create a luxurious
textile to enhance the richly decorated
interior of the Ottoman court.

214

ALBANIAN, late 19th century

Surcoat

Velvet embellished with metallic embroidery and brocade ribbon; silk lining. 45 x 15½

Gift of Phillip Adams. 73.086.3

This surcoat of wine-red velvet richly embroidered with gold and silver is a portion of a woman's ceremonial costume from southern Albania. It has stylistic affinities with the Turkish djubba, a sleeveless coat worn by women and girls of both the Christian and Moslem faiths. Like the djubba it would have been worn over an equally richly embroidered vest called a jelek, a shirt-style blouse, and a fully cut trouser-like skirt.

From the mid-14th century until early in this century, Albania was part of the Ottoman empire, which was a blend of the whole social and artistic legacy of Islam. The population of Albania has long been a mixture of Moslem, Eastern Orthodox, and Roman Catholic. All of these influences, with their social and political factors, have contributed to the character of the national costumes of the Balkan nations.

The costumes of Albania, especially the southern part, show the influences of the Ottoman empire most strongly. This coat, like the ceremonial garments of the Turks themselves, is made of sumptuous materials in the reds and gold favored in the Turkish palette. The motifs, in ogival arrangement so characteristic of Turkish embroidery, have been stylized and more highly organized in curvilinear form with an indigenous Albanian sense of design. The carnation and tulip, ubiquitous in Turkish art, have been replaced by a four-petaled flower, a frequent motif in Albanian embroidery. The decorative metallic braid-covered buttons with coral beads are similar to those seen on many Turkish garments.

While manufacture of woolen cloth for embroidered garments was common in Albania, the fine velvet as well as the

gold and silver purl (metallic thread made of several strands twisted together) and metallic brocade ribbon for this coat undoubtedly were imported from Italy, with which Albania had maintained strong trade relations for centuries. Although all these goods would have been available from itinerant peddlers, it is likely that the coat itself was cut by a professional tailor. Persian influence via the Ottoman empire is apparent in the enlarged skirt and nipped waist. The sleeves, which are open and hanging free, are probably of indigenous design. The embroidery could have been done by girls and women of a rank sufficiently high to have spent their time in seclusion (as was the practice for women in Moslem-dominated countries), with the leisure time available to prepare such elaborate embroideries for their dowries.

Color plate, page 82

215

ITALIAN, 1640–50

Velvet

Silk and silver rep weave, silk cut and uncut pile. 17½ x 9½

Gift of Mrs. Gustav Radeke. 06.140

Publication: Adèle Coulin Weibel, *Two Thousand Years of Textiles*, New York, 1952, p. 146, pl. 249.

According to legend, the secret of silk production was smuggled out of China and brought to Constantinople in the 7th century. By the 12th century, Arabs had begun a silk weaving industry in Palermo in Sicily. After 1266, when Sicily was taken over by the French, skilled weavers fled to Lucca in the north of Italy where fine silks were produced for the following several hundred years. Other important centers of silk production were Venice, Florence, and Genoa. While it is not definitely known whether velvet weaving originated in Italy or Persia, it began to appear in Italy in the 13th century. Velvet is distinguished by its lush raised pile surface which was accomplished by inserting fine brass rods in each row to hold the loops of thread in place as the weaving pro-

214

gressed; the brass rods had grooves into
which a blade was later inserted to cut
the pile. Patterns were created by
allowing the background weave to show
through in some areas or by contrasting
areas of cut and uncut pile. Because
painters, who also worked as textile
designers, frequently moved from one
city to another and because good
designs were often copied, in most
instances it is not possible to identify the
city where the fabrics were produced.

In 16th century Italy, velvets with
large-scale pomegranate and ogive
designs in deep rich reds, purples, and
blues were woven for the clergy and
nobility of most of Europe for both garments and furnishing fabrics. In the 17th
century, while the bolder textiles
continued to be used for wall hangings
and upholstery, velvets with small scale
repeat patterns in more subtle colors
were made for garments for the nobility.

This sumptuously refined beige velvet
has a background woven with fine silver
threads, many of which have worn
away. Called *cisele,* meaning chiseled,
the surface consists of fine cut and uncut
loops. The cut pile has a deep soft color
tone, while the uncut loops give a
rougher texture and medium color value
to the basically monochromatic velvet.
The overall pattern of a trellis intertwined
with sprigs of acorns on a silver background would have lent luxury and
elegance to a simply-styled mid-17th
century gown.

216

216

ITALIAN, Milan, ca. 1650

Lace

Linen bobbin lace. 13 x 66

Museum Works of Art Reserve. 51.317

Provenance: J. G. Verdier, Paris, 1951

Publication: *Museum Notes/Bulletin,* RISD,
Supplement, 1952.

In 16th century Italy, lace was made for
the Church to decorate altar cloths and
alb flounces. Starting with fine linen
cloth, holes were cut or threads removed
and the empty spaces filled with
embroidery. As lace-making techniques

developed in the 16th and 17th centuries,
gradually more and more of the
foundation fabric was cut away. The
resulting needlepoint lace had a delicate
but bold geometric character.

Bobbin lace was made without a base
fabric; the solid areas were woven and
plaited as the lacemaking progressed.
Several hundred linen threads were
required, each weighted by its own
bobbin. Flax, grown mostly in northern
Europe, could be bleached and spun into
a fine, crisp linen thread with enough
body to hold its shape in the form of an
openwork fabric such as lace. The pattern was traced on parchment, which
was laid on a hard pillow; brass pins
held the thread in place to enable the
lacemaker to follow the design. Plain
woven and contrasting patterned areas
are connected with scrolls and bars of
twisted thread forming a delicate linear
tracery. The fact that the bobbins could
be used to weave in any direction
enabled the creation of a fluid design
with bold, free-flowing curves.

This spectacular lace from Milan
depicts a Renaissance garden with exotic
flowers, birds, and animals; the peacock,
falcon, and rooster, in particular, are
associated with royalty. Donkeys, foxes,
deer, and tiny unicorns are also present.
The image of the double-tailed mermaid
grasping her tails is also found carved on
stone capitals in medieval churches in
Europe. This image is of ancient origin
and has been found representing Scylla
in Greek, Etruscan, and Roman art. In
this context, the mermaid may represent
sin or temptation in a garden of paradise.
The total composition of the lace, made
up of individually formed motifs fitted
together and carefully joined, is a marvel
of design and workmanship.

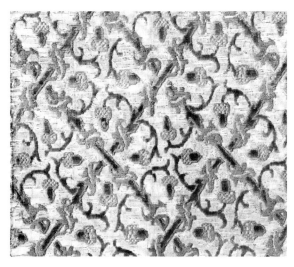

215

217

FLEMISH, Tournai, ca. 1530

Grand Verdure with Animals
Tapestry weave; linen warp, wool and silk weft. 90 x 137

Special Museum Reserve Fund. 43.259

Publications: Phyllis Ackerman, *The Rockefeller McCormick Tapestries,* New York, 1932, p. 17, pl. 32; *Museum Notes/ Bulletin,* RISD, November 1943.

While tapestry weaving began in other parts of Europe and was documented in Paris in 1303, it flourished in Flanders between the 14th and 18th centuries. Besides wall decoration and protection from cold drafts, tapestries were a form of capital investment and were used as diplomatic and political gifts. Tapestries with subjects from religion, history, and mythology were frequently woven in sets of up to ten pieces with individual dimensions of 16' by 33'. Many European rulers had enormous collections; for instance, in the mid-16th century, Francis I had more than 200 pieces in storage in Paris. Sets of tapestries were moved about from one residence to another, and were even taken on military campaigns.

Tapestries were woven on huge upright looms, where several weavers could work side by side. The cartoons were drawn by artists and held behind the warp as a guide to the weavers. Each color area was woven separately with discontinuous wefts which sometimes interlocked, at other times forming small slits which were sewn up after the piece was removed from the loom. Hatching was used to blend colors and eccentric wefts followed the curves and contours of the design rather than being woven in straight rows.

The image of this verdure tapestry is a fantastic garden of paradise populated with fanciful birds and animals. It is very similar to a large tapestry in the Rockefeller McCormick collection and may have been partly copied from the same cartoon. Here, some of the animals, such as the deer hidden among the branches, are treated naturalistically, while others, such as the heraldic lion and griffin, are more stylized. A luxuriant tree, with sinuous branches bearing imaginary flowers and fruit, forms the central axis of the composition. At some time, the original design was made smaller, perhaps to fit a particular wall space. Some of the blossoms on the right side are missing, leaving the tree about six inches off center. This delightful work, retaining most of its rich colors, combines decorative details characteristic of medieval architectural ornamentation, manuscript borders, and metalwork on a majestic scale.

Color plate, page 83

218

ENGLISH, mid-17th century

Casket
Silk satin with flat and raised embroidery in colored silks, with pearls, mica, metal purl, and metallic thread, on wood casket with brass feet. 8¼ x 9¾ x 11

Gift of Mrs. Gustav Radeke. 19.084

Provenance: Benquiat Collection, 1919

Publication: *Bulletin,* RISD, April 1920, pp. 16-18.

The courtship and marriage of Isaac and Rebecca is the theme of the series of silk embroideries which cover the top and sides of this 17th century casket. Old Testament subjects in 17th century costume placed in an exotic landscape were the most popular images found in the ornamental needlework that was the expected accomplishment of gentlewomen in the great households of the period. The raised embroidery on the top of the casket depicts Charles I, popularly regarded as a martyr after his execution in 1649, and his Queen, Henrietta Maria, in the guise of Isaac and Rebecca meeting at the well, here shown as a fountain at the upper left. For the 17th century Englishman, the camels alluded to the Holy Land, the site of Isaac's travels in search of a wife.

The designs for raised embroidery, sometimes called "stump work," and for other pictorial embroideries came from

217

engravings, manuscripts, herbals, and pattern books. A variety of elaborate stitches, twisted wire and crimped strips of metal were used to create differing textures in the raised work. Delicate faces and hands were held in shape by carved wood underneath, while flower petals and leaves were constructed separately using a variation of an interlocking buttonhole stitch and fastened in place when completed.

The front panel is executed in rococo stitch; the sides in satin stitch, and the back in a fine tent stitch. The casket, containing ink wells and writing materials, is trimmed on all edges with silver galloon.

One consistency throughout several centuries of English textiles and decorative arts is an extraordinary fondness for flowers and gardens. Here, not only are the delicate violets, roses, and tulips depicted on a grand scale, but, in addition, animals, birds, bees, butterflies, and snails are all competing for equal attention on the border around the top.

Color plate, page 83

219

ENGLISH, 1740'S

Shoes

Silk floral brocade with leather and kid soles, linen lining. 4 x 3 x 9

Bequest of Mrs. Hope Brown Russell. 09.840a, b

ENGLISH, 1740'S

Clogs

Wood with silk floral brocade, leather soles, kid lining and linen top-stitching. 3 x 8

Bequest of Mrs. Hope Brown Russell. 09.832a, b

These elegant silk brocade shoes with matching clogs are typical of the 1740's with their rounded toes, stout English heels, and lining of coarse linen canvas. They probably would have been fastened at the front with an ornamental buckle which was removed, like any other piece of jewelry, when not in use. Such ornamentation was usual on shoes up until the time of the French Revolution when it would have been abandoned as inappropriately ostentatious. The matching clogs are a sort of overshoe which protected the foot when a lady descended into the filthy streets from her carriage. A similar overshoe with an iron ring at the bottom which elevated the foot, called a patten, was used throughout the century as well by poor and ordinary people. The clog has a wooden wedge which fits beneath the arch and is covered with leather and lined with kid. It would have been fastened over the shoe by means of ribbon ties inserted through holes in the two front flaps. The elegant brocade material covering both the shoes and clogs was typical of the early 18th century, as were shoes with embroidered or lace trimmed cloth. This brocade was similar to, but probably did not match, dresses in the wardrobe of its owner.

218

219

220

FRENCH, mid-18th century
Fan
Painted ivory with mother-of-pearl.
14 x 18

Gift of Mrs. Livingston Hunt. 31.325

In the Museum's large collection of fans, none is more captivating than this "Vernis Martin" made in France during the middle of the 18th century. The brothers Martin were coach painters who, in their attempt to emulate oriental lacquer, discovered a varnish with unusual transparency and hardness which made it a highly suitable protective surface for painted fans. The pristine beauty of many an 18th century fan has been preserved thanks to the quality of their varnished coats.

Vernis Martin fans are always of the *éventail brisé* type; that is, they have no mount, but consist solely of sticks, usually made of ivory, on which a decoration has been thinly painted successively, then covered with a clear varnish. They are held together by a rivet at the bottom and a lacing ribbon at the top. At either end are guard sticks which are usually gilded or carved. Vernis Martins were carried at court by ladies of distinction.

This fan, like many other Vernis Martins, was undoubtedly a wedding gift. Its iconography is romantic, looking to the past with a true 18th century mélange of oriental and Renaissance motifs. On the front is a marriage scene painted in rich, warm colors. The wedding party is gathered in a grandiose Renaissance rotunda; in the lower semi-circle, near the rivet, is Chinoiserie decoration. On the back of the fan is a harbor scene in the grand romantic manner of Claude, showing a gorgeous sunset suffusing everything with its golden light. In the lower semi-circle are dogs chasing a stag, all surrounded by flowers. The guard sticks are painted with Chinese ladies, vases, and Italianate buildings in medallions, each with applied mother-of-pearl at its head.

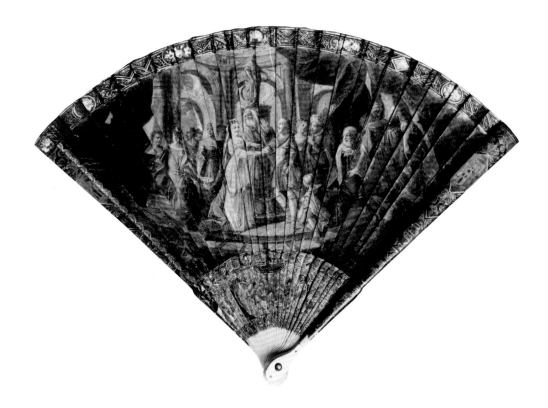

221

FRENCH, ca. 1775

Ballgown
Brocaded and embroidered silk faille.
51 X 13

Gift of the Museum Associates in honor of Eleanor Fayerweather. 82.287.1 a-c

FRENCH, ca. 1775

Man's Suit
Printed silk velvet. 54 x 17

Gift of the Museum Associates in honor of Eleanor Fayerweather. 82.287.2 a-b

Publication: *Museum Notes*, RISD, 1983, p. 16.

The basic components of 18th century costume were established late in the 17th century. For men this meant the coat, waistcoat, and breeches. Women wore a robe, which was open down the front, with a matching petticoat. A triangularly shaped stomacher covered the open bodice. Some robes were fitted close to the waist all the way around in the English style, and others, like ours, were detached behind and flowed away from the body in a wide fold called a Watteau pleat. This was the French style, or robe à la française.

These essential elements changed little during the 18th century; innovation came through changing materials and trims, and, in the case of women, dramatic changes in shape. With the aid of tightly laced corsets pushing the breasts up and forward and wide underskirts of linen-covered whalebone ellipses, the 18th century woman achieved a highly sculptured silhouette. Robes worn à la polonaise, pulled up from the hem with drawn strings, added billowed panniers to already enormous hips. (This exaggerated shape reached its zenith at mid-century and gradually fell more in line with the natural body shape as the century progressed.) The shape of men's clothes, on the other hand, changed little, the most noticeable difference being a gradual shortening in the length of the coat and waistcoat.

Extravagant use of materials and trims characterized the costume of both men and women. Corded silks, damasks, velvets, and rich brocades gave the look of splendor desired by both sexes. Embroidery, elegant ribbons, and costly buttons were the signs of high style that might change overnight and kept men and women of fashion in constant touch with their dressmaker and milliner or tailor.

By 1775, heightened social and political distress had its effect on fashion; wisdom had begun to dictate against ostentation. Our elegant but simple velvet suit with its fabric covered buttons reflects this trend. Earlier days would have required it to be of silk or a rich brocade trimmed with embroidery and layers of lace. Our ball gown is likewise rich but not ostentatious. They mark the end of an era, closed by the French Revolution, after which the good and prudent citizen chose to assert virtue, rather than splendor, through dress.

Color plate, page 84
Color plate, page 85

JEAN-DEMOSTHENE DUGOURC
French, 1749-1825
Camille Pernon et Compagnie

The Pheasants, ca. 1785
Brocaded silk satin weave; silk
embroidery. 93 x 17¾

Mary B. Jackson Fund. 47.194

Provenance: French and Company,
New York, 1947

Publication: Adèle Coulin Weibel, *Two
Thousand Years of Textiles*, New York,
1952, pp. 161-2.

By the mid-17th century, France had
become the leader in the textile arts,
producing magnificent tapestries at
Gobelin and Aubusson, beautiful laces
at Alençon and Argentan, and luxurious silks at Lyons. French kings of the
17th and 18th century patronized the silk
industry at Lyons, where silk brocades
and cloths of gold were woven especially
for splendid court ceremonies and balls.

Many of France's best painters and
designers were commissioned to design
silks to be woven on the drawloom, a
complex loom operated by a weaver and
an assistant, a "draw boy," who pulled
the cords which controlled the intricate
pattern mechanism. Jean-Démosthené
Dugourc was an outstanding interior
designer of his time. In addition to
textiles and interiors, he also designed
costumes and sets for the Paris opera,
and, for a time, was chief architect to the
King of Spain. Camille Pernon, the
manufacturer, worked with Dugourc as
well as other exceptional artists and
weavers to produce magnificent silks for
the royal courts all over Europe.

The extraordinary silk brocade is part
of a series of wall panels designed and
woven especially for the Royal Palace of
Madrid. An elaborately embroidered
birdcage, the only part not woven on the
loom, is surrounded by a brocaded
garland of roses with ribbons and
strands of beads below. Two confronting
pheasants, holding a double strand of
pearls in their beaks, are perched on
cone-shaped baskets. Above is a tall vase
of asters flanked by scrolling foliage. The
colors range from the intense reds and
browns of the pheasants to the delicate
pastels of the floral garlands, all on a
shimmering ivory-colored satin ground.
The delicate handling of so many diverse
and elaborate motifs forms a delightful
transition from the 18th century Rococo
to the more stylized period of the early
19th century.

223

FRENCH, ca. 1790–1800

Waistcoat
Satin with silk pointe de chainette
embroidery, wool twill back and linen
lining. 24 x 17

Gift of Francis Whitehead. 71.109.48

More waistcoats have survived over the
years than perhaps any other man's
garment. Because most of the color and
ornamentation in men's clothing has
been concentrated there, they have
always been regarded as useful documents of both the fashion and decorative
arts of their time. This charmingly
embroidered example would have been
part of an elegant man's costume at the
end of the 18th century when there was
a virtual mania for embroidered waistcoats. It would not have been uncommon
for a man of style to have as many as 100
in his wardrobe. Although by 1789 the
French Revolution had put an end to the
ostentatious use of rich fabrics and
colors which until that time had characterized both men's and women's
clothing, white or cream satin continued
to be a favored background for the
embroidered ornamentation of waistcoats and remained popular in Europe
until well into the 19th century.

As the embodiment of elegance and
sophistication, embroidery was a reflection of 18th century taste. It was a status
symbol which persisted through a
period ostensibly preoccupied with
democratic ideals. On a professional
level, patterns for embroidery were
created by designers and then executed
to shape on uncut fabric which later
would be made up into the garment in
workshops by skilled hands. Embroidery
was a popular amateur pastime as well.
For a woman, to be skilled as an embroi-
deress was synonymous with being well
educated. It was one of the few labors
allowed the rich. The pointe de chainette
stitch was popular among amateurs and
this waistcoat may as easily have been a
labor of love as a product of commerce.
Its motif of a humble traveler would
have suited the democratic values of the
day and its inclusion on such an elegant
garment would have matched the
French 18th century penchant for irony
through juxtaposition. Floral motifs
were ubiquitous and exemplify the
naturalism and delicacy which dominate
design considerations throughout the
century. Overblown flowers in full
bloom placed symmetrically all over the
surface were popular early in the century; natural size flowers on a geometric
grid followed, and toward the last third
of the century, as our waistcost exemplifies, patterns become small, delicate,
and confined to the borders, with buds
scattered all over the field.

224

JEAN-BAPTISTE ISABEY
French, 1767–1855

Court Train, 1804
Velvet embroidered with silver purl,
lined with satin. 132 x 63

Gift of Mrs. Harold Brown. 37.215

Designed to convey the importance of
the wearer and to allude to the greatness
of Napoleon, this orange velvet court
train with white satin was worn by
Madame Henri Gratien Bertrand, wife of
Napoleon's aide-de-camp, to Napoleon's
coronation in 1804.

The train would have been worn high,
immediately below the bust which was
the "waistline" of the Empire style.
Almost 11 feet in length, it would have
been at the height of fashion in 1804.

Orange, not an appropriate color for
everyday wear, was a symbol of social
rank and correct for ceremonial use. It
would have been worn with a white
gown and must have created a dynamic
and emphatic effect. The borders, as
have been characteristic of ceremonial
garments since medieval times, are
heavily embroidered with silver purl. In
a candlelit hall it would have had its own
luminosity. The embroidered palmettes
refer to Napoleon's victorious Egyptian
campaign which inspired the use of
Egyptian and Turkish motifs in European
embroidery and furniture.

The appearance of luxury and opulence on state occasions resumed only
gradually after the French Revolution.
When the bourgeoisie were in control
and fashion's aim was to have women of
all ranks dress as much alike as possible, make-up and rich dress were
proscribed. Instead, plain cotton and
chintzes were worn, inspired by
Rousseau's natural ideal and the antiquities discovered by Winckelmann in
the 18th century. But the years of
austerity were not long; fashion began to
show itself again in small ways – usually
making political references, such as
trimming hats with tricolor ribbons to
honor the new nation. By 1795 the Reign
of Terror was over, the Directory was
formed, and social life marked by social
distinctions had resumed.

With his elevation to First Counsel,
Napoleon established a court which
became increasingly regal. He expected
his wife Josephine and all the other
women of the court to dress to a high
standard of luxury with lavish displays
of jewels. To that end Josephine even
managed to retrieve Marie Antoinette's
pearls and in 1803 appeared in the crown
jewels during a state visit to Belgium.
And for the most splendid of state
occasions, the coronation of Napoleon,
Josephine spared no effort, calling upon
the greatest artists and artisans of the
day. This court train, designed by the
painter Jean-Baptiste Isabey, was part of
the glittering spectacle.

Color plate, page 85

225

FRENCH, 1870'S

Parasol
Silk covered with chantilly lace;
carved ivory handle; steel shaft and ribs.
22 x 25

Gift of Miss Emily Buch. 58.025.9

Unlike her 20th century counterpart, a lady in the 19th century was careful to protect her complexion from the rays of the sun. Not only was darkened skin extremely unfashionable, but it was thought to be unhealthy as well. Too much sun could cause vertigo, epilepsy, sore eyes, and fevers, according to contemporary medical wisdom. When Queen Victoria came to the throne, a lady typically wore a bonnet whose brim encircled her face and, more likely than not, had a veil. If she were fashionable as well, she carried a parasol.

This third line of defense from the sun originated in the Orient and had an illustrious history of sheltering digni-taries and persons of wealth. Often the parasol was so large and cumbersome that a servant was necessary to support it. Brought to Europe as an artifact from the Grand Tour, it became common for both men's and women's use in Europe during the 1700's. During the 19th century, it had diminished in size and could be carried with ease. By then it had gone well beyond its original function to become an instrument of coquetry and social intercourse rivaling the power of the fan.

Early construction utilized bamboo, rattan, or oak ribs. Whalebone was an early substitute which was more functional but expensive. After 1826 steel ribs were used, and as these became lighter in weight the parasol became smaller and its cover made of finer materials. Much creative energy was put into its trim and the elaboration of its handle. Several individuals working separately were responsible for its manufacture: a ribmaker, a trained artisan who carved or fabricated the handle, and a milliner who covered and trimmed it up in the very latest fashion. It was an elaborate and expensive fashion accessory.

The utilitarian aspect of the parasol predominated until the 1840's, but a growing middle class who could afford carriages in which to be out and about acquired objects for elegant display. The way a parasol was used in the skilled hands of a lady not only indicated her wealth and social position, but communicated very directly her disposition towards others she encountered. A slight tilt to the left or right might not only shelter her eyes from the sun but from social inferiors as well. A deft twirl might attract the attention of a handsome man and encourage an acquaintanceship.

The elegant, elaborately carved, twisted rope design handle of our parasol was inspired by Oriental models. Its folding stick, a device common throughout the century, made it very convenient to carry along in the carriage. The small pagoda top of silk covered with chantilly lace undoubtedly coordinated with its owner's costume, but was probably only one of many in her wardrobe.

226

JEAN-PHILIPPE WORTH (HOUSE OF WORTH)
French, 1856–1926

Evening Gown, ca. 1919
Gold lamé covered with silk chiffon; silk
bodice covered with metallic
embroidered tulle; rhinestone accessory.
51½ x 13

Gift of Mr. and Mrs. Archer Iselin.
81.287.2

Publication: *Museum Notes*, RISD, 1982,
p. 11.

In 1856, with the then startling innovation of using live mannequins wearing model garments, Charles Frederick Worth established the House of Worth, the first of the great institutions of haute couture as we know them today.

Prior to Worth's time a woman would first have selected her material and then gone to a dressmaker, who would make up a gown according to her customer's instructions which, more often than not, came from a current fashion plate. Worth, instead, presented his own inspiration to a customer on a model which allowed her to see exactly what her dress would look like before it was made up.

Securing the patronage of a favorite of Napoleon III, Princess Pauline de Metternich, Worth gained the attention and favor of the Empress Eugénie. With the court as his client, his workrooms were often required to produce as many as 1,000 dresses within a week's time for a single event. Since the guests would know each other well, each dress had to be unique. This enormous undertaking was made possible only by Worth's ingenious establishment of a system of standardized interchangeable parts which allowed diversity through permutations of sleeves, bodices, skirts, and trims.

Besides the French court, the House of Worth came to be patronized by almost every woman famous (or infamous) by birth, wealth, or scandal. Worth's name was magic through the 1860's and into the 80's and, as a large-scale producer of luxury goods, his house was one of the mainstays of the French economy. But by the late 1880's times had changed: the court of Napoleon III had met its demise; the House of Worth had come under the directorship of Worth's son, Jean-Philippe; and strong competition was coming from other houses that had followed Worth's lead – Doucet, Raudnitz, Callot-Soeurs, and Rouff. Continuing the uncompromising line of elegance that had made his father's reputation, Jean-Philippe designed now for a wealthy, but no longer elite, clientele. By the turn of the century, the House of Worth, following the lead of others (Poiret in particular) had established branches at fashionable resorts and created liaisons with the great department stores of London and New York.

This gown has the elegance of line that made the House of Worth famous, but reflects the fashion realities of the period after World War I. The draped overskirt was always one of Worth's favorite ploys, but the use of chiffon and lamé was influenced by Isadora Duncan. It is a dress made for a wealthy client, who valued the tradition of elegance associated with the House of Worth but accepted the possibility of meeting someone wearing a duplicate of her lovely gown.

226

227

227

MARIANO FORTUNY Y MADRAZO
Spanish, 1871–1949

Printed Textile, 1920–30
Cotton twill, stenciled and handpainted.
104 x 27½

Gift of Barbara Deering Danielson.
82.308.48G

Publication: *Museum Notes,* RISD, 1983,
p. 18.

Mariano Fortuny was a gifted artist who
worked in many media. First a painter
and engraver, he later went on to design
theatre costumes, stage sets, interiors,
and textiles, in addition to his well-
known pleated gowns inspired by Greek
and medieval garments. As an inventor,
he developed many unique dyeing and
printing processes along with the necessary machinery, as he oversaw every
phase of production in his Venetian
workshop.

Although these processes have
remained secret, here it appears that to
recreate the lush colors and textures of a
17th century Italian velvet, Fortuny used
stenciled and hand-painted pigment
with bronze powder on red cotton along
with discharge dyeing, a carefully
controlled method of removing color.
This piece is a striking example of the
use of modern means to create a timeless
quality of color and texture that blends
the present with the past.

Fortuny, whose collection of antique
textiles from Persia, Turkey, Italy, China,
and Japan provided a constant source of
inspiration, designed his fabrics to be
draped wall coverings in museums,
hotels, palaces, and private homes.

228

AMERICAN, probably Boston, mid-18th
century

Canvaswork Picture
Linen plain weave; wool and silk
embroidery. 23¾ x 24½

Gift of Mrs. Jesse H. Metcalf. 23.075

Publication: *Bulletin,* RISD, vol. XVI,
No. 2, 1928.

Although in the 18th century canvaswork
embroidery was used primarily to cover
furniture, this embroidered picture was
probably done by the daughter of a
prosperous family at a finishing school
when she was in her late teens or early
twenties. The picture is related to a
series of embroideries known to have
been made in Boston between 1746 and
1791. Because the works depict so many
similar motifs, it is thought that perhaps
there was a girls' school in Boston where
this type of needlework was taught.

Some common elements in these
pieces are idyllic landscapes of rolling
hills with figures in 18th century dress,
with buildings in the background and
birds and animals scattered about to fill
the empty spaces. The embroideries
show a concern with many interesting
details, rather than with the unity of the
total composition.

While American needlework of the
early 18th century shows a strong
English influence, the English work
tends to be more sophisticated in
approach. The figures in the pictures
were often taken from English and
French engravings, and the animals in
the background were traced directly
from needlework pattern books. The
patterns consisted of design units which
were meant to be combined according to
the whim of the needleworker; this
accounts for the variety in the size and
treatment of the animals and other
design elements, and the lack of
perspective.

Although some of the embroideries in
this series depict scenes of Boston
Common, the place and time shown
here cannot be identified. The focal
point is a charming couple playing
backgammon in the foreground with a
young woman standing by. The tree
with the parrot perched on a branch
lends an exotic touch to the composition.
While the buildings and the windmill
appear to be European, the treatment
and lack of sophistication seem typically
American.

228

229

NABBY MARTIN
American, East Windsor, Connecticut,
1775–1864

Sampler, 1786
Linen plain weave, silk and metallic
embroidery. 15 x 10¼

Museum Appropriation. 17.361

Publications: Glee Krueger, *New England
Samplers to 1840,* Sturbridge, 1978, pl. 44;
Betty Ring, *Let Virtue Be a Guide to Thee,*
Providence, 1983, p. 33.

The original purpose of embroidering a sampler was for a girl to practice decorating household linens and marking them with initials. In the 17th century, samplers tended to be long and narrow with space to record new stitches as they were learned. In the late 18th and early 19th centuries, after mastering embroidered alphabets, a girl would go on to create a pictorial sampler incorporating a verse and floral border in a wider format. This work was considered to be an important accomplishment of a well-educated young lady, and was often framed and displayed in a prominent place in her family's home.

Certain girls' academies, whose popularity increased during the prosperity following the Revolution, developed distinctive styles of needlework. Mary Balch's school in Providence (1785–1831) made a unique contribution to American needlework. The work of the school is more elaborate than most others of the period, employing a large variety of stitches with great attention to detail. Miss Balch's advertisement of 1825, "Taught as usual . . . Reading, Penmanship, English Grammer, Geography . . . , Arithmetick, Philosophy, Astronomy, and Chemistry. Painting, Embroidery, and most kinds of useful and ornamental work," shows that she took a girl's education seriously and that much more than needlework was taught at her school.

Eleven-year-old Nabby Martin, whose sampler illustrates a typical Balch School format, stitched a piece bordered on each side by an urn of large flowers. Rhode Island College, now University Hall at Brown University, appears at the top, with the Old Rhode Island State House in the center. Well-dressed figures promenade about on a dark green background filled with animals and birds. The saying, "Let Virtue be a Guide to Thee," and the row of strawberries above are both frequently found on needlework of the Balch School. Especially noteworthy are the four large flowers done in rococo stitch. Though Nabby Martin worked under her teacher's guidance, she created a charming sampler which still retains fresh, rich colors and has its own unique character.

Color plate, page 86

230

AMERICAN, early 19th century

Corset
Wool and linen, linen, leather and iron.
33 x 16½

Given in memory of Mrs. Lemuel H.
Arnold by her children. 10.044

The earliest references to corsets, fashion's instrument for controlling "the chaos of the flesh," are literary descriptions of Greek women wearing a band of linen or leather known as a zoné or girdle over their dress in order to control the torso. Its first visual representation is found among the Cottonian manuscripts at the British Museum which show a fantastic creature clothed in women's dress which features a tight-fitting bodice laced up the front. Extensive development came later when Queen Elizabeth I established the cult of the long, slim torso. At first a stiff linen underbodice, known as a cotte, was worn. As the mode progressed, this garment was made more figure-defining and rigid by use of paste stiffening between two layers of linen. By the 16th century it was fortified with whalebone – a material which coupled flexibility with tremendous strength along its narrow shafts. Catherine de Medici, who dictated fashion in the late 16th century, declared a thick waist to be the height of bad manners for a woman and prescribed the 13-inch waist as the feminine ideal.

Emphasis on the slim waist continued almost without exception for the next two centuries. Men as well as women wore corsets. Children, who were considered to be miniature adults, wore them too, in imitation of the adult ideal. Even the Puritans commended the use of the corset on the grounds that it disciplined the body (which it accomplished by displacing organs, inhibiting bone growth, and forbidding movement.) It was so disruptive to normal physiological functioning that a corset was considered to be an effective means of contraception and an inducement to abortion.

The French Revolution, under the intellectual enlightenment of Rousseau, put the waistline into temporary eclipse as the focus of attention shifted to the breasts, which, in their unfettered state, were thought to be symbolic of the virtues of Motherhood, Fertility, and Nature. The corset did not disappear but was modified in dimension in order to shape the body to the Neo-classical ideal of small hips and uplifted bosom of the true Grecian form. By the 1840's, however, and for the remainder of the 19th century, fashion focused its attention back on the waistline.

This early 19th century corset is made of a bright yellow combination of linen and wool and lined with a coarse linen which is typical of its time. It is singularly rigid and compressing. Its bottom border is cut into tabs so that it could fit across the waist and shape the hips. The back is higher than the front which now supports rather than flattens the breasts. The sides are hollowed out beneath the armpits. The back laces with a single thread which would have been done up by a personal maid or a close friend. One contemporary article advises a mother to have her daughter lie flat on the floor with the mother's foot in the small of her back so that she can get more purchase for lacing the corset. The eyeholes are bound in silk – an indication of its age, since metal rings were not used until 1828. Iron rods provide the stiffening that prompted reports of women falling and being badly bruised by their "vulcanian stays." Iron was a substitute for the more flexible whalebone which now was in short supply. This corset would have been worn over, not under, a chemise – quite possibly because of the rust problem which would have been presented by laundering a corset with iron stays.

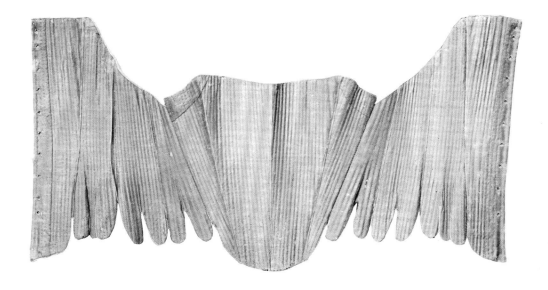

231

AMERICAN, ca. 1835

Bandbox
Pasteboard covered with wallpaper.
20 x 16 x 12

Gift of Stephen Minot Pitman. 17.368

Colorful, ornamental, and often witty, the decorative and functional character of bandboxes has been appreciated by collectors since the 1920's when American folk art was "discovered." Used by both men and women as storage units and travel accessories, bandboxes reached the height of their popularity between 1825 and 1850, by which time first class hotels and improved roads serviced by reliable transportation had made travel relatively easy and accessible to an increasing number of people.

Bandboxes came in a variety of sizes which were popular at different times throughout the century. The largest, often rectangular or oval, were popular as status symbols in the 1840's with young girls who traveled between their homes and the newly available jobs in nearby factories. Medium size boxes

could store miscellaneous accessories and were a virtual necessity during the 1830's for the protection of the large frilled daycaps that were the height of fashion at that time. The smallest sizes were often workboxes or for the use of children. While some boxes were home-made, more often they were manufactured. Usually when a costly dress or hat was purchased, a bandbox to carry and store it in came with it.

Men used bandboxes to protect their costly beaver stovepipe hats, the box often being identical in shape with the hat to offer maximum protection. As early as the 17th century men used bandboxes to protect their frilled neck ruffs. In fact, the term "bandbox" was derived from its usefulness for carrying men's neckbands.

Some bandboxes were made of wood with their decoration painted on, often by the local coach painter. Boxes of this sort were in use in Pennsylvania in particular. But most bandboxes were like this one, made of pasteboard covered with decorated paper with the parts stitched together with strong linen cord, and often lined with newspapers which have made them easy to date. Usually the covering was wallpaper, frequently imported from Europe, or of paper

produced especially for bandboxes. It might be hand decorated using a gouache paint or, like this one, printed with woodblocks using four or more colors in the manner of Japanese prints. These papers are among the first examples of color printing done in America.

Made in every conceivable color and design, bird and animal as well as floral patterns were very popular. So were scenes of local interest and public · buildings. Travel themes such as the steamboat and the railway on which contemporary public interest was focused were frequently seen, as were pictorial celebrations of the great events of the day. The paper covering of our box depicts the balloon voyage of a young English adventurer, Richard Clayton, from the Cincinnati Amphi-theater on April 8, 1835, 350 miles east to Monroe County, Virginia. This was a record-breaking achievement in a popular contemporary sport. Our box is one of many depicting this historic event and preserves in pictorial form a record of the infancy of aerial navigation in America.

232

AMERICAN, 1884

Dress
Silk compound brocade and satin,
trimmed with chenille and lace. 52 x 14

Gift of Miss Beatrice McCloy.
60.068.2 a,b

As in any period, parallels existed
during the 1880's between interior
decoration and women's dress. Probably
at no other time, however, was there
such a close resemblance in the way
windows, furniture, and women were
dressed. Layering of surfaces, neo-
mannerist exaggeration of form, ostentatious display of rich colors and fabrics
reached a peak during the 80's in all
these contexts. Trims, ruching, pleats,
drapery, elaborate fitting, folds draped
across pleats, pleats across fringe, velvet
on satin, and fringe over brocade were
everywhere the height of fashion.

The number and complexity of the
pieces comprising a dress such as this
one were astounding, and it was during
this last third of the 19th century that the
dressmaker's art truly came into its own.
The fullness fashionable at mid-century
was replaced with a passion for closeness
of fit. The bodice was long and tightly
buttoned over a torso-distorting corset,
ending as this one does with a point at
the waist. The bustle which had
disappeared in the 1870's reappeared as
a steel-banded extension to the derrière
with a sort of camel's hump shape to it,
giving the effect of a platform behind
and making the female figure look as
though it had four legs like a centaur.
With the bustle came the elaborately
draped skirt, pleated and flounced,
often with elaborate panniers falling off
in a waterfall effect behind. With its
ponderous folds, the dress of the 1880's
exaggerated William Morris's dictum of
the preceding decade that no dress can
be beautiful that is stiff. Even daytime
materials were generally heavy, and
with the tight-fitting bodice high at the
neck and pointed at the waist, the whole
ensemble took on the upholstered look
usually associated with furniture.

233

234

ADRIAN (ADRIAN ADOLPH GREENBERG)
American, 1903–1959

Woman's Suit, 1950
Men's wool suiting. 44 x 16

Gift of Mrs. Ella-Mae Manwarring.
68.151

This suit is not only representative of the famous "coat hanger" silhouette devised by Adrian (broad shouldered jacket with pencil slim skirt), but is one of the high points in the trend towards masculinization of women's clothing that had its start early in the century. Adrian chose the Modernist aesthetic of streamlined severity with attention to architectural detailing to dress the competent female moving and living in a man's world. Down to its use of wool suiting, it resembles a man's suit, but its yoked jacket with intricate insets belies the impression of simplicity.

Adrian made his name in the world of fashion through his career as a costume designer for Hollywood, where he always thought of his creations as vehicles to help the actor realize his role. Reportedly his "coat hanger" silhouette was originally developed in response to the problem of dressing Joan Crawford for a contemporary film role, for her broad shoulders made anything other than exaggeration impossible. Her look became the fashion of the 1940's, conveying the casual elegance, competence, and discreet femininity of the contemporary ideal. The Second World War brought hard times to Hollywood and Adrian made the difficult choice to leave a successful career to open his own house, Adrian Ltd., in Beverly Hills, where he produced what he felt were distinctly American designs.

With Paris cut off from the fashion world by the Nazi occupation, Adrian seized the opportunity to push his name and those of other American designers into the limelight. Department stores could not stock enough of his suits, expensive as they were. At the end of the war, however, with the assistance of *Vogue* and *Harper's Bazaar,* Paris recaptured the fashion headlines with Dior's ultra-feminine New Look of corseted waists and crinolined skirts. Adrian continued his success, however, through the 1950's; his suits, with slightly diminished shoulders, became the "classical" look.

233

H.F.MALLINSON AND CO.
American

Franklin's Key to Electricity, ca. 1926
Printed silk. 33 x 39. Half drop repeat,
16 x 18¾

Gift of the Society for the Preservation of
New England Antiquities. 57.083.100D

Franklin's Key to Electricity is one of a series of designs of *Early and Modern America* produced by Mallinson and Co. for the Sesquicentennial celebration in 1926. Mallinson was a leader in the silk industry in developing plain and multi-colored silks in an unusual variety of weaves and textures with trade names such as "Silkyway Brocade" and "Butterfly Velvet Voile." Their sheer "Indestructible Chiffon Voile" was guaranteed for at least two seasons.

This series of textile designs reflects the avant-garde art of the period as a reference for important American historical events. Here images such as a laboratory, electric lights, a printing press, construction sites, power lines, dams and hydroelectric plants, a city-scape, cars, and trains were combined to create a dynamic pattern symbolizing Franklin's experiments with electricity and the industrialization of America.

The American silk industry, which developed mainly in Paterson, New Jersey, began in the 1840's when individual entrepreneurs and skilled textile workers from Europe sought new opportunities in this country. Experienced designers and silk weavers, who lost their cottage industry jobs because of industrialization in Europe, contributed the knowledge and skills handed down in their families for generations to the development of the American silk industry, which was at its peak during the first quarter of the 20th century. The mid-20's was a period of great energy and optimism, and this design reflects that vibrant spirit. This textile is part of a study collection which documents the American textile industry of the 20th century.

235

CHARLES JAMES
English, 1906–1978

Ballgown, 1949
Velvet, catoir sateen, and taffeta. 66 x 14

Gift of Mrs. William Randolph Hearst.
57.084.1

CHARLES JAMES (Boucheron)
English, 1906–1978

Helmet Hat, 1929
Balibuntal straw. 10 x 12 x 7

Gift of Mrs. John Lincoln. 66.344

Charles James, once called the Frank Lloyd Wright of fashion, was an architect, sculptor, and engineer in his approach to design and a quixotic figure in the history of fashion. Born in 1906, he spent his formative years in England and then moved with his family to Chicago, where, in 1925, he began his design career as a milliner. The Museum's collection includes a now rare example of his early work in the form of a straw helmet hat made by James under his pseudonym, Boucheron. He moved his business back to London in 1928 but soon left it to go to Paris, determined to teach himself dress design. A few years later, James, beset by creditors (a state of affairs to be repeated many times throughout his career), came to New York where he formalized his couture establishment as Charles James, Inc. Through his early association with Elizabeth Arden, James was catapulted into the forefront of fashion design.

Although many James designs were produced for mass market consumption (the Museum's collection contains several such examples), his contribution to fashion is most significant in the area of haute couture; his clientele were the tastemakers of the time. It was his series of ballgowns, which consumed only five of his productive years, that made his reputation as a designer's designer, an architect of fashion.

James designed this gown for Mrs. William Randolph Hearst to wear at the Truman Inaugural Ball in 1949; it is a sculpture expressed in fabric. James the engineer planned and outlined the precise dimensions of its silhouette over a wire and padded structure he built himself. He did not create a specific size, but a shape into which various sizes were made to fit through corseting and underpinning.

234

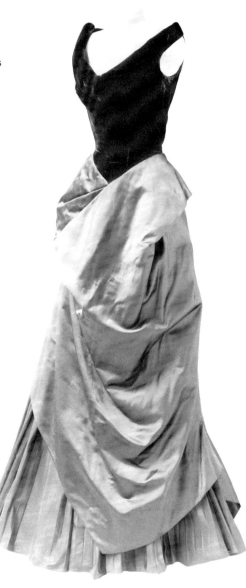

235

BONNIE CASHIN
American, b. 1915

*Sportswear Ensemble: Coat, Tunic,
and Skirt,* 1969
Wool trimmed with leather. 39 x 20

Gift of Phillip Sills. 80.171.23 a–c

Designed primarily to serve the needs of
the contemporary woman whose lifestyle is both affluent and active, this
ensemble is typical of the designs of
Bonnie Cashin. It is part of a large collection of her work at this Museum.

Always a believer that simple geometry provides maximum mobility,
Cashin's clothes are organic in conception with as few darts and seams as
possible. It is the character of the
material, in this case a bold wool plaid
trimmed with leather, hanging gracefully and naturally, that gives the air of
casual elegance that Cashin feels is the
essence of the well-dressed American
woman.

Like many American designers,
Bonnie Cashin started her career designing costumes for the theater and then
moved on to the movies and Hollywood,
coming to prominence during the
Second World War when Paris was cut
off from its fashion markets. She has
always conceived of her creations as a
means of assisting a specific type of
woman who is playing a specific role.
For the physically active and varied
lifestyles of her clientele, Cashin
developed the layered look of many
simply cut parts which could be shed or
added as the weather or occasion
demanded.

Cashin's inspirations, for the most
part, came from the Orient; the No coat
of this ensemble is her signature silhouette and was derived from Japanese
theater robes. Like most of her clothes, it
wraps the body rather than defining it.
The matching tunic was inspired by the
design of a traditional Chinese under-
coat. Other designs have come from the
work clothes of other ethnic groups; she
introduced the poncho early in the
1950's, inspired by the traditional
Mexican garment. Her early introduction
of the jump-suit was adapted from
workmen's overalls.

237

VERA MAXWELL
American, b. 1904

Travel Suit, 1974
Tie-dyed Ultrasuede and polyester.
47 x 16

Gift of Vera Maxwell. 80.065.8 a–c

After the 1930's, haute couture turned its attention from its traditional clientele to a new social phenomenon whose needs promised both lucrative and challenging prospects to a dwindling industry: the working woman. A product both of the Depression and of a rapidly industrializing society which promised a higher standard of living, her multifaceted life and financial limitations necessitated clothes that had both style and practicality and a look that would not fall out of fashion in just one season.

Vera Maxwell was one of the earliest designers to see a solution to the modern woman's dilemma by adapting the concept of sportswear to everyday living. Her wardrobe of separate but interchangeable parts done in elegant fabrics offered style as well as the freedom and comfort of clothing designed especially for sports. Her cut, borrowed from British methods of tailoring, was coupled with an affinity for rich and unusual fabric combinations to offer a wardrobe of practical elegance to the working woman.

The classic lines of Vera Maxwell's designs are expressed in three basic silhouettes: the peasant style with tight waist and full shirred skirt; the straight Chinese line; and, in between, what she referred to as her "boyish silhouette." Different fabrics, colors, combinations of materials and trims provide the contemporary touch. It is her use of tie-dyed fabric or perhaps Indian embroidery, not the timeless shape, that identifies the specific date of the garment. This wine red travel ensemble, from a collection of works by Maxwell spanning the late 1940's through the 1970's, has classic sportswear lines enlivened by the combination of polyester and Ultrasuede – a material of great ease and practicality as well as visual appeal which was introduced by Maxwell in 1971, but ignored by the fashion industry until several years later.

Vera Maxwell's innovation in the fashion world, like that of her contemporary, Coco Chanel, was less in the style of her garments than in the philosophic position that clothes should adapt to the needs of the wearer rather than the other way around. The essential realism of her vision is expressed by the fact that her clothes could be worn by a variety of individual figures rather than by an ideal type.

238

AMERICAN, Navajo, Third Phase, 1870–1890

Chief's Blanket
Tapestry weave, wool warp, wool weft.
55 × 73

Gift of Mrs. John Sloan. 42.088

The Navajo chief's blanket, which actually could have been worn as a mantle by any member of the tribe, was a garment of enormous prestige. The Navajos, with their semi-nomadic way of life and unstructured social organization, had no actual chiefs, and the name "chief's blanket" may refer to the fact that these blankets were widely traded and worn by chiefs of other Plains tribes.

The Navajos were one of the many Athabascan tribes which migrated from Alaska and Western Canada to the American Southwest sometime around A.D. 1000. The Navajos, traditionally nomadic raiders, proved highly adaptable to their new environment and borrowed numerous cultural elements from other tribes. According to Navajo legend, the art of weaving was given to them by Spider Woman, one of the Holy People. Archaeological research has revealed that prehistoric weaving in the Southwest was done with yucca and other wild plant and animal fibers. Cotton was introduced from Mexico betwen A.D. 100 and 600, and when the Spanish arrived in the 1500's, there was already a thriving industry producing cotton textiles for domestic use and for export. The more settled and peace-loving Pueblos learned to weave with wool and to raise sheep traded by the Spaniards, and it was from this source that the Navajos learned to weave woolen blankets.

Early Navajo blanket design was based on an intricate, subtle pattern of stripes of white and dark brown natural wool and deep blue yarn dyed with indigo. In the late 18th century, small amounts of red yarn dyed with cochineal were obtained by unraveling woolen bayeta cloth imported by the Spanish from England, and these small bands of red added a vibrant note to the restrained power of the striped blanket. Red yarn gained increasing importance in the Navajo palette, partly as a result of its availability from England and later from New England and Pennsylvania. Examination of the types of yarn found in a blanket serves as the most important means for dating. Here red is used with natural dark brown wool to weave a pattern of stepped diamonds, a design characteristic of the third phase, and which here appears to float on the striped background. The aniline red, a chemical dye which became available to the Navajos in the last quarter of the 19th century, was obtained from several dye lots and has faded to shades of salmon pink. The blanket was intended to function as a prestigious mantle enclosing the human figure, with geometric shapes along the edges meeting in front to complete the design. When seen today on a museum wall, its rich color variations of dyed and natural tones take on the impact and immediacy of contemporary abstract painting.

239

PERUVIAN, Paracas Peninsula,
1st century A.D.

Embroidered Mantle
Wool plain weave, cotton borders;
wool embroidery. 50 x 93

Museum Appropriation. 40.190

Provenance: John Wise, New York

Publications: *Bulletin*, RISD, December
1940, p. 80, pl. 51; Pal Keleman, *Medieval
American Art*, New York, 1946, II, pl.
177b; George Kubler, *The Art and Architecture of Ancient America*, Baltimore,
1962, p. 148b.

In Peru, before the Spanish conquest, the bodies of important persons were prepared for burial seated in a basket and wrapped with many layers of textiles to form a large bundle which was often decorated with a false head, mask, and wig. These elaborate mummy bundles were buried in the desert along the coast. Many beautiful textiles survive because of this method of burial and because of the extremely dry climate. The typical garments found in graves were tunics, breech cloths, kilt-like skirts, turbans, and large mantles, such as the one pictured here.

Weaving is an ancient art in Peru. The earliest evidence is of twined and darned textiles decorated with birds and animals and made before the invention of the simple heddle loom. By the 1st century A.D. the predominant textiles from the Paracas Peninsula on the south coast were a plain weave embroidered with elaborate figures representing myths of fertility and immortality. The embroidery was painstakingly done in a simple stem stitch. Along the border, the stitches are so dense that they resemble the texture of weaving. The richness and variety of color are remarkable and no two figures have the same color arrangement.

The mythological flying figure repeated on this mantle in a checkerboard pattern is perhaps a shaman, wearing a mask, headdress, and face paint with root vegetables and beans attached to serpent-like appendages. Along the bottom of his tunic are tiny representations of trophy heads, important symbols in ancient Peru. The exact meaning of such figures still eludes us today. Rituals concerning death, fertility, and regeneration were an important part of Peruvian culture and quantities of elaborate textiles played an important part in those rituals.

Color plate, page 86

240

BOLIVIAN, Tarabuco, early 20th century

Aksu (overskirt)
Warp-faced weave; wool and cotton
warp, wool weft. 38 x 29

Gift of Eleanor Fayerweather. 79.145

Provenance: Gale Hoskins, Stamford,
Connecticut

Bolivian costume in the 20th century, particularly women's garments, still retains features established before the Spanish conquest. This aksu is an overskirt worn at the back and held in place by a belt or sash. The horses, which commonly appear on textiles from Tarabuco, are of European origin, as is the custom of wearing black for mourning. Garments woven for mourning are characteristically of the same design as everyday garments; it is mainly the color black which distinguishes them. Here the horse motif is combined with geometric patterns to produce an elegant and restrained design.

Weaving in highland Bolivia is a highly developed art with roots reaching back to pre-Columbian times. The tradition of spinners and weavers using simple looms and drop spindles to create complex warp-patterned textiles continues even today. These two-sided weavings have the colors reversed on the opposite side. Typically, traditional garments have four selvages and are finished with a separately made edging which becomes an integral part of the piece as it is woven. The fine yarn is spun several times to give it an over-twist which makes it strong and durable. Along the border of this piece, subtle stripes were created by using S and Z (clockwise and counter-clockwise) twisted yarn. The Z twisted yarn is said to bring good luck and ward off evil. This special effect, which is difficult to detect at first glance, is reserved mostly for important ceremonial textiles.

240

241

241

ZAIRE, Kuba tribe, Bushong clan,
early 20th century

Ceremonial Skirt
Raffia plain weave; raffia embroidery.
26 x 66½

Mary B. Jackson Fund. 81.079

Provenance: Marie-Elaine d'Udekem
d'Acoz, New York

This Kuba ceremonial skirt can be appreciated as a work of art in itself and also
as one of the elements of a complex
dance costume. The characteristic geometric designs, combined in a way that
allows for variation within the overall
repeat pattern, have been beautifully
executed. The designs relate to those on
tribal wood carvings, metalwork, and
woven huts. The embroidery was probably done by the wives of a Bushong
king, the Bushong clan being dominant
within the Kuba ethnic group. The
sculptural quality of the total costume,
as well as its sheer bulk, contributed to
the prestige of the dance in which the
struggle for the royal succession was
enacted.

The traditional textile fiber in central
Zaire is raffia, made from palm leaves
which are shredded and beaten to make
them soft and pliable. Both men and
women had a role in textile production,
with men weaving the foundation fabric
and women embroidering the pattern of
linear and raised pile stitches. The pile
embroidery is so fine that it has often
been referred to as "velvet." The colors
are mostly limited to shades of beige,
black, brown, dark red, and rose. The
texture of the pile creates color changes
like those in this skirt, which is totally
wine red except for the black linear
border. Textiles imported from Europe
were very slow to be accepted by the
Kuba people; thus, traditional textiles
still remain important for ceremonial
occasions.

242

INDONESIAN, Sulawesi (Celebes), Toradja
tribe, ca. 1900

Ceremonial Cloth
Cotton warp ikat. 52 x 60½

Walter H. Kimball Fund. 83.186

Provenance: David Lantz, New York

Cloth has an important ceremonial
function in most parts of Indonesia.
Particularly in Sulawesi, cloth plays a
significant role in Toradja burial
ceremonies. Until the mid-20th century,
the Toradja were quite isolated in the
mountainous central part of the island of
Sulawesi. The remoteness of the small
highland valleys allowed the Toradja to
maintain a Bronze Age culture with an
animistic religion until relatively recent
times. Their belief in the continuous
presence of ancestral spirits required
that proper respect be shown for the
dead. Magnificent resist-dyed textiles
were used as shrouds and as decoration
on the pavilion for honored guests at the
funeral of an important personage. A
procession in which gifts of textiles,
animals, and food were presented to the
hosts preceded a feast where much

drinking and dancing gave a festive
rather than a somber mood to the
proceedings.

The production of the cloth involved
rituals related to the lengthy dye
preparation, the scarcity of the dyestuffs,
and the seasonal nature of the work. The
blue and red dyes from indigo and the
root of the morinda tree were only
available during certain seasons of the
year; the deep brown is obtained from a
mixture of these two colors. The pattern
of elongated geometric figures is bonded
to the threads by a method of resist
dyeing called ikat. The threads are tied
with fiber bindings and dipped in successive dye baths to create the pattern.
When the bindings are removed from
the thread, it takes the practiced eye of
the weaver to arrange the confusing
mass of threads into a coherent design
on a simple back-strap loom.

In spite of its complex production
method, this ceremonial textile has a
great visual clarity and energy derived
from the ikat technique itself. The
positive and negative attenuated shapes,
which give equal weight to the background and foreground, were executed
on an impressive scale. The expressive
angularity and strength of the simplified
interlocking forms have a strong visual
impact.

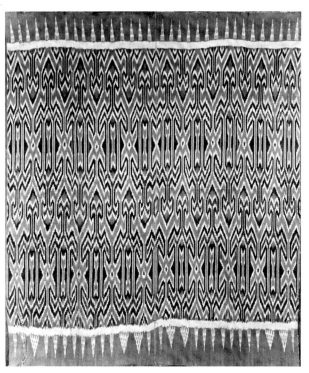

242

243

243

SOUTH GERMAN, ca. 1420

Candleholder

Brass. 12⅛ x 6⅜ x 6⅞

Helen M. Danforth Fund. 49.068

Publication: *Museum Notes*, RISD, January 1950.

Small statuettes of the 15th and 16th century often served utilitarian purposes. Recorded examples include inkwells and oil lamps as well as candlesticks. In designing this candlestick, the artist's purpose was primarily practical, yet he attained a mastery of both form and function. This expressive little man stands upon a triangular footed base and is dressed in the fashion of 1400. He originally held a pricket in each outstretched hand on which a candle could be stuck. Candles were used for lighting as early as the 6th century, though they were always very expensive and oil lamps were more common in ordinary households.

Candlesticks with a spike first appeared as simple, unadorned stands. Torchères for the floor consisted of an iron rod on three feet with the top sharpened to form a pricket. The corona – or crown of light – was a later form that held a ring of prickets, or sockets, for a number of candles. Servants also held torches at the table or carried them ahead to light the way at night.

The human figure, bearing a candleholder of some sort, was a favorite form of candlestick. In fact, the stance of this figure perhaps represents a torch-bearing servant and illustrates an early chapter in the history of illumination.

244

ITALIAN, Venice, late 15th – early 16th century

Bowl

Glass. 1¾ x 6

Gift of Mrs. Harold Brown (by exchange). 73.033

Publication: Landman/RISD, 1974, p. 30.

Fused mosaic canes were probably first made in the lands bordering the southeastern Mediterranean in the 3rd century B. C. By the time of the Empire, Roman glassmakers were producing such canes in wonderful and varied forms. This art was lost when the Western Empire fell; however, in the 15th century the skillful glassworkers of Venice revived the intricate process. Our bowl dates from the time of that revival.

Making fused mosaic canes is time-consuming. They have to be built up through a process of layering and tooling until the separate parts are one fat, solid bundle. The design runs through the whole length. Then, to reduce the bundle to the desired size, it is heated until its viscosity is fairly low. At this point the ends are rapidly pulled apart. The glass is stretched, but retains the design in the original proportions. When cooled, short lengths can be cut off to create a multiplicity of identical rods. (Paperweight rods are made the same way.)

To make our bowl, which is a good example of the elegant style of the period, a selection of several cane designs were placed in a form along with chips of colorless glass to fill the gaps. A convex cover was placed on top and the mold fired until the separate parts fused. As the mold had 31 ribs, so does the bowl. Polishing was employed at the end of the process to smooth the rough surface.

Color plate, page 87

244

245

GERMAN, 16th century

Casket
Steel. 5½ x 9 x 5½

Gift of Mrs. Henry D. Sharpe. 63.046.6

Ingenuity and complexity characterize this fine casket that rests on four ball feet. The locking mechanism, which one might normally expect to be concealed, is the most ornate design feature once the casket is open. The large, symmetrical mechanism occupies most of the underside of the lid. The sweeping curves of its steel springs are themselves decorative, yet they have been further embellished with engraved and stippled designs, including two heads in profile.

The exterior decoration of the casket consists of engraved panels with figures separated by strapwork and arabesques, a decorative scheme derived from a mixture of Classical and Near Eastern ornament that was developed in Italy in the 16th century but whose popularity quickly spread throughout northern Europe with the birth of the printed book. Similar "grotesque" ornament (from the grottoes among the ruins of Rome where these ornaments were first rediscovered around 1500), strapwork, and arabesques also appeared on contemporary stone-, metal-, and leatherwork, ceramics, and textiles.

Because the interior compartments of this box no longer survive, it is difficult to determine its original function, except that it probably safeguarded small and precious objects. The panels on the front of the box depicting a gentleman proffering some object to the woman at the opposite side suggest that this may have been some kind of wedding coffer, perhaps intended for a lady's jewels. The two female figures on either end of the casket are further evidence of some feminine purpose, perhaps to hold dressing accessories.

In any case, this coffer remains an excellent example of Renaissance ornament in the North and speaks for the value of portable and secure storage containers in an era before the invention of bank vaults or furniture with drawers.

245

246

AUSTRIAN OR SOUTH GERMAN, possibly
Innsbruck, ca. 1590

Wrangelschrank
Wood with inlay and iron mounts.
17⅝ x 23¹⁵⁄₁₆ x 13⅛

Anonymous gift. 75.023

This type of table cabinet has become
known as a "Wrangelschrank" because
during the Thirty Years War (1618–1648),
Count Wrangel, commander of the
Swedish army, removed a similar cabinet
(or "Schrank") from Augsburg as war
loot. In southern Germany, Augsburg
and Nuremberg were centers of great
commercial and artistic activity and
became famous for the elaborate writing
desks or cabinets produced there.
Craftsmen continued for more than a
century to produce these showpieces.
Loosely derived from the writing desk,
the Wrangelschrank evolved primarily
as an elegant cabinet for the storage of
curiosities.

The overall use of marquetry is the
dominant feature of this cabinet. Its
front, back, sides, and top are inlaid
with imaginary architectural views in
perspective within a marquetry border.
The inner surfaces of the fall front are
inlaid with designs of musical instruments enclosed by a floral band. When
open, the fall front reveals an inner
cupboard consisting of a central door
surrounded by ten small drawers, each
inlaid with townscapes and animals,
secular themes derived from the Italian
Renaissance.

247

JOHANN JOACHIM KANDLER
German, 1706–1775

Dancing Lady, ca. 1740
Porcelain. H. 7¾

The Lucy Truman Aldrich Collection of
European Porcelain Figures of the 18th
Century. 55.177

Publication: Casey/RISD, 1965, p. 108.

This exquisite figure was made about
1740 at the Meissen porcelain factory in
Germany, the first in Europe. Much of
the success of the Meissen factory can be
attributed to its chief sculptor, Johann
Joachim Kändler, who between 1733 and
1775 was responsible for modeling over a
thousand different subjects, including
this work. Such figures were at the
height of their popularity between 1740
and 1750, when they were used as table
decorations, especially with desserts.

The Meissen figures can be dated by a
study of their coloring and type of
decoration, as well as by the marks. The
earliest painted flowers, which may be
seen on this piece, were called *Indian-
ische Blumen,* or Indian flowers, after
those on imported oriental porcelains.
The low mound base with applied
flowers and leaves is also characteristic
of the earlier works. Later figures show
softer overall coloring, more naturalistic
flowers, and Rococo bases.

This graceful embodiment of the
Rococo style forms part of the Lucy
Truman Aldrich Collection of European
Porcelain Figures of the 18th Century,
which particularly emphasizes English
and German examples. It is appropriately
housed in a period Georgian room from
Chipstead Place, a country house near
Sevenoaks in Kent, which was presented
to the Museum by members of Miss
Aldrich's family as a permanent setting
for her important collection.

Color plate, page 87

246

248

SOUTH GERMAN, ca. 1750

Stein
Tin-glazed earthenware with hinged
pewter lid. 9⅞ x 4¹⁄₁₆

Gift of Eugene L. Garbaty. 49.178

The stein, a single-handled, cylindrical
mug with a hinged metal cover, is a form
of drinking vessel which has been popular in Germanic lands for many centuries.
The hinged lid is an unusual feature
possibly derived from a 16th century law
requiring the covering of food and
beverage containers in an attempt to
prevent the spread of disease by flies.
This example is of tin-glazed earthenware, also known as majolica, faïence,
and Delftware, and was created by
dipping the molded earthenware body
into a lead glaze that was whitened by
the addition of tin oxide. Enamel colors
were then hand-painted onto the white
surface. These colors (blue, green,
yellow, purple, and orange) are known
as the "high temperature colors,"
because of their ability to withstand the
high kiln temperatures necessary to fire
them.

Tin-glazed earthenware was originally
developed in Islamic countries in the 9th
century as an attempt to recreate the
white body of porcelain. Once oriental
porcelains were being imported into
Europe in large quantities, starting in the
16th century, tin-glazed earthenware
became an inexpensive substitute for
porcelain, and was popular with the
middle and peasant classes.

The decoration of steins often reflects
the pursuits and interests – such as
waging war, drinking, and hunting – of
the robust Germanic men who drank
from them. This example depicts an elk
rearing back on his hind legs amidst a
group of palm trees. The scene has been
painted in a lively but primitive manner,
indicating less skilled workmanship.
The inclusion of exotic foliage reflects
the Rococo fascination with faraway
lands, as well as the artist's desire to
imitate the designs found on high-quality
porcelain wares, such as those produced
at Meissen.

247

248

249

249

AUGUSTE PIGNET, printer
St. Génis-Laval, France

Le Palais Royal, ca. 1790
Block-printed paper. 74 x 56⅞

Mary B. Jackson Fund. 34.952

Provenance: M. and Mme. Charles
Huard, Versailles

Publication: Nancy McClelland, *Historic
Wallpapers*, Philadelphia, 1924, pp. 296–
297.

"Le Palais Royal" is one of 360 examples
of French wallpaper from the extraordinary Huard collection which constitutes the backbone of the Museum's
wallpaper collection. The golden age of
wallpaper occurred in France in the late
18th and early 19th century. Available to
a growing public was a wide range of
landscapes, Chinese and Middle Eastern
motifs, floral and bird designs, flocked
papers, papers simulating marble or

wood, gold-finished papers, over-door
panels, and wainscot papers. Dominating the market were panoramic and
mythological scenes, some requiring
over 3000 blocks to print a single series.
Polychromed scenic papers such as this
example were the most desirable of all
wallpapers. They created convincing
illusions of space and offered access
through illusion to remote corners of the
earth.

The impact of the painted wall decorations that had been discovered in the
mid-18th century at Pompeii and Herculaneum is obvious. The Neo-classical
elements in these designs especially
appealed to Americans who associated
them with the virtues of Greek
democracy and the Roman republic. In
America, where wallpaper printing had
started as early as 1756 in New York,
patterns were based on imported
examples, but they never attained the
same popularity as foreign papers.
Examples of "Le Palais Royal" have been
found in the Forrester House in Salem,
Masssachusetts (now removed), and in a
house on Nantucket.

250

CLAUDE CHAPUIS
French, active 1797–1818

Sewing Table, ca. 1800
Mahogany with ebony veneer and brass
inlay. 28¼ x 22 x 16½

Gift of Mrs. Harold Brown. 37.140

Provenance: Harold Brown, Newport,
Rhode Island

Publication: C. P. Monkhouse,
"Napoleon in Rhode Island," *Antiques*,
January 1978, pp. 192–201.

The ancient Greek *klismos* (chair) with its
four gracefully curved saber-like legs
inspired the Parisian cabinet- and chair-
maker Claude Chapuis when designing
this exquisitely proportioned and
detailed Neo-classical sewing table at the
beginning of the 19th century. As the
technology available to Chapuis for
bending wood was still limited, he
achieved the desired curved profile by
cutting each of the legs out of a solid
piece of mahogany. He then reinforced
them both structurally and visually by
applying thin strips of ebony veneer to
the inner side of the legs. As Chapuis
became more adept at bending and lam-
inating wood, he was able to avoid the
necessity of cutting curved forms out of
solid wood, as a pair of fully bent and
laminated armchairs, ca. 1810, in the
Museum's collection attests. His experiments in France, together with those of
Samuel Gragg in Boston, at the beginning
of the 19th century presaged the somewhat later work of the Austrian furniture
designer whose name has become synonymous with bentwood, Michael
Thonet, all of whom are represented by
examples of their respective work in the
Museum's collection.

251

GUILLAUME BENEMAN
French (b. Germany), active 1784–1811

Secretary Desk, ca. 1800–1810
Mahogany with ormolu mounts.
50 x 44½ x 17½

Helen M. Danforth Fund. 80.106.

Provenance: Edward Nickerson,
Providence; Providence Art Club

Publications: *Bulletin*, RISD, March 1956,
p. 13; Henry Hawley, *Neo-Classicism:
Style and Motif*, The Cleveland Museum
of Art, 1964, pl. 137.

This fall-front secretary desk of
mahogany with ormolu and patinated
bronze mounts was made in Paris
between 1800 and 1810 by the cabinetmaker Guillaume Beneman, who
stamped the piece four times, including
twice on the exterior. The latter practice
is unusual, but may have been suggested
by an older cabinetmaker, Jean-Henri
Riesener, who exercised a great influence
on Beneman's early work. Although
German-born and trained, Beneman
settled in Paris about 1784 and became a
maître ébéniste in 1785. He eventually
superseded Riesener in popularity, no
doubt owing to his more reasonable
prices, and despite the fall of the *ancien
régime*, remained in favor through the
Directoire and Empire. Napoleon commissioned Beneman to make a strikingly
similar commode and fall-front secretary
desk now at Fontainebleau. The overall
form and proportions of the desk are still
heavily indebted to Louis XVI examples,
while the mounts reflect Napoleon's
Egyptian Campaign of 1800–1801 as
reinterpreted by the foremost formu-
lators of the Empire Style, Charles
Percier and Pierre-François-Léonard
Fontaine, through the publication of
their highly influential *Recueil des
décorations intérieurs* (1801, re-issued
1812).

The desk was acquired in the 1870's by
the Providence architect and bibliophile,
Edward Nickerson, who was well ahead
of the revived interest in the Empire
Period that occurred in the late 1880's. In
the early 1890's another Rhode Islander,
Harold Brown, brought together a
remarkable group of Napoleonic decorative arts for use in his Newport home.
His widow, Georgette Wetmore
Sherman Brown, donated this collection
to the Museum in 1937. The Beneman
desk serves as the centerpiece for one of
the most significant holdings of French
Empire decorative arts to be found in an
American museum.

250

251

252

252

CLICHY GLASSWORKS
Clichy-la-Garenne, France

Paperweight, 1846–1860
Glass. 2¾ x 2¼

Gift of Alan Symonds. 69.200.9

Publication: Landman/RISD, 1974,
pp. 126–127.

Paperweight production in France is one
of the most delightful episodes in 19th
century glassmaking. The inspiration
came from Venice in the early 1840's and
by 1846 three French glassworks, Bac-
carat, St. Louis, and Clichy, were
making superb weights.

Their excellence and mastery of complex cane-making set the three French
companies apart from other paperweight
makers in Europe, at least during the
period of the art's first great flowering,
about 1860. (For an explanation of the
process of cane-making, see catalogue
entry no. 244.) Each factory developed
distinctive canes and designs. At Clichy,
the "rose" cane, seen here along the
edge, has four green outer leaves and
alternating quarter-rings to simulate
petals. The Clichy rose was imitated, but
never equaled, by factories in Bohemia
and at Sandwich, Massachusetts. Also
typical of Clichy are the so-called cookie-
cutter canes, several of which are in the
center area of this unusual weight and
appear larger at the base than at their
tops. More unusual, though, are the
variegated red and white sided canes.
The "moss green" ground on which the
contrasting 19 canes lie is composed of
yellow-tipped green canes surrounding
white stars with red centers. The great
amount of effort required to produce
such a background is indicative of the
meticulous care taken to make these
paperweights.

253

HECTOR GUIMARD
French, Paris, 1867–1942

Window, 1896–1897
Glass and lead cames. Each panel 26⅝ x
20⅛

Gift of Mrs. Harold Brown (by exchange).
73.016a-f

Provenance: M. Roy, Les Gévrils, near
Montargis, France

Publication: Landman/RISD, 1974, pp.
136–137.

The French Art Nouveau style lives and
moves in this striking window. It was
designed by the architect Hector
Guimard while in his late 20's for Les
Gévrils, the country home of friends in
the town of Montargis near Orléans.

Guimard began his long and influential
career after graduating from the Ecole
des Arts Décoratifs in 1885. He was
known from the start as a rebel, and he
embraced the Art Nouveau style as the
most successful way of uniting architecture with interior decoration.

His early work, to which our window
belongs, is notable for its lyric sense of
lightness. Guimard spoke in 1895 of
abandoning the flower and leaf,
retaining only the stems in his designs.
One can see this idea expressed in his
work, as his buildings from this period
fairly throb and writhe. The series of
entrances he designed for the Paris
Métro (1900) are typically flamboyant.
He achieved his intricate effects through
the use of wrought iron for gates,
window grills, balconies, stairways, and

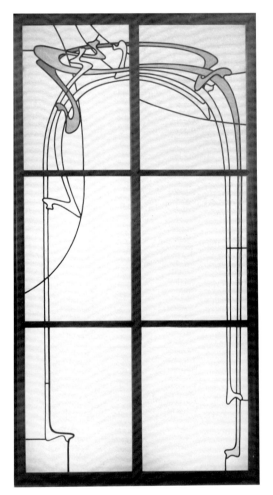

253

lanterns. His interiors also received careful attention, down to the door knobs.

Compared with the contemporary work of L. C. Tiffany, this window is simplicity itself. The glass throughout is quite thin and, no doubt, was commercially machine-made. The actual maker of the window is unknown. Thus the design is the most important aspect and every line has meaning within the composition. Its pastel colors intertwine in a subtle fashion and seem to add depth to the flat surface. The window must have been even more striking in its original setting, where it framed an outside view.

254

HUGNET FRERES
French, Paris

Fireplace Surround, ca. 1900
Walnut, ceramic and copper. 140 x 84 x 24

Georgianna Sayles Aldrich, Helen M. Danforth, Mary B. Jackson Funds. 83.152

Provenance: Mme. Petit; Patrick Just, Paris

Publications: Charles Massin, *Le Mobilier 1900–1925*, Paris, 1977; *Museum Notes*, RISD, 1984, pp. 14–15.

With the Art Nouveau style given such a resounding endorsement at the Paris Exhibition of 1900, French interiors from the turn of this century generally incorporate sinuous lines and asymmetrical

254

forms inspired by studies from nature. In the case of the country house near the town of Le Tréport on the coast of Normandy, which served as the original setting for this fireplace surround, the Parisian interior design firm of Hugnet Frères in Faubourg St. Antoine developed a comprehensive scheme throughout the house in this style. More robust and sculptural than the School of Nancy under Emile Gallé, where decorative detailing consists mainly of flat marquetry inlay, and less abstract and ethereal than Belgian work under Hector Guimard's influence, Parisian Art Nouveau tends to emphasize the natural materials at hand: in this case, walnut timbers punctuated by knots and enlivened by graining. Since the contemporaneous English Arts and Crafts style was similarly inspired, the fact that Le Tréport faces the English Channel makes the Parisian interpretation of Art Nouveau particularly appropriate here.

With the sunflower serving as the symbol of the house, that particular blossom came to play an important role in the decorative scheme for the dining room. A photograph showing that room before it was recently dismantled indicates that a pair of corner cabinets flanked the fireplace. While the cabinets were decorated with diminutively carved sunflowers in keeping with the furniture's relatively small scale, the sunflowers in the pediment of the chimney breast are by necessity much larger and bolder in scale in order to be appreciated from below, the distance from the floor to the sunflowers being about 12 feet. These same sunflowers also frame a subtly carved landscape view of the environs of the house in Normandy. The central sunflower in the pediment becomes a metaphor for the sun by sending its rays over the landscape below. The sunflower theme is further reinforced by the design of the colored ceramic tiles surrounding the horseshoe-shaped opening of the fireplace. In addition to flowers, two rather willowy bare-breasted women reminiscent of the work of the sculptor François-Rupert Carabin recline on either side. As they flank the fireplace opening and also support the chimney breast, they link visually the two portions of the composition and strengthen its overall organic flow.

Color plate, page 88

255

255

AUGUSTE DELAHERCHE
French, 1857–1940

Vase, ca. 1910
Earthenware. 8⅜ x 7

Bequest of Ellen D. Sharpe. 54.147.33

Auguste Delaherche was one of several French studio potters strongly influenced by Japanese ceramics, as well as by the English Arts and Crafts Movement. Both of these influences shared similar tenets: simplicity, functionalism, and craftsmanship. Delaherche's early forays into *Japonisme* produced wares decorated with floral motifs derived from Japanese prints and oriental pottery. When Delaherche moved his workshop in 1894 from the Haviland Pottery Studio, of which he had been the owner since 1887, to Armentières, he shifted his concentration to the shape of the ceramic body and the effects of monochromatic glazes with varying surface textures. This vase is from the period after 1904 when Delaherche created ceramic pieces himself rather than designing the pieces and leaving the execution to his studio assistants, who numbered over 400 by that time. Delaherche contrasts the textures of a deep turquoise matte underglaze with a mottled golden glaze dribbled over the body to create the decorative patterning. As with all art pottery, he emphasized contour, texture, and strong colors.

Delaherche won several awards for his ceramic work during his career and was honored by a retrospective exhibition in 1907 at the Musée des Arts Décoratifs in Paris. Many American art potters were inspired by Delaherche's pottery on display at the World's Columbian Exposition held in 1893 in Chicago. The Grueby Faïence Company of Boston was particularly impressed by Delaherche's *oeuvre* and began the production of wares with a similar emphasis on glaze texture and body contour.

256

256

WILLIAM GOULD
English, active 1732–1760

Pair of Candlesticks, 1734–1735
Silver. H. 6½

Gift of Mrs. John Nightingale in memory of John Trowbridge Nightingale.
75.117.23–24

The study of English silver candlesticks is as interesting and diverse as that of English wine glasses. In both instances there is infinite variation within the bounds of basic simplicity.

This pair of candlesticks from about 1734–35 shows skillful handling of their raised decoration, cyma curves, and baluster stems. They sit firmly on their bases and appear to reach upwards effortlessly, uniting utility and art. For their date, and in comparison to candlesticks by Gould's great French contemporary DeLamerie, our sticks are very plain and conservative. DeLamerie would probably have embellished every curve with shells or leaves or gadrooning. Gould, on the other hand, achieves his effects with understated elegance.

William Gould's career spanned almost three decades of the 18th century, and his hallmarks appear most frequently on candlesticks. Today he is better remembered for a deception. In 1752 he made a large and beautiful silver chandelier, which still hangs, for the Fishmonger's Company in London. Unfortunately, it was discovered that Gould had used silver-plated copper instead of the solid sterling for which he was paid.

257

257

BOW PORCELAIN FACTORY
English, Stratford-le-Bow, ca. 1747–1776

Pair of Sphinxes, ca. 1750
Porcelain. Each, 4⅝ x 4½ x 2

Gift of Mrs. Sigmund J. Katz.
58.187.2a, b

Publication: George Savage, *English Pottery and Porcelain*, New York, 1961, pp. 266–269, 305, pl. 129.

It was not until the 1740's that a factory for the production of porcelain opened in England, over 30 years after the secret of making true porcelain was discovered at Meissen. The Bow Porcelain Factory, located in London's East End, was founded by Thomas Frye, an Irish painter and engraver, in collaboration with Edward Heylyn, a local glass manufacturer. Their first porcelain patent was taken out in 1745 and lists unaker, a china clay imported from Virginia, as one of the components. Subsequent experiments in the composition of the clay body resulted in Frye's 1748 patent for a porcelain body containing bone ash. Bone china, as it is known, is more stable in firing, reducing kiln wastage, as well as more durable, making it more practical for everyday tablewares. This was to be Bow's major contribution to the history of ceramics.

The quality of Bow porcelain was never as high as that of the firm's major local competitor, Chelsea. Bow's products were consequently aimed at a middle-class market. In addition to dishes, Bow produced figures depicting biblical and mythological subjects, or contemporary celebrities, to be used as table centerpieces or mantle garnitures, such as this pair of sphinxes. The features of Peg Woffington, a popular Irish actress who made her debut at Covent Garden in 1740, are displayed on these sphinxes. The practice of portraying a woman, especially an actress, on the body of a lioness was popularized in France by Jean Bérain (1637–1711), a designer at the court of Louis XIV, probably because of the sphinx's association with the imagery of the *femme fatale*. In this piece, the Baroque practice was adapted to Rococo taste by a lighter and more lively treatment, particularly in the swirling waves on the base and the playful, coquettish turn of the figure's head.

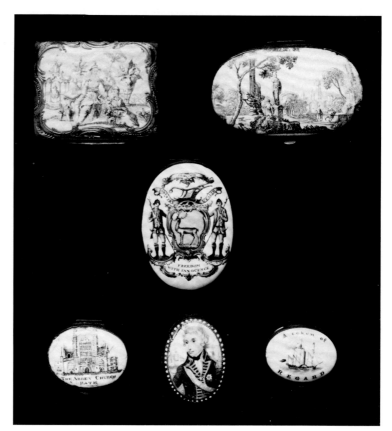

259

258

ENGLISH, Staffordshire, ca. 1750–1760

Sweetmeat Dish
Lead-glazed earthenware. 16 x 10 x 9

Bequest of Charles L. Pendleton. 04.355

Provenance: R. Soden-Smith, England

Publication: Lockwood/RISD, 1904, pl. 25.

This sweetmeat dish from the Pendleton Collection is one of many pieces of English and Oriental ceramics that Charles Pendleton acquired to complement his collection of American and English 18th century furniture. Sweetmeats were a popular confection, usually candied fruits or nuts, and would have been served in this elegant dish at the end of a long and elaborate meal along with a glass of Madeira or port, or for a special occasion to accompany a festive punch. In the design of this dish, a green dolphin finial surmounts a tiered arrangement of nine graduated scallop shells which are decorated with a lustrous brown lead

glaze and divided by arched dolphins and clusters of tiny seashells. The finely modeled details and the combination of rich soft colors attest to the work of a master potter.

Lead-glazed earthenware had been in use in England since the Middle Ages, and by the 18th century it rivaled in popularity the salt-glazed wares. The difference was in the clays used for the body and in the manner of firing and glazing. Often such lead-glazed wares were built up of solid masses of different colored clays. Certain types of these are usually known as "Whieldon wares," after the potter Thomas Whieldon of Fenton Low (1719–1795), who used glaze colorings extensively. Actually many other craftsmen made lead-glazed wares. Josiah Wedgwood and Josiah Spode are only two of the many Staffordshire potters who used and perfected the technique.

258

259

ENGLISH, ca. 1760–1830

Enamel Snuff and Patch Boxes
Enamel on copper, various sizes.

Gift of Miss Elizabeth Hazard and Mrs. Edward W. McVitty, in memory of their mother, Mrs. Elizabeth Hazard. 60.044.2, 19, 79, 113, 121, 138

Although still commonly referred to as "Battersea Boxes" after those produced by the short-lived partnership of Janssen, Delamain and Brooks at the Battersea Factory, York House, London (1753–56), the vast majority of these English copper enamel snuff and patch boxes were manufactured elsewhere. Birmingham, Bilston, Wednesbury, and Liverpool, as well as London, had factories operating for different lengths of time, making boxes of this specific type between 1740 and 1830. Attribution to any particular center is difficult, since boxes never bear a factory mark.

The fashions of taking snuff and of applying "beauty patches" to one's face resulted from a desire of the English upper classes to emulate cultivated French ways. It is not surprising, then, that initially these boxes imitated, stylistically and thematically, Continental examples such as those from the porcelain factories of St. Cloud and Sèvres. Pastorales inspired by Watteau and Boucher were commonly used to decorate the lids, as were chinoiserie and floral motifs, framed by "rocaille" (C-scroll) borders.

The snuff box (upper left) demonstrates its debt to French design and to English technological advancements that facilitated its manufacture. In the 1720's, machinery was developed in England that could roll copper to a thinness suitable for immediate enameling. Then in the 1750's John Brooks developed transfer printing, a process enabling the transfer of an image from an engraved copper plate to paper, then to the box's surface in the form of a monochrome print. Both of these innovations were milestones in mass production, and most factories adopted these time- and labor-saving methods.

The Neo-classical taste gained favor in England in the 1760's, and monochrome transfer prints were compatible with the austerity of this style. An example of this treatment is the snuff box (upper right) depicting an Italian landscape. Color was introduced to the snuff box (center) by painting over the print of the Liverpool Society's arms. It was not until the late 18th century that English manufacturers of enamel boxes completely broke away from Continental precedents. The patch boxes (bottom), distinguished by their interior mirrors, are less than two inches in length, and therefore had no practical function. They have become instead a reflection of contemporary Georgian life: (left to right) a souvenir from Bath; the profile of Admiral Nelson; and a token of friendship.

260

ENGLISH, ca. 1790

Cellaret
Mahogany. 22 x 26½ x 19½

Gift of Mrs. Guy Fairfax Cary. 56.001

Publication: *Bulletin*, RISD, 1956, pp. 13–14.

The drinking of wine greatly increased during the 18th century, and long evening hours were commonly spent after dinner conversing over wine glasses filled repeatedly. It was natural, therefore, that designers turned their attention to drinking accessories. During the 18th century when wine was stored in the cellar in barrels, the cellaret was one of the most important dining room accessories. Free-standing, it could hold a few bottles of wine which had been previously filled from the kegs in the cellar. It was generally kept under the central section of a sideboard or side table.

The cellaret, also known as "garde de vin," took various forms in keeping with the furniture style of the period of its manufacture. One of the chief sources of inspiration in this period was a renewed interest in Classical antiquity stimulated by the archaeological discoveries at Herculaneum and Pompeii. Stylistically, the cellaret shows many similarities to the furniture designs of Robert Adam, the Scottish architect who popularized a Classical aesthetic in England. A wine cistern appearing in his drawing of a sideboard for "the Rt. Honble. W. G. Hamilton's house at Brighton" of 1789 closely resembles the Museum's cellaret in its form and richly carved ornament.

The oval body is made up of six solid mahogany staves bound together at top and bottom by broad brass bands. The vigorously carved strigil fluting appears only on the front staves. Since the piece could be seen only from the front in its normal position under the sideboard, the back is undecorated and also lacks the gilded metal lion masks and rings found on the front and ends. The inside of the cellaret is divided into six circular metal-lined compartments that hold up to six bottles. Four finely carved lion feet with concealed casters support the body. The lockable cover with its fine fan carving distinguishes the cellaret from a wine cooler, which was usually made without a cover and was lined with removable water-tight liners.

260

ENGLISH, ca. 1810

Nest of Three Tables
Rosewood with boxwood and ebony
inlay. 29¼ x 15½ x 11 (largest table)

Gift of Mrs. Harold Brown. 37.150

Provenance: Napoleon Bonaparte, St.
Helena; Gen. Henri Gratien Bertrand;
Mme. Amadée Thayer; Marquis de
Biron, Paris; Harold Brown, Newport,
Rhode Island

Publication: C. P. Monkhouse,
"Napoleon in Rhode Island," *Antiques*,
January 1978, pp. 192–201.

Nests of four graduated tables became
popular in England at the very end of
the 18th century. Known appropriately
as "quartetto tables," their design may
well have been the invention of the
English cabinetmaker Thomas Sheraton,
best known for his authorship of highly
influential furniture pattern books. At
the least he can be given credit for
popularizing the quartetto table form
through its publication as a plate in his
Cabinet Dictionary of 1803. Through such
features as attenuated columnar legs,
the Neo-classical style achieved under
Sheraton's influence a truly remarkable
degree of delicacy and refinement.
When combined with exotically grained
woods, such as rosewood, and further
enlivened by string inlays of contrasting
woods, such as boxwood and ebony, the
result is a rich medley of materials
expressive of England's colonial wealth,
achieved through control over a wide
variety of natural resources. Further
befitting the colonial lifestyle of
administrators who were continually on
the move, the quartetto table form
served the need for furniture which was
both lightweight and readily reducible in
size for ease of transport.

In light of these social, economic and
political factors, this particular nest of
tables fittingly belonged to Napoleon,
although he does not appear to have
acquired them until the end of his
empire-building days, when in exile
between 1815 and 1821 at Longwood on
the island of St. Helena. There they saw
service in his bedroom, and upon his
death immediately achieved status as
significant historical relics, with the
largest of the four tables ending up at
Malmaison in 1924 by way of a descendant of Louis Marchand, Napoleon's
valet. The remaining three tables were
acquired by Napoleon's aide-de-camp,
Gen. Bertrand, and descended in his
family until acquired in Paris in the
1890's by Harold Brown.

261

262

262

ENGLISH, ca. 1810–1815

Sewing Table
Burl walnut, ivory, silver, mother-of-pearl. 38½ x 18½

Gift of Mrs. Henry D. Sharpe. 65.065

Provenance: Henry Sharpe; Mrs. Jesse H. Metcalf; Henry Sharpe

Although some globe-shaped work tables were made in Austria, it was in London that a patent was taken out on the furniture form in 1808. Morgan and Sanders, one of the most important firms of furniture dealers, acquired the 20-year patent from George Remington. Multi-purpose furniture was a specialty of the firm, and the Museum's example served as both a sewing table and a dressing table. Inside the globe are two removable compartments which conceal a series of hidden drawers. One compartment is outfitted with a sewing tray, ivory spools, and a pincushion. The second compartment has a back-drop mirror, allowing the stand to function as a dressing table.

The overall design of the table is based on Classical forms. The three curved legs have carved goat hoofs which rest on a trifid base and goat heads which support the globe. The table belongs to a small group of similar tables. Some of these, such as the one owned by the Metropolitan Museum, are much more ornamental and have Adamesque inlaid bands of marquetry and ivory. RISD's sewing table is a more simple, restrained version that relies upon burl veneer and clean, precise lines for its decoration and design.

263

263

ENOCH WOOD AND SONS
English, Burslem, Staffordshire, 1818–1846

Teapot with view of India Wharf and Exchange Coffee House, Boston, ca. 1820–30
Earthenware with transfer-printed decoration and lilac luster trim.
6 x 5¾ x 10½

Gift of Miss Alice Brownell, Mrs. Ernst R. Behrend, and Alfred S. Brownell. 29.234

Provenance: Collection of Mrs. Harriet F. Brownell, Providence

Publication: Hayden Goldberg, "Two Newly Identified American Views on Historical Blue Staffordshire," *Antiques*, January 1984, pp. 281–283.

This teapot by Enoch Wood and Sons, with views of two architecturally and commercially important buildings in 19th century Boston, is a typical example of what is known to collectors as "historical Staffordshire china." The pottery firms located in the Staffordshire district of England, an area long noted for producing commonplace earthenwares, found themselves with a plethora of dishes at the beginning of the 19th century due to recent improvements in the manufacturing process. Transfer printing had replaced hand-painted decoration and the assembly line sped up production time. Capitalizing on Americans' civic pride following their naval victories over England in the War of 1812, the potteries created dishes with views of American accomplishments, architecture, and scenery, shipping them across the Atlantic in large quantities.

The Staffordshire potters produced sets of dishes unified by a particular border, which surrounded vignettes focusing on a central theme. With this in mind, the unmarked teapot can be attributed to Enoch Wood and Sons by the existence of a marked plate bearing an identical flower-and-leaf border and a view of another Boston landmark, the State House. While the maker may be identified, the sources for the two engravings have not been. Since the Exchange Coffee House burned to the ground in 1818 and the India Wharf buildings were pulled down in 1962, the existence of these otherwise unknown views is of interest to architectural historians, as well as to collectors of "Old Blue."

Large collections of historical Staffordshire earthenware were formed by Americans in the early part of the 20th century. These collectors were fascinated by the depictions of the life and times of their forefathers. Several of these large collections were donated to the Museum, probably through the enthusiasm generated by Director Earle Rowe, who had an extensive collection himself. This teapot is one of many in a collection of teapots of all types and materials donated by the Brownell family, longtime tea and coffee merchants living in Providence.

264

AMERICAN, Connecticut Valley, 1680–
1720

Chest
Oak and pine. 35 x 44 x 18½

Museum Works of Art Fund. 19.293

Publications: Clair Franklin Luther, *The
Hadley Chest*, Hartford, 1935, p. 139, no.
70; Patricia E. Kane, "The Seventeenth-
Century Furniture of the Connecticut
Valley: The Hadley Chest Reappraised,"
*Arts of the Anglo-American Community in
the Seventeenth Century*, Ian M. G.
Quimby, ed., Charlottesville, 1974, pp.
79–122, no. 25.

There are approximately 125 known
chests which, along with the example at
RISD, form the group known as Hadley
chests. Although some of the chests are
directly associated with Hadley, Massachusetts, they were made up and down
the Connecticut River Valley between
1680 and 1740. The chests are linked by
their method of construction and their
distinctive carved decoration of scrolls,
tulips, and lobed leaves. The repeated
motif seems to have been brought to the
Connecticut Valley from Lancashire and
Yorkshire, as related examples of carving
have been found in these two areas.

Chamfering is a distinctive construction technique on Hadley chests and was
the first step in their construction. The
edges of the stiles, rails, and muntins
were beveled along their entire length.
The ends of the drawers and rails were
then shaped to cover the bevel. Where
the bevel is not covered by other framing
members it appears as a decorative
element (around the three decorative
panels and on the inner edge of the
feet). After shaping the various parts
necessary for the chest, the unidentified
maker painted the outer face of the parts
red or black. The rigid scroll, tulip, and
leaf design was then laid out over the
paint and carved, leaving the flat design
painted and the chipped-away "negative" surface unpainted. On many chests
this color scheme is reversed. In the case
of the RISD chest, the original surface
has been stripped entirely.

Hadley chests were usually intended
as hope or marriage chests. The
Museum's example, with the initials
"H S" prominently carved into the
center panel, was probably made for
Hester Smith, who was the daughter of
Chileab and Hannah Hitchcock Smith of
Hadley. Hester was born in 1674 and
married Nathaniel Ingram in 1696. If the
chest were indeed made for Hester
Smith it probably was made in the
1690's.

265

264

265

JOHN TANNER
American, Newport, Rhode Island,
1713–1785

Pepper Box or Dredger, 1735–65
Silver, marked I T. 4 x 2

Museum Purchase. 43.347

Provenance: "EC/To EB" (engraved on
bottom); "Family Relic/to E. B. Folger.
XX" (engraved on side)

Publications: *Museum Notes*, RISD, May
1944; *The New England Silversmith*,
Providence, 1965, no. 305.

This dredger, or pepper-box as the
shaker was often called in old inventories, is octagonal in form, flaring
slightly from the molding bands at top
and bottom. The cover is also octagonal
and is pierced in flower petal forms
alternately in straight and whirling
patterns. The octagonal form is carried
into the finial which is surmounted with
a rounded bead; the simple scroll handle
resembles those found on cream pots of
the period. Its balanced design is just as
pleasing as its perfect balance in the
hand.

Fine silver was a luxury in America
until well after the Revolution. But from
the 17th century on, silversmiths worked
in the large cities along the East Coast to
satisfy the demands of the rich for
decorative ways of displaying and using
their precious metals. One would not
expect to see an English dredger like
ours made after 1725. But in Newport
and elsewhere in New England, this
remained a popular traditional form as
late as 1765.

John Tanner was born in Westerly but
settled in Newport in his youth. He was
a prosperous silversmith and a trusted
citizen, serving as Newport's town
treasurer in 1763 and for two terms as a
justice of the peace in 1765–6 and 1771.
Tanner exemplifies the successful
artisan-entrepreneur who held public
office and became a prominent civic
leader after the Revolutionary War.

266

AMERICAN, Philadelphia, 1740–1760
Side Chair
Walnut; walnut and pine. 42 x 20¼ x 17¼

Charles L. Pendleton, by exchange.
68.167

Provenance: Descended in the Bonschur
family; Israel Sack, New York

Hogarth's "line of beauty" is fully
defined in this graceful Philadelphia
Queen Anne side chair, as its entire
design is an interplay of curved lines. To
create a successful chair is a true design
challenge, and this Philadelphia
example represents one successful solution. The skillful repetition of line and
motifs links the various planes of the
chair, allowing them to flow together as
a unified whole. Bringing the scrolls and
shells of the crest rail forward to the
knees of the chair further tightens the
design. The trifid feet, a hallmark of
Philadelphia furniture, also act as an
inversion of the carved shell on the
knee.

The construction of the side chair is
typical of Philadelphia. Its seat frame is
of horizontally laid boards forming an
inner square rather than following the
balloon curve of the seat. The tenon of
the side rails runs through the stiles,
which change from a square shape
below the seat to a round shape above
the seat.

Although the form and construction
are distinctive of a specific region of
manufacture, this chair shares with
Queen Anne chairs from other regions a
new concern for comfort. Hogarth's
"line of beauty" becomes not only a
cabriole leg but also a curved splat that
fits the sitter's back.

266

267

268

AMERICAN, Philadelphia, 1760–1780

Pier Table

Mahogany, pine, marble. 31⅞ x 54 x 26¾

Bequest of Charles L. Pendleton. 04.008

Publications: Lockwood/RISD, 1904, pl. 5; Hedy B. Landman, "The Pendleton House at the Museum of Art, Rhode Island School of Design," *Antiques*, May 1975, p. 929.

Large marble-top tables were a popular furniture form among the well-to-do in 18th century Philadelphia. Occurring alone or frequently in pairs, they stood against the wall (pier) between windows, beneath tall looking-glasses. Household inventories of the period indicate that similar tables often stood in the dining room, where marble served a practical function on a sideboard or serving table.

The quality of the carving on the legs and frame, and the richly veined marble top shaped to match the contour of the frame, suggest the collaboration of several specialized craftsmen. Price lists for Philadelphia cabinetwork refer to "sideboard tables" and "frames for marble slabs." One of Philadelphia's several woodcarvers probably carved the foliate and scroll ornament as well as the massive claw-and-ball feet. Finally, a stonecutter must have shaped and molded the edge of the marble slab, which could have come from the quarries in nearby Chester County, or may have been imported.

It is not known for whom this table was originally made or the names of the craftsmen who produced it, yet its massive scale, superior carving, and richly colored marble attest to the opulence of fashionable Philadelphia interiors of the later 18th century.

Color plate, page 89

268

AMERICAN, New York City, 1760–1780

Card Table

Mahogany, pine, oak, and tulip poplar.
27 x 34¼ x 16 ¾

Bequest of Charles L. Pendleton. 04.131

Provenance: Wendover collection,
Kinderhook, New York

Publications: Lockwood/RISD, 1904, pl.
99; Helen Comstock, *American Furniture*,
New York, 1962, no. 368; Morrison H.
Heckscher, *Antiques*, May 1973, pp. 974–
983; Hedy B. Landman, "The Pendleton
House at the Museum of Art, Rhode
Island School of Design," *Antiques*, May
1975, p. 925.

The New York card table purchased by
Charles Pendleton from the Wendover
collection is one of a body of approximately 25 examples of the most accomplished furniture design emanating from
the New York area between 1760 and
1780. New York furniture from this
period is often awkward in its design.
New York card tables, on the other
hand, transcend awkwardness with a
design that is elegant, bold, and
assured. The serpentine lines, and the
swinging fifth leg that conceals a small
drawer for dice and chips, are probably
based on an English form. There is
currently no known documentation
which traces the entry of this form into
New York cabinet shops, and there is
equally little documentation to connect
the Pendleton card table to a specific
craftsman. Five other tables exist which
are similar in construction and carved
detail to the Pendleton example, and
probably this sub-group of the larger
group of 25 is the work of one cabinet
shop.

Although unlabeled, this card table
with its distinctive grapevine motif on
the edge of the skirt and unusual C-
scroll carving on the knee is a testament
to one brilliant moment of design in 18th
century New York.

269

TOWNSEND AND GODDARD SCHOOL
American, Newport, Rhode Island

Bureau Table, ca. 1760–1790
Mahogany, pine, chestnut, and tulip
poplar. 33¾ x 36½ x 19¼

Gift of Mary Lemoine Potter. 33.216

Provenance: Thomas Mawney Potter,
Kingston, Rhode Island

Publications: Joseph K. Ott, *The John
Brown House Loan Exhibition of Rhode
Island Furniture*, Providence, 1965,
pp. 118–119; Hedy B. Landman, "The
Pendleton House at the Museum of Art,
Rhode Island School of Design,"
Antiques, May 1975, p. 931.

Of all the different forms of Newport
furniture associated with the Townsends
and Goddards and incorporating the
characteristic block and shell, none
seems to have enjoyed greater popularity
than the knee-hole bureau table, judging
from the remarkably high survival rate
of 25 or more examples, two of which
are in the Museum's collection. Although
the majority of these bureau tables are
thought to have served as dressing
tables, three of them have the top
drawer designed as a fall-front desk,
which opens to reveal an interior writing
surface and block-fronted document
drawers.

The most fully developed example of
this latter group is illustrated here. Not
only does it have two convex shells
flanking a central concave one, but the
latter is again repeated on the cupboard
door below, although that shell is carved
without a center design. The strong
sculptural statement made by these
projecting and receding forms is continued in the blocking of the ogee
bracket feet which terminate in scrolls. A
set of reticulated brasses with bale
handles and a dense mahogany selected
for its lively grain further contribute to
its highly successful design. Although it
is not known for whom this bureau table
was originally designed, by the middle
of the 19th century it had entered the
collection of the pioneer collector of
Rhode Island furniture, Thomas
Mawney Potter of Kingston, as had
other significant pieces, some of which
have also found their way to the Rhode
Island School of Design.

269

270

TOWNSEND AND GODDARD SCHOOL
American, Newport, Rhode Island

Desk and Bookcase, ca. 1760–1790
Mahogany, pine, tulip poplar, chestnut,
and cedar. 104 x 42 x 24

Bequest of Charles L. Pendleton. 04.042.

Publications: Lockwood/RISD, 1904,
pl. 57; Hedy B. Landman, "The
Pendleton House at the Museum of Art,
Rhode Island School of Design,"
Antiques, May 1975, p. 936.

This desk and bookcase of lustrous
mahogany is an extraordinary product of
the cabinetmaker's craft, one of approximately nine known examples made in
Newport, Rhode Island, by the
Townsend and Goddard families. The
desk has the solidity of form and grace

of line and proportion associated with
their work. Typical of Newport is the
use of the blocked front combined with
the deeply carved shell motif, giving the
piece a richly sculpted surface along its
entire height. The play of light on the
carved wood is varied by the alternating
convex and concave surfaces and a
densely grained "plum pudding"
mahogany. An even darker colored
mahogany has been carefully selected
for outlining its upper scrolled silhouette,
while the gleaming brasses provide a
lively contrast throughout the design.
The desk is capped by a reverse broken
scroll pediment, echoing the architectural
frameworks of so many doorways found
on Providence and Newport houses.
Also characteristic of Rhode Island
pedimented furniture are the corkscrew

finials emerging from fluted urns, while
the stop-fluted quarter columns that
flank the bookcase are frequently
encountered in the construction of the
best Rhode Island case furniture.

Although it is not known at present
from which of the Townsend or Goddard
shops it was originally commissioned, a
second desk and bookcase bequeathed
to the Museum in 1967 by Mr. and Mrs.
Arthur B. Lisle comes from the same
unidentified source. Several of the
drawers in each desk are so similarly
constructed as to be virtually interchangeable. The identity of the original
owner of the desk likewise remains a
mystery. Since four similar desks and
bookcases were made for the four
brothers of the great Providence mercantile family of Brown – Nicholas, Joseph,
John, and Moses – it seems reasonable to
assume that the owner of this desk was a
prosperous Rhode Island merchant as
well. Furthermore, the equal attention to
interior and exterior details strongly
suggests that the original owner enjoyed
seeing his wealth distributed throughout
the desk's construction and not simply
used on the front for show. In this
respect he was unlike Joseph Brown,
who may have the singular distinction of
having ordered the only desk and bookcase with nine shells, but at the expense
of the interior, which is exceedingly
plain.

Color plate, page 90

270

271

271

TOWNSEND AND GODDARD SCHOOL
American, Newport, Rhode Island

Tea Table, ca. 1760–1790
Mahogany. 26½ x 31½ x 20½

Gift of Mr. Harold Tarbox in memory of
Gertrude Rebecca Reynolds Tarbox.
81.155

Provenance: Sweet or Abbott family, by
descent to Gertrude Rebecca Reynolds
Tarbox, Wakefield, Rhode Island

Publication: *Museum Notes,* RISD, 1982,
p. 13.

In addition to this tea table's tray top
and the crisp profile of its cabriole legs,
the undercut talons of the claw-and-ball
feet are distinctive features of Rhode
Island furniture. This rare detail
occasionally occurs in English furniture,
but on this side of the Atlantic seems to
be unique to Newport. Taken together,
these features produce a tea table which
in point of elaboration falls midway
between two distinctive groups of tray-
top tea tables from Rhode Island. On the
simpler end of the design scale are
found tables virtually identical to this
one, save for the feet, with a slipper foot
used as a substitute for the claw-and-ball.
In view of the high survival rate of tables
meeting this description, including one
already in the Museum's collection given
by Mrs. Gustav Radeke, it must have
been an exceedingly popular model. At
the other end of the scale falls a group of
tray-top tables with elaborately shaped
aprons and stylized acanthus carving on
the knees, the most famous of which
was made for Jabez Bowen in 1763 by
John Goddard, and is now part of the
collection at Winterthur. Like the
Museum's table, those tables are supported on claw-and-ball feet with the
distinctive undercut talon. The
Museum's table is therefore a synthesis
of two clearly defined styles of Rhode
Island tray-top tea tables, and as only
two other examples are known – one at
Bayou Bend and the other ex-Gershenson
collection – it is probably among the
rarest forms to come out of the Townsend
and Goddard school of cabinetmakers.

272

AMERICAN, Boston, ca. 1755–1795
Chest of Drawers
Mahogany; pine. 32½ x 38½ x 19½

Bequest of Charles L. Pendleton. 04.079

Provenance: Dexter heirs, Providence

Publications: Lockwood/RISD, 1904, pl.
81; Verna Cook Salomonsky, *Masterpieces
of Furniture,* New York, 1953, pl. 72;
Hedy B. Landman, "The Pendleton
House at the Museum of Art, Rhode
Island School of Design," *Antiques,* May
1975, p. 934.

The bombé or "kettle base" chest of
drawers in the Pendleton Collection is
part of a group of similarly shaped
American case furniture, including
desks, desks and bookcases, and chests-
on-chests which are unique to Boston
and date from the second half of the 18th
century. While the source of the bombé
form is Continental, and more
particularly the lofty Rococo cabinets
and desks made of veneered walnut in
the Netherlands around 1750, refine-
ments occur on this side of the Atlantic.
The introduction of extended claw-and-
ball feet by such Boston cabinetmakers
as John Cogswell and George Bright
(whose signatures appear on two
examples of bombé furniture) tends to
raise the case higher from the floor.
Furthermore, the elongated serpentine
curves of the sides of the case are
repeated and reinforced by shaping the
ends of the drawers to conform with
their swelling profiles, unlike European
examples where the drawer ends remain
straight. Here the serpentine curves of
the sides of the case are repeated across
the front, the mahogany has been
especially selected for its lively graining,
and the cut "Chippendale" brasses lend
a bold scale and vigorous sihouette.
These elements, along with the molded
top and skirt and the cock beading of the
stiles and rails framing the drawers,
result in a superlative statement,
animated yet controlled, of the Rococo
style in America.

272

273

273

CHINESE EXPORT, ca. 1785–1800

Punch Bowl
Porcelain. 6 x 14⅜

Gift of Hope Brown Russell. 09.343

Provenance: Anne Allen Ives

Publication: Kee Il Choi, Jr., *The China Trade: Romance and Reality,* Lincoln, Mass., 1979, pp. 48–50.

This punch bowl is not only a monumental example of Chinese porcelain made for the export market, but its decorative program refers directly to an aspect of the trade of which it was a product. Depicted around its outer surface is a series of "hongs" or "factories" along the Canton waterfront where the foreign merchants were confined to transact their business in rented premises. While the lower floor of each hong was devoted to counting rooms, storerooms, and quarters for the *comprador,* or intermediary, the two upper floors provided living quarters for the merchant. Even though tea, spices, and silks were the focal point of this trade, only the porcelain has survived in any significant quantity to suggest the extent of it. In turn, the export porcelain was supplied almost exclusively by the potteries at Ching-te Chen, some 500 miles away in the province of Kangxi.

Among the several punch bowls decorated with hongs, six variants have been identified, of which this example and one at Winterthur have been classified as forming the second variant. Consisting of a continuous frieze of tightly packed buildings, the various hongs are identified by their national flags in front, reading from left to right: Denmark, Spain, France, America, Sweden, England, and Holland. The presence of the American flag indicates that bowls of this type must be assigned to the period from 1785 to 1800 because the first American vessel did not arrive in Canton until 1784. It is interesting to note that another example of this type was brought back to Providence as a souvenir by the first local merchant to engage in the China trade, John Brown. Indeed, when his ship *George Washington* entered the port of Providence on July 5, 1789, the event signaled the beginning of an active trade which was to bring prosperity to many of the town's merchants and ultimately a rich legacy of Chinese export porcelain to the holdings of this Museum.

Color plate, page 91

274

AMERICAN, Rhode Island, ca. 1790

Windsor Chair
Ash and pine. 40 x 22⅛ x 22⅝

Gift of the Estate of Mrs. Gustav Radeke. 31.427

Publication: Charles Santore, *The Windsor Style in America, 1730–1830,* Philadelphia, 1981, p. 113.

The delicacy and grace of this Rhode Island continuous-arm windsor chair makes it one of the finest examples of the many windsors that Mrs. Radeke collected and left to the Museum.

First made in 17th century England for the market town of Windsor, windsor chairs had acquired the names "oval back" or "bow back" by the 18th century. The English appropriated the chair for outdoor garden and porch use, which may be the reason that the most popular paint color for windsors was the green seen on the RISD chair.

Several types of wood were used in the construction of windsors as the bent back, spindles, and seat imposed different requirements on the construction material. Springy hickory and ash might be used for the bows and spindles, pine for the seat, and maple for the lathe-turned legs. A coat of paint was the

274

easiest way to bring uniformity to the assorted woods. If skillfully made, the chairs needed no nails or screws, for the spindles and legs would be set into the unseasoned wood of the seat. As the wood dried it tightened on the spindles and legs, locking them into position.

In America, windsors seem to have appeared first in Philadelphia. Due to their versatility and low cost, their popularity quickly spread throughout the colonies, with some chairmakers specializing in windsor chairs. Americans brought them in from outdoors, using them as seating in public buildings as well as in the best parlors. In their use and construction, windsor chairs were the forerunner of the Federal period fancy chair and indeed many fancy chairs are essentially modified windsors.

275

AMERICAN, Providence, ca. 1800–1820

Canopy Bed

Mahogany, cherry, beech or maple, and ivory. 99 x 66 x 81

Gift of Mr. and Mrs. Frank Mauran III. 80.281

Provenance: Edward Carrington or Sullivan Dorr by descent to Frank Mauran, Providence

Publications: Joseph K. Ott, *The John Brown House Loan Exhibition of Rhode Island Furniture*, Providence, 1965, pp. 136–137; *Museum Notes*, RISD, 1981, p. 15.

This four-post mahogany bed is a superlative American interpretation of Thomas Sheraton's designs, with its richly turned and carved posts and carved and gilded ornaments in the form of Prince of Wales feathers and cornucopias of fruit supporting the canopy's swag draperies. Although beds of comparable quality and design can be found in the collections of Bayou Bend (the closest parallel), the Metropolitan Museum, and the Museum of Fine Arts, Boston – attributed to or documented as coming from Salem or Boston – none has the additional use of ivory escutcheons to cover up the bed bolts, or ivory cups to cover up the casters mounted to the bed's feet. On the other hand, the use of ivory by Providence cabinetmakers is well documented through the papers of the cabinetmaker Thomas Howard, Jr., and hence there is good reason to believe this bed was made in Providence, especially as it was owned by either Edward Carrington or Sullivan Dorr, both of whom were prominent Providence merchants. Unfortunately, it has thus far been impossible to find a specific reference to the bed in their extensively interrelated family papers. If it eventually turns out to have been made for Sullivan Dorr, it then bears comparison with the architectural design of his house at 109 Benefit Street. In 1810, Dorr's architect, John Holden Greene, created a portico which freely combines Classical and Gothic elements in much the same way as the unidentified designer of the bed has done with the ogee Gothic arches sandwiched in between Classical swags and tassels.

275

276

Attributed to JOSEPH RAWSON, SR.
American, Providence, 1760–1835

Dressing Bureau, ca. 1813
Mahogany, chestnut, tulip poplar, and ivory. 72 x 38 x 21

Mary B. Jackson Fund and Furniture Exchange Fund. 77.020

Provenance: Matthew Perry family by descent; Shreve, Crump & Low, Boston

Publication: C. P. Monkhouse, "American Furniture Recently Acquired by the Museum of Art, Rhode Island School of Design," *Antiques*, July 1980, p. 127.

Prior to the Federal period, mirrors and chests of drawers were treated as quite separate elements. Once united, however, they became an essential part of the design of suites of bedroom furniture down to the present day. Boston, Salem, and Providence seem to share the credit for the development of this new furniture form in America.

This example has a Rhode Island provenance, having descended in the family of Matthew Perry, the younger son of Oliver Hazard Perry, and is nearly identical to one that bears a manuscript label stating that it was made by Joseph Rawson as part of Mary Wheaton's dowry when she married Thomas Rivers in Providence in 1813. In support of the attribution is the use of chestnut and tulip poplar for their respective secondary woods, and ivory for their drawer pulls, keyhole escutcheons, and finials on the stiles upon which the mirrors pivot. The only notable difference is that the Museum's dressing bureau is further enlivened by additional ivory rosettes affixed to the scrolled stiles which support the mirror, while in the other example they are executed in mahogany. The lunette or semi-circular inlays which embellish their respective skirts are the one aspect of design which traditionally suggests Boston workmanship, in particular the work of John and Thomas Seymour, whose trademark it was once thought to be. Recent research, however, has demonstrated that inlays as a rule were fabricated in specialized shops in Boston, and thus available to any cabinetmaker. These dressing bureaus are therefore proof that strips of lunette inlay were sold to cabinetmakers working as far afield as Providence.

277

SAMUEL TROXEL
American, Upper Hanover Township, Montgomery County, Pennsylvania, ca. 1803–70

Plate, 1827
Earthenware with *sgraffito* decoration. 2 x 11⅜

Gift of Mrs. Gustav Radeke. 11.778

The first Pennsylvania German settlers were farmers busy clearing land for cultivation, but their descendants had time and money to open small businesses and factories, which were often passed from father to son. Such was the case with the pottery begun in 1799 by Henry Troxel and run from 1824 to 1846 by his son Samuel, who made this plate in

1827. Many signed wares by father and son have survived and can be found in other public collections, including the Philadelphia Museum of Art and the Metropolitan Museum of Art.

This plate is an example of both conservatism and patriotism, ideas often reflected in household wares created by the Pennsylvania Germans. Conservative in pottery technique and design, the plate was created by the clay being pressed into a mold to form the body, after which the face was covered with a white slip, or liquid clay. Through the wet slip were incised the linear decorations, a technique known as *sgraffito*. Then the decoration was enhanced by the inpainting of red iron oxide and a sprinkling of green copper oxide. The decorative motifs chosen by the potter include a trio of stylized flowers,

276

perhaps to symbolize the Trinity, as well as the spread eagle of the Great Seal to proclaim the maker's pride in America. Encircling the plate is an inscription in the Pennsylvania German dialect "Samuel Troxel Potter, 1827, Und mägden haben die buben gern; anfang in der Scheisel städ ein stern" ("And the maids like the boys; in the beginning in the plate there was a star"). This ceramic piece is an excellent example of the liveliness and naiveté which characterize virtually all the Pennsylvania German domestic wares.

278

EASTERN MASSACHUSETTS, perhaps the New England Glass Co., Cambridge

Sugar Bowl, 1830–1835
Glass and silver coin. 7½ (with cover) x 5

Given in memory of Mrs. Anita W. Hinckley by her five children. 73.051a, b

Publication: Landman/RISD, 1974, p. 86.

Sugar bowls with embedded coins are extremely rare and have always been highly prized by collectors of American glass. The coin in this bowl, an unworn silver 1830 U.S. 10¢ piece, dates the glass more closely than is usually possible. The New England Glass Company of Cambridge is known to have made a number of presentation pieces with coins during the 1830's and 40's, although the possibility of its having been made at any of the other eastern Massachusetts glassworks cannot be ruled out since they all worked in the same styles.

The bowl itself, which is unusually pleasing and well-proportioned, is in a form widely used in America from about 1820 to the 1850's. The gallery rim sits above a fine bulbous body. Below that is the thick-walled hollow knop with its coin and heavy flat foot. The cover repeats the bulbous form of the bowl and rests easily within the gallery rim. An applied finial, polished on its top to remove the rough pontil scar, surmounts the cover.

277

278

279

280

Sugar Bowl, 1839–1841
Pewter. 5¼ x 6½

Bequest of John F. Street. 40.017.257

Provenance: A. B. A. Bradley, New York

Publication: John Barrett Kerfoot,
American Pewter, Boston, 1924,
frontispiece, fig. 306.

A classic form in American pewter, this
Richardson sugar bowl was made at the
Glennore Company, owned by the
Olney family, in Cranston, Rhode
Island. It is marked on the bottom "G.
Richardson / Glennore Co. / No. 2 /
Cranston, R. I." The Glennore Company
was in business from 1839 to 1841.

George Richardson was born in
England, began his career in Boston in
1818, moved to South Reading, and then
settled in Rhode Island in 1836. Besides
sugar bowls, he made a wide range of
objects including tea and coffee pots,
dishes, pitchers, mugs, bowls, and
spoons. In a number of examples where
the design allowed, and following the
standard practice of pewterers, he used
castings from the same mold to make
elements of different objects. Thus we
find one mold making the body of our
sugar bowl as well as the lower half of a
water pitcher.

In 1845 Richardson moved to Providence, where his sons continued in
business after his death in 1848.

280

LYMAN, FENTON & CO.
American, Bennington, Vermont

Washbowl and Pitcher, 1849
Earthenware with flint enamel glaze.
Bowl: 4 1/16 x 12 9/16. Pitcher: 12 1/16 x 9

Gift of Mrs. Davenport West.
64.001.12a, b

This washbowl and pitcher, richly colored in mottled shades of brown, yellow, and green, bear the rare 1849 mark of the Bennington, Vermont firm of Lyman, Fenton & Co. Forming an offshoot of the first and longest-lived pottery works in Bennington established by Capt. John Norton in 1793, Christopher Webber Fenton continued the tradition of Bennington-made wares that were straightforward and functional. The Fenton firm went on to produce a new and remarkable array of ceramics in Parian and blue and white porcelain, Rockingham, and flint enamel. Although first produced in England, American Rockingham denotes a coarse ware with a brown tortoise-shell mottled glaze that was spattered on. Another glaze used on this washbowl and pitcher was flint enamel, a new process patented in 1849 by Fenton. While the brown color in American Rockingham is inherent in the glaze itself, in Fenton's new glazing process a clear glaze was applied to the biscuit piece before sprinkling on his new powdered metallic oxides (cobalt for blue, copper for green, manganese for brown). When fired, the colors melted and fused with the underglaze, flowing over the surface of the piece. In our example, color was sprinkled lightly, and the appearance is that of a Rockingham glaze with color added.

These two Bennington potteries produced items in more than a dozen types of pottery and porcelain, in an endless variety of household accessories and fancy articles, and this variety significantly influenced other American manufacturers.

281

ALEXANDER ROUX
American, New York City (b. France),
ca. 1813–1886

Bronze Cabinet, ca. 1866
Rosewood, mahogany, walnut, maple, gilt bronze, and porcelain. 44 x 51 1/2 x 19

Jesse Metcalf Fund. 78.052

Provenance: Unidentified house on Bellevue Avenue, Newport, Rhode Island; McDonough & Larner, Newport

Publication: C. P. Monkhouse, "American Furniture Recently Acquired by the Museum of Art, Rhode Island School of Design," *Antiques*, July 1980, p. 131.

In the middle of the 19th century this type of case furniture would have been referred to as a "bronze cabinet" in light of its supportive role for bronze sculpture. The cabinet and the sculpture in turn would have provided the drawing room with its focal point; so positioned, they would have served as a secular altar for the worship of culture. In order for a piece of furniture to live up to such a lofty role, the cabinetmaker felt compelled to embellish it with elaborate panels of floral marquetry, ornately cast gilt bronze mounts, and an oval decorated "Sèvres" porcelain plaque, all of which would have been described as in the style of Louis XVI. But in keeping with the eclecticism of the day, this ornament was then applied to a case in the Renaissance revival mode characterized by heavy proportions and angular profiles, deeply incised lines, and contrasting veneers.

Although these cabinets were made on both sides of the Atlantic, the American examples are almost invariably from New York City, owing to the presence of several French émigré cabinetmakers who seem to have made a specialty of this type of richly veneered furniture. Such a source is quickly confirmed by a label affixed to the back of this cabinet: "From / Alexander Roux / 479 Broadway / 43 & 46 Mercer St. / New York, / French cabinetmaker, / and importer of / fancy buhl / and mosaic furniture / Established 1836."

281

282

SYDNEY R. BURLEIGH
American, Providence, 1853–1928

Shakespeare Chest, ca. 1900
Cherry. 21¾ x 40 x 21⅞

Gift of Ellen D. Sharpe. 28.046

Provenance: Conant collection,
Providence

Publication: Kathleen Pyne, ed., *The Quest for Unity, American Art Between World's Fairs, 1876–1893*, Detroit, 1983, pp. 171–173.

The Providence artist Sydney Burleigh designed and decorated this simple post and panel chest around 1900. In the process Burleigh was able to address several themes of interest to the artistically minded at the end of the 19th century, namely, the Colonial Revival, *Japonisme*, and the Arts and Crafts movement. In Burleigh's selection of a 17th century American chest as the prototype for this chest, he shows an appreciation of Colonial furniture which may have been first awakened at the time of the Centennial Exhibition in Philadelphia in 1876, where there were a number of displays devoted to antique furniture. But when Burleigh decided to have the chest made out of cherry, he deviated from the prototype, which more likely would have been of oak. His reason for doing so can be explained by

his desire to apply a black stain to some of the wood in order to simulate ebony. The dense grain of cherry is well suited to this effect. Burleigh's enthusiasm for ebonized wood was in keeping with the prevailing taste for Japanese objects which Matthew Perry had done so much to promote when he opened up trade between Japan and the West in 1854. Burleigh, however, reserved the panels on the chest for paintings from his own hand. In this respect he was following the example of William Morris, the English artist and designer who did more than anybody else to promote the Arts and Crafts movement. Like Morris, Burleigh's paintings adhered to a flattened format, which he reinforced by bold outlining and a brightly colored palette in order to avoid any suggestion of perspective and thus any compromise of the fact that the picture was painted on a two-dimensional panel. As characters from Shakespeare's plays served as the theme for Burleigh's panels, the English connection with Morris and the Arts and Crafts movement was made even more explicit. In another chest that Burleigh designed in carved oak, now also in the Museum's collection, he turned to the theme of King Arthur, a further example of his interest in English literature.

283

LOUIS COMFORT TIFFANY
American, New York City, 1848–1933

Vase, 1901
Glass. 11½ x 4⅝

Gift of Mrs. Gustav Radeke. 20.349

Publication: Landman/RISD, 1974, p. 139.

Louis Comfort Tiffany, son of the founder of the New York silver and jewelry firm, was a successful and much-traveled painter before he was seized by the urge to make beautiful objects. His experiments with glass, pottery, bronze, textiles, rugs, wallpaper, and stone made him the chief exponent of the Art Nouveau style in America.

This tall flower-form vase is more beautiful than useful. The bowl is opalescent, to which pale red, purple, and lime green elements have been added and combed to give the illusion of petals. The stem is drawn down to an attached, domed opalescent foot.

The underside of the foot bears the lightly engraved series number "01914," the "0" indicating the piece was made in the first half of 1901. The original paper label, "TGDCo" in monogram (for Tiffany Glass & Decorating Company) surrounded by "Tiffany•Favrile•Glass Registered•Trade•mark," is attached to the bottom.

By its form and coloring, this vase stands with the best of Tiffany's glass in the Art Nouveau style.

282

283

284

WILLIAM C. CODMAN
English, 1839–1912

Lady's Writing Table and Chair, 1903
Ebony, mahogany, boxwood, redwood,
ivory, mother-of-pearl, tooled leather,
and silver. Table: 50 x 50 x 28. Chair: 30 x
14 x 19

Gift of Mr. and Mrs. Frederick B.
Thurber. 58.095

Provenance: Gorham Company,
Providence; August Heckscher; the
Viscountess Esher

Publication: Charles H. Carpenter, Jr.,
Gorham Silver 1831–1981, New York,
1983, pp. 207–209.

Only in the context of international
competition and gold medals at world's
fairs is it possible to comprehend fully
how the lady's writing table and chair
William C. Codman created for Gorham
came into existence. Made in 1903 as the
centerpiece of the Gorham display at the
St. Louis World's Fair of 1904, they took
nearly 7,000 man hours to complete. In
the process an incredible variety of
materials was used, ranging from redwood, boxwood, and ebony to ivory,

tooled leather, and mother-of-pearl. For
sources of design, Codman drew
inspiration from diverse cultures and
historical traditions, including luxury
furniture created by André-Charles
Boulle in late 17th century France,
Rococo designs for furniture and
decoration published by Thomas
Chippendale in mid-18th century
England, and Art Nouveau objects in
silver and ceramics designed by Félix
Bracquemond in late 19th century
France. Codman also relied heavily on
Hispano-Moorish design sources,
especially for the sinuous floral inlays
which enhance its surface.

Before creating the St. Louis lady's
writing table and chair, Codman had
designed and made a solid silver
dressing table and stool for the Gorham
display at the Paris Exposition of 1900.
Perhaps even more significant in
Codman's career was a suite of music
room furniture for the New York art
collector Henry G. Marquand. While
designed by the English artist Sir
Lawrence Alma-Tadema, it was Codman
who actually oversaw its execution in
England before he came to work for
Gorham in 1891. Like our writing table
and chair, it incorporated a rich medley
of materials, not to mention stylistic
sources. Indeed, no single experience
could have better prepared Codman for
the creation of great exhibition pieces on
behalf of Gorham, culminating in the
design of the St. Louis desk and chair.

Color plate, page 91

284

285

FREDERICK CARDER
American, Corning, New York
(b. England), 1863–1963

Intarsia Bowl, 1920–1930
Engraved signature: Fred'k Carder
Glass. 2¾ x 5¼

Gift of the Estate of William E. Brigham.
63.011.95

Provenance: Frederick Carder; William
E. Brigham

Publication: Landman/RISD, 1974, p. 141.

Frederick Carder, unlike the more
famous L. C. Tiffany, was a practical
glass blower. He was born in Staffordshire, the son of a potter. In his mid-teens
he forsook an academic career for one of
artistic creativity in glass. In 1903 he
came to Corning, New York, where he
remained active as a craftsman and
designer until his official retirement in
1933. The difference between his
working and retired years was barely
discernible, for he continued designing
and experimenting at the Corning Glass
Works until shortly before his death at
100.

Innovation was a Carder trademark,
but occasionally a new process proved
too impractical for sustained commercial
production. This piece of Intarsia glass,
one of about a hundred known, falls into
this category. In the period in which

Intarsia glasses were made, production
amounted only to about ten a year. Each
piece was apparently a great challenge to
make. Economically, too, Intarsia glass
took its toll, for it was never a source of
profit. With the onset of the Depression,
production at Corning was limited to
such wares as would keep the company
solvent.

Our bowl of colorless glass with deep
blue flowers and an applied foot is
delicate and a little mysterious. Its walls
are thin, making the floral network seem
to float within. The technique involved
layering a colorless gather of glass with
colored glass. It was then allowed to cool
slowly. The design was painted onto the
colored surface with a wax product
resistant to hydrofluoric acid. When the
glass was exposed to the acid, the
colored glass was etched away except for
the resistant design. This reaction
stopped when the acid reached the
colorless layer. Then, the glass was
heated again, the design side cased with
another layer of colorless glass, and the
piece expanded and tooled into its final
shape. The bowl was completed by
adding its foot.

Today the surviving Intarsia pieces are
highly prized as much for their skillful
execution and beauty as for the unusual
circumstances of their production.

286

WILLIAM E. BRIGHAM
American, Providence, 1885–1962

Warming Ladle, ca. 1940
Silver and carnelian. 2½ x 10⅞

Gift of the Estate of William E. Brigham.
63.011.80

Designed and executed by William
Brigham, former head of the design
department at the Rhode Island School
of Design, this silver warming ladle is
representative of one facet of Brigham's
work. Born in North Attleboro, Massachusetts, Brigham grew up in the midst
of jewelry factories. His father worked in
one and he, too, was employed there.
From the factory Brigham went to RISD
and upon completion of his course work
went to Harvard to study under
Denman Ross. After teaching in Cleveland for several years, Brigham returned
to his alma mater to head up the design
department. Because of his early stint in
the factory, Brigham realized the
importance of the designer and believed
that one who designed an object should
also execute it. His first love was jewelry
design, and his creations were whimsical
and intricate objects, beautifully crafted.
On his many foreign travels he watched
for the unusual item – be it stone, shell,
or other material – which he could
incorporate into his work.

Brigham's silver is somewhat reminiscent of his jewelry, as he often incorporated a semi-precious stone into the lid
or handle, as in the case of the ladle.
However, in his silver designs Brigham
transcended whimsy and designed
objects of beautiful verve and line. The
Museum is fortunate in having a number
of these silver pieces, for Brigham left
his estate to the Museum. The estate
included not only works of his own
hand, but also the many objects amassed
during his trips abroad and his design
portfolio, which illustrates how he used
his collection as inspiration for his own
creations.

285

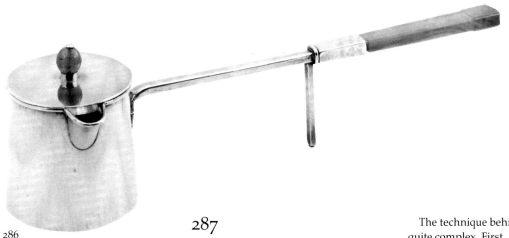
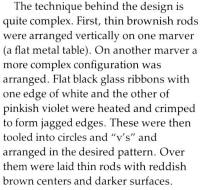

286

287

DALE CHIHULY
American, b. 1941

"First Eye Dazzler" Vase, 1976
Glass. 8¾ x 6¾

Museum Purchase. 76.167

Provenance: The artist

This imposing cylinder vase was made by Dale Chihuly in 1976 while he was a professor in the glass department at RISD. It is one of a number of similarly shaped pieces whose design is inspired by Navajo woven rugs and blankets.

The technique behind the design is quite complex. First, thin brownish rods were arranged vertically on one marver (a flat metal table). On another marver a more complex configuration was arranged. Flat black glass ribbons with one edge of white and the other of pinkish violet were heated and crimped to form jagged edges. These were then tooled into circles and "v's" and arranged in the desired pattern. Over them were laid thin rods with reddish brown centers and darker surfaces.

The opaque inner surface of the cylinder was cased with the thick color-less glass, and while still hot was first rolled onto the vertical brown rods and expanded slightly. Then the larger rug design was similarly applied. When all these rods had been picked up, the hot glass was rolled on the marver one last time to make the surface smooth. The strands of glass on each side then tended to collapse, revealing their lighter colored centers. Doing all this while keeping the very heavy cylinder at the right temperature and shape took a great amount of control and skill.

287

288

JUDY KENSLEY MCKIE
American, b. 1944

Chest, 1980
Limewood. 31 x 36 x 22

Albert Pilavin Collection of 20th Century
American Art. 81.024

Provenance: The artist

Publication: *Museum Notes*, RISD, 1981,
p. 17.

Although trained as a painter at RISD in
the 1960's, Judy McKie discovered
woodworking when she found it
necessary to furnish an apartment
inexpensively, and hence started making
her own furniture. In the catalogue for
an exhibition of her furniture at the
Addison Gallery of American Art, the
author characterizes her work as "clearly
in the Egypto-Assyrian, African, Ionian,
Pre-Columbian, très moderne tradition
of carved sculpture." Elements of all
these traditions can be found in this
chest, along with strong references to
19th century American folk art. In
conjunction with superior workmanship
and arresting decorative detail, McKie's
ability to enhance the formal properties
of her furniture by way of its functional
requirements is particularly well demonstrated by the incorporation of the
chest's handles into the arch formed by
the pelicans' feathers. It is a most
engaging object which is both a usable
piece of furniture and a striking piece of
sculpture, and hence a rare synthesis of
the useful and fine arts.

289

BETTY WOODMAN
American, b. 1930

Mussel Server, 1981
Glazed ceramic. 4½ x 35½ x 10

Marken Scholes Shedd Memorial Fund.
81.063

Provenance: The artist

Publications: Jacquelyn Rice, *Clay*,
Providence, 1981, pp. 38–39; *Museum
Notes*, RISD, 1982, p. 17.

One of a small but growing collection of
contemporary American ceramics whose
acquisition was made possible through
the Marken Scholes Shedd Memorial
Fund is this mussel server by Betty
Woodman. Her use of highly fired glazes
gives the impression that the clay is still
wet. The close identity with the creative
process which this effect conjures up is
further enhanced by the seemingly
random way in which the colored
decoration has been applied. The results
are decidedly aquatic, very much in
keeping with the function of the piece.
Indeed, empty mussel shells placed
along the server's broad rim blend in
with the camouflaged surface. Although
the piece is very much her own creation,
Woodman emerges as a highly creative
reinterpreter of the work of the 18th
century English potter Thomas Whieldon, an historical precedent which in no
way diminishes the vitality and originality of her own work.

288

289

290

HUGO ALVAR HENRIK AALTO
Finnish, 1899–1976

Arm Chair, 1929–1932
Laminated birchwood painted black.
26¼ x 24 x 30¼

Anonymous acquisition. 84.018

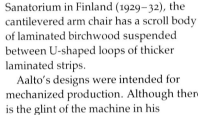

Shortly after he adopted the International Modern Style for his architecture, Alvar Aalto began to concern himself with the objects within a building. The classic bentwood chair in the RISD collection was part of this first experimentation with furniture design. One of several pieces intended for the Paimo Sanatorium in Finland (1929–32), the cantilevered arm chair has a scroll body of laminated birchwood suspended between U-shaped loops of thicker laminated strips.

Aalto's designs were intended for mechanized production. Although there is the glint of the machine in his furniture, there is also a softness which Aalto purposely retained. He was aware that a totally mechanical design was cold and uninviting and that natural texture and organic form were important in the reception of a piece. Hence Aalto often left his furniture in the natural wood color and gradually eliminated metal parts in favor of all-wood construction.

Black paint conceals the birchwood of the RISD example, yet the paint does not conceal the inherent strength of this wood which, when laminated, is as resilient as steel. Learning from Thonet's experience and partaking of the designs of Marcel Breuer and the manufacturing technology of wooden skis, Aalto developed a chair elegant in line, simple in manufacture, and appealing to the public.

290

Publications of the Permanent Collection

Luke Vincent Lockwood, *The Pendleton Collection*, 1904.

Stephen Bleeker Luce, *Corpus Vasorum Antiquorum* (U. S. A. Fascicule 2, Providence, Fascicule 1), Cambridge, Harvard University Press, 1933.

Lucy T. Aldrich Collection of Japanese Costumes, 1937.

Heinrich Schwarz, *Studies, Museum of Art*, 1947.

Elizabeth Temple Casey, *The Lucy Truman Aldrich Collection of Porcelain Figures of the Eighteenth Century*, 1965.

Daniel Robbins *et al.*, *Nancy Sayles Day Collection of Modern Latin American Art*, 1966.

Daniel Robbins *et al.*, *Nancy Sayles Day Collection of Modern Latin American Art. Supplementary Catalogue*, 1968.

Daniel Robbins and Susan Platt, *Works of Art from the Albert Pilavin Collection: Twentieth Century American Art*, Vol. 1, 1969.

Stephen E. Ostrow *et al.*, *Raid the Icebox with Andy Warhol*, 1970.

Susan P. Carmalt, *Selection I: American Drawings and Watercolors from the Museum's Collection*, 1972.

Malcolm Cormack, *Selection II: British Watercolors and Drawings from the Museum's Collection*, 1972.

Diana L. Johnson, *Selection III: Contemporary Graphics from the Museum's Collection*, 1973.

Brunhilde S. Ridgway, *Catalogue of the Classical Collection: Sculpture*, 1973.

Stephen E. Ostrow, *The Albert Pilavin Collection: Twentieth Century American Art II*, 1973.

Hedy Backlin Landman, *Selection IV: Glass from the Museum's Permanent Collection*, 1974.

Kermit S. and Kate H. Champa, eds., *Selection V: French Watercolors and Drawings from the Museum's Collection, ca. 1800–1910*, 1975.

David Gordon Mitten, *Catalogue of the Classical Collection: Bronzes*, 1975.

Ann Ashmead and Kyle Phillips, *Catalogue of the Classical Collection: Vases*, 1976.

Tony Hackens, *Selection VI: Catalogue of the Classical Collection: Jewelry*, 1976.

Patricia C. F. Mandel, *Selection VII: American Paintings from the Museum's Collection, ca. 1800–1930*, 1977.

Masterpieces from the Museum of Art, Rhode Island School of Design, 1981.

L. Candace Pezzera, *How Pleasant to Know Mr. Lear, Watercolors by Edward Lear from Rhode Island Collections*, 1982.

Rolf Winkes, *Roman Paintings and Mosaics*, 1982.

Deborah J. Johnson, *Old Master Drawings from the Museum of Art, Rhode Island School of Design*, 1983.

Index of Artists

The page numbers in parentheses indicate that a work is reproduced in color as well as black and white.

Index of Donors and Funds

The page numbers in parentheses indicate that a work is reproduced in color as well as black and white.

Three thousand copies of this handbook,
designed by Gilbert Associates, typeset
in Mergenthaler Palatino, have been
printed at Eastern Press in May 1985 for
the Museum of Art, Rhode Island School
of Design.